Realities and Relationships

Kenneth J. Gergen

Realities and Relationships

Soundings in Social Construction

Harvard University Press
Cambridge, Massachusetts, and London, England 1994

To my brother David
with love and admiration

This book is printed on acid-free paper, and its binding
materials have been chosen for strength and durability.

Library of Congress Cataloging-in-Publication Data

Gergen, Kenneth J.
Realities and relationships : soundings in social construction /
Kenneth J. Gergen.
    p.   cm.
Includes bibliographical references and index.
ISBN 0-674-74930-8 (acid-free paper).
1. Social psychology.   2. Knowledge, Sociology of.
3. Interpersonal relations.   4. Discourse analysis.   I. Title.
HM251.G3475   1994
302—dc20   94-27463
CIP

Contents

Preface

It was after the publication of my book *Toward Transformation in Social Knowledge* that my engagement in social constructionism took a serious turn. I had long been involved in a critical analysis of empiricist psychology, but in this volume I found the elements of a social constructionist alternative slowly taking form. As these ideas began to color subsequent readings and conversations, I found myself immersed in what might be characterized as a relational epiphany. In extending constructionist dialogues, I began to realize, with exhilarating frequency, novel turns of theory and creative forms of practice. And this searching exploration resonated across disciplines, professions, and continents. The present writings largely grow from this immersion and reflect some of its major trajectories. In a sense, these are frozen artifacts, but my fond hope is that they can inject the spirit of past conversations into the future.

Let us place these developments in broader historical context. In *Discourse on Method,* René Descartes voiced sentiments that reverberate across the centuries. There was first the voice of anguished incertitude. If we adopt a posture of systematic doubt, is there any way to locate a foundation? Are there any grounds on which we can rely for firm and dependable knowledge? Authorities claim knowledge, proposed Descartes, but they are subject to error, nor is there compelling reason to trust the vagaries of our senses, for they often deceive us. The ideas that enter our minds from various sources can also mislead us. In what then can we place our trust? The painful question now posed, Descartes moved on to furnish the precious voice of reassurance: I cannot doubt that I am the one who doubts. Although my reason may lead me to doubt all that I survey, I cannot doubt reason itself. And if I can rest my trust in the existence of reason, I may also be certain of my own existence. *Cogito ergo sum.*

It is the celebration of the individual mind—its capacity to organize sense data, reason logically, and speculate intelligently—that has served over the centuries to insulate Western culture from the disabling assaults of doubt. It is encouraging to believe that individuals endowed with powers of reason and attentive to the contours of the objective world can transcend the ambiguities of continuously changing circumstance and move toward a self-determined prosperity. And it is largely through this faith in reason that we are led to search for rational foundations of knowledge. From the positivism of the nineteenth century to the transcendental realism of the present century, scholars have sustained the foundationalist tradition, ensuring that individual reason remains securely at the helm of action.

Let us reconsider but a single link in Descartes' compelling thesis. While we may resonate with his declaration of doubt, on what grounds does he go on to equate the process of doubt with that of reason? On what basis does he conclude that the process of doubt is an activity of the individual *mind,* removed from the world but reflecting upon it? Why was this equation itself not subjected to Cartesian skepticism, for is it not more obviously compelling that doubt is a process carried out in language? To write of the fallibilities of authorities, the senses, incoming ideas, and the like is to enter into a discursive practice. Whether the practice also proves to be an emanation or expression of some other realm, a ratiocinative one, remains open to conjecture. However, one can scarcely doubt the discourse on doubt.

Yet, if doubt is a discursive process, we are drawn to conclusions of a far different character than those reached by Descartes. For we also find that discourse is not the possession of a single individual. Meaningful language is the product of social interdependence. It requires the coordinated actions of at least two persons, and until there is mutual agreement on the meaningful character of words, they fail to constitute language. If we follow this line of argument to its ineluctable conclusion, we find that it is not the mind of the single individual that provides whatever certitude we possess, but relationships of interdependency. If there were no interdependence—the joint creation of meaningful discourse—there would be no "objects" or "actions" or means of rendering them doubtful. We may rightfully replace Descartes's dictum with *communicamus ergo sum.*

It is this latter point of departure that furnishes a unifying basis for a variety of recent attempts, spanning the scholarly disciplines, to generate an alternative to foundationalist accounts of human knowledge. These attempts—variously labeled post-empiricist, poststructural, nonfoundational, or postmodern—place language in the vanguard of concern. Regardless of our methods of procedure, what we call knowledgeable accounts of the world (including ourselves) are essentially discursive. And because disquisitions on the nature of things are framed in language, there is no grounding of science or any other knowledge-generating enterprise in other than communities of interlocutors. There is no appeal to mind or matter—to reason or facts—that will lend transcendental validity to propositions. (Indeed, both "mind" and "world" are themselves integers within the Western linguistic code.) Equally, the attempt to articulate universal principles of the right and the good, which stand above and outside the hurlyburly of daily interchange, is misleading. In the end, all that is meaningful grows from relationships, and it is within this vortex that the future will be forged.

Although they vary in detail and emphasis, a number of widely shared assumptions within these widespread discussions are conveniently captured by the term "social construction." In the chapters composing this volume, I attempt to articulate and synthesize major elements of a viable social constructionism; to answer various challenges to this perspective; to illustrate its potential through theory, research, and application; and to open debate on the future of constructionist pursuits in psychology and in the human sciences more generally. To these ends, I have organized these essays into three groups. Part I provides an introduction to constructionist thought. The first chapter clears the way by demonstrating why the individualist view of knowledge, exemplified by contemporary cognitive psychology, has reached an impasse. The second chapter then charts the emergence of the social constructionist alternative to the individual view of knowledge. It outlines sweeping critiques of recent decades and from these distills a set of propositions that enable us to move beyond critique to the possibilities of human science in a constructionist mode. The third chapter takes up a variety of critiques of social constructionism. For many, constructionism is tantamount to nihilism; to others its relativism—both ontological and moral—is seriously objectionable. In replying to these and other charges, I hope to elaborate on the contours of the perspective. So serious are the critiques of moral and political anemia that I devote all of Chapter 4 to this issue. Here I explore both the shortcomings of the critique and the positive potential inhering in a constructionist relativism.

Central to a constructionist view of human science is the importance of critical appraisal, not only of contemporary cultural pursuits, but of the endeavors of the scientific community. Critique not only expands the possibilities for construction, it also forms a significant origin for cultural transformation. In this context, the essays featured in Part II are primarily critical in focus. Echoing themes developed in Part I, I explore in Chapter 5 significant flaws in the cognitive account of human action and outline the outcomes for psychology when this view is replaced by a social epistemology. Chapter 6 focuses on the production of deficit discourse in the mental health professions and its deleterious effects on the culture. In constructing both the "pathologies" and the "cures," the professions launch us on a course that is as devastating as it is uncontainable. Chapter 7 turns critical attention to the means by which scientific worlds are made palpable and objective. My aim here is not only to reveal the rhetorical artifice by which objective worlds are constructed but to open discussion on possible alternatives.

In Part III, the emphasis shifts from critique to transformation. These chapters attempt to move beyond the programmatic and the critical to engage in theoretical reconstruction. Constructionism replaces the individual with the relationship as the locus of knowledge. Yet so captivated is Western tradition by the significance of the individual, that the discourse of relatedness has been little developed. These chapters attempt, then, to generate resources for constructing the reality of relationship. Three of them extend the earlier emphasis on rhetoric, now turning it into a descriptive tool. They focus on the narrative basis of self-understanding. Identities are constructed largely through narratives, and these narratives are properties of communal interchange. The emphasis on narrative is extended into Chapter 9, where I take up the topic of the emotions. Here I propose that the emotions are not possessions of individual minds but constituents of relational patterns—or lived narratives. In Chapter 10 the discussion of narratives moves into the practical domain of therapy. After applying several of the preceding arguments to client-therapist relationships, I argue for the transcendence of narrative reality. The implications of this proposal go far beyond the therapeutic context.

The final chapters further extend the reach of relational theorizing. The central concern of Chapter 11 is human communication. How do we generate and sustain meaning? The critical problem here is to replace the unworkable view of meaning as intersubjective with a relational answer. Although poststructural literary theory appears to make understanding an impossibility, a social recasting of the deconstructionist metaphor allows significant progress to be made. With the groundwork for a theory of meaning in place, Chapter 12 confronts the problem of deceit. If constructionism challenges the concept of objective truth, then how are we to understand the cultural construction of falsehood? A relational answer to this question opens new vistas for confronting problems of deceit in public and private life.

It is my special hope that these essays can serve as resources for psychologists and scholars concerned with the critical challenges now confronting the human sciences more generally. As resources, the chapters may speak to a variety of different audiences. The chapters comprising Part I are addressed most directly to those who find themselves uneasy with traditional behavioral science and interested in possible alternatives. These chapters also attempt to make intelligible to the traditional scientist a series of intellectual movements, which together, pose a profound challenge to established practices. These movements, once restricted to small sectors of the academy, now burst their boundaries and provoke exhilarated discussion throughout the scholarly world. For those social scientists recently embarked on these paths, these chapters point beyond the deep skepticism fostered by these movements. They attempt to replace the rubble of deconstructive critique with efforts toward reconstruction and to grapple productively with significant criticism.

Parts II and III will prove more useful to scholars already engaged in constructionist pursuits. Here I explore a variety of pathways invited by a constructionist standpoint. My hope is first to demonstrate the advantages of breaking disciplinary boundaries, of entering the interrelated dialogues now connecting scholars around the globe and offering new and interesting avenues of departure. In addition, I hope to contribute substantively to several active dialogues within the existing confluence and to open discussion on what I believe to be one of the most important challenges for future theory and practice, namely, the replacement of the individualized orientation to understanding and action with a relational investment. These chapters mark only one beginning of this attempt, and I am deeply excited by the prospects of future dialogues.

I am well aware that many of the issues addressed in this volume are the subject of an enormous and rapidly expanding body of scholarship. To achieve the broad and integrative line of thinking that was often my goal, it has been necessary to skate rapidly over thin ice, often neglecting the many fine cracks under foot. I have tried not to suppress major lines of critique, but I have had to make many difficult judgments regarding "the weight of the arguments" to date. There is little that is not subject to continued controversy, but the same holds for the many texts that truck in qualification. At the same time, for the reader who wishes to press more deeply, or who simply wishes to explore the broader context in which these arguments figure, I have provided a liberal body of citations.

The essays in this volume have benefited greatly from the reactions of friends, editors, and colleagues, to whom the ideas have been presented in more primitive form. The initial chapter grew out of a 1983 presentation to the Boston Colloquium on the Philosophy of Science. Sections of Chapter 2 were stimulated by a 1983 conference presentation at the University of Chicago on Potentialities for Knowledge in Social Science (subsequently published in Fiske and Shweder 1986). Sections of Chapter 3 have been sharpened from discussions at various meetings of the Society for Theoretical Psychology, where many of these ideas were first presented. Conferees at the 1991 Georgetown conference on Values in the Social Sciences were a strong impetus to the ideas appearing as Chapter 4. Chapter 5 is an extended revision of a paper presented at the 1987 Paris conference on The Future of Social Psychology, whose proceedings were published in the *European Journal of Social Psychology*, 19 (1989). Chapter 6 grew from discussions at the Heidelberg conference on Historical Dimensions of Psychological Discourse, where it was presented in 1991. Similarly, Chapter 7 revises a series of arguments developed for a special issue of *Annals of Scholarship*, 8 (1991) devoted to the problem of objectivity.

Mary Gergen gave invaluable assistance in generating many of the arguments in Chapters 8 and 9, portions of which were published in *Advances in Experimental Social Psychology*, 21 (1988). John Kaye, a scholar and therapist, was a valuable ally in generating an earlier version of Chapter 10 (now published in McNamee and Gergen 1992). Chapter 11 owes much to discussions at the 1991 meetings of the Jean Piaget Society, where the ideas were initially presented. Similarly, Chapter 12 was exposed to intensive critique by conference participants at the Bad Hamburg meetings on Societal Social Psychology in 1988.

I am deeply indebted to several institutions for furnishing the time and resources necessary for pursuing these topics. Most appreciated were fellowships from the Netherlands Institute of Advanced Study, the Alexander von Humboldt Foundation, the Fulbright Foundation, and the Rockefeller Study Center in Bellagio. An academic leave from Swarthmore College as a Eugene M. Lang Professor was also invaluable, as was the warmth and support of the faculty during my tenure at Fundacion Interfas in Buenos Aires. There are many individuals who have contributed to the preparation of these chapters. In their insightful comments, critiques, enthusiasm, or abiding intellectual presence I am especially grateful to Al Alschuler, Tom Andersen, Harlene Anderson, Mick Billig, Sissela Bok, Pablo Boczkowski, Ben Bradley, Jerome Bruner, Esther Cohen, David Cooperrider, Peter Dachler, Wolfgang Frindte, Saul Fuks, Gabi Gloger Tippelt, Carl Graumann, Harry Goolishian, Rom Harré, Lynn Hoffman, Tomas Ibanez, Arie Kruglanski, Jack Lannamann, Gerishwar Misra, Don McClosky, Sheila McNamee, Shepley Orr, Barnett Pearce, Peggy Penn, John and Anne Marie Rijsman, Dan Robinson, Wojciech Sadurski, Dora Fried Schnitman, Gun Semin, Richard Shweder, Herb Simons, Margaret and Wolfgang Stroebe, Diana Whitney, and Stan Wortham. Without the secretarial and bibliographic assistance of Lisa Gebhart and Joanne Bramley, this volume would scarcely have materialized. To Linda Howe at Harvard University Press I owe an enormous debt for her enthusiasm and outstanding editorial efforts. John Shotter has been a continuing source of support and inspiration to me. To Mary Gergen I owe my deepest gratitude, for her catalytic companionship, unfailing encouragement, and capacity for positive reconstruction.

Part One

From Individual Knowledge to Communal Construction

1   The Impasse of Individual Knowledge

In recent decades psychology has undergone a major revolution in its view of individual knowledge. As this account will reveal, psychological science now confronts an impasse, a point at which both the knowledge claims of the profession and the individualist view of knowledge sustained by these claims cease to be compelling. A retreat to the presumptions of earlier times seems precluded. What is needed is an alternative conception of knowledge and related forms of cultural practice. It is to exploring a social constructionist alternative that the remainder of this volume is devoted.

In Western culture the individual has long occupied a place of commanding importance. Cultural interests are virtually absorbed by the nature of individual minds—their states of well-being, their tendencies, their capacities, and their shortcomings. Individual minds have served as the critical locus of explanation, not only in psychology, but in many sectors of philosophy, economics, sociology, anthropology, history, literary study, and communication. The interior condition of the individual also serves as a prominent criterion in determining public policy. Our beliefs about the single individual furnish the rationale for most of our major institutions. It is the individual who acquires knowledge, and thus we invest in educational institutions to train and expand the individual mind. It is the individual who harbors the capacity for free choice, and on these grounds we erect both informal practices of moral accountability and formal agencies of justice. Because the individual has the capacity for reason and evaluation we can place our faith in democratic institutions. Because the individual is motivated to seek gain and minimize loss we believe the free market can prosper. Because individuals harbor the capacity for love and commitment, the institutions of marriage and the family can form the building blocks for community.

These beliefs and associated institutions have emerged and grown powerful within a cultural context of relative insularity. Over the centuries it has been possible to distinguish a uniquely Western cultural tradition, conversant with but fundamentally separated from other traditions throughout the world. And while Western culture has exchanged goods and services, views and values, and armed excursions with those outside, it has been unwilling to see other cultures as superior or even equal. If there was to be cultural diffusion, it would be primarily "from the West to the rest." Yet world conditions have changed dramatically within the past century. A spate of emerging technologies—the telephone, the automobile, radio, jet transportation, television, computers, and satellites among them—bring the peoples of the world into greater intimacy and interdependency than ever before. Never before have we been confronted so fully and intensively by the values, views, investments, and practices of those "not quite like us." Increasingly the networks of interdependence expand in the worlds of politics, business, science, communications, and more. Where allegiances, mergers, joint inquiries, and networks are not yet formed, more subtle interdependencies—in matters of ecology, energy, economy, and health, for example—creep increasingly into consciousness.

In light of these dramatic changes, it no longer seems possible to sustain the insularity, the sense of superiority, and the hegemonic tendencies of previous centuries. We cannot presume out of hand that Western traditions are suited to a context of intensifying globalization, that they lend themselves to the processes of mutual understanding, appreciation, and tolerance increasingly demanded. We cannot rest easy in the assumption that the Western heritage, with its emphasis on the single individual and its requisite institutions, can effectively participate in a world of thoroughgoing interdependence. Required, then, is a self-reflexive assessment of the traditions, an inquiry into the benefits and shortcomings of our beliefs and practices, and an exploration of alternative possibilities. This is not to opt for radical transformation, a disjunctive leap into the alien and unfamiliar. It is rather to favor a process of inquiry that may enhance the possibility of selectively salvaging and absorbing—of determining what we should retain from these traditions and how we may soften the edges of our commitments so that others may be heard more fully.

It is in this spirit that I wish to reconsider the presumption of individual knowledge, which is in many respects a cultural keystone. Without believing that individuals can accurately reflect on the world around them, it is difficult to see what value derives from individual decision making in the arenas of morality, politics, economics, family life, and so on. If knowledge is not an individual possession, then individual choices in these domains can be little trusted. The institutions built on this trust would simultaneously lose their warrant. At the same time, there is growing concern in many sectors of the academy that the presumption of individual knowledge is on the brink of bankruptcy. So deeply is it flawed that Western culture is in danger of striding the earth unclothed. Some of these flaws will become focal in later chapters. However, because this book grows first and foremost from the soil of psychology, here I wish to consider the status of individual knowledge within this discipline. Given a century of scientific commitment to the exploration of individual knowledge, its acquisition and its deployment, what has been gained? Where does the discipline now stand, and what hopes can it have for the future?

There is good reason for this assessment. Scientific psychology, more than any other discipline of ordered inquiry, has accepted the challenge of rendering valid and reliable accounts of individual mental processes. With this mandate, the discipline attempts, insofar as is possible, to provide the culture with useful insights into the processes of knowledge acquisition and utilization—to inform the culture of the most effective means by which persons can gain cognizance of their surroundings, collect and store information, think through contingencies, recall needed facts, solve problems, make rational plans, and put those plans into action. All the ancillary institutions mentioned above, from education, law, and the economy to religion and family life, should stand to benefit from such insights. Thus, to take account of the peregrinations of psychological science in the present century is to peer into the inner sanctum of cultural justification. It is to enter the Fort Knox of individualism and assay our condition of wealth.

The conclusions of this inquiry will not be sanguine. As I shall argue, a century of scientific inquiry essentially leaves us in a conceptual cul-de-sac. Psychological inquiry has emerged as the byproduct of two major traditions of Western thought: the empiricist and the rationalist. The former was most fully expressed in the behaviorist movement that dominated psychology for the greater part of this century. The rationalist tradition, now manifest in the hegemonic pulsations of the cognitive movement, confronts the point of termination. And when the rationalist impulse is exhausted, there are few remaining resources within the tradition. Neither retreat to the behaviorist (empiricist) past nor further evolution of the rationalist orientation seems possible. By exploring the emergence of this condition, we are better positioned to consider alternative conceptions of knowledge, fresh discourses of human functioning, new vistas for human science, and transformations in cultural practice.

To Know about Knowledge

A discipline committed to understanding the nature of individual knowledge is haunted by dislocating irony. On the one hand, the pursuit is lodged in the assumption of ignorance about the processes and mechanisms at stake: "Because we are ignorant about how people acquire knowledge, we require research." On the other hand, in making claims for the research process, we deny our state of ignorance. By claiming that the research process produces knowledge, the scientist is claiming knowledge of knowledge. If one knows nothing about knowledge, its acquisition, its adequacy, its utilization, and the like, then one can scarcely claim to know. If one claims the privilege of knowledge, then we must presume that this claim is grounded in an awareness of the knowledge-generating process. Psychologists have softened the impact of this irony by claiming the need to investigate this vital aspect of human functioning (the claim to ignorance), but draw their justification for their claims to knowledge from other sources. It is to other disciplines, more sure of foot and more captivating in power of argumentation, that psychologists have turned to warrant their assertions.

These ancillary or supportive bodies of discourse have primarily been of two varieties, the first *metatheoretical* and the second *methodological*. In the former, philosophic understandings of science—and most particularly those of the logical empiricists—offered a convenient and compelling means of justification.[1] Not only were such philosophical foundations consistent with a great deal of commonsense understanding, but they were linked to important philosophical traditions (namely British empiricism and continental rationalism) that themselves presumed a world of mental life worthy of exploration. Second, these disciplines relied on the logic of empirical methodology and, most particularly, the laboratory experiment. Because of the manifest success of the natural sciences and the seeming reliance of these sciences on empirical methods, one might reasonably place trust in a discipline that employed such methods. In effect, to achieve discursive power psychologists have wedded their explanations of mental life to both metatheoretical and methodological justifications.

Let us first consider each of these bodies of discourse—psychological theory, scientific metatheory, and theory of methodology—as constituting an *intelligibility nucleus*. A theory of mental life, like a theory of science or a theory of method, ideally forms a set of interrelated propositions that furnish a community of interlocutors with a sense of description and/or explanation within a given domain. To participate in the intelligibility nucleus is to "make sense" by the standards of a particular community. Such nuclei may be unbounded and totalizing (as in the case of universal cosmologies or ontologies) or localized and specific (as in a theory of the educational process at Swarthmore College); they may command broad agreement (as in common understandings of the democratic process) or appeal to a small minority (as in a religious sect). Further, such forms of intelligibility are typically embedded within a broader array of patterned activities (writing papers, doing experiments, voting, praying, and so on). In effect, propositional networks are essential constituents of more inclusive forms of action, a topic to which I shall return in later chapters.

Central to our present purposes, although such intelligibility nuclei may exist in relative independence of each other (war strategists, for example, seldom speak with spiritual advisors), they may also be related. On the most elementary level, they may vary in the extent to which they lend support to one another, either acting as full endorsements for each other at one extreme, or as thoroughgoing antagonists at the other. In large measure, the extent of support provided by a neighboring intelligibility nucleus will depend on the degree to which propositional constituents are common to both nuclei. For example, various Protestant religious sects can act in mutual support for reasons of shared suppositions, but they tend to be more supportive of each other than of the Catholic faith because the domain of common suppositions is less extensive. At the same time, because of shared beliefs in the Holy Trinity, Christian denominations tend to be more supportive of each other than, for example, of Islam or Buddhism.[2]

Placed in this context, psychological research into individual knowledge can be justified by ancillary networks of discourse to the degree that assumptions are held in common. Thus, scientific psychologists cannot derive support from a spiritual ontology, since the suppositional networks are largely independent or antagonistic. (There is no place in the scientific world of systematic cause and effect for God as an "unmoved mover.") Similarly, a commitment to phenomenological methodology (stressing the organizing function of human experience) would be inimical to psychological theory viewing individual knowledge as the accretion of inputs.

I propose that within the first half of the century there was a close and mutually supportive alliance between psychological theories of individual functioning and available accounts at both the level of metatheory and theory. The nucleus of behaviorist theory was able to thrive in a context of strong justificatory discourses: empiricist metatheory on the one hand and the discourse of experimental methodology on the other. Yet, as the dialogue has moved on, psychological theory has undergone a major transformation from a behavioral to a cognitive base. This transformation at the level of theory has not been accompanied by shifts at the level of either metatheory or methodology. Transformations in both of these registers are stymied by a barrage of criticism. Thus, cognitive accounts of individual knowledge are largely isolated and vulnerable; because they lack any compelling justification—either in terms of a foundational theory of knowledge or a theory of methodology—they live on borrowed time. As contemporary critique becomes more fully articulated and adequate justifications cannot be located, trust in the cognitive perspective will wither. The very idea of individual knowledge becomes suspicious.

The Discursive Dimension of Paradigm Shifts

In order to appreciate the basis for these views, it is necessary to sketch out the broader frame of understanding from which this analysis proceeds. This preliminary sketch is doubly important, as it contains the ingredients of several critical themes that both organize and influence the course of later chapters. For present purposes I will frame the issues in terms of the familiar idea of paradigm shifts. More narrowly, how are we to understand stability and change in the theoretical perspectives occurring in knowledge-generating communities? There is now a voluminous literature on this topic, and I am not proposing here to offer either a full critique or a successor to the many views currently extant. Rather, I wish to focus on one particular dimension of scientific activity infrequently treated in the literature to date. Where such analyses often center on particular personalities, values, discoveries, technologies, or sociopolitical conditions, I wish to foreground the discursive processes operating within scientific communities. If scientific communities indeed acquire their status as communities by virtue of their shared languages of description and explanation, then we may gain significant insights into theoretical transformation by concentrating on the character of discursive practices.

Let us return then to the intelligibility nucleus, a body of interrelated propositions shared by participants in various scientific enclaves. Virtually all scientific discourse proposes an array of existents (along with sundry explanatory propositions to account for their character). In effect, the language creates an imagined ontology and a structure for rendering intelligible how and why constituents of the ontology are related. As discursive domains, such systems of understanding stand equivalent to both mathematics and theological eschatology. In all cases, the propositional world stands intelligible without necessary linkages to events outside the nucleus. Children can master versions of the Big Bang theory of the origins of the universe or what might await them in heaven in the same way they learn their multiplication tables. These clusters of intelligibility *can* be related to events outside themselves in various ways—ways not given within the systems themselves. Thus, one can learn when and where to apply the tables of multiplication or the concept of the Holy Spirit. However, the nucleus does not require these linkages in order to be understood or to be compelling. (Darwinian theory remains active and vital within the culture despite the fact that there is little common agreement about how and to what it now applies.)

Yet the self-sustaining character of the intelligibility nucleus is only an apparent one. In important respects the very formulation of a discursive nucleus simultaneously establishes the potential for its dissolution. The asserted ontology (along with its network of putative relationships) furnishes the grounds for its own demise. Why is this so? Consider Kant's argument in the *Critique of Practical Reason.* As he proposed, one cannot make one's way in society without a conception of what one "ought" to do. Yet to have a conception of what one ought to do also entails understanding that it is possible to act otherwise—that is, to act in contradiction to "ought." Action proceeds and is only intelligible against the backdrop of its negation. This line of argument is also reflected in Hegel's (1979) writings on being and negation. The very comprehension of being requires a simultaneous grasp of nonbeing or absence. To understand that something is the case requires the realization that it might be otherwise. More recently, we find a similar argument in Saussure's (1983) semiotic formulation. As he proposes, linguistic signifiers gain their meaning by virtue of their differentiation from other signifiers. Language, and thus meaning, depends on a system of differences. For most structural semiotics, these differences have been cast in terms of binaries. The word *man* gains its communicative capacity by virtue of its contrast with *woman, up* as it contrasts with *down, emotion* with *reason,* and so on. To extend the implications of these various arguments, let me propose that any system of intelligibility rests on what is typically an implicit negation—an alternative intelligibility that stands as a rival to itself. Whether a religion, a political theory, or a scientific perspective, all are distinguished by virtue of what they are not.

The tensions produced by a given intelligibility nucleus can be appreciated more fully by drawing from A. J. Greimas's (1987) concept of the "semiotic square." Rather than focus on the single binary basis of meaning (object and opposition), the "square" graphically demonstrates the possibility of alternative forms of difference. Consider the structure in Figure 1.1. As indicated, the term *empiricist* is typically cast in opposition to *rationalist.* The enormous epistemological battles in philosophy over the past several centuries can largely be cast in terms of this binary. Analyses within one domain are often sustained or vindicated by demonstrating fallacies within the other. Yet, in addition to the traditional tension, the transversals also indicate additional possibilities: *empiricist* can be cast against *all things nonempiricist* (which might, but need not, include philosophical positions), and *rationalist* may be contrasted with *all that is nonrationalist.* There is a final distinction to consider, one that will come to figure centrally in the closing arguments of this chapter. That is, one can collapse the elements constituting the traditional tension—both the empiricist and rationalist philosophies being uniquely *Western*—and contrast them with the polarity Buddhism–Shintoism, collapsed as *Eastern* philosophy.

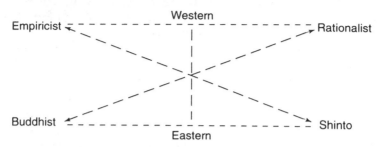

Figure 1.1   Possibilities for Contrasting Intelligibilities

As we find, the elaboration of any given nucleus of intelligibility depends for its meaning and significance on that which it is not—including its contraries, its absences, and those positions made possible from its various pairings. As the ontology within the nucleus is established, so are multiple possibilities for its negation. To propose a theory of human functioning, a philosophy of knowledge, or a theory of methodology is simultaneously to establish multiple grounds for challenge. In many cases intelligibility systems can be sustained without threat of antagonism. Communities sharing in a given system of intelligibility often cut themselves away from those who "spoil the party" by rebelling against the prevailing understandings. For example, the structure of professional communication systems (journals, electronic mail systems), along with the physical layout of the typical university (with each department housed in separate quarters), virtually ensures that members of the constituent knowledge-generating communities will seldom conflict. Sanctioning devices of both informal and formal varieties (such as promoting and tenuring "right thinking" faculty or awarding research grants to the "promising" researchers) also function to retain the sanctity of existing paradigms.

In Foucault's (1980) terms, there is a close connection, then, between knowledge and power. Knowledge structures (here intelligibility nuclei) are fundamental to the ordering of various cultural enclaves and thus to the distribution of outcomes in which some people are favored over others. The discourses of a discipline are constituent features of its structures of punishment and privilege. At the same time, as hierarchies of privilege are established, so the discourses of negation may be set in motion. The dominant discourse, by its very domination, may activate the binaries. This may be increasingly so as any given discourse becomes codified and canonized; in their more ambiguous and porous composition, discourse arrays more easily incorporate the marginals. It is their formal institutionalization that typically serves to exclude. A tendency toward negation may also be exacerbated as means are found within marginal enclaves for generating a coherent voice. As the marginal groups find ways of cementing otherwise disparate intelligibilities, so the voice of critique may be amplified.[3]

From Critique to Transformation

With the stage thus set, we may consider the possibility of theoretical transformation within the sciences. There are many implements available in the struggle against hegemonic discourses, honorable and dishonorable, cunning and crude. However, for knowledge-generating communities nurtured in the soil of Enlightenment thought, the major grounds for challenge are rational or, in contemporary terms, guided by discursive conventions. It is discursive exchange that should reveal the promise and peril of any given position, theory, or ontology. The rules of such exchange—definitions of what constitutes a winning argument—are matters of continuous debate.[4] But if we view the matter in terms of intelligibility nuclei, at least one general surmise is clear: attempts to contain, reduce, or nullify the power of any given discourse structure must optimally take place in terms falling outside the structure itself. To use the terms of an ontology against itself is either self-contradictory or succeeds only in reinstating the terms of the ontology. In the above example, empiricism cannot be proven untrue via empirical research, nor can phenomenology be discredited by appeal to personal experience. In both cases, to win the argument would be simultaneously to lose it.

Thus, to return to the alternatives laid out in the semiotic square, we find that effective counters to any given nucleus of intelligibility must optimally rely on suppositions contained within alternative nuclei—either linked by binary opposition, furnished by contrast, or derived from new distinctions. To withstand the hegemonic thrust of empiricist discourse, for example, one can develop arguments in terms of a rationalist philosophy (as binary), phenomenology (as difference), or Buddhism (as non-Western). Let us view each of these counters as *conventions of negation,* essentially argumentative strategies intended to displace a given system of intelligibility. To assert a given state of affairs is thus akin to an invitation to a dance. Others may join the dance through affirmation, but the invitation both activates and legitimates a body of conventions of negation.

Let us focus more fully on the capacity of conventions of negation to displace a given form of intelligibility. In the early stages of exchange, conventions of negation gain impact through their critical attacks on the dominant discourse—by pointing to factors or processes it excludes, demonstrating shortcomings according to various criteria, decrying various oppressive effects, condemning underlying motives, and so on. Here we may speak of a *critical phase* of paradigm shift, in which conventions of negation are employed to undermine confidence in the dominant form of intelligibility. During this phase, however, critique will necessarily employ language fragments from an alternative nucleus, from the range of propositions lending intelligibility to the critique. To justify a negation will require fragments not given in the nucleus under attack. In effect, critique admits into the dialogue terms in an overlapping or contrasting nucleus of intelligibility. Thus, to criticize a theory of cognition because it takes no account of the emotions simultaneously presumes and substantiates an ontology in which the emotions are central. To fault scientific theory on the grounds of its ideological underpinnings is to inveigh against the traditional presumption that facts are ideologically neutral. These interjections of an alternative reality are significant harbingers of a *transformational phase* in the shifting of discursive paradigms. In pursuing critique alone, the terms of the alternative intelligibility remain skeletal. The full impact of critique is only achieved with the articulation of the unspoken subtext, the body of discourse upon which the critique depends for its coherence but which is itself unspecified within the critique. One may effectively argue against cognitive theories for their insensitivity to the emotions. Yet, the cognitive view is only replaced when the full "reality of the emotions" is made palpable (for example, by dividing the mind between cognitive and emotional domains and demonstrating the biological priority of the latter). A full transformation in theoretical understanding would thus depend on unpacking the implications of the "emotions critique" in such a way that an "alternative world" became palpable.[5]

In schematic form, we begin with a given system of intelligibility (*Intelligibility A* in Figure 1.2) containing an array of interrelated propositions concerning a given domain (for example, a theory of astronomy, human reasoning, aesthetic taste, and so on). This array of propositions in the ideal case is coherent and self-contained; that is, its propositions are noncontradictory and do not substantiate other worlds. The critical phase begins with various conventions of negation. One or more of the propositions con-

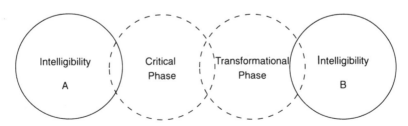

Figure 1.2   Phases in the Transformation of Intelligibility

tained in system A are challenged by arguments making use of terms not included in A. The critical phase gives way to the transformational phase when the discursive implications of the critical forms are elaborated. As the implicational network is progressively articulated, an alternative system of intelligibility emerges (B). As this system is increasingly employed in the "ontology" of the world (for example, in naming and interpreting what there is), its credibility gradually rivals that of Intelligibility A; it approaches the status of plain talk or common sense. Thus, within the sciences, if the alternative intelligibility can be attached to successful products (such as predictions, technology, or cures), the heretical may slowly give way to the plausible, and the plausible to the certain. The sense of knowledge in progress becomes palpable.

Of course, I am speaking here of an idealized course of theoretical transformation rather than the messy and disjunctive proceedings of scholarly life. This idealization will prove useful, however, in understanding the life course of theories in contemporary psychology. Before making this application, a brief comparison of alternative accounts of paradigm change might be useful. I am hardly proposing the above schema as a general account of theoretical transformation, but its scope and implications are sufficient that certain comparisons are useful. At the outset, the analysis owes a clear debt to the arguments of Quine (1960) and Kuhn (1970), which stress the problematic relationship between accounts of the world and their putative objects. With Quine, scientific theories are not and cannot be "data determined," a point I will pursue more fully in the next chapter. With Kuhn I can see little reason to argue that scientific revolution is in any profound sense driven by the systematic application of rules for hypothesis testing and revision. Similarly, the present approach is highly consistent with history of science and sociology of science accounts that stress the importance of social process in changing conceptions of reality, again a subject for future discussion. The present account differs from most sociological and historical analyses, however, in its major emphasis on processes of argumentation as opposed, let's say, to issues of economic context, power, personal motivation, or social influences. Although issues of economics, power, and the like can be transformed into discursive representations and thus treated as integers in the argumentation process, the present analysis is necessarily restricted in its emphasis.

In my view, the present account also helps to compensate for certain shortcomings in Kuhn's formulation. For Kuhn, the driving force in paradigm change is the intrusion of the anomalous—facts that are independent of prevailing systems of intelligibility. As Kuhn proposes, factual anomalies that are not intelligible in terms of (or predicted by) the prevailing paradigm begin to emerge. At some point, as these anomalies accumulate, a "Gestalt shift" in theoretical perspective occurs. A new theory emerges that can account for the range of anomalies and, if truly effective, for all the findings generated within the previously existing paradigm. Yet such a view suffers on several counts. First, there is no way of explaining the genesis of anomalies. Kuhn characterizes anomalies as "unsuspected phenomena," "fundamental novelties of fact," and "extended episodes with a regularly recurrent structure" (p. 52), in effect as forms of brute data that cause the scientist to recognize "that nature has somehow violated the paradigm-induced expectations that govern normal science" (pp. 52–53). Yet if paradigms of understanding determine (as Kuhn also holds) how we construct, construe, or render a fact, then how are "unsuspected phenomena" to violate or challenge the accepted understandings?[6] In effect, a paradigm of intelligibility must precede the discovery of an anomaly rather than vice versa. From the present standpoint, the anomaly as driving force is replaced by a tension among intelligibilities, that is, by negations standing against assertions. Such tensions are an inevitable byproduct of naming and explaining, and virtually ensure an instability in theoretical understandings.

As this view makes apparent, paradigm shifts in science are in significant degree matters of evolution in socially negotiated forms of meaning. Facts, anomalies, or technology may play a significant role in altering forms of scientific understanding, but their significance is largely achieved because of the forms of intelligibility by which they are constituted. The criteria of logic, comprehensiveness, and the like do not render science rational; such criteria are essentially moves within various domains of discourse—rhetorical devices for achieving discursive efficacy. This does not mean that anything goes—at least in practice. Conventions of discourse are often sedimented, restrictive, and wedded to social practice in compelling ways. However, from the present perspective one is invited to scrutinize with care the warranting conventions of any given era. One must be perpetually sensitive to the inimical and potentially debilitating consequences of existing conventions and constraints.

Theoretical Transformation in Psychological Science

During the past century professional psychologists have formulated an impressive if not staggering array of theoretical perspectives. At the same time, many of these theories fall into overlapping clusters—instances of shared intelligibility—and such clusters vary greatly in their centrality to the profession (for example, their coverage in textbooks, representation in course requirements, or claim on research funds). As is widely recognized, during the greater part of the present century a certain cluster of *behaviorist* theories dominated the scientific landscape. Virtually all other theoretical perspectives occupied positions of marginal significance. Yet within the past several decades, behaviorist theory has withered substantially. It has been succeeded by a cluster of *cognitive* theories. In effect, a discursive transformation of enormous scope has taken place. The immediate task is to elucidate this transformation in terms of the discursive process I have just described: What is the relationship between the behaviorist and cognitive intelligibilities, from whence comes their discursive support, and why was transformation necessary? As I hope to show, because of the character of this transformation, the cognitive venture—along with all individualist accounts of human knowledge—is emptied of justification. A vacuum is created for the emergence of a new perspective on knowledge.

The Behavioral Period: Symbiosis and Sonority

First we must consider the enormous popularity of the behaviorist perspective during the first half of this century. Although one can explain this ascendancy in a number of ways, the present approach sensitizes one to aspects of the discursive context. What other intelligibilities, we might ask, were in ascendance during this period, and in what ways was the behaviorist movement rationalized or supported by these views? What is most striking in this case is that a high degree of overlap may be recognized between *behaviorist theory* and the prevailing account of *experimental methodology*, along with the *metatheoretical perspective* articulated by logical empiricist philosophers. During these decades the three bodies of discourse were mutually supportive and sustaining. Theoretical accounts of human functioning could be justified by recourse to both the methodological and metatheoretical intelligibilities. Truth claims about human behavior could be sustained through the ancillary discourses, the one justifying the factual basis of the claims ("experiments demonstrate the causal relations between stimuli and responses") and the other the philosophic probity of the scientific effort ("science rests on rational foundations").

To elaborate, we may first consider the relationship that exists between the received view of logical empiricism and behaviorist theory in psychology. The scientific metatheory first asserts a fundamental independence between the natural world and the scientific observer. It is the task of the scientist to develop theory that maps with fidelity the contours of the world as given: "The essential task of the scientist is to identify facts with the highest possible precision, for they form the stock in trade of all his work" (Brown and Ghiselli 1955). The received view also endows the scientist with several major capacities through which objective knowledge may be acquired. Among the most important of these are the capacities for accurate observation and logic. Initial observation is intended to furnish the scientist with a rudimentary acquaintance with the phenomena of interest. Such observation, when combined with canons of inductive logic, enables the scientist to formulate a series of tentative hypotheses concerning the conditions under which various phenomena occur. The scientist should ideally derive from observation a set of propositions (normally of the variety, "if X antecedent . . . then Y consequence") to account for regularities in the relationship among observed events. In the case of psychology the focus of interest is the behavior of the individual. Individual behavior thus serves as the consequence for which real world conditions function as antecedents. Given general, lawlike propositions concerning the relations between antecedents and consequences—along with hypothesized explanations for their relationship—the scientist is then to employ deductive logic to derive predictions about patterns of nature as yet unobserved. These predictions are also stated in the "if . . . then" format.

On the basis of these deductively derived hypotheses the scientist again enters the world of nature, using controlled observation to test the validity of the initial set of propositions. The results of this new set of observations serve to sustain, modify, or invalidate the propositions initially propounded. Thus, through observational test, scientists gain confidence in, amend, or discard their initial propositions. This skeletal account of what is often termed the *hypothetico-deductive* process is diagrammed in the upper half of Figure 1.3. Ideally the process of observation-proposition-test-refine can be sustained indefinitely, resulting in an increasingly precise, well-differentiated, and well-validated network of interrelated propositions. These propositions are said to carry or convey "objective knowledge" insofar as it is obtainable, and should facilitate the prediction and control of human activity. In Brown and Ghiselli's terms, "The object of the scientist is to understand the phenomenon with which he [sic] is working. He considers that he understands it when he can successfully predict its expressions . . . or when his knowledge enables him to control its expression to achieve certain ends" (1955, p. 35).

Given this sketch of the hypothetico-deductive orientation to knowledge, we may now examine its relationship to behaviorist conceptions of human functioning. As I will demonstrate, the essential narrative of progressive knowledge portrayed in the metatheory is reincarnated in behaviorist accounts of human learning. When psychologists set out to "observe" and "discover" the nature of human behavior, their senses unencumbered by theoretical commitments—or, at least, so they believed—they effectively "derived from nature" the same theory of knowledge that rationalized their activities as scientists.

Consider: At the outset behaviorist theory possesses a strong environmentalist bias. From the behaviorist perspective human activity is viewed as a series of "responses" guided, controlled, or stimulated by environmental inputs. Thus, we find "stimulus inputs" at the level of theory serving as a substitute for the "state of nature" at the level of metatheory. Stimulus inputs as preeminent determinants of human activity are virtually identical in their function to the state of nature (as a stimulus to theory construction)

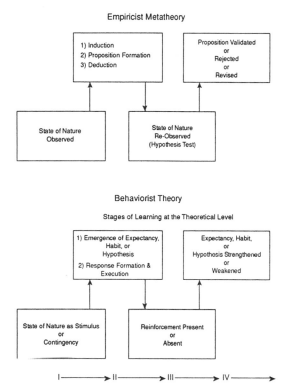

Figure 1.3   Parallel States in Advancing Scientific
Knowledge and Behavioral Learning

within the metatheory (see Figure 1.3). With respect to the processes of
observation and logic (Phase II), we must distinguish between the two
prominent paradigms within the behaviorist movement. *Radical behaviorists* such as Watson and Skinner had so thoroughly assimilated the "lore of
science" and its concern with observables that they avoided statements
about the hypothetical realm of psychological states. Thus, within radical
behaviorism, reinstigation of the second state of the hypothetico-deductive
process is not readily apparent. Equivalences to psychological processes
such as "observation" and "logic" are difficult to locate. However, the
second stage does manifest itself, not in statements about the internal workings of organisms, but as descriptions of the *ends* served by behavior. Although nothing is said about internal processes of rational thought, the
human species acts so as to maximize its adaptiveness—that is, it acts in a
rational manner. As Watson (1924) described it, "although born more
helpless than almost any other mammal, [man] very quickly learns to out-

strip other animals by reason of the . . . habits he acquires" (p. 224). And as Skinner (1971) advanced: "The process of operant conditioning . . . supplements natural selection. Important consequences of behavior which could not play a role in evolution because they were not sufficiently stable features of the environment are made effective through operant conditioning during the lifetime of the individual whose power in dealing with his world is thus vastly increased" (p. 46). In effect, although no specific mental processes are identified, radical behaviorists describe human behavior as rational and problem-solving in its effects. The second step of the hypothetico-deductive process is thus achieved covertly.

Owing in large measure to the liberalization of logical empiricist metatheory (Koch 1966), radical behaviorism was slowly supplanted by neobehaviorist (S-O-R) theory. The early empiricist tenets, which laid great importance on the precise correspondence between theoretical terms and real-world observables, were found too rigidly constraining. As it was argued, mature sciences do have a place for theoretical terms not directly referring to observables. Terms such as "gravity," "force field," and "magnetism" are all highly serviceable within the natural sciences, and yet they are without immediately observable referents. This liberalization on the metatheoretical level enabled psychologists to develop the concept of "hypothetical constructs" (MacCorquodale and Meehl 1948), terms that referred to hypothetical psychological states intervening between stimulus and response. With the door thus open to introduce talk about "the mind," the behaviorist was free to develop terms that stood in functional correspondence to the processes of observation and logic so central to the metatheory. Thus, for Clark Hull (1943), such terms as "habit strength," "incentive strength," and "inhibitory potential" operated in concert to produce adaptive responses to given circumstances. Within expectancy-value formulations (Rotter 1966; Ajzen and Fishbein 1980), the term "expectancy" furnished a parallel at the theoretical level for "hypothesis" at the metatheoretical level. Social learning theorist Albert Bandura (1977) employs the concept of "expectancy" in the same way but adds additional processes of "covert problem solving" and "verification through thought" to the psychological arsenal.

Where scientific metatheory now calls for the hypothesis test as the next step in advancing knowledge (Figure 1.3), learning theorists substitute the concept of reinforcement. For theorists such as Skinner (1971), Thorndike (1933), and Bandura (1977), reinforcement selects and sustains certain response patterns while discouraging or "stamping out" others. Patterns of the former variety are often termed "adaptive" while those of the latter are "maladaptive." In this sense, the results of the hypothesis test serve the same function as reinforcement: they are nature's means of informing one of the adequacy of one's actions. It follows from this analysis that the fourth stage of the hypothetico-deductive model, theory extension and/or revision, is but a later stage of the process of "behavior shaping" for the Skinnerian, or a single step in a process of "expectancy confirmation" for the more cognitively oriented learning theorist. In both cases the mental functioning of the individual is rendered increasingly adequate to the environmental surroundings. The entire hypothetico-deductive system finds its coordinates in various forms of behaviorist learning theory.

Perhaps there is no more fitting conclusion to the present argument than a pair of quotes from Clark Hull's *Principles of Behavior*. Speaking first of the nature of science, Hull recites the hypothetico-deductive litany (stages are indicated in margin):

I. Empirical observation supplemented by shrewd conjecture, is the main source of the primary principles or postulates of a science. Such formulations, when taken in various combinations together with relevant antecedent conditions,

II. yield inferences or theorems, of which some may agree with the empirical outcome of the conditions in question, and some may not. Primary propositions yielding logical deductions which consistently agree with the observed

III. empirical outcome are retained whereas, those which disagree are rejected or modified. As the sifting of this trial-and-error process continues, there gradually emerges a limited series of primary principles whose joint

IV. implications are progressively more likely to agree with relevant observations. Deductions made from these surviving postulates, while never absolutely certain do at length become highly trustworthy. (Hull 1943, p. 382)

The similarities between this account of science and Hull's theory of learning are striking. With regard to the latter, Hull summarizes his views as follows (again, parallels with stages in the hypothetico-deductive model are noted in the margin):

The substance of the elementary learning process as revealed by much experimentation seems to be this: A condition of need exists . . . initiated by the action of

I. environmental stimulus energies. This . . . activates numerous

II. vaguely adaptive reaction potentials . . . laid down by organic evolution. In case one of these random responses, or a sequence of them, results in the reduction of a need dominant at the time, there follows an indirect effect

III.   that is known as reinforcement. This consists in (1) a strengthen-
        ing of the particular receptor-effector connections which originally
        mediated the reaction and (2) a tendency for all receptor dis-
        charge(s) occurring at about the same time to acquire new connec-
        tions with the effectors mediating the response in question. The
        first effect is known as primitive trial-and-error learning; the sec-
        ond is known as conditioned-reflex learning. As a result, when the
        same need again arises in this or a similar situation, the stimuli will
        activate the same effectors more certainly, more promptly, and
        more vigorously than on the first occasion. Such action, while

IV.   by no means adaptively infallible, in the long run will reduce the
        need more surely than would a chance sampling of the unlearned
        response tendencies . . . Thus the acquisition of such receptor-
        effector connections will, as a rule, make for survival—i.e., it will
        be adaptive. (Hull 1943, pp. 386–387)

Both science and human learning processes thus work in an analogous manner toward similar ends. The theory of human learning replicates the theory
of science.

    During these decades both metatheory and theory were also synchronous
with the prevailing conception of methodology. Of course, observational
methods and controlled experimentation in particular were themselves favored by empiricist philosophy. For psychologists, the properties of the real
world ("material antecedents" for the logical empiricist, "stimulus world"
for the behavioral theorist) were captured in the methodological language
by the concept of the "independent variable." In effect, experimental conditions exist independent of the organism and logically prior to its behavior
in these conditions. The scientist's manipulations of the independent variable release causal forces that direct or constrain the behavior of the organism. The "resulting activity" of the organism is captured by the concept of
the "dependent variable"—caused by and therefore dependent on the manipulation of the independent variable. The dependent variable in methodological terms thus parallels the concepts of "material consequent" in the
logical empiricist metatheory and "behavioral response" in behaviorist theory. In effect, the account of what takes place within an experiment, along
with the choice of terminology for describing experimental particulars, was
fully resonant with the metatheoretical and theoretical perspectives of the
period. The metatheory presumed an orderly world of mechanically related
entities, the method promised a precise tracing of the causal linkages, and
the resulting picture of human functioning was one in which human behavior is dependent on its antecedent conditions. Metatheory, theory, and
method all played in sonorous harmony.[7]

The Critical Phase: Deteriorating Intelligibilities

Very little of the optimism and sense of mission that pervaded this period of mutually supportive discourses remains today. Each of the interdependent bodies of discourse has undergone extensive criticism. The critical phase of the transformation process has been broadscale and compelling at all three levels. First, on the level of metatheory, logical empiricism had always fared better in its translation to other disciplines than within its own philosophical ranks. There was long-standing philosophic debate concerning the place of personal experience in science, the relationship of material events to experience, the possibility of linking observables to language, and more. However, from midcentury on, the philosophy of science became dominated by an increasingly articulate and incisive range of critiques. Effective arguments were formulated against the full range of empiricist assumptions, including the traditional separation of analytic from synthetic propositions (Quine 1953), induction as a method for developing theory (Hanson 1958; Popper 1959), the logic of verification (Popper 1959), the possibility of operational definitions (Koch 1963), word-object correspondence (Quine 1960), the interdependence of theoretical understanding and prediction (Toulmin 1961), the commensurability of competing theories (Kuhn 1962), the separation of fact and value (MacIntyre 1973), the possibility of theoretically unsaturated or brute facts (Hanson 1958; Quine 1960), the foundational rationality of scientific procedures (Barrett 1979; Feyerabend 1976), the possibility of falsifying theory (Quine 1953), the nonpartisan character of scientific knowledge (Habermas 1971), and the applicability of the covering law model to human action (White 1978). As many philosophers now conclude, the philosophy of scientific knowledge has entered a *post-empiricist stage* (Thomas 1979). Outside a few straggling survivors, the attempt to ground science in a foundational rationality is largely moribund.[8]

At the level of theory, psychologists have also conducted a full-scale assault on behavioral theory. Much of the early criticism was either articulated or orchestrated by Sigmund Koch (1963). Problems with the intervening variable (or the S-O-R) account, the linking of constructs with observables, mounting "defining experiments," and the generality of behavioral laws were among his early targets. Later critiques challenged the behaviorist assumptions of cross-species generality in the laws of learning, the historical contingency of behavioral principles, and the ideological underpinnings of behavioral theory. Most dramatic in the pervasiveness of its impact has been the amplification of nativist arguments similar to those posed by Gestalt psychologists of the late 1930s, which claim that one cannot account for human activity in terms of stimulus inputs alone. As

Chomsky (1968) effectively demonstrated, capacities for the skilled use of language could not, in principle, be derived from environmental reinforcement. For Piaget (1952) and his colleagues, capacities for abstract thought were not acquired through learning but developed through the natural unfolding of the child. More generally, the organism appears to have its own inherent tendencies—for searching for and processing information, formulating hypotheses, moving toward goals, and so on. With the emergence of such arguments, the unidirectional chain of causality—from stimulus world to behavioral response—is broken. In many respects, it was argued, the organism harbors its own autonomous causes.

Finally, accompanying the deterioration of commitment to empiricist metatheory and behavioral theory was a widespread discontent with the experimental method. Early critics stressed the extent to which experimental findings were subject to experimenter bias or demand characteristics established by the experimenter (see Rosnow's 1981 summary). Critics also expressed concern with the ethics of experimental manipulation (Smith 1969; Kelman 1968), the manipulative attitude of experimenters toward their subjects (Ring 1967), the ecological validity of experiments, and the extent to which experimental results are achieved through skilled stagecraft (McGuire 1973). Still others, including critical psychologists and feminists, raised ideological issues, arguing that experiments replicated the system of domination and control inherent in capitalist society, or the male personality, or both (Hampden-Turner 1970; Reinharz 1985). Substantial segments of the research community now seek viable alternatives to experimental methodology (including field research, qualitative research case methods, dialogic methods, and so on).

The Transformational Phase: Cognition without Consensus

As we find, the closely blended fabric of the previous era—metatheory, theory, and method—begins to unravel. Empiricist metatheory, behavioral theory, and experimental methodology have all suffered from broad critique. The critical phase of discursive transition is thus fully mature. But has a transformational phase occurred in which a new set of interlocking intelligibilities has been forged? What is our present condition and what may we anticipate from the future? To explore these questions it is useful to return to the semiotic square (see Figure 1.3). Here we may try to locate alternative intelligibilities upon which the existing critiques are premised and consider the possibility of a successful transformation.

Let us first consider the possibility of transformation at the level of metatheory. With the demise of empiricist foundations, what alternative philosophy of science can be generated from the penumbra of understandings on which the critiques were founded? In my view, most of the anti-empiricist arguments can be clustered in three major categories. There are first *within paradigm* critiques, that is, attempts to revise certain assumptions in the existing metatheory but without sacrificing the presumption of the foundational rationality of the scientific effort. This was clearly Popper's (1963) attempt as he inveighed against the inductivist presumptions of traditional empiricism, but he replaced it with the equally foundational view of "critical rationalism." Although arguable in several respects, I would also place central works by Lakatos (1970), Laudan (1977), and Bhaskar (1978) in a similar category. That is, while abandoning various tenets of empiricist foundationalism, they retain certain key assumptions (such as subject-object independence) and simultaneously sustain the search for transcendent rationale. In effect, such criticism fails to provoke what I would view as a radical transformation in perspective.

Second, there are strands of *binary critique* woven into the critical phase, that is, arguments that derive largely from the standpoint most traditionally antagonistic to empiricism, namely, the rationalist. As commonly argued, the history of Western theories of knowledge can largely be written in terms of pendulum swings between accounts of human knowledge as a repository of experiential inputs and accounts holding the mind to be an originary source of knowledge. Thus, for major philosophers in the empiricist tradition (Locke, Hume, the Mills) individual knowledge is largely built up from experiences of environmental events. The individual comes to know through observation; without experiential contact with the world there is little that the individual can be said to know. In contrast, for philosophers more commonly identified within the rationalist tradition (Spinoza, Descartes, Kant) the inherent character of the human mind is critical to the development of knowledge. Without a native capacity for rationality or for organizing the world in certain ways, we could scarcely be credited with possessing knowledge. In these terms, a logical empiricist philosophy of science largely represents a twentieth-century refinement of traditional empiricist conceptions. Thus, given the history of debate across the binary, critiques of rationalist stripe were to be anticipated. To illustrate, in certain respects the critiques of both Hanson (1958) and Kuhn (1962) have made use of assumptions springing from the soil of the rationalist tradition. For Hanson, mental concepts must precede the identification of facts; for Kuhn, paradigm transformations are akin to Gestalt shifts—driven not by data but by inherent mental tendencies.

Can the discursive implications of rationalist critiques be fleshed out to form an alternative theory of scientific knowledge? It is interesting that no philosopher has stepped forward to extend the underlying assumptions into a full-blown theory of knowledge. In my view, this possibility is virtually precluded by the past three centuries of debate in philosophy. Problems of solipsism, innate knowledge, mind-material separation, and political conservatism, among others (see Chapter 5), have effectively discouraged this pursuit. In effect, the replacement of empiricism by a rationalist foundationalism is unlikely.

Finally, at the metatheoretical level, one discerns critique from *alternative modalities,* that is, from perspectives that differ from both the logical empiricist and the rationalist accounts and collapse them into a single unit itself now the pole of a new binary. Such critiques are at once the least and most effective. They are ineffectual to the extent that they simply do not speak to those within the dominant systems of intelligibility in a way that is cogent to their concerns. In effect, they often appear as "critiques from nowhere," tangential, or outside the dialogue. At the same time, such critiques are most effective, inasmuch as (1) those under attack have little means of defending themselves, and (2) the grounds of argument begin to offer significant alternatives to existing views. For empiricists, critiques of the rationalist form are virtually ritualistic; the arguments and counterarguments have played back and forth over the centuries with such repetitiveness that "yet another round" is scarcely unsettling. The alternative intelligibility is well understood and its shortcomings apparent. However, in the case of critiques from outside the binary, neither of these conditions pertains. Rebuttals have not been well prepared, and the problems inherent in the alternatives are beyond comprehension.

In my view, two of the major lines of anti-empiricist critique find their roots in an alternative modality. These are the genres of *ideological* and *social critique.* Critiques of the ideological variety center on the moral and political biases inherent in the empiricist view. Both MacIntyre (1981) and Habermas (1971), for example, point to ways in which empiricist conceptions of knowledge are inimical to human welfare. In effect, they fail to measure up by moral and political standards. Empiricists have no well-developed means of demonstrating that they are without moral and political biases; in fact, they have systematically avoided participating in dialogue on moral and political goods. Much the same may be said of the social critique, that is, criticism that points to various social processes at work in generating scientific intelligibilities. Thus, in his stress on the communal basis of paradigm commitment, Kuhn (1962) is essentially arguing for a social account of scientific knowledge. The same outcome is favored by Feyerabend's (1976) discussion of rationality as a form of cultural tradition. Again, the empiricist is unprepared for rebuttal; social processes are ineffectually declared to be either uninteresting, interfering, or irrelevant, and conditions are thus prepared for social process to become the basis for an alternative theory of knowledge. In the following chapter, I shall fold the ideological critique into the social and, with additional resources, lay the groundwork for a full-blown successor project: *social constructionism.* In this case, both empiricism and rationalism will form the rejected pole of a new binary—both hold knowledge to be an *individual* possession, while the new polarity will take knowledge to be a byproduct of *communal* relationships.

In striking contrast to the inability of philosophers to mount a compelling alternative to empiricist foundationalism, psychologists have moved rapidly into a period of theoretical transformation. In large measure this is because critiques of behaviorist theory were lodged within the traditional empiricist-rationalist binary and relied on various assumptions born of the rationalist tradition. They argued for the incapacity of behaviorist theory to take inherent rational propensities into account, to consider the domain of thought processes, or to grapple with such issues as consciousness and intentionality—all congenial arguments within a rationalist frame. Most important for our purposes, psychologists began to unpack the assumptive forestructure of such critiques, thus transforming criticism into an alternative ontology. Thus, for example, when Chomsky (1968) argued that language production (and by implication, human action more generally) cannot be understood in terms of environmental reinforcement, he was making an important contribution to the literature of critique. As he went on to account for the child's enormous flexibility in constructing well-formed sentences in terms of inherent tendencies (the "deep structure" of grammatical knowledge), the positive ontology of a rationalist theory was under way. It is the flowering of the positive ontology that constitutes what we now see as "the cognitive revolution." In its emphasis on schemas, information processing, environmental scanning, and schema-driven memory, for example—all inherent in the individual "mind"—the cognitive movement represents a contemporary reemergence of the rationalist philosophic tradition. In the case of psychological theory, then, the transformation in theoretical intelligibilities is virtually complete.

Turning finally to the prevailing account of methodology, we find a trajectory similar to that of empiricist metatheory. While effectively reducing confidence in the experimental method, critique has failed to produce an alternative of broad credibility.[9] The chief reason that transformation has failed is that most of the existing critiques have been "within paradigm." That is, to assail the experiment for its lack of external validity, the operation of experimenter bias and demand characteristics, and its ethical improprieties is not to conclude that experiments are problematic in principle. Nothing is said in this case that impugns their knowledge-producing potential. Thus, the critic's invitation is not to abandon experimentation as a failed program but to locate a means of improving its efficacy (for example, through field experimentation, double blind procedures, research ethics boards). Further, those attempting a transformation in methodology confront a common problem: the very concept of methodology as a warranting device is wedded to the empiricist tradition and its emphasis on "truth through method." Thus, feminists, phenomenologists, interpretivists, and others seeking a genuine alternative to empiricist methods find themselves struggling to demonstrate that their methods are adequate to empiricist standards of rigor (such as validity, reliability, neutrality, and so on). Failing to demonstrate their adequacy on these (empiricist) grounds, they have found it difficult to convince the scientific community that they are indeed conducting scientific research. For example, dialogic methodology (which attempts to generate new insights through subject-scientist dialogue) does not seem credible as a tool of "scientific" research. And, of course, attempts to demonstrate an equality with empiricist methods typically fall short of the mark. Indeed, the very attempt to demonstrate, for example, that qualitative methods are as rigorous as questionnaire or observational methods only lends silent sanction to the empiricist conception of science.

By the same token, there has been no flowering of what might be called "rationalist research methods." No one has explored the kinds of methods that would result if the view of the individual as inherently rational, information searching, and concept sustaining were extended to the level of scientific practice. In the behaviorist era, psychologists fashioned the individual in much the same mold as the scientist. The common person was simply a scientist operating less systematically and less rigorously than the professional. Science and human psychology formed a coherent whole. But there has been no attempt in the era of the cognitive revolution to generate such coherence—no deliberation on the nature of scientific knowledge should the prevailing view of human functioning be taken seriously. The result is a peculiar disjunction between contemporary methodology (congenial with an empiricist view of science and a behaviorist view of the person) and prevailing cognitivist theory.

This disjunction between contemporary method and theory belies an ironic incoherence. The cognitive theorist conceptualizes human functioning in a way that essentially destroys the warrant for empiricist methods. To the extent that theorists claim that cognitive processes are fixed by genetics and operate in "top down" fashion—with the individual sifting and sorting information on the basis of inherent, structural requirements—the individual loses his or her ability to claim accurate knowledge of an independent world. In this case, the individual's representations of the world are not determined by experience—what is "out there"—but by the requirements of the cognitive system itself.[10] Applying this view of human functioning at the level of scientific practice, we find that the scientist loses credibility as an "authority on nature." Experimental methods could not "correct for cognitive biasing," because the experimenter would inevitably conduct research in ways required by the demands of the cognitive system—thus, for example, employing experiments in the service of schemas already embraced and interpreting all data in precisely the ways required by one's proclivities for information processing. In addition, the experimenter loses justification for speaking of experimental manipulation and control. Rather, from the perspective of cognitive theory, subjects bring to experiments processes that will determine what they must take away or derive from the conditions; experimenters in turn will make interpretations consistent with their own initial schemas and problematically related to the activities of their subjects. Thus, the entire logic of "independent" and "dependent" variables is obviated. In effect, cognitive psychologists are in the uncomfortable position of embracing theories denying the possibility that they be subjected to empirical evaluation. And to rely on empirical methods is, by logical implication, to deny the very conceptions of human functioning on which the cognitive revolution is grounded.

Whither Individual Knowledge?

This chapter began with concern over the long-standing presumption of knowledge as an individual possession. Can this view be sustained, and in light of shifting global conditions, should it remain robust? We hoped to gain insight into these matters by exploring the condition of scientific psychology—that discipline most systematically engaged in generating firm knowledge about the individual's knowledge-generating capacities. As we have found, over the century mainstream psychology's position on matters of knowledge has changed markedly. A major transformation in assumptions has occurred in the replacement of behavioral theory with cognitive theory. However, as Figure 1.4 demonstrates, this transformation is accomplished at enormous cost.

Behavioral theory emerged in a discursive context fully congenial with its major tenets. It was largely supported by the dominant philosophy of science and buttressed by a felicitous discourse on methods. Both the foundational philosophy and the prevailing confidence in methods have now eroded, yet there have been no significant successors to render support to the individualist conception of knowledge. Thus present-day cognitive theory exists in a precarious position. It is a perspective on knowledge without a supporting philosophy of science (metatheory) and one which employs a methodology antithetical to its basic suppositions. In effect, cognitive psychologists are bereft of two major forms of sustaining discourse: a philosophy of science to justify the rationality of cognitive theory and a methodology to properly warrant its claims to truth.

In this light, we may anticipate that cognitive psychology, like its nineteenth-century predecessor mentalism, will soon run its course. It is possible, of course, that even when shorn of supporting rationale, the cognitive movement can remain self-sustaining. In my view the present vitality of the movement can be attributed to its alliance with the computer, both as

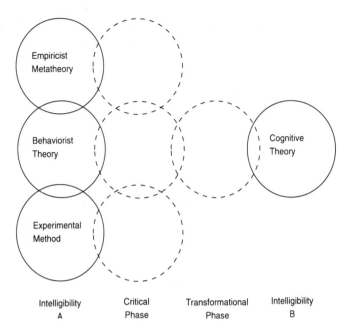

Figure 1.4   Cognitive Theory without Ancillary Support

a metaphor for theory construction and a technological testing ground. By equating cognitive processes with computational functioning, using the computer as a means of modeling human decision making, and concluding that successful computer models demonstrate that the mind operates in just this way, cognitivists have developed an effective, albeit viciously circular, means of lending credibility to their endeavors. Then too, the academic landscape is strewn with self-sustaining enclaves that continue to trade on icons long since absent from common exchange.

The possibility of an enduring hegemony, however, seems doubtful. Drawing from the preceding analysis, assertions in the cognitive modality establish the conditions for negation, and as these negations are progressively articulated, there are few resources available for resistance—no obdurate facts, no foundational philosophy, and few suppositions that can be sustained in the face of the philosophic arguments yielded up by preceding centuries. Even now the computer metaphor is stimulating an array of criticisms, and as I shall outline in Chapter 5, the corpus of self-critical literature is now bringing the paradigm close to implosion.

As the new critical phase runs its course, can we anticipate a return to some form of behaviorism? Such a return might be anticipated by the preceding history of psychology, moving as it did from nineteenth-century

mentalism to twentieth-century behaviorism and then giving way to cognitivism. It might also be anticipated in terms of the debates in philosophy
between those of empiricist and rationalist stripe—debates that have see-
sawed back and forth over the centuries without resolution. What is to
prevent yet another swing of the intellectual pendulum? In my view, such a
swing is contraindicated. First, it would be essential to locate ways of transcending the array of critique to which behaviorism has already been exposed—from within the paradigm, from the rationalist pole of the binary,
and from the ideological and social sectors. Further, as the present analysis
suggests, there would be no undergirding philosophy of science upon which
to rest such views of human functioning. Finally, it would be necessary to
deflect the rising tides of intellectual change, currents that together favor the
replacement of the individualist view of knowledge with a communal formulation. We now confront the possibility of transcending the Enlightenment heritage and its empiricist-rationalist binary. It is to this pursuit that
we turn in the following chapters.

2 Crisis in Representation and the Emergence of Social Construction

As the view of knowledge as individual possession reaches an impasse, transformations are taking place in other scholarly domains. These shifts in sensibility share certain common themes, which suggest an alternative to the individual conception of knowledge, namely, a view of knowledge as lodged within the sphere of social relatedness. This chapter first outlines these emerging dialogues and their implications for a social constructionist view of human science. I give primary attention to the deterioration of traditional beliefs in true and objective representation of the world. Ideological, literary-rhetorical, and social critiques are foregrounded. After distilling from these critiques a number of central constructionist assumptions, I explore the contours of inquiry invited by such assumptions. As I shall propose, constructionism does not necessitate the abandonment of traditional pursuits. Rather, it places them within a different frame, with a resulting shift in emphasis and priorities. More important, constructionism invites new forms of inquiry, substantially expanding the scope and significance of the endeavors of human science.

The mandate of the sociobehavioral sciences has traditionally been to render objective accounts of human conduct and to explain its character, concerns that extend to the actions of all people from all cultures and across history. The sciences offer accounts of love and hostility, power and submission, rationality and passion, illness and well-being, work and play, along with wide-ranging explanations of their functioning. And, when they are suitably confident, scientists often hazard predictions—suggesting how children will develop, prejudices be reduced, learning prosper, intimacies deteriorate, the gross national product increase, and so on. Like their colleagues in the natural sciences, sociobehavioral scientists communicate these accounts to each other and to society primarily through language. To language the sciences entrust the duty of depicting or mirroring the results of their inquiry. It is language, then, that must bear objective truth—both now and for future generations. And if it is language that carries truth across cultures and into the future, one might reasonably conclude that species survival is dependent upon the functioning of language.

Although this much seems comfortably conventional, let us pause to reconsider the duties traditionally assigned to language. Can language bear the ponderous responsibility of "depicting" or "mirroring" what is the case? Can we be certain that language is the sort of vehicle that can "convey" truth to others? And when it is stamped into print, can we properly anticipate that it will "store" the truth for future generations? On what grounds do we rest such beliefs? Doubt begins when we consider everyday descriptions of people. We describe them as "intelligent," "warm," or "depressed," while their bodies are in a state of continuous motion. Their actions are protean, elastic, ever shifting, and yet our descriptions remain static and frozen. In what sense, then, is language *depicting* their actions? Or, if we use the term "hostile" to refer to Sarah's facial expression, Ted's tone of voice, and the relationship between Irish Catholics and Protestants, precisely what is the term "hostile" a picture of? Actual photos of the events would bear no resemblance to each other. In what sense, then, is the term mimetic?

Similar disjunctions between word and world can be discerned on the professional level. In psychoanalysis, for example, practitioners demonstrate an uncanny ability to apply a restricted vocabulary of description to an unusual and ever-changing array of actions. In spite of the vicissitudes of life trajectories, all analysands can be characterized as "repressed," "conflicted," and "defended." Similarly, in the behavioral laboratory, investigators are capable of retaining a given theoretical commitment regardless of the range and variability of their observation. From white rats to college sophomores, the theorist maintains that all make the same response (such as avoidance) to patterns of punishment. And in spite of the rigorous methods of observation employed in such laboratories, we can scarcely locate a behavioral theory that has been abandoned because it has been disproven by observations.

Our initial concern, then, is the relationship between descriptive language and the world it is designed to represent. The problem is of no small consequence, for as philosophers of science have long been aware, theory acquires value in the marketplace of scientific prediction to the degree that theoretical language corresponds to real-world events. If scientific language bears no determinate relationship to events external to language itself, its contribution to prediction becomes problematic, and scientific theory is closed to improvement through observation. The hope that knowledge can be advanced through continuous systematic observation proves futile. More generally, one may question the fundamental objectivity of scientific accounts. If such accounts do not correspond to the world, then what provides their warrant? This question is a critical one, since the claim to objectivity has furnished the chief basis for the broad authority claimed by the sciences over the past century.

It is in these many respects that logical empiricist philosophers were keen to establish a close relationship between language and observation. At the heart of the positivist movement, for example, lay the "verifiability principle of meaning" (called "meaning realism" in revised form), which held that the meaning of a proposition rests on its capacity for verification through observation; propositions not open to corroboration or emendation through observation are unworthy of further dispute. The problem, however, was to account for the connection between propositions and observations. Russell (1924) proposed that objective knowledge could be reduced to sets of "atomic propositions," the truth of which would rest on isolated and discriminable facts. In contrast, Schlick (1925) proposed that the meaning of single words within propositions must be established through ostensive ("pointing to") means. Carnap (1928) proposed that thing predicates represented "primitive ideas," thus reducing scientific propositions to reports of private experience. For Neurath (1933), propositions were to be verified through "protocol sentences," which were themselves linked to the biological processes of perception. All such statements on this view are reducible to the language of physics. In effect, there was a fundamental unity among all branches of science.

Yet such attempts to establish secure and determinate relationships between words and real-world referents left a variety of problems essentially unsolved. Were the propositions entering into the verifiability principle themselves subject to verification? If not, in what sense are they meaningful or trustworthy? If the object to which a proposition refers is in a state of continuous change, or ceases to exist, is the proposition only momentarily true? Propositions have meaning over and above the referential capacity of the individual words that make them up. How is such meaning to be understood? Are propositions subject to verification, or only single terms? Is verification a state of mind, and if so, in what sense are propositions about states of mind themselves verifiable? On what grounds are the factual atoms to be distinguished one from another? These and other nettlesome questions have remained recalcitrant to broadly compelling solution.

For many, the arguments of Popper (1959) and Quine (1960), in particular, gave reason for reconsidering the empirical basis of scientific claims to description. The former argued that there was no logical means of inducing general theoretical statements from observation, that is, of moving in a logically grounded way from a linguistic account of particulars to a general or universal account of classes. This led Popper to embrace Reichenbach's distinction between a "context of discovery" and a "context of justification." The context of discovery—that space in which the scientist makes initial claims to correspondence—was, for Popper, "irrelevant to the logical analysis of scientific knowledge" (p. 31). In effect, the means by which the scientist establishes the ontological claims to be put to study are not in themselves rationally justified. Quine's (1960) critique raised havoc with even the possibility of solid grounding in the context of justification. What, he asked, is the possibility of ostensive definition, that is, of defining scientific terms through public designation of material referents? Can the terms of a scientific ontology be grounded by the stimulus characteristics to which they refer? In his famous *gavagai* example (pp. 26–57), Quine demonstrated the impossibility of doing so. If such a term is used by natives to refer to a running rabbit, a dead rabbit, a rabbit in a pot, or simply the signs of rabbit presence, then what precise stimulus configuration secures the translation of the term as "rabbit"? In the extreme case, each time the native uses the term he may be referring to an assemblage of rabbit parts, while the translator is referring to the rabbit as a whole. We find, then, no means of ostensively linking terms and precise characteristics of the world. Ostensive definition may work for many practical purposes, but scientific description cannot be grounded or made firm by stimulus meaning. For Quine, scientific theory is "notoriously underdetermined" by what is the case.

It is now generally agreed that the manner in which objective representation is achieved in matters of description and explanation remains unsatisfactorily explicated (Fuller 1993; Barnes 1974). Meanwhile, outside the ranks of the philosophy of science, drumbeats of a different tempo are sounding with increasing intensity. These movements—sometimes labeled post-empiricist, poststructural, or postmodern—no longer seek a rationale for precisely linking word with world. Rather, in each case the arguments raise a more fundamental challenge to the assumption that language can depict, mirror, contain, convey, or store objective knowledge. Such critiques invite thoroughgoing reconsideration of the nature of language and its place in social life; more important, they begin to form the basis for an alternative to the presumption of individual knowledge. In the preceding chapter, we found that critical work in the philosophy of science yielded no successor to empiricist foundationalism, while in psychology it produced simply another iteration in a cyclical debate of centuries' duration. Neither did criticism of methodology yield viable alternatives. The present forms of criticism, however, emerge from discursive intelligibilities falling largely outside the philosophic-scientific domains. When their implications are elaborated and synthesized, they lay the groundwork for a full transformation in our view of language and of the allied concepts of truth and rationality. More specifically, they will provide a means of reinvisioning psychology and related human sciences.

Ideological Critique

For the better part of the century a strong attempt has been made—by both scientists and empiricist philosophers—to remove the sciences from moral debate. The task of the sciences, as commonly put, is to furnish objectively accurate accounts of "what is the case." Matters of "what ought to be" are not principally of scientific concern. When theoretical description and explanation are suffused with values, it is said, they are untrustworthy or prejudicial; they distort the truth. Whether scientific technologies *ought* to be used for various purposes (such as waging war, controlling the populace, or political forecasting) may be of vital concern to scientists, but as has frequently been made clear, decisions about such matters cannot be derived from science as such. For many social scientists, the moral outrage of the Vietnam War began to undermine confidence in this long-standing view. Somehow the jellyfish neutrality of the sciences seemed morally corrupt. Not only was there nothing about the scientific outlook that gave reason to reject imperious brutality, but the scientific establishment often lent its efforts to enhancing the technologies of aggression. There was ample reason to refurbish and revitalize the language of "ought."

For many scholars this quest for moral reformation inspired interest in a languishing form of philosophic analysis: the morally informed critique of Enlightenment rationality. The 1930s writings of the so-called Frankfurt School—Horkheimer, Adorno, Marcuse, Benjamin, and others—were particularly catalytic. First, these theorists drew from a significant intellectual lineage: Kant's emphasis on the primacy of individual freedom and moral responsibility over the scientifically conceived world of material contingencies, Hegel's view of both reason and morality as embedded in cultural practices, and Marx's demonstration of the ways in which forms of rationality are influenced by class interests. More pointedly, such writings effectively traced a broad spectrum of social and individual ills to the Enlightenment quest for a historically and culturally transcendent rationality. The commitment to positivist philosophy of science, capitalism, and bourgeois liberalism—contemporary manifestations of the Enlightenment vision—lent itself to such evils as the erosion of community, the deterioration of moral values, the establishment of dominance relationships, the renunciation of pleasure, and the mutilation of nature. This form of analysis, termed "critical theory," was aimed at the body of beliefs, or ideology, supporting or rationalizing these institutions. The purpose of such analysis was ideological *emancipation*. Scientific truth claims, for example, could properly be evaluated in terms of the ideological biases they revealed. Critical appraisal thus liberates us from the pernicious effects of mystifying truths.[1]

Although critical school writings were (and are) predominantly Marxist in their orientation, in that they seek to emancipate the culture from the thrall of capitalist ideology, this form of argument has since broken from its Marxist moorings. For any group concerned with injustice or oppression, ideological critique is a powerful weapon for undermining confidence in the taken-for-granted realities of the dominant institutions: science, government, the military, education, and so on. As a general form, ideological critique attempts to reveal the valuational biases underlying claims to truth and reason. To the extent that such claims are shown to represent personal or class interests, they are disqualified as either objective or rationally transcendent.

For example, now eclipsing the Marxist oeuvre in extensity and interest is an enormous body of feminist critique. To illustrate its deconstructive potential, consider Martin's (1987) analysis of the ways in which biological science characterizes woman's body. Martin's particular concern is the way biological texts, in both the classroom and laboratory, represent or describe the female body. As she reveals, the female body is typically treated as a form of *factory* whose primary purpose is to reproduce the species. From this metaphor it follows that the processes of menstruation and menopause are wasteful if not dysfunctional, for they are periods of "nonproduction." Consider the negative terms in which the typical biology text describes menstruation: "the fall in blood progesterone and estrogen *deprives* the highly developed endometrial lining of its hormonal support"; "*constriction* of blood vessels leads to a *diminished* supply of oxygen and nutrients"; and when "*disintegration* starts, the entire lining begins to *slough*, and the menstrual flow begins." "The *loss* of hormonal stimulation causes *decrosis*" (death of tissue). According to one text, menstruation is like "the uterus crying for *lack* of a baby" (emphasis added).

As Martin sees it, these scientific descriptions are anything but neutral. In subtle ways they inform the reader that menstruation and menopause are forms of breakdown or failure. As such, they have pejorative implications of broad consequence. For a woman to accept such accounts is to alienate herself from her body. The descriptions furnish grounds for negative self-judgment—both on a monthly basis for most of her adult years and then permanently after her years of fertility have passed. In addition, these characterizations could be otherwise. Such negative bias is not required by the "fact of the woman's body" but results from the exercise of the masculine metaphor of the woman as reproduction factory. For Martin, as for many other critics, science operates as politics by other means.[2] Or, as Butler

(1990) puts it, "ontology is . . . not a foundation, but a normative injunction that operates insidiously by installing itself into political discourse as its necessary ground" (p. 148).

This form of critical analysis—aimed at disclosing ideological, moral, or political purposes within seemingly objective or dispassionate accounts of the world—is now flourishing throughout the humanities and the sciences. It is used by blacks, for example, to discredit implicit racism in its myriad forms, by gays to reveal homophobic attitudes within common representations of the world, by area specialists concerned with the subtle imperialism of Western ethnography, by historians unsettled by the use of historical writing to valorize the present condition ("presentist history"), and by scholars concerned with the moral and political consequences of a broad variety of social and psychological theories.[3] For our purposes here, the most important consequence of this concatenating chorus is its threat to the presumption that language can contain truth, that science can furnish objective or accurate descriptions of the world. These forms of critique remove the truth claim from contention by shifting the site of consideration from the claim itself to the ideological or motivational basis from which it derives. They point to the underlying intent of the truth teller to suppress, to gain power, to accumulate wealth, to sustain his or her culture above all others, and so on, thereby undermining the suasive power of truth as presented. In effect, they reconstitute the language of description and explanation as motive language; they ask that claims to neutrality be viewed as "mystifying," that factual talk be indexed as "manipulation," and so on. In doing so they destroy the status of language as truth bearing.

Literary-Rhetorical Critique

A second threat to the mirroring capacity of description and explanation has been nurtured in different soil, namely, that of literary theory. Rather than destroy the semantic base of description and explanation by demonstrating their valuational origins, literary theorists attempt to demonstrate that such accounts are determined not by the character of events themselves but by the conventions of literary rendering. To appreciate the force of the argument it is useful to return to the Kuhn (1962) and Hanson (1958) critiques of the factual foundations of scientific theories. As Kuhn reasoned, a scientific theory is an amalgam of a priori beliefs that function to "tell the scientist about the entities that nature does and does not contain" (p. 109). It is not the facts that produce the paradigm but the paradigm that determines what counts as fact. Similarly, for Hanson the origin of factual accounts in the sciences lies within the observer's perspective. In effect, both Kuhn and Hanson view the a priori framework of observation as a *cognitive* one: the scientist literally *sees* the material world through the lens of the theory. For Kuhn, paradigm shifts, then, are akin to Gestalt shifts in perception (p. 111). For Hanson, "the observer . . . aims only to get his observations to cohere against a background of established knowledge. This seeing is the goal of observation" (p. 20).

Yet, in spite of their weight, these critiques of science as truth bearing do preserve fundamental aspects of an individualist view of knowledge. It is the individual scientist's cognitive disposition (point of view, perspective, construction) that serves to organize the world in particular ways. How, then, can the force of these arguments be sustained without simultaneously reinstantiating the individualist frame? The answer to this question lies in a reconsideration of the a priori. There is little reason to believe that we literally experience or "see the world" though a system of categories. Indeed, as I will demonstrate more fully in Chapter 5, there is no viable explanation for how the cognitive a priori could be established. However, we gain substantially if we consider the world-structuring process as linguistic rather than cognitive. It is through an a priori commitment to particular forms of language (genres, conventions, speech codes, and so on) that we place boundaries around what we take to be "the real." Nelson Goodman suggests this view in *Ways of Worldmaking*: "If I ask about the world, you can offer to tell me how it is under one or more frames of reference; but if I insist that you tell me how it is apart from all frames, what can you say? We are confined to ways of describing whatever is described" (p. 3). In Goodman's terms, it is *description* not *cognition* that constructs the factual world.

This contention prepares the way for the literary-rhetorical critique of the truth-bearing function of language. To the extent that description and explanation are demanded by the rules of literary exposition, the "object of description" fails to impress itself upon the language. As literary requirements absorb the process of scientific accounting, the objects of such accounts—as independent from the accounts themselves—lose ontological status.

The strongest case for textual absorption is made within the body of *poststructural* literary theory. To appreciate its significance, it is useful to consider briefly the structuralist dialogues from which this work emerged. For present purposes the structuralist movement in the social sciences and humanities can be seen as an early challenge to the presumption of language as mirror, the beginning of an argument to which more recent poststructural writings form the extreme conclusion. Structuralism as a general orientation carries a dual focus on an *exterior* (the apparent, the given, the observed) and an *interior* (a structure, force, or process). As frequently held, the exterior is given its shape or form through the interior and may only be understood with respect to its influences. Viewing spoken or written language in this way, we may distinguish between discourse (as an exterior) and the structures or forces that determine its configurations. In this sense, most structuralist theory subverts the view of language as object driven, where an inventory of an objective language would be an inventory of the world as it is. For the structuralist, primary attention is directed toward the way linguistic representations are influenced by structures and forces *other* than the represented world. For the structural linguist Ferdinand de Saussure, the duality is between *la langue,* "a grammatical system which . . . exists in the mind of each speaker" (1983, p. 14), and *la parole,* the externalization of the system in terms of the combination of sounds or markings necessary for communicating meaning. In effect, the sprawling, ephemeral, and variegated acts of overt communication are expressions of more fundamental, structured sets of inward-lying dispositions. From this standpoint, it is the linguist's task to move beyond the surface of the linguistic expression to discover the generative system or structure within.

Much of the inquiry in the human sciences is compatible with the structuralist endeavor. Freud's attempt to use the spoken word ("manifest content") to explore the structure of unconscious desire ("latent content") is illustrative. Marxist writings are often viewed as structuralist in their emphasis on the material modes of production underlying capitalist theories of the economy, value, and the individual.[4] More directly linked to the structuralist movement is the work of Lévi-Strauss (1969), which attempts to trace wide-ranging cultural forms and artifacts to a fundamental binary logic. Similar are Chomsky's (1968) attempts to locate a "deep" grammatical structure from which all well-formed sentences ("surface structure") may be derived. Foucault's early (1972) concept of the *episteme* shared much with the structuralist project in its presumption of a configuration of relations or conditions from which various forms of knowledge within a historical epoch might be derived.

For those holding that language can serve as a truth-bearing vehicle, structuralist thought begins to pose a challenge. To the extent that so-called "objective accounts" are driven not by events as they are but by structured systems (internal systems of meaning, unconscious forces, modes of production, inherent linguistic tendencies, and the like) it is difficult to determine in what sense scientific accounts are objective. Description thus seems to be *structure-* rather than *object*-driven. Interestingly, this challenge to the concepts of truth and objectivity was little developed within structuralist circles. Most structuralists wished to claim a rational or objective basis for their knowledge of structure. They wished to make objective claims about the determining structure—the unconscious, universal grammar, economic or material conditions, and so on. Slowly, however, the theoretical tide has turned against this presumption. Perhaps the pivotal point in the turn toward poststructuralism came from the self-reflexive realization that accounts of structure are themselves discursive. If discourse is not driven by objects in the world but by underlying structures, and if the accounts of these structures are also framed in language, then in what sense do such accounts map the reality of the structures? If they are pictures of the structures, then empiricist or realist views of language are correct and the structuralist claims to truth are circumscribed; if they are not accurate depictions, what is their status? This realization invites not the reinstantiation of a picture theory of language but the abandonment of the structuralist binary: a surface language versus a determining interior. More specifically, because our lodgment in discourse seems undeniable, the presumption of an "underlying structure"—a hidden force behind language—loses its appeal.

Semioticians have long flirted with the radical implications of this latter conclusion. For example, in his puckishly titled "autobiography," *Roland Barthes,* Barthes proceeded to violate virtually every rule for representing a life story. By avoiding chronology, speaking of himself in the third person, randomly inserting opinions on various topics, making little reference to the past, and so on, he attempted to demonstrate that what we take to be "real life history" is a product of linguistic artifice. More philosophically consequential, however, is the later work of Jacques Derrida and the deconstruction movement. For Derrida the structuralist enterprise (and indeed all Western epistemology) was infected with an unfortunate "metaphysics of presence." Why, he asked, must we presume that discourse is an *outward* expression of an *inward* being (thought, intention, structure, or the like)? On what grounds do we presume the presence of an unseen subjectivity inhabiting or present in the words? The unsettling implications of such questions are enhanced by Derrida's analysis of the means by which words acquire meaning. For Derrida, word meaning not only depends on *differences* between the auditory or visual characteristics of words (*bit, bet, bat,* and *but,* for example, all carry different meanings by virtue of vowel shifts), but also on a process of *deferral,* in which definitions are supplied by other words—oral and written, formal and informal—furnished on various occasions over time. Thus, a term such as *bit* may be used when saddling a horse, accepting a difficult task ("He took the bit in his mouth"), speaking of the theater ("She took a bit part"), referring to small sections or items ("This bit is the funniest of all"), and so on. Yet the meaning of each of these words or phrases depends on still other deferrals to other definitions and contexts. A "bit part" is a "small" part, and in Derrida's terms, "small" carries with it *traces* of uses in countless other settings.

In pursuing the meaning of a word, one thus encounters a steadily increasing expanse of words. To determine what a given utterance means is to be thrust back on an enormous array of language uses or texts. An utterance does not furnish us, then, with faint simulacra of the ideas in people's heads; rather, it invites us into an "infinite play of signifiers." Derrida coins the term *différance* to refer simultaneously to *difference* and *deferral,* thus ensuring that the meaning of the term itself is appropriately obscured. Through this analysis the author's presence (intention or private meaning) is obliterated. Inner meaning is replaced by immersion in systems of inherently obscure, undecidable processes of signification.

It is only a short step from the deconstruction of the author's intention to the disappearance of the object of language as well. The author's intention ceases to be an important locus of meaning, as does the world outside discourse. As Derrida attempted to demonstrate in the case of various lines of philosophy, such writing is indeed just that, a form of writing. It gains its meaning not from that which it supposes to exist or to which it putatively refers (logic, mental representation, a priori ideas, and the like) but by its reference to other philosophic texts. For philosophy, then, there is nothing outside the world of texts. The discipline can continue to exist indefinitely as a self-referring enterprise. This line of argument leads, in turn, to the analysis of philosophic texts in terms of the literary strategies by which their outcomes are achieved. Various lines of philosophic argument are shown to depend, for example, on the adoption of certain metaphors. If the metaphor is extracted from the argument, there is little argument or object of discussion left to pursue. It is this line of argument that lends power to Rorty's (1979) attack on the history of Western epistemology. The entire history, suggests Rorty, results from the unfortunate metaphor of mind as mirror, a "glassy essence" reflecting events in the external world. In effect, the long-standing debate between empiricists and rationalists is not about a realm existing outside the texts, it is a combat between competing literary traditions. Remove the central metaphors and the debate largely collapses.

Many other scholars are drawn to the literary devices out of which authoritative texts are constructed. Nietzsche's words are ever ambient: "What, therefore, is true? A mobile army of metaphors, metonymies, anthropomorphisms, . . . which after long use seem firm, canonical, and obligatory to a people; truths are illusions of which one has forgotten that they are illusions" (1979, p. 174). Thus, we find explorations of the literary basis of historical reality (White 1973; 1978), legal rationality (Levinson 1982), philosophic debate (Lang 1990), and psychological theory (Sarbin 1986; Leary 1990). Cultural anthropologists have taken a keen interest in the literary practices guiding ethnographic inscription, arguing that Western conventions of writing occlude our view of the very cultures we wish to understand (Clifford 1983; Tyler 1986).

Although literary analysis can have powerful catalytic effects, many see it as limited by its preoccupation with text in itself. Often lacking from such analysis is a concern with text as human communication, and particularly, with its capacity to move or persuade a reader. This much-needed supplement is supplied by rhetorical studies. As many hold, we are now experiencing a renaissance in this 2,500-year-old tradition. Such study has long been concerned with the means by which language acquires its suasive power. Traditionally, however, a sharp distinction is made between the *content* of a given message (its substance) and its *form* (or mode of presentation). Within the empiricist tradition this distinction is also used to discredit the study of rhetoric. Science, it is argued, is concerned with substance—with communicating pure content. The form in which it is presented (its "packaging") is not only of peripheral interest, but to the extent that persuasion depends on it, the scientific project is subverted. It is the content, not "mere rhetoric," that should suffice in scientific debate.[5] However, as the truth-bearing capacity of language is threatened by poststructural literary theory, the presumption of content—a true and objective portrayal of an independent object—gives way. All that was content stands open to critical analysis as persuasive form. In effect, developments in rhetorical study parallel those in literary criticism: both displace attention from the object of representation (the "facts," the "rationality of the argument") to the vehicle of representation.

To illustrate, consider the case of "human evolution," a seeming fact of biological life. As Landau (1991) proposes, accounts of human evolution are not governed by events of the past (and their manifestation in various fossils), but by forms of narrative or story telling. In particular, all the major paleoanthropological accounts—from Julian Huxley to Elliot Smith—"approximate the structure of a hero tale, along the lines proposed by Vladimir Propp in his classic *Morphology of the Folktale*" (p. 10). The hero tale, then, furnishes the necessary forestructure for the articulation of evolutionary theory. Without the story form in place, evolutionary theory would be essentially unintelligible. The various fossils and artifacts collected by scientists would not serve as evidence, because there would be no form of intelligibility for which they would stand as instantiations.

In the claim to content, scientists have also made a strong distinction between a literal language (reflecting the world) and a metaphoric one (altering the reflection in artistic ways); again the literal is privileged over the metaphor. Yet, if a literal language is removed from the field, then the entire scientific corpus is opened to analysis as metaphor. It is in this context, for example, that feminist critics have demonstrated ways in which male metaphors guide theory construction in biology (Hubbard 1983; Fausto-Sterling 1985), biophysics (Keller 1985), and anthropology (Sanday 1988). Psychologists have been especially concerned with the field's broad reliance on mechanistic metaphors (Hollis 1977; Shotter 1975). As it is reasoned, metaphors are not derived from observation, but rather, serve as rhetorical forestructures through which the observational world is construed. Once a theorist is committed to the metaphor of the human as a machine, for example, the theoretical account is constrained in important ways. Regardless of the character of the person's actions, the mechanist theorist is virtually obliged to segment him or her from the environment, to define the environment in terms of stimuli or inputs, to construct the person as responsive to these inputs, to theorize the mental domain as structured (constituted of interacting elements), to segment behavior into units, and so on. Other metaphors exist as alternatives to the mechanistic. For example, the organismic, the marketplace, the dramaturgical, and the rule-following metaphors are all available for intelligible explanation (Gergen 1991a). Each carries with it certain advantages and limitations, each favors certain ways of life over others, and most important for our purposes, each constructs a different ontology.

Major inquiries have also been launched to understand the rhetorical bases of economics (McClosky 1985), psychology (Bazerman 1988; Leary 1990), and the human sciences more generally (Nelson, Megill, and Mc-Closkey 1987; Simons 1989, 1990).

The Social Critique

The force of the ideological and literary-rhetorical assaults on truth, rationality, and objectivity is augmented by a third scholarly movement of pivotal importance for the emergence of social constructionism. One beginning to this story can be traced to a line of thought emerging in the works of Max Weber, Max Scheler, Karl Mannheim, and others occupied with the social genesis of scientific thought. Each was concerned in particular with the cultural context in which various ideas take shape and the ways in which these ideas in turn give form to both scientific and cultural practice. It is perhaps Mannheim's 1929 volume, translated as *Ideology and Utopia* (1951), that carries with it the clearest outline of the assumptions of reverberating significance. As Mannheim proposed, (1) theoretical commitments may usefully be traced to social (as opposed to empirical or transcendentally rational) origins; (2) social groups are often organized around certain theories; (3) theoretical disagreements are therefore issues of group (or political) conflict; and (4) what we take to be knowledge is therefore culturally and historically contingent.

The reverberations of and complicities with these early themes were broadly resounding. In Poland and Germany, Fleck's *Genesis and Development of a Scientific Fact* (originally published in 1935) developed the idea that in the scientific laboratory "one must know before one can see" and traced such knowing to the social surrounds. In England, Winch's influential little volume, *The Idea of a Social Science* (1946), demonstrated ways in which theoretical propositions are constitutive of "the phenomena" of the social sciences. For the French, Gurvitch's *The Social Frameworks of Knowledge* (originally published in 1966) traced scientific knowledge to particular frameworks of understanding, themselves the out-

;rowth of particular communities. And in the United States, Berger and Luckmann's *The Social Construction of Reality* (1966) effectively removed objectivity as a foundation stone of science and replaced it with a conception of socially informed and institutionalized subjectivity.

The profound implications of these views began to surface, however, only within the context of the moral and political upheaval of the late 1960s. Perhaps because of the parallels it drew between political and scientific revolution, Kuhn's *The Structure of Scientific Revolutions* (1962) served as the major catalyst for what became a discussion of sweeping consequence. (At one point, Kuhn's volume was the most widely cited book in the United States.) Kuhn's proposals were not dissimilar to those of Mannheim's some thirty years earlier, emphasizing as they did the importance of scientific communities in determining what counts as legitimate or important problems, what serves as evidence, and how progress is defined. However, they did demonstrate with clarity the problems in using traditional empiricist criteria to adjudicate among competing theoretical claims, when theoretical paradigms themselves define the array of relevant facts. And deriving the full dramatic potential from the problem of "paradigm incommensurability," Kuhn declared that indeed the scientific vision of truth seeking may be a mirage. "We may," he opined, "have to relinquish the notion, explicit or implicit, that changes of paradigm carry scientists and those who learn from them closer and closer to the truth" (p. 169).

The dialogues rapidly expanded in many significant directions. Feyerabend's (1976) caustic volume *Against Method* added significant force to the Kuhnian position. As he demonstrated, traditional standards of scientific rationality are often irrelevant (if not obfuscating) to scientific advances. Mitroff, in *The Subjective Side of Science* (1974), examined the emotional side of scientific commitments, exploring the ways in which various scientific judgments are based on personality and prestige. It was thus that by the mid-1970s, the sociologists Barnes (1974) and Bloor (1976) could outline possibilities for a "strong programme" in the sociology of knowledge. They proposed that virtually all scientific accounts are determined by social interests—political, economic, professional, and so on. In effect, to remove the social from the scientific would leave nothing left over to count as knowledge.

While the "strong programme" continues to stimulate debate, most inquiry now adopts a more circumspect posture. Particularly significant for the emergence of social constructionism are elaborations of the microsocial processes out of which scientific meaning is produced. It is in this vein that sociologists have explored the social processes essential for creating "facts" within the laboratory (Latour and Woolgar 1979), the discursive practices of self-legitimation within scientific communities (Mulkay and Gilbert 1982), scientific knowledge claims as forms of symbolic capital (Bourdieu

1977), the social practices underlying inductive inference (Collins 1985), group influences on the way data are interpreted (Collins and Pinch 1982), and the locally situated and contingent character of scientific description (Knorr-Cetina 1981).

Inquiry in these many domains has also proved highly congenial with the simultaneously developing field of ethnomethodology. For Garfinkel (1967) and his colleagues, descriptive terms within both the sciences and everyday life are fundamentally *indexical:* that is, their meaning can vary across divergent contexts of usage. Descriptions index events within particularized situations and are devoid of generalized meaning. The essential defeasibility (or undefinable character) of descriptive terms is demonstrated by wide-ranging studies of how people go about determining what counts as a psychiatric problem, suicide, juvenile crime, gender, state of mind, alcoholism, mental illness, or other putative constituents of the taken-for-granted world (see Garfinkel 1967; Atkinson 1977; Cicourel 1974; Kessler and McKenna 1978; Coulter 1979; Scheff 1966). In each case, it is argued, localized rules concerning what counts as an instance of the event in question develop within relationships. As is now widely accepted, the philosophic quest for indefeasible foundations for scientific methodology and the generation of truth is moribund. The "philosophy of science" has now been virtually eclipsed by "social studies of science."

Knowledge as Communal Possession

Each of the preceding lines of critique forms a powerful challenge to the traditional view of language as truth bearing. Each simultaneously sheds doubt on empiricist and realist claims that systematic science can yield culturally decontextualized accounts of what is the case—what is true without respect to human organizations of meaning. These forms of argument have evoked broad and sometimes vociferous interchange in philosophy (see for example, Trigg 1980; Grace 1987; Krausz 1989; Harris 1992). And these reverberations are indicative of the way in which such arguments have trammeled the borders of traditional disciplines, inciting dialogue, inviting innovation, and generating a giddy and optimistic presentiment of uncharted exploration. Indeed, the very assumption of academic disciplines—built around circumscribed or natural classes of phenomena, requiring specialized methods of study, and privileging their own logics and ontologies—has been thrown into critical relief. As many believe, this general ferment forms the basis for the *postmodern turn* in the scholarly world.[6]

Yet in spite of the similarity in their revolutionary conclusions, we find that the analyses themselves proceed along quite different trajectories. The semantic link between word and world, signifier and signified, is broken in different and even conflicting ways. For the ideological critic, it is not the world as it is but typically self-interest that drives the author's account of the world. Truth claims originate in ideological commitments. The literary critique also removes "the object" as the touchstone of language, replacing it not with ideology but with text. The meaning and significance of truth claims are derived from a discursive history. The social critique offers a contrasting account of language. It is neither underlying ideology nor textual history that shapes our conceptions of the true and the good. Rather, it is social process.

Not only do these accounts differ in important respects, there are also significant tensions among their proponents. Most ideological critics, seeing the value of their work as emancipatory, do not wish to relinquish the possibility of truth through language. Knowledge claims saturated with ideological interests are worthy of critique, it is ventured, because they mystify the unwitting audience. Emancipation occurs, however, when one understands the *true* nature of things—class, gender, and racist oppression, for example. Yet for both the literary and social analyst there is little room for an "unbiased" account. All tellings are dominated by textual-rhetorical traditions in the former instance and social process in the latter. There is no "true" description of the nature of things. Ideological critics counter with accusations that textual and social positions are politically and/or morally bankrupt, and are themselves the product of ideological interests (for example, bourgeois liberalism in disguise).[7] In a similar way, literary analysts stand ready to deconstruct the social account, seeing it as the product of a Western textual tradition. Likewise, the social analyst may readily expand the focus of analysis to include the literary guilds. Is deconstruction theory not itself the byproduct of social process? In effect, each orientation is capable of stripping the other of its ostensible authority.

We thus confront a double problematic. The first is obvious from the preceding: is there any means of mitigating these tensions and moving toward a unifying standpoint? The second is more subtle but equally substantial: if there is some means of retaining the force of these combined efforts, can we avoid the problem of incipient despair? Although these movements do form an enormously powerful antidote to the hegemonic thrust of empiricism and its associated theory of individual knowledge—and, indeed, to any claim to the last, the superior, or the incorrigible word. Yet these movements also leave us embroiled in doubt, absorbed by acrimony, and paralyzed with respect to future action. As critiques they are essentially parasitic on prevailing assertions of truth. Should the entire community of "truth-bearing" scholars tire of playing the fool and set off for the intellectual high ground of critique, no high ground will remain—all will be flat. If we wish to stop short of abandoning the entire effort at human science, we must venture beyond the critical impulse. A critical stage must give way to a transformative stage—deconstruction to reconstruction. What is desired, then, is a synthesis that can open more positive possibilities.

In my view, it is the third of these forms of critique, the social, that offers the most promising pathway toward a reconstructed science, and most particularly, a scientific practice understood as social construction. This is so because of certain shortcomings in the alternatives and because of the unique advantages offered by a social account. Consider first the problems of ideological critique. At the outset there is no way of vindicating such critique. Should the target of criticism (the industrialist, the male, the white) claim that his accounts are not self-serving but in the best interests of all, there is no means by which the critic can clinch the case. Is the critic to claim a more penetrating understanding of the actor than the actor himself possesses, or is the critic simply the victim of an alienating distrust? And how is the critic to claim clairvoyance, the possession of insights that are not themselves saturated with ideology? Are the critic's accounts accurate and objective? On what grounds can such claims be made? And if they are, does this not reinstate the possibility that language can indeed reflect reality? Should the conclusion be affirmative, then the critique of empirical science as knowledge generating is destroyed. The ideological critic must endorse in some form the very empiricist orientation that he or she has typically attempted to subvert.

As a unifying discourse the literary standpoint is also flawed. Its chief problem is its inability to exit from the self-created prison of the text. Here the answer to the Cartesian dilemma of doubt is a singular moment of certainty: there *is* text. This moment rapidly gives way, however, to the redoubt that the conclusion is itself a textual strategy. In the end, there is nothing outside of text, and most cogently, no promise of anything we might call a science. As a human scientist one could scarcely take an interest in poverty, conflict, the economy, history, government, and so on, for these are but terms lodged within a textual-rhetorical history. There is no social critique to be made, nothing to resist, nothing to champion, and, indeed, no action to be taken, for the very idea of "action to be taken" is an extension of linguistic convention. In addition to the unrelievable torpor invited by such a conclusion, literary-rhetorical analysis in its pure form can offer no account of human communication. Not only is doubt cast on the very idea of communication (it is simply a term within texts), but if we understand only through linguistic convention, there is no means of comprehending anyone who does not participate in the same conventions. In effect, authentic understanding can only take place with someone who is identical to oneself.[8]

Consider further: what is it to say that language (text, rhetoric) constructs the world? Words are, after all, passive and empty—simply sounds or markings of no consequence. Yet, words are active insofar as they are employed by persons in relationship, insofar as they are granted power in human interchange. A relationship between author and reader is required for us to speak of the textual construction of reality. In effect, there is good reason for privileging the reality of the social. If we do so we not only restore the textual-rhetorical critique to intelligibility, we also locate an exit from the dungeon of the text. We can retain the concern with the textual-rhetorical construction of reality and benefit from the insights derived from such analyses.

In addition, as we shall find, many concepts used in literary and rhetorical analysis can enrich the theoretical and practical spectrum of the human scientist. Concepts such as narrative, metaphor, metonomy, author positioning, and the like open new vistas for the human scientist in terms of both theory and various forms of practical work (such as research, therapy, community intervention). At the same time, literary analysis stands to be enriched in terms of the possibilities opened for understanding texts as they function within the broader social milieu, both reflecting and contributing to cultural processes. Indeed, this is precisely the direction taken by much literary analysis since the earlier romance with deconstruction theory (see for example, Bukatman 1993; DeJean 1991; Laqueur 1990; Weinstein 1988).

Just as a commitment to social process can absorb the vast share of the literary-rhetorical critique, a way can also be opened for sustaining the force of the ideological critique. This can be accomplished while simultaneously avoiding the problematic tendencies toward psychological reductionism or clairvoyant conceptions of the real. It is perhaps the work of Michel Foucault (1978, 1979) that provides the most effective means of securing the necessary link between social and critical analysis. For Foucault, there is a close relationship between language (including all forms of text) and social process (conceived in terms of power relations). In particular, as various professions (such as government, religion, academic disciplines) develop languages that both justify their existence and articulate the social world, and as these languages are placed into practice, so also do individuals come (even gladly) under the sway of such professions. In *Discipline and Punish,* Foucault was especially concerned with "the scientifico-legal complex from which the power to punish derives its bases, justifications and rules, from which it extends its effects and by which it masks its exorbitant singularity" (1979, p. 23). Most pertinently, Foucault singles out individual subjectivity as the site where many contemporary institutions—including the mental health professions—insinuate themselves into ongoing social life and expand their dominion. "The 'mind,' " he writes, "is a surface of inscription for power, with semiology as its tool" (1977, p. 102).

In this context, it is through a critical appraisal of language that we gain comprehension of our forms of relationship within the culture and thereby open a space for considering alternative futures. Rather than view critique as revealing the biasing interests lurking beneath the language, we may now see it as elucidating the pragmatic implications of the discourse itself. In this case, problematic issues of false consciousness and veracity are removed from consideration, and the focus shifts to the ways in which discourse functions in ongoing relationships. Putting aside issues of motive and truth, what are the societal repercussions of existing modes of discourse?

Social critique of this sort suffers from the same reflexive redoubt as both the ideological and the textual: its own truth is undermined by its very thesis. Critique of the social genesis of any account is itself socially derived. However, the result of this rejoinder is not a prison of infinite ideology or text—each ideological critique an expression of ideology, each textual deconstruction itself a text. Rather, with each reflexive reprise, one moves into an alternative discursive space, which is to say, into yet another domain of relatedness. Reflexive doubt is not then a slide into infinite regress but a means of recognizing alterior realities, and thus giving voice to still further relationships. In this sense, constructionist scholars may employ self-reflexive deconstructions of their own theses, thus simultaneously declaring a position, but removing its authority and inviting other voices into the conversation (see especially Woolgar, 1988).

Recalling the Chapter 1 account of paradigm shifts, we see that the elaboration of the implicit ontology of social critique now serves as grounds for the shift from a critical to a transformational stage in discursive development. It provides an opportunity for dialogue on the potential of a social constructionist outlook on human science. Such dialogue is now reflected in an extensive array of writings—cutting across the sciences and the humanities—which represent, I believe, the emergence of a common consciousness of how we can move from critique to a reconstituted science.[9]

Assumptions for a Social Constructionist Science

How is this emergent understanding to be characterized? If we elaborate on key assumptions derived from social critique, what are the components of a social constructionist view of knowledge and what are its promises for scientific practice? While not all those who carry out work in a constructionist idiom would agree on premises, and still others would entirely avoid freezing the dialogue, there are advantages to a momentary solidification of perspective. In these moments we glimpse the possibility for collective affinity, locate repositories of collaboration and contention, and foreground the *topoi* for further deliberation. Consider then the following suppositions as central to a social constructionist account of knowledge:

The terms by which we account for the world and ourselves are not dictated by the stipulated objects of such accounts. There is nothing about what is the case that demands any particular form of sound, marking, or movement of the kind used by persons in acts of representation or communication. This orienting assumption grows in part from the incapacity of scholars to make good either on a correspondence theory of language or a logic of induction by which general propositions can be derived from observation. It owes a special debt to Saussure's (1983) elucidation of the arbitrary relationship between signifier and signified. It benefits directly from the various forms of semiotic analysis and textual critique demonstrating how accounts of worlds and persons depend for their intelligibility and impact on the confluence of literary tropes by which they are constituted. It is also informed by analysis focused on social conditions and processes in science that privilege certain interpretations of fact over others. In its most radical form, it proposes that there are no *principled* constraints over our characterization of states of affairs. At a fundamental level the scientist confronts a condition of "anything goes." What is possible in principle, however, is beyond practical possibility. A second assumption furnishes one important reason:

The terms and forms by which we achieve understanding of the world and ourselves are social artifacts, products of historically and culturally situated interchanges among people. For constructionists, descriptions and explanations are neither driven by the world as it is, nor are they the inexorable outcome of genetic or structural propensities within the individual. Rather, they are the result of human coordination of action. Words take on their meaning only within the context of ongoing relationships. They are, in Shotter's (1984) terms, the result not of individual action and reaction but of joint-action. Or, in Bakhtin's (1981) sense, words are inherently "inter-individual." This means that to achieve intelligibility is to participate in a reiterative pattern of relationship, or if sufficiently extended, a tradition. It is only by virtue of sustaining some form of past relationship that we can make sense at all. And in this way, intelligible accounts of the world and the self are everywhere and at all times constrained.

In large measure, it is also cultural tradition that enables our words so often to appear fully grounded or derived from what is the case. If forms of understanding are sufficiently long-standing, and there is sufficient univocality in their usage, they may acquire the veneer of objectivity, the sense of being literal as opposed to metaphoric. Or, in Schutz's (1962) terms, understandings become *culturally sedimented;* they are constituents of the taken-for-granted order. Yet an emphasis on "truth through tradition" is incomplete without taking into account the forms of interaction in which language is embedded. It is not simply repetition and univocality that serve to reify the discourse, but the entire array of relationships of which such discourse is a part. It is thus possible to maintain a deep concern with "justice" and "morality"—terms with a high degree of referential pliability—because they are embedded within more general patterns of relationship. We carry out elaborate social procedures—such as "blame and forgiveness" on the informal level and court proceedings at the institutional level—in which terms such as "justice" and "morality" play a key role. To remove the terms would be to threaten the entire organization of proceedings. To remain within the accustomed array of procedures is to *know* that justice and morality can be achieved.

In the same way, scientific enclaves reach conclusions that carry the sense of transparent objectivity. By selecting certain configurations to count as "objects," "processes," or "events," and by generating consensus about the occasions upon which the descriptive language is to apply, a conversational world is formed of which the sense of "objective validity" is a byproduct (Shotter 1993b). Thus, as scientists we may come to agree that on certain occasions we shall call various configurations "aggressive behavior," "prejudice," "unemployment," and so on, not because there simply is aggression, prejudice, and unemployment "in the world" but because these terms allow us to index various configurations in ways that we find socially useful. It is thus that communities of scientists can reach consensus, for example, about "the nature of aggression," and feel justified in calling such conclusions "objective." However, cut away from the social processes responsible for establishing and negotiating reference, the conclusions lapse into mere formalisms.

This proposal is related to yet another argument of some significance. It is commonly said that scientific theories gain their value primarily in the context of prediction. Even philosophic instrumentalists, who disagree with empiricists concerning the capacity of science to reveal the truths of nature, place strong emphasis on predictive utility. A theory is rendered superior by virtue of its capacity to forecast. And even within branches of the social sciences where strong prediction has not been achieved, theories are credited for having applied value, that is, for conveying knowledge that can be applied in various practical settings. Kurt Lewin's dictum "There is nothing so practical as a good theory" is a general truism. Yet as the present arguments make clear, theories themselves do not make predictions, nor do they prescribe the conditions of their application. Theoretical propositions themselves stand empty, devoid of significance in what we call the "concrete world." In themselves, they fail to carry the culturally shared rules of instantiation necessary for prediction or application. Theories may be an invaluable adjunct to the scientific community in developing "technologies of prediction," or negotiating agreements as to what constitutes an "application." To the extent that predictions or applications are formulated in language and shared within a community, theories may be essential. However, to make predictions about aggression, altruism, prejudice, eating disorders, unemployment, and the like is simply an exercise in language unless one is a participant within the forms of relationship in which those terms have been granted reference. Thus, to convey abstract, decontextualized theories in journals, books, speeches, and the like is of limited practical consequence in terms of prediction or application.[10]

The degree to which a given account of world or self is sustained across time is not dependent on the objective validity of the account but on the vicissitudes of social process. That is to say, accounts of the world and the self may be sustained without respect to perturbations in the world they are designed to describe or explain. Similarly, they may be abandoned without regard to what we take to be the perduring features of the world. In effect, the languages of description and explanation may change without reference to what we term phenomena, and the latter are free to change without necessary consequences for theoretical accounts. This view owes a debt to the Quine-Duhem thesis that through progressive elaboration of ancillary and implied clauses a theory may be sustained across a sea of observations that might otherwise function as refutations. It further reflects much history of science lore on the social processes at play in periods of paradigm change. Further, it benefits from the sociology of knowledge emphasis on the negotiation of meaning in scientific laboratories. It is featured in the present summary primarily to underscore the implications of social constructionism for scientific proceedings. For as this position makes clear, methodological procedures, regardless of rigor, do not act as principled correctives to the languages of scientific description and explanation. Or, following the theme developed in the preceding chapter, methodology is not a knockdown device for adjudicating among competing scientific accounts. Politically speaking, this is to open the door to alternative voices within the culture, voices long scorned for their lack of an acceptable ontology, epistemology, and accompanying methodology. Such voices are no longer silenced because they lack the necessary data.[11]

At the same time, these arguments do not lead to the dangerous conclusions that traditional methodology is irrelevant to scientific description, could be abandoned without affecting the corpus of scientific writing, and has no bearing on the credibility of the scientist or the societal value of the scientific effort. What is being claimed here is that methodology does not furnish a transcendent or context-free warrant for holding certain descriptions and explanations superior to ("more objective" or "more true") than others. However, *within* scientific communities empirical methods can be (and typically are) used in ways that bear on truth claims, the confidence of conclusions, the veracity of the investigator, and the implications of the scientific effort for society. As outlined above, communities of scientists can forge local ontologies of substantial durability. Through continued negotiation, ritual practice, and the socialization of neophytes into these practices, communities can develop consensus over "the nature of things." Within these communities propositions can be verified or falsified. And because objects, instruments, and statistical representations are built into these practices (forming "the datum," the means of "recognition," the indicators of reliability), they enter into the process of verification and falsification. In this way scientists can establish the presence or absence of pheromones, short-term memory, personality traits, and other discursive realities. Methodological practices can be developed to ascertain the "existence of the phenomena," their co-occurrence with other established phenomena, and the probability of their existence within larger populations. Further, community members may build up mutual trust in the report of such events, and legitimately chastise or expulse those who play the game incorrectly or guilefully. The texts of science will amply express the results of such activities, and if one enters into the rituals, predictions can indeed result.

Language derives its significance in human affairs from the way in which it functions within patterns of relationship. In their critique of the correspondence view of language, the three lines of argument treated above also lay to rest any simple view of the semantic basis of language meaning. That is, we find that propositions do not derive their sense from their determinant relationship to a world of referents. At the same time, we find that the semanticist view can be reconstituted within a social frame. Following the treatment of reference as a social ritual, with referential practices as sociohistorically situated, the semantic possibilities for word meaning are brought into being. It must be underscored, however, that semantics thus becomes a derivative of social pragmatics. It is the form of relationship that enables semantics to function.[12]

When put in these terms, social constructionism is a congenial companion to Wittgenstein's (1953) conception of meaning as a derivative of social use. For Wittgenstein words acquire their meaning within what he metaphorically terms "language games," that is, through the ways they are used in patterns of ongoing exchange. The terms "batter," "pitcher," "bases," and "home run" are all essential in describing the game of baseball. In commonsense terms, the game of baseball exists prior to the act of description, and a given description can be more or less accurate (think of the abuse heaped upon the umpire who calls "strike" at what obviously is a "ball"). From Wittgenstein's view, however, the terms for baseball are not dissociated descriptors but constitutive features of the game. A pitcher is only a pitcher by virtue of one's acceding to the rules of the game. In effect, the terms acquire their meaning by their function within a set of circum-scribed rules. The act of "describing the game" is a derivative of the pre-ceding placement of the relevant terms within the game itself. "Now what do the words of this language signify?" asks Wittgenstein (1953). "What is supposed to show what they signify, if not the kind of use they have?" (6e). Apposite as well is Wittgenstein's concept of a *form of life,* that is, a broader pattern of cultural activity in which specific language games are embedded. The game of baseball, for example, generally functions as a "leisure-time activity" and is distinguished from the domain of work; it is a cultural pastime constituted by a variety of traditional rituals (such as betting, tak-ing one's son to his first game). Meaning within the game depends on the use of the game within broader cultural patterns.

This view of meaning as derived from microsocial exchanges embedded within broad patterns of cultural life lends to social constructionism strong critical and pragmatic dimensions. That is, it draws attention to the way in which languages, including scientific theories, are used within the culture. How do various "ways of putting things" function within ongoing rela-tionships? The constructionist is little likely to ask about the truth, validity, or objectivity of a given account, what predictions follow from a theory, how well a statement reflects the true intentions or emotions of a speaker, or how an utterance is made possible by cognitive processing. Rather, for the constructionist, samples of language are integers within patterns of re-lationship. They are not maps or mirrors of other domains—referential worlds or interior impulses—but outgrowths of specific modes of life, rit-uals of exchange, relations of control and domination, and so on. The chief questions to be asked of generalized truth claims are thus, how do they function, in which rituals are they essential, what activities are facilitated and what impeded, who is harmed and who gains by such claims?

To appraise existing forms of discourse is to evaluate patterns of cultural life; such evaluations give voice to other cultural enclaves. Within a given community of intelligibility, where words and actions are related in reliable ways, it is possible to appraise what we call the "empirical validity" of an assertion. Although this form of evaluation is useful in both science and daily life, it is essentially unreflexive; it offers no means by which to evaluate itself, its own constructions of the world, and the relationship of these to the broader and more extended forms of cultural life. For example, to the extent that they exist as communities of understanding, laboratory scientists may felicitously evaluate the credibility and acceptability of assertions within the relationships by which they are constituted. The same may be said of psy-choanalysts and spiritualists. However, the criteria of validity or desirability operating within these communities furnish no opportunity for self-appraisal and, what is more important, for assessing the impact these commitments have on the lives of those in related or overlapping communities. The scientist as such cannot ask about the spiritual value of science; the psychoanalyst per se has no means of debating the cultural assets and liabilities of believing in unconscious processes; and the terms and understandings of the military strategist offer no means of evaluating the morality of war.

A premium is thus placed on the critical evaluation of various intelligibilities from exterior positions, exploring the impact of these intelligibilities on the broader forms of cultural life. What does the culture gain or lose if we constitute the world in the terms of the economist, the military strategist, the ecologist, the psychologist, the feminist, and so on? How is cultural life improved or impoverished as the vocabularies and practices of these communities expand or proliferate? This is not to privilege the evaluation over the intelligibilities and practices in question; the moral or political lament, for example, does not constitute the "final word" on such matters. However, because such evaluations are essentially outgrowths of other communities of meaning—other ways of life—it is to open the door to a fuller interweaving of the disparate communities of meaning. If evaluations can be communicated in ways that can be absorbed by those under scrutiny, relational boundaries are softened. As the otherwise alien signifiers interpenetrate, so do otherwise alien communities begin to cohere. Evaluative dialogue, then, may constitute a significant step toward a humane society.

Human Science in Constructionist Perspective

The various assumptions collected here begin to form an alternative to the individual view of knowledge we found so deeply problematic in the preceding chapter. The question we must now address concerns the positive potential of these views. What do such assumptions suggest for a reconstructed human science? What is now favored? What must be rejected? For the traditional empiricist or security-seeking scientist, constructionist arguments may seem pessimistic, even nihilistic. However, they are so only if one remains glued to worn-out conceptions of the scientific enterprise, or obfuscating conceptions of truth, knowledge, objectivity, and progress. What we find is that in significant degree, traditional empiricist conceptions of the craft have narrowed its scope, truncated its methods, muzzled its possible expressions, and circumscribed its potential for social utility. In contrast, I propose that when properly extended, constructionist arguments contain enormous potential for the human sciences. New horizons emerge at every turn, and many are currently under exploration.

In the remainder of this chapter I wish not only to lay out several of the more prominent openings generated by a constructionist standpoint, but to resuscitate a number of traditional pursuits now in constructionist terms.

To appreciate the array of potentials, it is helpful to recall the attempt in the preceding chapter to account for transformations in human science perspectives. There I spoke of tendencies to maintain, to question, and to transform traditions. In keeping with these emphases, we may also consider various forms of scientific practice in terms of (1) their contribution to existing institutions or ways of life; (2) their capacity for critical challenge; and (3) their potential for transforming culture. This analysis is only suggestive, inasmuch as any scientific practice may function in different ways for different cultural groups, and practices often have multiple, contrary, and unintended effects. However, by arraying practices in this way, I hope to accentuate differing functions and effects.

Scientific Practice in a Stable Society

Let us first consider the potential of the human sciences under conditions of relative stability or enduring tradition. Here we may include forms of language, themselves inseparable from or constitutive of the relational patterns in which they are enmeshed. This language is likely to contain an implicit ontology, an inventory of "what there is," and an implicit moral code (criteria of "what ought to be"). Thus, whether we are speaking of biologists studying DNA molecules or the Supreme Court deliberating the First Amendment, there must be shared assumptions about what exists and agreement as to appropriate action. Without such conventions there would be no community of biologists or Supreme Court. Further, what may be said of local, face-to-face groups also holds to a certain degree on the national or continental level; thus we can speak of Japanese as opposed to Norwegian culture.

Put in these terms, the human sciences have a substantial contribution to make to the array of existing traditions. There are two major and interdependent functions to be served. First, human science inquiry can function to *sustain and/or strengthen the existing form of life;* and second, it can *enable persons to live more adequately within these traditions.* The first of these functions is most fully served by theoretical intelligibilities—the scientist's mode of describing and explaining the world. As articulate, respected, and visible elaborators and purveyors of language—and specifically languages about the human condition—human scientists can have a substantial impact on the dominant intelligibilities of the society and thus on its prevailing practices. Such intelligibilities place labels on human action, furnish causes for people's success and failure, and provide rationales for behavior. To explain human action in terms of individual psychological processes, for example, is to have far different implications for practices and policies than to explain the same actions in terms of social structures. Theories of the former stripe lead us to blame, punish, or treat the deviants in society, while those of the latter favor reorganization of the systems responsible for such outcomes. Theories of human learning implicitly suggest that aberrant behavior is subject to programmatic retraining, while nativist theories more often stress containment of the otherwise inevitable. Mechanistic theories tend to deny individual responsibility, while dramaturgic theories grant the individual powers of agency and thus of self-control. In each case, the theoretical intelligibility operates to sustain or reinforce a significant societal perspective and its associated ways of life.

The human sciences can also facilitate adaptive action within the confines of the conventional. Given certain relatively reliable patterns of action and the possibility of communal agreement in labeling, the human sciences can furnish the kinds of predictions that enable policies to be formed, programs put in place, and useful information disseminated to the culture. Within the common realities of the culture, the human sciences can generate, for example, reasonably reliable predictions of academic success, schizophrenic breakdown, rates of mental illness, voting patterns, crime rates, divorce rates, school dropout rates, abortion requests, product success, the GNP, and so on. They enable therapists to relate to clients in such a way that "cures" are achieved and organizational consultants to "solve problems" within organizational settings. It is in this domain of prognostication that the traditional empiricist technologies can play their most significant role. Sampling procedures, recording devices, survey questionnaires, experimental methods, statistical analyses and the like—the legacy of the behavioral sciences—are effectively crafted for enhancing predictive capabilities. So long as the traditions endure, one places value on them, and the codes of reference are broadly shared, actuarial forecasting does have advantages.

This is not, however, to argue for a sustained investment in testing general theories of human behavior. As we have seen, such research cannot be justified on the traditional grounds that it enables us to distinguish the accurate and predictive theories from the empirically specious. The research operates neither to validate nor invalidate general hypotheses, as all theories may be rendered true or false depending on one's negotiation of meaning in a given context. Nor is the vast share of hypothesis-testing research relevant to the challenge of social prediction. This is so because such research is typically driven by the desire to demonstrate the validity of the theory in question. The specific behavior under assessment is of peripheral interest—chosen merely because it is convenient or subject to measurement and control in the laboratory. Society has little need for better predictions of button pressing, pencil marks on questionnaires, success in contrived games, or performance on laboratory apparatus. In effect, the enormous numbers of hours consumed by such endeavors, the sacrifices made by vast hordes of subjects and of animal populations, the sums of national monies, the painstaking practices of publication, and the making or breaking of careers have little compelling justification. This is not to abandon all forms of hypothesis testing. A limited amount of controlled research may be useful in vivifying or lending rhetorical weight to general theoretical positions. But the present arguments champion theoretical intelligibility as perhaps the most significant contribution the human sciences can make to cultural life.

Destabilizing Convention

For the majority of society, contributions to the public good, as conventionally defined, are of no small consequence. Cultural values seem altogether too precarious, cherished patterns too quick to erode, and undesirable elements always in ascendance. At the same time, cultural realities are seldom univocal. We swim in a sea of competing intelligibilities, where discursive currents from dislocated periods of history—Greco, Roman, Christian, Judaic, and more—are forever surging one against the other, and the mingling of disparate pasts is forever generating new and appealing (or appalling) possibilities. Thus, regardless of the dominant cultural realities, and their related practices, there are always groups whose realities are scorned, suffering that goes unheeded, and visions of positive change that are muffled by the secure and the sanctimonious.

For the constructionist the languages of the sciences serve as pragmatic devices—favoring certain forms of activity while discouraging others. The scientist is inevitably, then, a moral and political advocate, whether willing or witless. To claim value neutrality is simply to blind oneself to the cultural modes of life that one's work sustains or destroys. Thus, rather than separating one's professional commitments from one's passions, trying to pry apart fact and value, the constructionist invitation is for a fully expressive professional life—for theories, methods, and practices that may realize one's vision of a better society. In this sense, constructionism offers a rationale for challenging the dominant realities and their associated forms of life. Let us consider three central forms of challenge: *culture critique, internal critique,* and the *scholarship of dislodgment.*

Perhaps the most direct and broadly accessible means of unsettling the status quo—from the discursive standpoint—is *culture critique*. For the greater part of the century, the empirically oriented sciences have assiduously avoided ethical or political partisanship. As we now find, value neutrality is a chimerical pursuit; the professional always and inevitably affects social life for good or ill by some valuational criterion. Thus, rather than function as passive minions to the "mirror of nature," the human scientists may legitimately and responsibly expand their investments. Rather than scratch matters of "ought" from the professional ledger, we should actively employ our skills to make intelligible the moral and political issues related to our professional domain. Social critique, while scarcely new to the human sciences, is one important form of such expression. Scholars in both the psychoanalytic and the critical school traditions furnished early and powerful demonstrations of the possibility of sophisticated and far-reaching societal analysis. And, while this potential was largely ignored (or disparaged) during the behavioral (or strong empiricist) era, it has begun to reemerge in multiple and highly variegated forms since the 1960s. The recent emergence of the cultural studies discipline attests to the vigor of this movement. More will be said about such work in Chapter 5.

Social critique must be supplemented in important ways. Such critique is essentially turned outward, challenging features of the culture at large. In so doing, it leaves the human sciences themselves unquestioned. Yet, because the human sciences are purveyors of languages and practices that affect the culture, they too require critical appraisal. In addition to social critique, a constructionist perspective favors a strong investment in *internal critique*. In effect, scientists are invited to monitor, criticize, and cast necessary doubt on the use of their own constructions of reality and associated practices. Again, internal critique is hardly new to the sciences. As set out in the preceding chapter, for example, critical appraisal of the behaviorist paradigm was essential to the cognitive revolution. From the present standpoint, however, internalist debate of this kind is of minimal significance in terms of its value to the culture at large. This is so because it fails to stand outside science itself. The values inherent in the sciences, and their corresponding implications for cultural life, are never brought into question. Favored here is a form of critique that represents interests or values other than those benefiting those generating scientific realities. I have described instances of such work in the preceding account of ideological critique, and I will explore further cases in Chapter 5.

A third form of destabilizing scholarship must be considered. Both cultural and internal critique are typically grounded in particular value commitments—equality, justice, conflict reduction, and so on. However, constructionism also invites a third form of inquiry, one less invested in a particular value position and more focused on the general disruption of the conventional. To the extent that any reality becomes objectified or taken for granted, relationships are frozen, options sealed off, and voices unheard. When we presume that there is equality, we are blind to inequities; when a conflict is resolved, we are insensitive to the suffering in the wings. In this respect, there is value to be placed on a *scholarship of dislodgment,* one that simply loosens the grip of the conventional. In certain respects literary deconstruction offers a model for such scholarship. When deconstructionists set out to locate the unsettling aporia at the heart of a given work, the result was a reverberating distrust of any transparent text, well-wrought principle, or well-formed plan. As the deconstructionist effort demonstrates, when closely examined, the clear, elegant, and compelling rationale unravels, its logic collapses, its meaning is indeterminant. Yet, while deconstructionist analyses are available to the human sciences as dislodgment devices, more rhetorically powerful are emerging efforts to demonstrate the constructed character of dominant discourses. Here the efforts of both the rhetorical and social critics are exemplary. As described, the rhetorical analyst focuses on the devices by which a given discourse acquires its persuasive power, its sense of rationality, objectivity, or truth. In locating the metaphors, the narratives, the suppressions of meaning, the appeals to authority, and so on, rationality and objectivity lose their regnancy. With consciousness of artifice, the discourse loses suasive power. Similarly, as social analysts explore the relational processes—the negotiations, power tactics, political dynamics, and so on—that annunciate various truths, such truths lose their generality. What seemed the "only way" of putting things— beyond time and culture—becomes local and particular.

There are other scholarships of dislodgment. Particularly noteworthy are cultural and historical recontextualizations. So often, it seems, what begin as local values, assumptions, and warrants become expansive. The values of a particular community or the truth of a particular science move in the direction of the universal—good and true for all people for all time. Inquiry into the cultural and historical location of particular values and truths is an effective battlement against the ravages of words gone wild. As anthropologists explore the local realities of other cultural groups, demonstrating the validity of these alien realities within their particular circumstances, so do they foreground the limitations of our own rationalities. When Winch (1946), for example, champions the cause of Szondi magic, he simultaneously blurs the distinction between Western science and tribal witchcraft. Historical work can accomplish the same results. As Morawski (1988) and her colleagues trace the changing interpretations of the experiment in psychology, and Danziger (1990) shows that the concept of the experimental subject depends on historical circumstance, they challenge the contemporary view of a fixed and universal methodology and subject.

Cultural Transformation: New Realities and Resources

The human sciences possess significant potential for both sustaining cultural institutions on the one hand, and placing them in reflexive doubt on the other. Yet a third array of challenges must finally be considered, namely those moving beyond critical and destabilizing inquiry to cultural transformation. If our conceptions of the real and the good are cultural constructions, then most of our cultural practices may equally be viewed as contingent. All that is natural, normal, rational, obvious, and necessary is—in principle—open to alteration. Although the scholarships of critique and dislodgment are valuable resources for generating ferment, in themselves they are insufficient. This is primarily so because of their symbiotic character; their intelligibility is dependent on what they oppose. Required for social transformation are new visions and vocabularies, new visions of possibility, and practices that in their very realization begin to chart an alternative course. Such transformative possibilities can grow from the soil of traditional social science: recognized modes of theory and research. However, because they are understood primarily in terms of the traditional intelligibilities, such innovations continue to sustain these traditions. Cultural transformation seems best served by new forms of scientific practice. Let us consider, then, the potential inherent in more audacious forms of theory, research, and professional practice.

Concepts of human conduct operate much like tools for carrying out relationships. In this sense, the possibility of social change may be derived from new forms of intelligibility.[13] The development of new languages of understanding augments the range of possible actions. As a language of unconscious motives was elaborated, so were new strategies of courtroom defense developed; as a vocabulary of intrinsic motives was enriched, so did we enrich our educational regimens; and as theories of family systems were developed so did we expand our ways of treating individual pain. In another context (Gergen 1994), I proposed the term *generative theory* to refer to theoretical views that are lodged against or contradict the commonly accepted assumptions of the culture and open new vistas of intelligibility. The theories of Freud and Marx were surely among the most generative of the past century. In each case the theoretical work posed a major challenge to dominant assumptions and served as the impetus to new forms of action. This is not to say, however, that such work retains its generative potential today; innovative and iconoclastic interpretations of the canonical texts would be necessary to sustain such vitality. (For example, the Lacanian revisioning of Freud provides a means for psychoanalytic theory to enter poststructural dialogues.) Although less resounding in impact, the work of Jung, Mead, Skinner, Piaget, and Goffman, for example, were generative in many respects; even more narrowly focused formulations such as Geertz's (1973) interpretation of a Balinese cockfight or Festinger's (1957) theory of cognitive dissonance have had significant generative effects. Each has transformed intelligibility to a certain degree and added importantly to the range of scientific and cultural resources.[14]

Yet in significant ways, such theoretical writing is also conservative. Sustained by these scholars, and indeed lending rhetorical power to their work, are cultural traditions of long standing. To be more explicit, theoretical writing is a social action *sui generis,* and as such, favors certain kinds of relations over others. In each of the above cases, for example, the writer adopts the posture of knowing authority, thus sustaining hierarchies of privilege; claims are made to individual authorship, thus sustaining the view of individuals as originary sources of thought; forms of educated or elitist argumentation are used, thus dismissing as irrelevant or inferior the persuasive idioms of the noneducated; each text objectifies its subject matter, thus privileging a realm of the real over the rhetorical. The invitation to transformation extends, then, to the form of scholarly expression. As the human sciences experiment with modes of expression—as they challenge traditional styles of writing, blur the genres, stir vision and sound into text—so do they transform the conception of the scholar, the academy, the nature of education, and ultimately the potential for human relationship.

It is in this context that great value must be placed on the new and iconoclastic forms of writing slowly making their way into the human sciences. Feminist writers are in the vanguard. For example, as French feminists Irigaray (1974) and Cixous (1986) demonstrate, most conventions of scholarly writing are phallocentric (linear, binary, dispassionate). Their writings experiment with alternative forms of expression, forms they believe are more congenial to a primordial feminine consciousness. Cultural anthropologists have become increasingly disturbed over the Western conventions of writing ethnography, reasoning that the very conventions themselves constitute a form of imperialism. Thus, experiments are launched, for example, to bring the "subjects of study" into the ethnography as collaborators, write ethnography as autobiography, use ethnography as critique of the home culture, and convert ethnography to poetry (thus revealing its basis in artifice rather than in fact). In other textual experiments Mulkay (1985) has explored the possibilities of writing as several different personas within the same work, Mary Gergen (1992) has penned a postmodern drama, and in a groundbreaking volume, *Death at the Parasite Cafe,* Pfohl (1992) has deployed a collage of theory, fiction, autobiography, and photography to carry out critical social analysis. Increasingly, scholars are also channeling their inventive talents into film, clearly the major challenge for the future.

Let us turn from theoretical expression to research methodology. In the transformative mode, the principal aim of research is to vivify the possibility of new modes of action. Research adds significant imagery to novel possibilities. As suggested earlier, even the laboratory experiment can serve in this role. For example, Milgram's (1974) still challenging research on obedience scarcely "tests a hypothesis" of any significant kind. However, in its capacity to shock the reader into consciousness of his or her own potential for "evil under orders," this vivid research provokes discussion of the desirability of hierarchies and the limits of obligation.

Despite the transformative power of conventional research practices, they share with traditional forms of writing a culturally conserving tendency. Although laboratory experiments can illustrate new potentials, their reliance on a mechanistic model of human functioning, their alienating treatment of the subject, and their control of outcomes lend themselves to traditions that many find otiose. More radical transformation is encouraged by alternative research procedures, methods that favor other values and views. As new research procedures are made intelligible, new models for relationship are encouraged. Such attempts now emerge with increasing frequency across the human sciences. Avoiding many of the ideological and intellectual problems of traditional research practices are flourishing explorations in qualitative research (Denzin and Lincoln 1994), hermeneutic or interpretive inquiry (Packer and Addison 1989), dialogic methodology (M. Gergen 1989), cooperative inquiry (Reason 1988), biographical or life history (Bertaux 1984; Polkinghorne, 1988), narrative analysis (Brown and Kreps 1993), appreciative inquiry (Cooperrider 1990), research as social intervention (McNamee 1988), and feminist scholarship as lived research (Fonow and Cook 1991). In each case, new research practices model new forms of cultural life.

Attention must finally be given to the realm of professional practice. In many respects, therapists, counselors, organizational consultants, educational specialists, and the like have a far greater impact on cultural life than the academician. Their actions can enter more deeply and directly into relational practices than the abstruse writings of the professional. In effect, they have enormous potential for cultural transformation. It is in the realm of model practices that their impact may be most powerful. When therapists develop new forms of interacting with clients, the culture may be informed of alternative ways of helping those in need; when consultants create dialogue across the strata of an organization (as opposed to offering authoritative solutions), they implicitly create the reality of interdependence; and when educational researchers pursue collaborative modes of evaluation, the stage is set for new forms of student-teacher relationship. The practitioner is not, then, a mere servant to the existing institutions or to logics and "findings" developed within the tower, but a potential agent for far-reaching change.[15] In my view the next decade will be one in which the scholar will benefit more from the contextualized skills of the practitioner, than the reverse.

In summary, for the human sciences in a constructionist mode, traditional research practices can make a valuable contribution. However, we also see that this contribution is highly restricted. A constructionist orientation substantially expands the agenda. The three most significant overtures to innovation are *deconstruction,* wherein all presumptions of the true, the rational, and the good are open to suspicion—including those of the suspicious; *democratization,* wherein the range of voices participating in the consequential dialogues of the science is expanded, and *reconstruction,* wherein new realities and practices are fashioned for cultural transformation. It is my hope that such investments can propel the sciences from their current status at the margins of cultural life to the center of its pursuits.

3 Constructionism in Question

To challenge prevailing assumptions about the generation and function of knowledge and to explore an alternative vision threatens long-standing and widely shared commitments to objectivity, truth, rational foundations, and individualism. It is not surprising that criticism of constructionist thought has been readily forthcoming—some of it lethal in intent. For many scholars the view that knowledge is socially constructed proves deeply problematic. It is not simply that cherished concepts of objectivity, unbiased inquiry, truth, authority, and scientific progress are put in jeopardy, nor that constructionism offers no clear and apparent foundation for an alternative science. These problems are further complicated by the threats of existential doubt, the immersion in continuous ambiguity, and the posture of jellyfish tolerance that the constructionist alternative seems to invite. At the same time, cherished concepts of intimacy, experience, consciousness, creativity, autonomy, integrity, and democracy also seem threatened. Although there is no one way in which all such threats can be subdued and all such doubts assuaged, no form of intelligibility that can fully accommodate the multiplicitous misgivings of all existing alternatives, we must address several pressing critiques of constructionism if dialogue is to proceed in productive ways. There is a particular need to reduce widespread misconceptions and respond to broadly vexing aspects of constructionist thought.

Because these queries arise in different quarters and for different reasons, there is no single narrative line around which argument can effectively be developed. Rather, to treat these critical issues I shall proceed with a series of related discussions, each directed toward a specific form of criticism. For the reader desiring a forecast of the questions, the following—in their more truculent form—will structure the discussion:

1. Is constructionism really new?
2. Does constructionism deny the reality of personal experience?
3. Does constructionism abandon all concern with the real world?
4. As a form of skepticism, isn't constructionism incoherent?
5. In its relativism, isn't constructionism morally vacuous?
6. On what grounds can constructionists claim that people differ in their constructions of the world?
7. If theory is unfalsifiable, as constructionism suggests, then what is the value of theoretical understanding; is there no sense in which science progresses?

Before proceeding further, I want to consider briefly a common reaction to such critiques among constructionists: Why bother to engage in debates such as these? These critiques defend a set of positions that constructionism has already found faulty. Is it not better to proceed in unpacking the positive implications of constructionism than to fight rearguard skirmishes with old traditions? In addition, all forms of critique are subject to the various deconstructionist methods that, as we have seen, give rise to constructionism. Thus, criticism may be dismissed on the grounds of its ideological consequences (for example, defending the status quo, an androcentric order, and the West over the rest); by elucidating its literary and rhetorical base, the undecidability of its meaning, and the means by which it persuades; and finally, by tracing its logic to historically and culturally situated communities.

Although attractive in certain respects, such rebuttals are also dangerous. There is a strong tendency among those sharing paradigms and practices to cut themselves away from the alienated. Over time antagonistic groups cease communicating altogether, viewing each other as hopelessly mistaken. Meanwhile, the interior discourses spin on, feeding upon themselves and becoming increasingly rarefied. The impact on "the profane life" outside the sacred circle is often minimal. There is good reason, then, to listen closely to the critics, to be sensitive to the community practices from which criticism grows, and actively to pursue dialogue with those differing in discursive preferences. In this way, constructionist discourse stands to be enriched, relations across otherwise alienated communities sustained, and the potential for constructionist discourse to inform broader cultural practices enhanced.

Constructionism: Roots and Tendrils

Many question the intellectual roots of the constructionist orientation. The historically curious wish to identify its earliest origins, while antagonists ask whether constructionism isn't simply a rehashing of earlier—and reputedly wiser—theory. In these untutored forms, both questions are flawed in the asking. The former often presumes an originary point for a body of thought—a single inspired genius or a date before which minds were dark. In its emphasis on the communal construction of meaning, and the continuous and unsystematic appropriation of past meanings to forge present understandings, constructionism subverts attempts to locate precise origins. For example, if we wished to understand the origins of the phrase "the ship of state," should we document the first usage of each word composing the phrase, the first attempt to force the scattered borrowings from the past into a single amalgam, the first usage of a vessel metaphor in speaking of government, the first appropriation of the phrase for purposes of political persuasion, or what? Similarly, to ask whether constructionism is a rephrasing of earlier ideas presumes that words are expressions of a fixed underlying meaning, that the same "thought" may be voiced in many different ways. For constructionists, however, the emphasis on the contextual basis of meaning, and its continuing negotiation across time, displaces this traditional assumption. The attempt to fix the meaning of a text is misguided.

Yet, to clarify constructionism through comparison and contrast, we need to locate—by current conventions—related or interdependent dialogues. From whence the conversations of construction? In some degree we approached this task in the previous chapter. As we saw, constructionist views can be traced to recent explorations in ideological critique, literary and rhetorical processes, and the social basis of scientific knowledge.[1] A full elaboration of constructionist roots would thus invite an exploration of the history of each of these enterprises—the roots of ideological critique in Hegel, for example, or the influence of Condillac or the French *ideologues* on the linguistic view of knowledge. It is also clear that in the development of constructionism, these enterprises too are not reproduced whole cloth; the relevant works are disfigured and rewoven in various ways. For example, in the case of ideological critique, the traditional emphases on "demystification" and "emancipation from invalid knowledge" are removed from the constructionist thesis, for each presumes the possibility of a true and objective representation of reality for which critique should serve as a correction. The definition of ideology as a psychological state is also removed from the constructionist ledger and replaced with social pragmatics.

In a similar manner, literary theory adds substantially to a constructionist view in its dismantling of a mimetic view of language and its removal of the logos as the central source of meaning. At the same time, while social pragmatics play little role in most literary theory, they play a central role in constructionist analyses. And, while the sociology of knowledge and history of science are of pivotal significance in the development of constructionist inquiry, explorations in these fields vary substantially in their assumptive base, and many would overlap only partially with my view of constructionism. For example, Berger and Luckmann's (1966) classic work in the sociology of knowledge, *The Social Construction of Reality,* is a constructionist icon. Its emphases on the relativity of perspectives, the linking of individual perspectives to social process, and reification through language continue to play a major role in constructionist dialogues. At the same time, the concepts of "individual subjectivity" and "social structure"—both central to Berger and Luckmann—have moved to the margins. To propose, for example, that "society exists as both objective and subjective reality" (p. 119) is not only to create an obfuscating dualism but to essentialize the material and the mental. Similarly, Thomas Kuhn's (1962) *The Structure of Scientific Revolutions* is of singular importance in its replacement of a foundationalist philosophy of science with a predominantly social account of theoretical "advances." At the same time, Kuhn's conception of shifts in worldview or perspective as fundamentally psychological— equivalent to a shift in visual Gestalt (pp. 110–120)—is incompatible with the present view of constructionism. Similarly, Kuhn's (1977) subsequent attempt to ground scientific practice in a set of epistemic values is regressive in terms of the views I am setting forth here.

There are other intellectual traditions to which constructionism bears an important intertextual relationship. Two of these deserve special attention, the first distinctly psychological in nature and the second uniting mind and society. In the former there is a class of psychological theories, often termed *constructivist,*[2] which place particular stress on the individual's psychological construction of the experiential world. They vary, however, in their concern with the world in itself. Thus, on the one hand, Jean Piaget's (1954) theory of genetic epistemology is frequently termed "constructivist." Its major theoretical emphasis is on the individual's construction of reality: reality is *assimilated* into the child's existing system of understandings. At the same time, however, through the additional process of *accommodation,* the cognitive system adapts itself to the structure of the world.

Somewhat more radical is the *constructive alternativism* of George Kelly (1955) and his followers. This view traces the chief source of human action to the processes by which the individual privately construes, cognizes, or interprets the world. However, in the end, it also voices a healthy respect for "the world as it is." The choice of constructs, as Kelly puts it, "favors the alternative which seems to provide the best basis for anticipating ensuing events" (p. 64). Most extreme is the radical constructivism of Ernst von

Glasersfeld (1987, 1988) and others within the second-order cybernetics movement. For von Glasersfeld "Knowledge is not passively received either through the senses or by way of communication, but is actively built up by the cognizing subject" (1988, p. 83). In effect, the individual never makes direct contact with the world as it is; there is nothing to be said about a world that is unconstructed by the mind.[3]

The constructivist literatures are congenial with social constructionism in two important respects. First, in their emphasis on the constructed nature of knowledge, both constructivism and constructionism are skeptical of foundationalist warrants for an empirical science. Further, each challenges the traditional view of the individual mind as a device for reflecting the character and conditions of an independent world. Each questions the view of knowledge as something "built up" within the mind through dispassionate observation. And thus, each questions the authority traditionally accorded to "behavioral science" and the methods of science that do not take into account their own effects in shaping knowledge.[4]

Yet, beyond these points of convergence, constructivist theses are often antagonistic to constructionism as I develop it here. From a constructionist perspective neither "mind" nor "world" is granted ontological status, thus removing the very grounding assumptions of constructivism. Nor do extreme forms of constructivism, which would reduce the world to mental construction, become a satisfying replacement. For the constructionist, terms for both world and mind are constituents of discursive practices; they are integers within language and thus themselves socially contested and negotiated. Social constructionism, then, is neither dualist nor monist (debates on such matters are, for the constructionst, primarily exercises in linguistic competence). It remains essentially mute or agnostic about such matters. Finally, the constructivist view remains lodged within the tradition of Western individualism. It traces knowledge claims primarily to intrinsic processes within the individual. But social constructionism traces the sources of human action to relationships and the very understanding of "individual functioning" to communal interchange.

Constructionism also bears an intertextual relation to theories concerned with the social basis of mental life (sometimes called "social constructivist"). Unlike constructivists, who posit a mental world and then theorize its relation to an external world, these theorists give priority to social process in shaping what is taken to be knowledge at the level of the individual mind. This privileging of the social over the personal is a hallmark of social phenomenology (Schutz 1962), symbolic interactionism (Mead 1934), and the work of Vygotsky and his colleagues (Wertsch 1985), and has begun to enter various sectors of cognitive psychology (see, for example, Arbib and Hesse 1986). In effect, individual knowledge claims are ultimately traced to social process, a position that is highly compatible with constructionism. In spite of the rich dialogic relationship born of this affinity, however, there are also substantial differences, beginning with the primary position accorded to mental processes within these various perspectives. Schutz held that concepts of "cognitive setting," "subjectivity," "attention," "reasons," and "goals" are pivotal to the explanation of action. Similarly, Mead and other symbolic interactionists richly elaborated such concepts as "symbolization," "consciousness," "conceptualization," and "self-concept." And Vygotsky paid special attention to mental processes of "abstraction," "generalization," "volition," "association," "attention," "representation," "judgment," and so on. In effect, all these theorists objectified a specifically mental world. In contrast, the chief focus of interest for the constructionist is microsocial process. The constructionist rejects the dualistic premises that give rise to "the problem of mental functioning." The site of explanation for human action moves to the relational sphere. I shall return to this issue shortly.

Constructionist arguments are thus textually related to a number of intellectual traditions, sharing much but often differing either in emphasis or in fundamental assumptions. An important question for the future concerns the desirability of domain sanctity, that is, the value of clear differentiations between one conceptual orientation and another. In the present analysis, I have paid my dues to traditional analytic demands, striving to achieve an internal coherence in the case of constructionism and showing where it is both similar to and different from other perspectives. However, many scholars now borrow various concepts and approaches from across the related genres, with little concern for purity. And, while problematic in terms of systematicity, aesthetics, and clarity, these very standards may also be contested on a number of other grounds. Further, "blurred genres" may also be both rhetorically powerful and catalytic in effect. Depending on pragmatic considerations, there are times when generic purity may be usefully sacrificed for alternative ends, and a continued mixing of the signifiers may be counted as desirable. This is also to say that any attempt, such as this one, to establish a coherent account of constructionism, must be viewed as situated—open to contest, subversion, and transformation. It is an account that serves the purposes of the present volume—attempting to reach particular readers confronting special problems at particular times. Constructionist arguments generally militate against fixed and final formulations, even those of their own making.

Experience and Other Psychological Realities

Many scholars welcome constructionism because it challenges the "cult" of the individual that is endemic to Western tradition. As the implications of a communal or relational ontology are developed, however, many also find the deemphasis on psychological processes unsettling. It places secure and trusted beliefs about persons, including ourselves, into question. The "individual mind" loses not only its ontological grounding but all of its traditional constituents—the emotions, rational thought, motives, personality traits, intentions, memory, and the like. All these constituents of the self become historically contingent constructions of culture. (The fuller implications of this view will unfold in later chapters; see especially Chapters 8 to 12). As a preliminary we must confront the loss of what, for many, is the central ingredient of personal existence: private experience. To paraphrase the common grievance, "It is one thing to view talk about the mind (thought, attitudes, motives, and so on) as Western constructions, but to deny me the reality of my own experience is going too far. Conscious experience is real; it is all I can really know; it precedes rather than follows construction. Without my experience I cannot enter into language and social life." Surely this line of argument is familiar and compelling. How should the constructionist regard it?

As a preliminary softening of the ontology, the constructionist might wish to engage in a deconstructive effort. What precisely is the referent for the term "experience" after all? What does the term signify? As Bruner and Feldman (1990) point out, the concept of conscious experience does not have a singular meaning; rather, different traditions anchor the conception in different and often conflicting metaphors. A major distinction can be made, for example, between traditions holding conscious experience to be "passive" (formed by events from the outside) and "active" (imposing itself on whatever it encounters).[5] Can we claim an objective—as opposed to subjective—account of experience? How can our language for describing conscious experience get beyond metaphor to depict "the thing in itself"? Further, by traditional standards, to claim possession of "experience" ("I experienced it") presumes an *awareness* of experience, or more bluntly, that "I experience my experience." And yet what are we to make of the assumption that experience can turn in upon itself and register its own existence? What arguments can we offer to render such an assertion reasonable? In addition, if I report on "my experience," am I not reporting on the contents ("I feel *cold*"; "I see *rain*") rather than the experience itself? If I remove all contents (whose referents are located in what I take to be "the external world") is there anything left over that I can term "pure experience"? And if it is difficult to determine what I am referring to within myself, how can I determine whether we are speaking of an identical phenomenon? I cannot have access to your subjectivity, nor you to mine. Do we mean the same thing when we each report what we are "experiencing"? Such issues have long troubled philosophers and remain unresolved even today.

A preliminary analysis of this kind reduces the force of the simple assumption that the word *experience* stands in an unambiguous relationship with a particular datum. In championing the existence of experience, we leave unclear what kind of claim we are making. Given the difficulty in locating a referent for the term "experience," let us adopt a constructionist standpoint and attend to *discourse about experience.* In considering such discourse, the paramount question is one of social consequence. What forms of cultural life are suppressed or sustained by such discourse? Such considerations move in two directions, one diachronic and the other synchronic. In the former instance, we should press toward an account of the historical vicissitudes of "experience talk," the conditions in which it gains or loses currency, the ways in which such words have been used (to denote private mental events, the relation between the mental and the material, the conflation of person and world, and so on), the kinds of discourse that have sustained it, and the patterns of relationship that it serves to constitute. Such queries would not only serve further to de-objectify the concept, to challenge the common presumption that the term pictures a reality outside itself. Synchronic inquiry would also carry the implications of such historical analysis into the present, exploring the pragmatic functions served by such discourse today. In Wittgenstein's terms, we might ask about the social function of claims to consciousness: "What is the purpose of saying this to myself, and how can another person understand me?" asks Wittgenstein. "Now expressions like 'I see, I hear, I am conscious' really have their uses. I tell a doctor now I am hearing with this ear again, or I tell someone who believes I am in a faint 'I am conscious again,' and so on" (1953, p. 416). In each case, the statement accomplishes a social end. It does so because of a particular history, and its ramifications in cultural life are many and noteworthy.

Yet it is important to stress that there is nothing about such explorations that militates against either a scholarly concern with the nature of experience or the common use of the term in everyday life. For the constructionist the lack of ontological grounding for language is no argument against its use. The value of psychological discourse lies not in its capacity to reflect truth but in its capacity to carry out relationships. Thus, for phenomenologists, feminists, or qualitative researchers, to "explore the character of people's experience" is not foreclosed as a move within the annals of scholarly or therapeutic dialogue. Indeed, there may be valuable functions served through the situated objectification of the term. For example, phenomenological accounts of individual experience may be credited for their richness of descriptive language (compared to the flat, technical argot of the quantitative researcher) and the humane concern for the individual that this language fosters. Similarly, feminist accounts of "women's experience" do not so much inform us about "women's internal world," as draw attention to a marginalized discourse and enable this discourse to acquire political currency. In the same way, I shall continue to speak of "my experience" in daily relations, not because such accounts reflect another plane of reality (an "inner world"), but because a failure to do so would reduce my capacity to participate in valued forms of relationship. Talk of experience figures in a great many cultural rituals—patterns of revelation, sharing, confirming, and the like. Constructionism scarcely challenges the lived validity of such usages.

Realism: "But There Is a World Out There!"

While many wish to hold fast to the reality of private experience, the more self-consciously scientific are quite willing to relinquish this "holdover from the prescientific era." Empirical psychology has scarcely been a friend to the concept of private experience since the nineteenth-century era of mentalism. For the empirically minded, yet another question takes prominence, the question of material reality. The typical objection leveled at the constructionist—often accompanied by a self-satisfied smirk or a display of righteous indignation—is its seeming absurdity in the face of an obdurate reality. The objection takes many forms: "Do you mean to say that if you placed a lighted match into a container of gasoline the result is undecidable?" "Are you denying the existence of poverty, disease, and hunger in the world?" "Death is an obvious part of human existence; it is pure nonsense to say it is a social construction." "Do you mean to say that there is no world out there? We are just making it up?"[6]

Although laced with the full rhetorical power of everyday convention, such objections are ultimately based on a misunderstanding of the constructionist position. Constructionism makes no denial concerning explosions, poverty, death, or "the world out there" more generally. Neither does it make any affirmation. As I have noted, constructionism is ontologically mute. Whatever is, simply is. There is no foundational description to be made about an "out there" as opposed to an "in here," about experience or material. Once we attempt to articulate "what there is," however, we enter the world of discourse. At that moment the process of construction commences, and this effort is inextricably woven into processes of social interchange and into history and culture. And when these processes are set in motion they will generally work toward the reification of the language. It is precisely the reified base that also lends to the realist the rhetorical power of the present line of critique. To illustrate, let us consider more closely the question of whether putting a lighted match to gasoline will produce an explosion. There are two specific questions the constructionist would ask: first, is there any alternative way of describing the same state of affairs? Clearly the answer is yes: the artist's account of colors shifting in hue and intensity, the poet's detailing of soaring spirits, the chemist's analysis of heated molecules, the shaman's account of magical forces, and so on. The multiplicity of accounts brings up a second question: is one account more objectively accurate than another? If so, on what grounds? As we saw in the preceding chapter, there is no way of listing words on one side of the ledger and "what there is" on the other, and then locating identities that transcend the conventions of a particular community. The adequacy of any word or arrangement of words to "capture reality as it is" is a matter of local convention.

Let us apply this line of reasoning to the frequent attacks made on constructionism for its insensitivity to issues of power. Putting aside for the moment the ideological issues at stake, critics will say that constructionst writings often seem "soft on power." They do not take into account the most basic fact—that power is inequitably distributed by class, gender, and/or race, and concomitantly, that in the cultural competition for voice there are enormous differences in resources. Consider, for example, who owns and controls the media, the class biases in educational curricula, and racial and class differences in literacy. And in personal relationships, constructionists can give no account of how power is manifest in such activities as the oppression of the poor, rape, or child molestation.

In my view, constructionism is not at all opposed to such concerns; they surely deserve our keenest attention. The hesitation is in presuming that power should be a grounding concept within the metatheory, a concept without which a constructionist sensitivity cannot be set in motion. To what does the concept of power refer? It is, after all, multiply constructed or, in Lukes's (1974) view, "essentially contested." The Machiavellian view of power differs from that of the traditional Marxist, which differs from that of Parsons (1964) or Giddens (1976), which likewise differ from the kinds of capillary theories that have emerged since Foucault (1978, 1979). Further, these various concepts are used by different interest groups (Marxists, political conservatives, feminists) for often contrary purposes. Within any group the concept of power can be reified, with significant consequences for that group's activities. Thus, in the same way that the constructionist would scarcely abandon such terms as "gasoline," "ignition," and "explosion" because of their constructed character, so, too, certain groups may find the concept of power invaluable at certain times—including constructionists.

The relentless critic continues: Perhaps these descriptions are the product of local convention, but aren't some of these conventions transcendentally better than others? Wouldn't you rather tell your child about possible "explosions" than "the color display" that will result from the lighted match? Or, more directly, if your son had pneumonia, wouldn't you rather take him to a doctor than a shaman? Don't the words of the doctor give us more useful and effective information than those of the shaman? Paul Feyerabend

(1978) deals with a similar argument in his *Science and a Free Society*. After his thoughtful critique of the rational foundations of science, he faces the problem of whether Western scientific medicine isn't more advanced than the practices of "prescientific" cultures, whether the former has knowledge superior to that of the latter. Feyerabend answers by celebrating the knowledge of the nonscientific cultures, and denigrating the claims of Western medicine. Western medicine only seems superior, he argues, "because *the apostles of science were the more determined conquerors, because they materially suppressed the bearers of alternative cultures*" (p. 102; italics mine). Feyerabend then goes on to extol the advances of Chinese healers, herbalists, masseurs, hypnotists, acupuncturists, and the like. Here he finds a "vast amount of valuable medical knowledge that is frowned upon and treated with contempt by the medical profession" (p. 136).

Yet, for a constructionist, this is not the appropriate answer to the query. The question is not whether scientific medicine represents more advanced knowledge than its alternatives, whether doctors know more than shamans or vice versa. Such issues can only be settled from a given perspective, and if one selects the perspective of Western medicine, it will—despite Feyerabend's remonstrations—prove the superior. If Western medicine is allowed to establish the ontology of infirmity and the criteria for cure, no competitor is likely to furnish a threat. For the constructionist, then, there is no culturally decontextualized crucible against which any two systems of medicine can be compared. More generally, it may be said that participants in each community develop their own practices, rituals, or patterns of relationship. Within one community certain "events" are selected out, given names, and treated in various ways. The medical profession delineates certain configurations, which it categorizes as "diseases" and sets out to eradicate. In the same way the shaman may fasten on other "entities," label them as symptoms of "voodoo," and seek to eliminate them. In Western medicine there simply are no "voodoo effects," just as for the shaman "pneumonia" does not exist. Further, Western medical treatments would be no more or less effective or "advanced" if doctors used the syllables *voodoo* in their work as opposed to *nu-mon-ya;* the results would be largely the same. Likewise the shaman would not be more effective in eliminating spell-like effects if he were to call them *nu-mon-ya*. The terms are not pictures of events, they are simply the local ways of talking used in coordinating relations among people within their environment. The words used in describing or explaining "events" and their "eradication" should not be confused with their putative referents. Western medical terminology does not cause its success in achieving what it calls "cures."

Thus, as a participant in Western culture, I would prefer to take my child to a Western doctor. I would do so not because Western medical knowledge is transcendentally superior, but because I participate in relationships where

Western values predominate, and I code events as "illness" and "cure" in ways that are congenial to local medical practices. It is because I participate in a community that values the practices of "cure" in Western terms that doctors are permitted to achieve what we call "success." At the same time, whether these values and associated practices are universally preferable is open to serious debate.[7]

Yet, these arguments don't exhaust the realist claims because there are many extant forms of realism. Material realists are only one such group to raise questions about constructionism. A second band of *transcendental realists*—including Bhaskar (1978, 1989), Harré (1988), and Greenwood (1991)—join constructionists in the critique of empiricist foundationalism. Their attacks on empiricist assumptions of value neutrality, along with the traditional predilection for Humean explanations of human conduct, are quite congenial with constructionism. However, rather than jettison the attempt at foundations, viewed with suspicion by most constructionists, transcendental realists press on to seek alternative grounds for scientific rationality. In this respect, transcendental realists have been antagonistic to the kind of constructionism represented here (see espccially Greenwood 1991, 1992; Harré 1992).

It is interesting that for transcendental realists the observable world, which is central to the empiricist, is of little concern. The critical dimension of reality is to be located within or behind observable events, in a realm of "generative mechanisms," "inherent tendencies," or "causal powers." The "objects" of science "are real structures which exist and act independently of the patterns of events they generate" (Bhaskar 1991, p. 68). Thus, the aim of science is to discover and elucidate the character of these hidden realities. Although attractive to many Marxist thinkers wishing to postulate underlying structures of economic and personal life, the realist program suffers as a foundational rationality. It does so not only by virtue of the problems inherent in any foundationalism, most notably the incapacity to justify its own grounding ontology and valuational investments, but also because it fails to supply a rationale for how the underlying structures could ever be identified, how one could ascertain which structures were related to what observable outcomes, and how one could establish the superiority of one structural account over another. Transcendental realism inherits all the problems discussed in the preceding chapter concerning the capacity of scientific theory to furnish accurate representations of reality.[8]

In the end one must be suspicious of all attempts to establish *fundamental* ontologies—incorrigible inventories of *the real*. As Margolis (1991) queries, "What reason do we ever have for supposing that there *are* discernible criteria—timelessly suitable . . . *for* matching truth-claims to truth and falsity *tout court,* or for reliably approximating to them?" (p. 4). Each carries with it a favored way of life, and a host of suppressive impulses. Each moves toward totalization, subjecting alternative discourses to ridicule, threatening alternative ways of life with extinction.[9] To proclaim that reality is constituted of material casts aspersions on those who speak of intentions, creativity, or spiritual depth and threatens those forms of life in which such terms are integral. Transcendental realism supports a hierarchy of labor that relegates engineering, actuarial prediction, "applied" research, and hands-on practice to the nether ranks. For the phenomenologist who views reality as fundamentally experiential, the materialist takes on the demeanor of a Philistine. And for psychoanalytic theorists who hold that experiential reality is but a pawn to the deeper energies of the psyche, all claims to empirical knowledge are psychodynamically suspect. Are the debates among these and other foundational claims of substantial moment? How would one set of foundational claims ever establish superiority over another outside its own peculiar language commitments, and how can we locate a mode of language that is uncontested? And why, from a constructionist standpoint, should we press toward closure of all intelligibilities save one? Why set out to impoverish the landscape of language as opposed to enriching it? [10]

Ontological Relativism: The Incoherence of Skepticism

The constructionist critique of ontological claims is not without its costs. One of the most important of these is the invitation to yet another line of critique, Platonic in origin and savage in efficacy. All forms of ontological skepticism, on this account, suffer death by incoherence. To paraphrase the critique, "If the skeptic argues there is no truth, objectivity, or empirical knowledge, then on what grounds should these claims be accepted? On its own account, the skeptic's attack cannot be true, objective, or empirically based. Skepticism is thus incoherent." Constructionist theses fall heir to this critique because if all intelligibilities are socially constructed, as earlier arguments suggest, then the same must be said of constructionist theses themselves. Social constructionism, then, cannot be true.

For the constructionist there are several significant rejoinders to such charges of incoherence. Let us consider two particular forms of the critique and the constructionist reply:

1. *Is the social constructionist position not itself a social construction?* To this the coherent constructionist can only respond yes. The arguments for constructionism are, after all, social artifacts: tied together by metaphor and narrative, historically and culturally bounded, and used by persons in the process of relating. However, in taking such a stand, the aspiring critic has essentially vindicated the constructionist position. That is, the attempt to undo constructionism in this case is based on the same constructionist

premises that the critic strives to undo: it seeks to establish the socially constructed character of the constructionist arguments. As a result, the critic first fails to put forward an alternative to constructionism; that is, no arguments are presented that are antithetical to a constructionist position. Second, and more important, the critic embraces constructionist premises in order to move the dialogue forward. The critic now stands in the same ontological space as the target of the putative attack—thus adding further weight to the constructionist thesis.

Most important, for the constructionist the process of dismantling constructionist "rhetoric" is an end much to be valued, for it is just such incursions—questioning the pragmatic implications of constructionism, unveiling the literary devices from which its rhetorical power is derived, elucidating the social processes from which it has emerged, inquiring into its cultural and historical roots, and challenging its implicit values—that are called for by constructionism itself. Through such refutations, otherwise silenced voices gain entry into the conversation, and the dialogue is expanded.[11] And when self-critical explorations are opened to assessment, the conversation expands once again.

2. If social constructionism abandons the concept of truth, how can it make truth claims for itself? Although a more trenchant form of criticism on the face of it, the sound and fury are short-lived. At the outset, it is important to realize that commitments to a premise of truth—whether empirical, rational, phenomenological, or spiritual—do not themselves contribute to the truth of these premises. That empiricists are committed to a belief in objective truth does not itself bear on the truth value of empiricist propositions; commitments to analytic truth do not render analytic proofs true. In effect, making truth claims is an exercise in warranting or justification, in inviting others to accept a set of propositions by virtue of a particular juxtaposition of words. Such justifications do not themselves render a body of propositions true; they are simply ancillary or accompanying assertions. To warrant a set of justifications as "truth giving" would require yet another range of justification (such as a reason why we might believe that empiricist metatheory guaranteed the truth of empirical propositions).

More generally, it may be argued that there is no theory of knowledge—whether empiricist, realist, rationalist, phenomenological, or otherwise—that can coherently furnish warrants for its own truth or validity. The aspiring theorist of knowledge is confronted in each case with two equally problematic choices: First, he or she can attempt to use *the same arguments* proposed by the theory of knowledge to validate the theory itself (for example, use empirical data to justify empiricism or rationalist techniques to justify rationalism). However, as is quickly apparent, such attempts are inherently circular. They simply reassert their initial claims, but the claims themselves remain without justification. To have confidence in the empirical data used to support empiricism it would be necessary to embrace the theory of knowledge in question beforehand. Rational argumentation as support for a rationalist theory of knowledge would, by the same token, simply be redundant ("rationality is true because rationality is true").[12] The second alternative is to employ *an alternative basis* for the truth of one's theory of knowledge. That is, the empiricist might seek a rationalist foundation for empiricist claims to truth, or the rationalist search for empirical data to support rationalism. To select this option, however, is to destroy the validity of the favored theory of knowledge, for if a theory of knowledge is warranted by a second theory of knowledge, its claims to warrant are replaced by the source from which its claims are derived. If empiricism is only true by virtue of rationalist foundations, for example, then rationalist foundations displace empiricism as the primary means for establishing truth.

Yet there is a more substantial answer to the question of constructionism's validity, and it concerns the suppressed grounds of the critique. The criticism of incoherence in this case ultimately rests its rhetorical weight on its own premises. It reinstates as a criterion of theoretical acceptability the very concept (for example, "objective truth") that is thrown into question by the constructionist. To illustrate, the critic argues that (1) there are ample grounds for establishing the truth conditions for various propositions; (2) objective validity should serve as the appropriate basis for accepting or rejecting a given theory; and (3) since constructionism offers no possibility for its objective assessment, its truth is indeterminant. Yet the constructionist arguments of the preceding chapter undermine the legitimacy of the first of the premises. Little sense can be made of the view that propositions can be matched against the world in such a way that their truth-bearing capacities can be determined. As a result, it is no longer tenable to use "correspondence with reality" as the criterion by which constructionist arguments—or any others—should be evaluated. For the constructionist, "objective truth" as a foundational criterion for the adequacy of various assertions, a foundation beyond communal convention, is simply irrelevant to their acceptance or rejection.

This is to say that constructionism offers no foundation, no ineluctable rationality, no means for establishing its basic superiority to all competing views of knowledge. It is, rather, a form of intelligibility—an array of propositions, arguments, metaphors, narratives, and the like—that welcome inhabitation. All constructionist analyses engage in a form of "selective realism," privileging certain "objects of analysis." They all require a form of "ontological gerrymandering" (Woolgar and Pawluck 1985) in order to achieve rhetorical impact. At the same time, such analyses do not ask for an application of the true-false binary. Rather, they invite the reader to enter in: to collaborate in giving the array a sense and a significance, to play with the possibilities and the practices coherent with this intelligibility, and to evaluate them against alternatives. Constructionist views function as an invitation to a dance, a game, or a form of life. Unlike the foundationalist, who attempts to restrict the range of proper tellings, the constructionist does not seek to abolish the alternatives. For an empiricist foundationalist, the phenomenological view is suspect, rationalism moribund, and spiritualism anathema. For the empiricist, then, the competitors could be abandoned with no loss to humanity. By the same token, phenomenologists and spiritualists might be pleased to see the eradication of empiricism, and so on across the spectrum of existing metatheories. Yet, because constructionism makes no claim to be "true"—a position beyond question—it does not thereby remove the alternatives from the field. Rather, it prompts one to ask, What are the gains and losses to our way of life that follow from each view? In what sense do these discourses contribute to our well-being and in what sense do they obfuscate our ends? And indeed, this discussion itself should have no terminus.

Moral Relativism

One of the most formidable attacks against constructionist views is voiced by those with deep ethical convictions. The constructionist orientation is all too laissez-faire, they say. It seems to tolerate everything and itself to stand for nothing. It discourages commitment to any set of values or ideals and seems to advocate an amoral free-for-all. Constructionism offers no grounds for societal critique and renewal, and at worst, fails even to inspire the kind of principled indignation that is necessary to prevent the kinds of atrocities our civilization has so often perpetrated. How can any theoretical orientation that "tolerates" the annihilation of millions of people be acceptable? Such accusations surely demand a reply. The present discussion will thus serve only as a prelude to a more extended account in Chapter 4.

   At the outset, whether constructionist views, when fully extended, contain a moral or political standpoint remains an open question. Although no explicitly moral or political vision has been explicated in the present work, constructionist texts are inherently porous: with little effort, one can locate within these lines of argument strong moral and political preferences.[13] At the same time, the nature of these views remains open to question. Many find constructionst arguments implicitly feminist in their challenge to traditional social hierarchies and the totalizing discourse of empirical science. Others see them as antifeminist in their critique of feminist standpoint epistemology. Certain readers find constructionism to be implicitly Marxist in its emphasis on communal interdependence, while others see it as vintage liberalism in its emphasis on freedom and equality. Some find constructionism profoundly moral in putting relatedness before self, while others will see its critique of individual reason and intention as the end of moral responsibility. Is constructionism, then, morally shallow or morally profound? The outcome depends both on constructionist theory and the reading one makes of its arguments.

For the moment, however, let us avoid forging any determinant linkage between constructionism and any specific set of values or political investments. Let us not use valuational commitments as a justificatory base for a constructionist standpoint. Let us, in effect, explore the outcome of a constructionism that fails to "take a moral stand." What rejoinders are then possible to the critique of moral relativism?

Here it is important to realize that there is no well-defined, well-defended, and broadly accepted view of morality against which to oppose a constructionist relativism. In fact, many would maintain that moral certainty has, if anything, been in a state of long-term deterioration. The ability of the Church to dictate on moral matters has steadily eroded since the Enlightenment, the subsequent separation of Church and State, and the hegemony of science. Nor have philosophical contributions over the centuries elucidated compelling alternatives to religious orthodoxy. Toward the end of the nineteenth century there was widespread hope that science, then gaining ascendance, might furnish the comfort of moral clarification. Yet as scientists became increasingly aware that "ought" cannot be derived from "is," they abnegated virtually all responsibility for declaring what people *should* do. And, as philosophers shifted their attention to the clarification of language and the foundations of science in the present century, moral philosophy became virtually defunct. In the present century, moral discourse has, until recently, fallen on hard times. To fault constructionism for failing to generate moral foundations is scarcely a lethal condemnation when broadly accepted foundations are nowhere else apparent.

It is in this respect that constructionist impulses may, in fact, be lauded for the space they have opened for moral deliberation. As we have seen, Kuhn's (1970) devaluation of foundationalist views of scientific knowledge, Berger and Luckmann's (1966) analysis of knowledge as a social artifact, and Habermas's (1971) exploration of the relationship between knowledge and human interests all stood as challenges to the factual or rational grounding of established "bodies of knowledge." In this way each formed important bases for subsequent constructionist thought. At the same time, as they served to undermine scientific authority, they invited reconsideration of the moral, ethical, or valuational concerns that empiricism had so stridently discredited as sources of bias. In effect, these contributions gave rhetorical weight to the ideological critiques of equal rights exponents, antiwar activists, feminists, humanists, Marxists, and many others concerned with valuational deliberation. The constructionist demystification of the claims of the "knowledge class" breathed new life into the moral languages of recent decades.

Yet, while a constructionist posture invites moral deliberation, it does not in my view necessarily champion one set of moral suppositions over another. Constructionism can furnish a mandate for feminists, ethnic minorities, Christians, Muslims, and others to speak boldly on issues of value, but it does not thereby grant the validity of their claims, or claim certain moral verities to be superior. At this point, however, we need to ask whether a theory of knowledge that establishes a hierarchy of values (or champions certain virtues above others) is desirable. Do those who fault constructionism for its moral relativism truly desire a fixed standard of the good? In my view, those who criticize the moral shallowness of constructionism are usually not interested in replacing it with just any theory of the good. They do not want simply a moral commitment of *some* kind, they want one that duplicates their own. The Marxist critic would not be silenced by a constructionist commitment to free enterprise, nor a feminist by a valorization of male dominion. In this sense, the charge of moral vacuity is disingenuous; it masks the frustration that the arguments fail to support the inquisitor's own preferences and simultaneously protects the inquisitor from revealing the vulnerability of his or her own valuational standpoint. In Rorty's (1991) terms, "The ritual invocation of the 'need to avoid relativism' is most comprehensible as an expression of the need to preserve certain habits of contemporary European life" (p. 28).

As a more general surmise, few would wish to have a theory of the good and the right that did not justify or sustain the way of life they already valued. And herein lies the critical problem, for there is no single value, moral ideal, or social good that, when fully pursued, will not trammel upon the alternatives and obliterate the social patterns these alternatives support. Pursue justice to its limits, and mercy is lost; favor honesty above all, and personal security is threatened; champion community well-being, and individual initiative may be destroyed. Who then is to establish the hierarchy of the good, and by what right? In effect, if constructionism were to seek justification by recourse to a specific code of moral values, it would be faulted for arrogating an otherwise parochial standpoint to the status of universal ethic both totalizing and oppressive. Would such a code be serviceable in stemming the tide of evil in the contemporary world—in convincing those whose actions we find reprehensible that they are morally wrong, in fostering apologies and retreats, and in sustaining the order we desire? It seems doubtful, for our code would not be their code, and could be readily dismissed as irrelevant or even malevolent. We find, then, that virtuous standpoints are not unproblematic; they frequently operate to reduce trust and foster alienation. And, given the problems associated with the hegemony of any particular code, is it possible that a theory choosing not to advocate a hierarchy of the good holds greater promise for human-kind than one that is morally committed?

In saying this, I must echo a now familiar refrain: simply because our ontologies—and in this case our value systems—are socially constituted is no argument against bearing them into action. In fact, that they contribute to ongoing cultural patterns may be their best justification.[14] The culture may be ill served by the view that rational foundations are required—for either the good life or the moral society. I shudder to think that we must await the agreement of the learned or the inspired before we can know how to go on. I am not advocating here an ethical standpoint of relativism, a position from which other positions can be judged as good or bad, or one which itself dictates action (or, as Haraway [1988] puts it, yet another "God trick"). In terms of the arguments developed thus far, construction-ism could offer no such position. Or, in Fish's (1980) terms, there is no position of relativism in itself, a space from which one can peer at other positions free of cultural tradition. Of necessity, we live by our existing intelligibilities, which include comparative as well as ethical discourses. Whether ethical discourse serves valuable purposes in society will be ad-dressed in the next chapter.

Conceptual Relativism

A final form of relativism is embodied in many constructionist writings, and like relativisms of any kind, it has evoked broad criticism. Constructionist writings—including this volume—frequently emphasize variation in under-standing. They call attention to the multiplicity of ways in which "the world" is, and can be, constructed. They challenge any attempt to establish first principles, a grounding ontology, or an epistemological basis for the universal prioritizing of any given reality posit. Against this line of argu-ment, critics respond with the following form of redoubt: In order to claim that there are differences in construction, there must be a criterion or stan-dard of comparison. We should have to possess a criterion of what is the case in order to demonstrate that there were differences with respect to its construction; we should have to posit a common rationality that would enable us to recognize that ways of thinking were incompatible. In David-son's terms, "the dominant metaphor of conceptual relativism, that of dif-fering points of view, seems to betray an underlying paradox. Different points of view make sense, but only if there is a common coordinate system on which to plot them; yet the existence of a common system belies the claim of dramatic incomparability" (1973, p. 6). These arguments are of-ten coupled as well with the rejoinder that if constructionism were true, there would be no possibility for intercultural understanding. We should each be locked within our local systems of construction.[15]

In my view, these related forms of criticism are all premised on a particular conception of language, a tradition holding that (1) language is an instrument for bearing truth, on the one hand, and (2) for conveying rational thought (internal concepts or meanings) on the other. To paraphrase, "When I make accurate observations of the world and share my conceptions with you via language, you too will know the world." On these grounds, indeed, I could scarcely say that another culture's conception of reality differed from my own without presuming a common datum against which comparisons could be made: if the natives say *gavagai* when we say *rabbit,* for example, there is a common denominator—an unconstructed datum—to which we both refer. Or, if pronouncements are made about conceptual differences between cultures, then I must presume the possibility for a common rationality: if I can show you that the Nuer concept of *kwoth* is different from the Western concept of god, then I must understand the Nuer concept, and the Nuer must in principle be able to understand ours. If so, there must be a common form of rational thought.

Let us consider two replies to the critic, the first of which grants the premises of the critique and the second of which does not. If the constructionist admits the validity of these arguments and forsakes the presumption of differences, what can then be asserted? The constructionist can make no strong claim to differences in perspective, but how is the critic then to claim knowledge of the shared similarities—of the nature of the world from all standpoints or the rationality of universal proportion? Such claims would have to be lodged in some form of clairvoyance concerning the world and rationality beyond a cultural standpoint—from a god's eye view of the true and the rational. In effect, even if the premises are granted, the critique fails to do any significant work. No propositions or insights are forthcoming. Thus, one ends the debate in a standoff—a state of full indeterminacy in which no assertions of comparability are possible.[16]

Consider now a second line of rebuttal, one that rejects the premises of the critique of difference. In previous chapters I have set constructionism against the traditional view of language, upon which the present critique depends for its intelligibility. I have outlined profound problems inhering in the view that language is an instrument for bearing truth, on the one hand, and rational thought on the other. The constructionist is more likely to favor a pragmatic view of language, one in which the meaning of terms or propositions is dependent on its social usage. On this account, to say that another system of meaning differs from one's own is to assert that the composite of meaning-making conditions across different groups, times, and language histories is not identical. To reach agreement regarding the similarity of propositions or rationalities, then, is always a local achievement, and this achievement is no less relevant to matters of daily life than it is to scholarly argument. That is, academic assertions about the similarities and differences in meaning systems are themselves discursive achievements. And in the present context, assertions to the effect that Aristotelian physics differs from Newtonian physics and that the Western conception of magic differs from that of the Szondi are more easily demonstrated than assertions about their identity. Differences can be convincingly demonstrated by contemporary standards with a mere show of texts or practices; in contrast, to declare an identity requires arduous interpretive work. Constructionist declarations of contextual differences are not then grounded in empirical fact, but are simply more congenial to our contemporary forms of argumentation than their opposite. Most important, rather than reach an impasse of indeterminacy, the outcome of such arguments for the human sciences is a substantial broadening and enrichment of practices.

Theoretical Utility and the Problem of Progress

We must finally turn to a handful of interrelated questions that concern the practice of science, its past accomplishments, and its future potential. The preceding chapters have done much to discredit foundational views of scientific rationality, scientific progress, and the possibility of establishing theoretical proof through observation. As we have found, there is little to support the long-standing claim that science can progress by abandoning theories falsified by observation, and that theories in themselves can make predictions. These critiques of theory leave us in an uncomfortable position in trying to account for what we must view as enhanced capacities for prediction within the sciences. Most would agree that our capacity to travel in space, harness energy sources, and cure disease has been markedly improved over the centuries. Could such augmentation take place without theory? Could scientists have produced a bomb without atomic theory or perform gene splicing in the absence of genetic theory? How, then, are we to understand the function of theory within the sciences? Are there criteria by which we can say that certain forms of theory are better than others? Is there any sense, from a constructionist standpoint, in which scientific work is progressive?

Description as Performative

To develop this account successfully we require a precis concerning the character of scientific description. In this instance, it is useful to return to the distinction made by J. L. Austin in 1962 between *constative* propositions, those used for the description of the world, and what he termed *performative* propositions, linguistic formations that do not describe or report on states of affairs, that cannot be verified as true or false but are themselves actions in the world. For example, the sentence "The tag is on the bag" would be considered constative; one can verify the utterance through observation. In contrast, the utterances "On your mark, get set, go . . . ," "Hello," or "Here's to you" are performative. Starting a race, greeting, and toasting are significant social actions in themselves. Austin's distinction is useful because it shifts attention from the descriptive capacities of language to its pragmatic functions in relationships. But it is also problematic, for all those arguments lodged against the correspondence view of truth (and the picture theory of language) simultaneously serve to undermine the assumption of the constative—of truth-bearing propositions. Yet, it may be asked, are there no important distinctions to be made between a description of the approaching enemy and a curse on them? Doesn't the former have pragmatic implications the latter does not, and isn't this accomplishment central to the conduct of science? Perhaps what we require is an alternative way of conceptualizing the constative.

By exploring the implications of Austin's proposals, we can locate an auspicious way of doing so. Austin proposed that performatives are to be evaluated not according to correspondence with fact but according to their *felicity* within a *procedure*. A procedure is essentially some form of social convention: a felicitous utterance fits appropriately or congenially into a conventional state of affairs, but an infelicitous utterance does not. To shout "On your mark, get set . . ." suddenly and spontaneously while chatting with a companion would be regarded with deep suspicion; the utterance would be infelicitous. But its felicity would be restored should we relocate it in the context of a children's race. In effect, a proper understanding of the performative character of language requires that we focus our attention less on the linguistic acts themselves and more on the broader patterns of interaction in which they occur. To put it more directly, the performative value of an utterance is derived from its position within a more extended pattern of relationship.

Austin's analysis also implies that these more extended procedures or conventions are not merely verbal. In Wittgenstein's (1953) terms, we may view utterances as constituents of more extended forms of life, which may include both actions (other than verbal) and objects or environments. The point is illustrated in matters of gesture and facial expression; both contribute to the context that renders speech meaningful, giving it status as a particular kind of performative. There are only a limited number of nonverbal expressions, for example, that may felicitously accompany the statement "I love you" and successfully achieve the relational pattern we call romance. A grimace, a sinister laugh, or a dazed look will not generally qualify the remark in this way. It also follows that various actions, such as running, lifting, or striking at a moving object, can all be constituents of interpersonal procedures or life forms. Their performative value is determined by a felicitous context of words just as much as the performative capacity of words depends on the patterning of such actions. The game of tennis is illustrative. Here various utterances are indeed constituent elements of the game. Such phrases as "your serve" and "thirty-love" are essential components of the event. Their performative value typically depends on an extended set of physical actions both preceding and following; in turn, the actions require such utterance for them to proceed effectively. It is also important to notice in this case that in addition to words and actions the procedure includes extended sets of objects—balls, rackets, nets, and so on. Objects, actions, and words must all be coordinated for the social achievement of the game or the form of life to occur.

Let us return now to the problem of description. We began with Austin's distinction between constatives and performatives, and we bracketed the problem of how words, including theoretical propositions in the sciences, could be said to furnish pictures of an independent reality. With an expanded analysis of the performative function of words we can recognize the importance of the distinction, but significantly reformulated. In particular, when we engage in actions such as "describing," "explaining," or "theorizing" we are also engaging in a performative activity or form of life. That is to say, the first term in Austin's distinction, the constative or descriptive, is more properly considered a special case of his second or performative mode.[17] Thus, when we say that a certain utterance is "accurate" or "inaccurate," "true" or "false," we are not judging it according to some abstract or idealized standard of correspondence; pictorial accuracy is not at stake. Rather, we are indicating its degree of felicity or infelicity in particular circumstances. The proposition that "the world is round and not flat" is neither true nor false in terms of pictorial value—its correspondence with the objective world. By current standards, however, it is more felicitous to play the game of "round-world truth" when flying from Canton to Kansas and more felicitous to "play it flat" when touring the state of Kansas itself.

It follows that description can function *as* picture or mirror, but only within a local game or procedure in which we invest it with this function. We can develop a local ritual in which a correspondence view is vindicated; however, this vindication is not a function of the mimetic capacity of words but a historically and culturally situated agreement. Let me illustrate this idea more fully. As an impecunious adolescent I once served as a summer assistant to a wall plasterer. When Marvin climbed to the top of a ladder, his arms working the plaster to perfection on the ceiling overhead, it was crucial that I provide mixtures of water and plastering compound exactly to his specifications. At times the mixture had to be moist so it could be subtly worked and reworked; at others it had to be dry so that it could rapidly seal the desired contours. Thus, depending on his progress, he would bellow, "skosh" (for a wet mixture) and "dry-un" (for a drier compound). Of course these words were quite alien when I began my servitude, but within a few days I became proficient in producing the desired mixtures. In effect, "skosh" and "dry-un" became part of a relational dance in which we were engaged—words around which we coordinated our actions in order to achieve a perfect finish.

Yet, let us consider what has been achieved as a byproduct of this primitive dance of words, actions, and objects. If Marvin and I were exposed to a series of mixtures after two weeks of immersion in this procedure, with very little error we could have agreed on which were "skosh" and which "dry-uns." If I said "dry-un cumin' up," this would also inform Marvin of what he might predict at that moment. This prediction could have been confirmed or disconfirmed. In effect, by virtue of their function within the relational form, such terms as "skosh" and "dry-un" developed the capacity to function within the game of description and verification. The words themselves do not describe the world, but because they function successfully within the relational ritual, they come to serve as "descriptors" within the rules of that game. Because of their success in coordinating relationships, various utterances come to occupy a useful place in those rituals by which we determine truth and error, make predictions, and so on. To say that words describe, picture, or map (in this case, the world of plastering) must be seen as a byproduct of their embeddedness within the joint achievement of a relationship. What are the implications for the function of theory within science?[18]

Scientific Theories and the Pragmatics of Prediction

At least one major goal of scientific activity, as traditionally understood, is successful prediction. This is most obviously the case in the so-called "natural sciences," in which existing technologies permit us to do things unimagined in previous centuries. The predictive capacity of the social sciences is far less awesome, but we have developed technologies that enable prediction, at better than chance, of voting patterns, crime rates, divorce rates, performance in a variety of settings, and so on. In all these various cases, the process of generating predictive technology essentially relies on a community of scientists who develop various measures, employ them in different populations and contexts, apply or develop various statistical devices, and so on. Within these contexts theories as proposed do not themselves make these predictions; acts of prediction cannot in any way be logically derived from the theoretical premises. What then is the role of theory within the predictive process?

As I have suggested, the primary function of theories can be traced to the collaborative process operating within scientific communities. That is, theoretical language is constitutive of the pragmatic interchange of which predictions are the ultimate achievement. Like "three-love" and "my add" in tennis, they serve as the common argot that enables scientists to coordinate their activities one with another. If I join a group of scientists concerned with the prediction of what they call "academic performance," I must employ not only this term but a series of additional indexicals, including, for example, "IQ tests," "anxiety indicators," "achievement motivation," and the like. Such terms must also be embedded both within a set of relationships with my colleagues and within sets of objects—papers, pencils, scoring keys, students, and the like. The resulting function form, which relates IQ, achievement motive, and anxiety predictively to academic performance, serves as an iconic realization of our capacity to make predictions. The function form itself does not predict, but it enables the community of practitioners to represent and communicate so that predictions are constituted.

We have now identified two major functions of theory within the sciences, the first operative in the context of social transformation (see Chapter 2) and the second in the context of prediction, and are now positioned to consider the problem of theoretical evaluation. For if theory is valued for these pragmatic capacities, then specific criteria of evaluation can be derived—criteria that can replace "truth value" as the crucible for theoretical assessment. However, given the multiple functions of theory, a proper stance toward evaluation requires a diachronic view of science. That is, if the scientific process can be viewed as a roughly ordered sequence in which theory plays different roles at different times, then a univocal set of evaluative criteria may be unpropitious. Theoretical accounts may be differentially evaluated, depending on where they occur in the sequence. To put it another way, differing forms of theory may be required at different points in scientific development. This possibility becomes more fully apparent if we return to the Chapter 1 account of transformation in scientific intelligibilities.

Evaluating Theory in a Stage of Normal Science

Following that analysis, it is useful to view scientific transformations as occurring in three hypothetical stages: *normal science,* a stage during which there is common intelligibility among scientists at both the theoretical and practical level, and two further stages, first a *critical* stage in which rhetorics of negation challenge the dominant discourse, and then a *transformational* stage in which the discursive implicature of critique is elaborated. Although normal, critical, and transformational activities may occur at any time, in various combinations or in different wings of a discipline, it is useful to retain the hypothetical division for our purposes here, because it allows us to appreciate the possibility of multiple theoretical functions, and thus, the relevance of differing criteria for theoretical evaluation across time and circumstance.

First consider the phase of normal science. As proposed, one of the chief aims of the sciences—the natural sciences more significantly than the social—is that of generating reliable predictions. During this normal phase of scientific activity, a primary use of theory may be that of coordinating the actions of scientists around the task of prediction. As we have seen, theoretical accounts serve as the major pragmatic vehicle for conjoining the efforts of individuals in achieving this common end. It is also within this context that many of the traditional criteria for evaluating theory acquire their relevance. Within the conventions of discourse-action-object established by a community of scientists, the *predictive relevance* of a theory may be of critical importance. Does a rocket trajectory confirm or disconfirm predictions indexed by a given theoretical language or not? Within the same domain of conventions, *theoretical differentiation* may also be prized. Terms that are undifferentiated or imprecise make it difficult to forge reliable linkages to particulars and discourage useful distinctions among actions and objects. During this stage, *logical coherence* also becomes a valuable asset in codifying and giving communicable order to the otherwise informal understandings within the community. In a similar fashion, the *explanatory range* of a theory (for example, its capacity to integrate "findings from multiple domains") is valued for its capacity to bring otherwise disparate communities of scientists into collaborative unity. Finally, the traditional demand for *theoretical parsimony* gains currency: in the same way a complex rhythm challenges the coordination of a dancer's movements (unlike a simple one), a conceptually elaborate theory impedes the mutual adjustment of activities within a community of scientists.

What we find, then, is that many of the empiricist ideals for developing scientific theory can be justified—with two significant caveats. First, according to the present account, these theoretical desiderata have no transcendental value; their sanction derives not from a foundational account of scientific rationality but from a concern with the pragmatic utility of language within scientific communities. If language is the vehicle for coordinating action around a series of events, then certain language forms will be more practically advantageous. Second, these values are not generalizable across the spectrum of scientific activity. Their utility is largely restricted to a specific context, one in which generating predictions within a restricted domain is paramount. We may speak, then, of a *context of prediction,* in which certain qualities of a theoretical formulation are superior to others. Let us broaden the range of considerations.

There is a second major function of theory in this stage of normal science. As advanced, scientific intelligibilities also enter into the culture as practical resources. They furnish ontologies, values, rationalities, and justifications within ongoing cultural life. We may speak of theories, then, not only in terms of their function in coordinating the community of scientists, but also as they function within a *context of cultural participation*. Here the ideals for theory favored in the context of prediction are of arguable utility. Predictive relevance, differentiation, logical coherence, and parsimony, for example, are largely irrelevant and possibly counterproductive. Highly differentiated theories, for example, may be cumbersome and difficult to export across wide-ranging cultural circumstances; the strict demands of logical coherence also place restrictions on the number of communities that can resonate with a given form of intelligibility; and the demand for parsimony works against the possibility of richly evocative theory. Immaculate theory within the conventions of the scientific community may have precious little cultural currency, an important point in terms of the previous emphasis placed on fashioning intelligibilities as opposed to predictions in the human sciences.

In the context of cultural participation one can scarcely be definitive about the criteria of evaluation. This is so because of the rich range of valuational perspectives—moral, political, religious, and so on—extant within the culture. All furnish discourse frames from which theoretical accounts in the human sciences can be assessed. Christians wish to retain a spiritual dimension in human makeup; Marxists justifiably use political grounds in selecting organismic as opposed to mechanistic theories; feminists see severe ideological limitations in theories favoring self-contained individualism; humanists hold that deterministic theories have deplorable effects on the common consciousness and thus prefer accounts in which agency plays a pivotal role. It seems unwise to delimit the range of valuational criteria brought to bear on scientific formulations. The most significant requirement at this juncture is dialogue within the human sciences that confronts the challenge of cultural participation. How can scholarly intelligibilities be made available to the culture in ways that allow their practical potentials to be realized; how can scholarly communities be opened to permit the voices of the culture to be heard; what self-reflexive processes can be set in motion so that the cultural value of scientific intelligibilities can be properly explored? We are only beginning to appreciate the magnitude of such challenges.

Theory in Critical and Transformational Stages of Science

As I am proposing, during a stage of normal science, theories may properly be compared with respect to their ability to coordinate the scientific community around the task of prediction and their capacity to reflect and express the cultural commitments of a scientific community. Theories that enhance the coordination of the scientific community and are most fully coherent with one's commitments within the culture may be viewed as superior within this phase. Should scientific activity be fixed in a given path of prediction, however, or committed to traditional visions of the good, we might view the sciences as both stagnant and parochial. Recall that theories are constitutive of broader patterns of relationship both within the science and within the society more generally. Remaining fixed to a circumscribed range of theories constrains the potential of science and culture alike.

To illustrate, theoretical stability favors pattern maintenance among scientists. What this effectively means is that the range of interesting or compelling predictions will also be delimited. Refinements and derivations will demand attention, but not "factual domains" outside the circumscribed ontology. For example, to the extent that psychological theories of perception remained "bottom-up," as they did for many years, scientists paid exclusive attention to the effects on perception of variables in the stimulus world. The more recent development of "top-down" formulations generated interest in genetic antecedents of perception, in the possibility of native proclivities. With the shift in theoretical perspective, from environmentalism to nativism, new research challenges emerged. With regard to the effects of theoretical discourse on cultural practice, theories of well-being primarily concerned with psychological processes (such as psychoanalysis and cognitive therapy) have led to an almost exclusive concern with individual actions. Aberrant behavior is the result of problematic psychological processes, and treatment is directed at the defective individual. Yet, as theories of social systems enter into the vocabulary of the scientist (and thus into the culture more generally), we gain the option of viewing an individual's problems within the context of defective groups—families, educational systems, economic institutions, and the like. In effect, to remain in the phase of normal science is to circumscribe the range of prediction, delimit the possibilities for solving problems, and reduce the opportunity for realizing human potential.

It is in this sense that I employed the concept of generative theory in the preceding chapter. A generative theory is designed to undermine commitment to the prevailing systems of theoretical construction and to generate new options for action. It is the generative criterion that can, in my view, most effectively bring about a transformational shift. Generative theorizing frequently begins with critiques of existing accounts. Then, as the conceptual implications of the critique are progressively elaborated, the contours of a new ontology or world construction can slowly emerge, inviting and/or rationalizing new options for action. The characteristics of generative theory will differ substantially from those required of theory within the phase of normal science. Normal science thrives on *literal* terminologies, vocabularies so fully sedimented by common usage that they seem to map the world and so useful to coordinating action that they cannot be sacrificed. (Rocket technicians presume the existence of *O rings*, and strict agreements about such matters are essential to life and property.) In contrast, during the critical and transformational stages greater value is placed on forms of expression that dislocate the conventional languages, loosen the hold of the taken-for-granted, and offer fresh images and alternatives. In this sense, generative theory may eschew the common ontology, reconstitute existing modes of expression, subvert the common binaries, and articulate new realms of reality.

We may thus envision the scientific process as composed of two opposing tendencies. The first opts toward stabilizing meaning systems, sharpening prediction, and affirming traditional values. In Bakhtin's (1981) sense, meanings move in a *centripetal* direction, toward uniformity and exclusion. The second aims toward a transformation in which established patterns and values are challenged and the range of available alternatives, within both science and society, is broadened. A *centrifugal* thrust is set in motion, unsettling convention and admitting new discourses. Under conditions of stabilization, the optimal criteria of theoretical evaluation differ from those under conditions of transformation. Stabilization favors theories that lead to maximum social coordination and value articulation. But when transformation has priority, the theorist may approach the borders of absurdity, unsettling the sedimented presumptions, and arguing critically and audaciously. At the same time, successful moves toward transformation will, in the end, give way to stabilization. As the audacious becomes commonplace, the metaphoric becomes literal, value possibilities are realized in new institutions, and transformational theory becomes normalized. Ideally, the human sciences should move through periods of stabilization, decay, challenge, growth, and subsequent stabilization. Although our theories do not thus move inexorably toward greater fidelity with nature and we come no nearer to "truth" through this process, we do offer to the culture an increasing range of predictive capacities and, most important for the human sciences, an increasing range of intelligibilities and practices.

In Conclusion

I have attempted to respond to a number of major questions frequently addressed to constructionists. These entries into the dialogues will scarcely serve to extinguish those various concerns—nor should they. Critiques of constructionism derive from investments in various forms of life that appear to be threatened by its arguments. In my view, however, constructionism should function not as a destructive but as a transformative force. The point is not to obliterate forms of language or life but to supply conceptual and practical means by which peoples may more fully and less lethally coordinate themselves with each other. Thus as critics and constructionists continue to explore the potentials and perils of constructionism (see, for example, Stenner and Eccleston 1994; Stein 1990; Young and Mathews 1992), it is my hope that the result will not be exacerbated polarization but an enriched sensitivity among the interlocutors.

4   Social Construction
and Moral Orders

In the preceding chapter I opened discussion on the problem of moral and political commitment in a constructed world. As I argued, although constructionist views are significant in stimulating moral and political deliberation, and constructionist arguments powerful in challenging dominant and dominating discourses, no particular commitment is finally favored. One can locate various ideological implications within constructionist writings, and certain scholars are willing to endorse these consequences. However, any such commitments also bring travail, for if social constructionist theses prove moral or political on any grounds other than those preferred by a particular reader, they soon become oppressive and cease to communicate. This is not at all to argue against moral and political commitment; to abandon moral and political action would be to step out of cultural—and therefore meaningful—life. However, it is to avoid using constructionism itself as a univocal ideological wedge.

At the same time, however, this line of argument fails to give a satisfactory reply to the charge of moral decrepitude: social construction is evil in its very incapacity to take a position. Its relativistic stance is itself immoral. It is this issue I wish to address in this chapter. First I wish to consider briefly some of the most prominent contenders for moral guidance. What resources for moral edification are furnished by major scholarly investments of the past century, particularly those most closely associated with the human sciences? Then I shall consider the pragmatic consequences of various moral discourses: do they function effectively in generating what we might view as "the moral society"? Finally, I wish to consider the positive potentials in a constructionist alternative. In effect, I wish to challenge the view that constructionist relativism is morally impoverished. On the contrary, the culture might be well served if the scholarly community could overcome its long-standing hysteria over relativism and begin to explore its positive possibilities.

In the Western tradition the single individual serves as the atom of moral concern—that essence without which matters of ethical debate would have little point and without whose commitment the civilization might indeed disintegrate. Thus, philosophers seek to establish essential criteria for moral decision making, religious institutions are concerned with states of individual conscience, courts of law establish criteria for judging individual guilt, educational institutions are motivated to instill personal values, and parents are concerned with the moral education and character of their offspring. In effect, in matters of ethics, morality, and, ultimately, the good society, Western peoples are *psychologists.* It is the virtuous mind that propels meritorious conduct, and with sufficient numbers of individuals performing worthy acts, we achieve the good society. In this context, we find that psychology and its allied disciplines play a pivotal role in the culture's concerns with moral action, since such disciplines possess the means by which the secrets of the virtuous mind (and more cogently, the iniquitous mind) can be disclosed. Thus, the history of moral philosophy—from Kant's categorical imperatives, through Rawls's (1971) *Theory of Justice*—has largely been a deliberation on the potentials of the individual agent. Similarly, from Freud's early work on the formation of the superego, through social learning formulations of modeling and contemporary theories of moral decision making, psychological inquiry has played (and continues to play) a pivotal role in describing the basis of moral action and furnishing insights into its genesis.

It is within this context that I wish to consider two major views of moral action emerging within recent history in terms of what they say about individual functioning and what they offer to society more generally. These views, which I shall call the *romanticist* and the *modernist,* have both figured prominently in various psychological formulations, and both have multiple implications for societal action. However, as I shall argue, both the romanticist and modernist conceptions of moral action are flawed in important ways. Neither can deliver what is promised, either in terms of a viable conception of human functioning or of ethical foundations for a viable society. As we shall find, while constructionism does not dictate an alternative foundation for moral action, its very silence may best serve human well-being.

Romanticism and Inherent Morality

Although there are many stories to be told about the romanticist movement in nineteenth-century art, literature, philosophy, and music, I shall offer here only a brief summary of romanticist presumptions of moral being.[1] For the romanticist, the most significant domain of human functioning—a domain I have characterized elsewhere (Gergen 1991b) as a "deep interior"—was beyond the immediate grasp of consciousness. Herein were to be found the primordial powers of the passions, inspiration, creativity, genius, and, as many believed, madness. At the center of the deep interior was the human spirit or soul, related on the one hand to God (and thus touched with a divine element), but rooted at the same time in nature (thus possessing instinctive force). Most important, within this deep interior were to be found inherent values or moral sentiments—guidance for a worthy life, inspiration for virtuous works, resources for resisting temptation, and naturalized foundations for philosophical and religious formulations of the good. As Shelley rhapsodized, "the essence, the vitality of [moral] actions, derives its color from what is in no way contributed to from any external source. The benevolent propensities are . . . inherent in the human mind. We are impelled to seek the happiness of others."[2] This view is echoed as well in G. E. Moore's turn-of-the-century volume *Principia Ethica*. Moore trusts to the individual's deeply nurtured intuitions as sources of moral action. "They are incapable of proof or disproof," he writes, "and indeed no evidence or reasoning whatever can be adduced in their favour or disfavour." For Moore, "personal affections" and "aesthetic enjoyments" were among the greatest goods imaginable. Various traces of the romanticist legacy can also be located in the philosophies of "expressivism" or "emotivism." While romanticism ceases to play a commanding role in the intellectual world, it is probably the central means by which persons currently justify their moral positions in daily life. Our actions intuitively and compellingly "feel right."

The Waning of Romantic Morality

In my view, neither the romanticist conception of the human being nor its allied view of moral direction continue to be compelling, in large measure because of the advent of alternative discourses—arguments of strong rational and rhetorical appeal. Four lines of argument deserve attention.

INHERENT EVIL AND THE PROBLEM OF TRUST

The optimistic belief in an inherent basis for moral action surely finds its source in religious history. If humans are creatures of a divine creator—

possibly created in "His image"—surely their instincts are to be trusted. However, with the advent of Enlightenment thinking, and the associated erosion of religious influence, there was also much reason for doubt. One can find abundant evidence of evil within the natural world, which is difficult to reconcile with the religious tradition. Such suspicions were also fueled by numerous romantic writers and scholars who, after peering into the deep interior, reacted with frightened awe. For Baudelaire, Poe, and Nietzsche, for example, the deeper forces of the psyche were indeed daunting. The thesis of naturalized evil was given further impetus in the writings of Freud. For Freud, the infant is wholly self-indulgent, "polymorphous perverse," and without conscience. One's moral tendencies (the superego) are acquired, and represent a compensatory defense against immoral urges and fears of castration. Under the influence of such dramatic texts, the presumption of inherent morality could scarcely remain robust.

THE DARWINIAN THESIS

It is difficult to overestimate the impact of Darwin's *On the Origin of Species* on intellectual and cultural life at the turn of the century. There are also important ways in which Darwin's view was deeply inimical to romanticist views of morality. At the outset, Darwin's thesis favored a thoroughgoing secularism in moral matters. In discrediting creationist views, it placed the presumption of the Creator in jeopardy and unsettled any spiritual basis for the urges of the deep interior. At the same time, Darwinian theory lent itself strongly to what was to become the modernist standpoint. For Darwin the various species of life are essentially locked into a Hobbesian struggle of all against all. The survival of the human species thus demands that humans hold an adaptive edge over their competitors in the animal kingdom. And if adaptation requires objective knowledge of the environment and a systematic assessment of various courses of action, it also favors a view of human functioning that grants humans just these capacities. In the Darwinian view, the optimally functioning human being would be one who relies most heavily on powers of observation and reason. Such a conception of human functioning was at odds not only with the romanticist view of the individual but with its companionate view of moral principles. The romanticist is not ideally fitted for survival: an individual driven by sentiments, passions, or raptures would simply be nonadaptive. And because moral sentiments operate on the basis not of the real but of the ideal—they are tied to conscience, not to contingencies—then they are also suspect as guides to action.[3]

THE RISE OF SCIENCE

Coupled with and congenial to the sway of Darwinism was the blossoming of the scientific perspective. During the nineteenth century, impressive strides were made in the medical sciences, chemistry, and physics, and the technological byproducts were becoming widely evident. Science could thus be seen as that institution ideally fitted for survival. In effect, scientism served as a choral accompaniment to the Darwinian perspective. At the same time, science traced its origins to the Enlightenment and to the significance of individual observation and rationality. Moral sentiments were, by definition, nonrational (and by implication irrational). Effective action in life, as in science, demanded astute observation and logical reasoning. To justify one's action according to moral sentiments was no better than proclaiming one's personal tastes or desires.

CULTURAL CONSCIOUSNESS

As both Darwinism and scientism gained increasing sway, scholarly interests were drawn toward the objective study of the human species, both historically and cross-culturally. The 1871 publication of Edward Burnett Tylor's *Primitive Culture* in particular set the stage for inquiry into contrasting systems of ethical or religious belief. These studies served in many ways to replace religious with scientific authority. As such work demonstrated, the range and variety of religious and moral commitment were enormous. And given this variety there was little means by which Christianity, or indeed any form of "intuitive knowledge of the good," could lay claim to superiority. Claims to ethical probity were thus reduced to little more than cultural bias. Attempts to establish universal systems of value or ethics based on moral sentiments or intuitions came to be seen as Western imperialism in disguise.

Modernism and Morality

As Western culture moved into the twentieth century, the romantic conception of the moral being was essentially losing its grasp on the intellectual imagination. Not only was it difficult to reconcile the romantic view of the deep interior with Darwinism, scientism, and the spread of cultural consciousness, but the romantic conception of fundamental or universal moral sentiments also proved unconvincing. Perhaps the death knell for romanticist ethics was saved for later in the twentieth century. Of those various movements claiming transcendental probity in matters of human good or moral superiority, two of the most outspoken were Communism and Nazism. Marx and Engels's *Communist Manifesto,* in its condemnation of an economic system that promotes a "naked, shameless, direct, brutal exploitation" and its championing of human bondedness and freedom from oppression, gains its persuasive force from its inherently moral claims. Yet the enormous oppression that resulted from the communist movement enabled the world to glimpse the apocalyptic potential inherent in these claims. We might consider as well the romanticist appeal in Adolf Hitler's *Mein Kampf,* in which he speaks of his people as "sighing beneath the intolerable burden of an existing condition" and condemns "nations which no longer find any heroic solution for such distress" as *"impotent."* For him it is essential to struggle toward "a people's liberation from a great oppression, or for the elimination of a bitter distress, or for the satisfaction of its soul, restless because it has grown insecure" (1943, pp. 509–510). One shudders at the outcome.[4]

This is hardly to say that the rhetoric of moral sentiments is dead. There are many significant movements demonstrating that concepts such as justice, equality, and rights retain a powerful capacity to move human action. However, little remains in the way of foundational justification for such movements. The successor project, at least within the world of science and letters, is prefigured by the critiques of romanticism I outlined earlier. To fault the romanticist conception of the moral being on the grounds of species survival and scientific rationality in particular is to suppose that there is a form of human being who, by virtue of observation and reason, is effectively equipped for building the good society. It is this conception of the human being—rational, observant, and thus capable of enhancing the human condition—that has become dominant within the present century. As Habermas (1983) views it, this modernist conception of the human being is largely a reinstantiation of the Enlightenment view. It is a view that has played a major role in shaping the discourse of empiricist philosophy of science, theories of economic man, discourse on liberty and democracy within political science, and sociobiologic formulations among others. It is this same view that has been normalized by most of the psychological theory and research of the present century. While learning theory formulations constituted the person as an adaptive organism tuned to the contingencies of the environment, the cognitive revolution succeeded in moving rational processes to the center of human functioning. In effect, both endeavors served to objectify the modernist (or neo-Enlightenment) conception of human functioning.

What is the place of moral (ethical, ideological) action in the modernist conception of the human as rational-instrumental being? In my view, any answer to this question must distinguish between two major Enlightenment influences on modernist views of the person. The first is a domain of modernist discourse informed by the *empiricist* tradition from the works of Locke, Hume, and the Mills through Comte in the nineteenth century. In its emphasis on the environmental antecedents of mental functioning, the empiricist tradition laid the groundwork for a twentieth-century conception of the individual as a cog in the one great and universal machine. The individual, according to this account, is little more than the result of systematic inputs. And if all human activity is understood as a function of environmental antecedents—a view substantiated by much logical empiricist philosophy along with the behavioral view in the social sciences—then the issue of "moral choice" is subverted. To the extent that people act morally, their behavior must be traced to preceding conditions, such as family socialization, religious education, or character-building programs like the Boy Scouts and the YMCA. Yet precisely what constitutes *moral* action is not a matter most philosophers of science, behavioral scientists, and others within the empiricist tradition wish to confront. For empiricist philosophers and scientists, the important and answerable questions are matters of "what *is* the case." Concern about "what *ought* to be" is beyond answer— mere metaphysics or worse. Adequate functioning within the sciences, as in daily life, requires observing, reasoning, and planning and testing hypotheses in the world. Personal values, ethics, and political passions simply obfuscate the process. They act as biases that interfere with the kinds of impartial judgments necessary for effective action, both in science and, by implication, in daily life.[5]

It is largely for these reasons that many scholars today find the modernist conception of human functioning morally vacuous. The view of the ideal individual as empiricist-scientist is one that leaves the individual with no sense of ethical direction, no means of evaluating right and wrong, and no motive for challenging the status quo. The scientist qua scientist has no moral standpoint. Scientists may generate knowledge of sophisticated weapons systems, but there is nothing in science itself that admonishes (or invites) their use. The only means by which *good* actions can be guaranteed, from this standpoint, is through socialization and education—essentially by stamping them in. Thus, questions of value are always solved at a one-step remove from the individual actor. The single individual is destined to act as others have designed, and they in turn as still others have dictated. At no point is unfettered deliberation of the good made possible. Nor is it clear what useful outcomes would be achieved through such consideration, since there are no standards of "the good" necessarily favored by empirical study, no means of deriving what should be from what is. Questions of value are, in effect, abnegated.

Yet, there is a second tradition that contributes to the modernist conception of the individual, one that is usually identified as *rationalist* (see also Chapter 1). The writings of Descartes, Spinoza, and Kant among others placed emphasis not on observational skills, but on the inherent rationality of the individual and the signal importance of rationality in determining the nature of the good. Basing their arguments on the assumption of inherent rationality, modernist philosophers have set out to develop rational foundations for moral action. John Rawls's (1971) *Theory of Justice* and Alan Gewirth's (1987) *Reason and Morality* are among the most celebrated recent exemplars.[6] The rationalist orientation to moral action is also reflected and normalized within scientific psychology, which uses empirical observation to justify its position ("the human as astute observer") but simultaneously asserts that a given line of thinking is morally superior because it is more sophisticated. Thus, rather than see themselves as scientists offering solutions to the problem of the good, such psychologists presume the individual's natural capacity for moral thought. The challenge then is to determine empirically the nature of moral decisions—how, by whom, and in what circumstances do persons reason in a morally sophisticated way?

The most ambitious attempt of this variety is embodied in Kohlberg's (1971) theory of moral development. Kohlberg posits a nativist theory of moral reasoning, in this way drawing from the romanticist presumption of an inherent capacity for moral direction, but he substitutes "rational capacities" for the romanticist's "sentiments." The epigenetic unfolding of the individual mind, argues Kohlberg, will necessarily lead in the direction of abstract moral reasoning. At the early and more rudimentary stages of development—preconventional and conventional—the individual will make those decisions that are rewarded by the social environment or which he or she has absorbed from the social group. (In effect, the empiricist account is given credence, but only at the more rudimentary stages of development.) At the most mature stage of cognitive development, the individual will come to generate his or her own abstract principles of ethics.

That said, I would point out that neither the philosopher's attempt to lodge moral action in a foundational rationality nor the psychologist's attempt to locate superior forms of moral decision making are broadly compelling. On the philosophic side, how can one justify any particular rational scaffolding? Must a commitment to justice, for example, not rest on an elaborate set of reasons as to why justice is to be preferred, and if we ask why these reasons are foundational, will the advocate not again resort to a set of reasons that themselves require justification? If, in the end, the justification proves to be grounded in desire ("my feeling for what is right"), then we have returned to romanticist romanticism. As we shall explore in later chapters (especially Chapter 9), a range of problems also inheres in traditional Western individualism. Narcissism, alienation, and exploitativeness are among them. To the extent that there is a close link between individualism on the one hand and moral thought on the other, all the flaws of individualism stand as potential condemnations of a moral theory in which the thinking individual stands at the center.[7] In the same way, the entire range of arguments against knowledge as the possession of individual minds (see Chapters 1 and 5) operates as a major impediment to the modernist view of rationally derived morality. To locate flaws in the binary separating an "inner mind" from an "external world" is to problematize the concept of "the moral decision maker."

In the case of psychology, there are further problems. There is, for example, a deep incoherence in using a scientific, deterministic worldview to prove the existence of the individual's capacity for moral decision making. The empiricist perspective makes no room for an "independent decision maker" (capable of reaching a decision undetermined by environmental inputs), and to the extent that the rationalist tradition is reflected in the psychologist's penchant for cognitive and information processing mechanisms, the concept of voluntary agency (decisions beyond the requirements of the cognitive system) is repudiated. To use the scientific perspective to prove a view antithetical to science is mischievous. Kohlberg's theory of moral development appears to escape this problem, but the solution is deceptive. That is, the theory of developmental stages is fully deterministic, as are the processes in operation at every stage—except the final stage of postconventional moral reasoning. Here individual autonomy is subtly restored, but so is the possibility of a deterministic science undone.

However, there is another problem at stake that is relevant to both philosophic and psychological attempts to base morality on processes of rational principle. If we grant to individuals the capacity for abstract moral thought and a commitment to a set of principles—let us say, justice, honesty, and equality—would the result of these capacities and commitments be a moral society? Would increasing the number of such persons, either by dint of heredity or education, necessarily enhance the quality of cultural life? I think not. The chief problem of abstract principles of morality is that they are empty of significant content. Within themselves they contain no rules of instantiation; they fail to determine when and where they apply. One can thus be committed to the principle "Thou shall not kill," but the principle itself stands empty of implications for action. To whom or what does it apply? Under what conditions? What does "kill" mean in terms of actual movements of the body?

One may attempt to improve matters by searching the mental compendium for a precise definition from which action could be derived. "To kill," one finds on deliberation, means "to deprive of life." Such a definition might initially seem replete with determinant implications. Yet closer inspection reveals that this more exacting definition is in itself abstract. What, after all, does "deprive of life" mean over an array of concrete settings? Are my acts of eating and breathing not depriving others of oxygen and nutriments? Are my intimacies with others not threatening them with potentially harmful bacteria? What if it is a question of my life versus theirs? The exacting definition proves grossly imprecise. As we quickly surmise, when abstract principles are defined, their definitions are also in the abstract, themselves failing to indicate when, where, and how they apply. And so are the further explications of definitions and the explications of the explications in infinite regress—from which there is no exit to moral action.[8]

One may opt at this point for a social or communal designation of particulars: one may not be *directly* guided by abstract proposition, but after extensive immersion in the culture one comes to learn (in practice) the range of relevant actions. One learns, for example, that "Thou shall not kill" has little to do with "killer cakes," persons "dressed to kill," or smiles "that kill softly," that it does forbid certain actions toward one's kith and kin, and that it applies contingently to those of other religious, political, or racial persuasions. However, to thus rescue moral principles from the shoals of infinite regress is to remove the psyche from the center of moral action. That which is moral is defined not according to the individual's principles, but according to the cultural standards for how the moral principle applies. If the culture defines it as immoral to kill children except when they are the children of one's enemies, there is no further room for individual deliberation (unless by virtue of some other cultural standard). Cultural convention replaces ethical reflection as the fulcrum of moral action.

I further submit that it is precisely this conventional character of moral principledness that enables courts, governments, and religions to maintain laws, constitutional bases, and theological principles over the centuries; for as social, economic, and material exigencies shift over time, so also can the conventions be renegotiated. The meaning of the principles of justice, honesty, and equality—in terms of behavioral applications—can vary. It is in this way that the abstract principles embodied in the Constitution, the courts, or the Bible can remain relevant; their meaning is under continuous repair. At the same time, moral rules neither determine nor guarantee what any particular group will favor as moral action. Constitutional guarantees were of little protection to Japanese Americans during World War II, and their implications for blacks, women, homosexuals, or pregnant teenagers are in continuous contention today. What is at stake in such cases is not the principles—they may remain obdurate—but issues of how and when they apply are in continuous motion. In this sense, cultural conventions do not stand in opposition to transcendental moral principles; rather, without this social determination of meaning such principles cease to be germane.

Moral Action from a Constructionist Standpoint

Thus far I have outlined the contours of a romanticist and a modernist perspective on moral being and have underscored significant shortcomings in their potentials for generating a moral society. To open consideration on a social constructionist alternative, it is useful to consider a line of argument developed by Alisdair MacIntyre (1984) in *After Virtue*. MacIntyre lends strong voice to those who find both romanticist and modernist attempts to generate universal moral precepts to be failed enterprises. Contemporary moral debate for MacIntyre is both "interminable and unsettlable" (p. 210). It suffers in particular in its attempt to establish principles or values that transcend the contexts of their usage. Without a context of usage, these abstractions lose practical consequence and susceptibility to assessment. MacIntyre traces moral action to communal tradition. It is when individuals are embedded in communal life, and develop self-identifying narratives that render them intelligible to others and to themselves, that moral action is possible. It is because of the self-identifying narratives and their embeddedness in communal life that the individual can be held morally responsible. "To be the subject of a narrative that runs from one's birth to one's death is . . . to be accountable for the actions and experiences which compose a narratable life" (p. 202). On this view, what we take to be virtues are inseparable from the tissue of social relations: "The virtues find their point and purpose not only in sustaining those relationships necessary if the variety of goods internal to practices are to be achieved . . . but also in sustaining those traditions which provide both practices and individual lives with their necessary historical context" (p. 207).

With these arguments MacIntyre succeeds in moving the fulcrum of moral action from the individual mind to relations among persons. It is only persons within relationship who can sustain (and be sustained by) a view of moral action. In my view, however, MacIntyre does not extend the case to its full potential. When its implications are pressed further, the individual is removed as the central concern of moral deliberation. More explicitly, if the narratives in which we are embedded are products of ongoing interaction, then problems of moral action may be separated from issues of mental state. Moral action is not a byproduct of a mental condition, a private act within the psyche, but a public act inseparable from the relationships in which one is (or has been) participating. According to this account, morality is not something one possesses *within,* it is an action that possesses its moral meaning only within a particular arena of cultural intelligibility. One participates in the cultural forms of action as in a dance or a game; questions of why one is moral or immoral do not require a specifically psychological answer any more than questions of why one moves in three-quarter time when dancing a waltz or plays tennis with balls rather than shuttlecocks. Such actions can be fully understood as sequences of coordinated action within particular communities. A moral life, then, is not an issue of individual sentiment or rationality but a form of communal participation.[9]

From the constructionist vantage point, how are we then to understand individual moral sentiment, moral reasoning, personal values, intentions, and the like? Are we wholly to abandon concern with such states? Although this question is complex, let me propose for now that for the constructionist these various terms are not abandoned so much as reconstituted. This reconstitution requires both an ontological deconstruction and a discursive reconstruction. Again to extend MacIntyre's thesis, if the narratives by which we understand ourselves and our relationships are forms of social accounting, then so is their content. This content would include what we take to be states of mind—matters of "intention," "moral feelings," "values," and "reason." To speak about one's mental life is thus to join in a form of cultural story telling; to claim an "intention" or to possess a "value" is to relate intelligibly to other participants in Western culture (see also Chapters 6 and 9). When psychologists and philosophers speak of the necessary psychological ingredients for a moral life, they are participating in a form of cultural narration. The psychological ingredients—the major locus of concern for romanticists and modernists—are thus de-ontologized. The language of moral sentiments and moral deliberation does not then refer to mental events located within the minds of single individuals and directing their actions. Rather, we can reconstitute them as linguistic (poetic, rhetorical) forms of communal practice.

If mental language does not acquire its meaning and significance from mental states, how does it function? What is its bearing on issues of moral action? From a constructionist perspective, accounts such as "I feel this is right," "such an action would violate my principles," or "I think this is immoral" are in their very saying constitutive features of everyday life. Such sentences are used by people in carrying out various social rituals, patterns of interchange, or cultural projects. They operate within relationships to prevent, admonish, praise, and invite various forms of action; they can also establish one's identity, furnish others with guides to one's future conduct, and achieve unity within a group. In effect, moral and ethical languages are among the resources available for playing the games and participating in the dances of cultural life. They are moves or positionings that enable persons to construct the culture in what we take to be a moral or ethical way.

In certain respects these arguments are congenial with the thesis developed in Taylor's (1989) *Sources of the Self*. Taylor attempts to resuscitate the assumptions underlying the Western conception of self, assumptions which, from his perspective, serve as the implicit basis for moral action. These implicit "frameworks provide the background . . . for our moral judgments, intuitions or reactions . . . To articulate a framework is to explicate what makes sense of our moral responses" (p. 26). It is not simply that this attempt to lay out the "moral topography" of Western culture may "counteract the layers of suppression of modern moral consciousness" (p. 90). Rather, as Taylor sees it, the languages of self-understanding—and thus of moral action—serve as "moral sources." They are "constitutive of human agency," such that "stepping outside these limits would be tantamount to stepping outside what we would recognize as integral, that is, undamaged human personhood" (p. 27).

In proposing that moral language is essentially a resource for generating and sustaining actions that we hold to be moral within the culture, Taylor's position is congenial to the constructionist thesis developed here. However, in its valorization of the language of individual morality, and the underlying supposition that this language is uniquely suited for generating the moral society, the constructionist might raise substantial questions. With Taylor, the constructionist would join the enterprise of tracing moral discourse through history; however, the constructionist would not necessarily champion such languages, but try to account for the conditions and circumstances in which such linguistic conventions came to play a functional role in social (and intellectual) life.[10] For the constructionist the languages of individual morality would be resuscitated, not because they are essential to a moral life, but because they may open up or remind us of potentially useful modes of speaking (and acting) that might otherwise be lost or destroyed in the hurly-burly of contemporary life. At the same time, the constructionist would be alerted to the possible dangers inherent in these same languages and actions. It is to this prospect that we now turn.

Moral Discourse: Necessary and Desirable?

Although the language of individual morality plays a significant role in the organization and coherence of social life, and the revitalizing of traditional moral languages enriches the range and potential of our interchanges, we cannot thereby conclude that moral language is both essential and desirable for agreeable forms of social life. Such discourse may figure prominently in our daily actions, enabling us to intercede, give significant pause, and consider the broad consequence of our actions. However, as we have seen, this is not to say that the terms of morality (ethics, values, rights) are essential to the formation of a "good society." Rather, we must ask whether—and which—communal interests are best served by these sorts of performatives. Does talk of "the good" and "the moral" necessarily improve the likelihood of valued actions?

In the first instance, are the languages of "ought," "duty," "rights," "principles," and the like essential to agreeable forms of social life? It seems doubtful. For example, a smooth and unproblematic parent-infant relationship may be achieved without the benefit of specifically moral discourse. In the same way, most friendships, collegial relationships and business proceedings take place with little recourse to a vocabulary of moral approbation. There is little reason to believe, then, that without moral language, society would deteriorate or regress to savagery. People are fully capable of coordinating their actions without moral performatives.

More speculatively, I propose that such languages owe their development primarily to breaches in the acceptable patterns of interchange. Should an individual or group violate common customs, moral language can be employed as a means of correcting or rechanneling the offending action. In effect, moral language functions largely as a means of sustaining patterns of social interchange in danger of erosion. Such languages are not so much responsible for the generation of agreeable forms of society as they are rhetorical means for reinforcing lines of action already embraced. Satisfactory relationships require neither persons with moral states within their heads nor social institutions with moral credos.

This is not to say that moral languages are of small consequence in sustaining the existing order. However, if moral language chiefly serves performative functions—and particularly those of sustaining particular traditions—we must question whether such language is the most useful or effective vehicle for enhancing the quality of cultural life. If moral language is not essential, how does it function in comparison to other possible means of achieving the same ends? Here it is useful to consider Felson's (1984) research on convicted criminals. Individuals convicted for crimes of aggressive assault were asked to describe the incidents leading up to their assaultive actions. As these narratives revealed, the majority traced their actions to incidents in which someone (often the victim) was seen as acting immorally (breaking a proper rule), there was often a verbal admonishment (typically made by the offender), and the putative rule breaker often attempted to save face through a hostile reaction. Such hostility would then trigger the aggressive assault. In effect, when principles of the good were introduced into the situation, the human condition was not enhanced but rapidly deteriorated.

In my view this deterioration is often intensified by that very tradition fostering the search for moral foundations for society—from early theology and romanticist intuitionism to modernist attempts at rational foundations. And here I am speaking of traditions attempting to establish universal standards of the good—principles of right and wrong, codes of ethics, constitutional principles, bills of universal rights, and so on that aspire to speak beyond time and place. The problematic repercussions of such approaches are revealed in Gewirth's (1987) attempt to secure a rational basis for moral action. In his preface, Gewirth first attacks conventionalist forms of morality, that is, principles or rules that simply capture or express one's cultural tradition. As he points out,

> This approach ... incurs a severe difficulty. For so long as the rightness or correctness of the principle itself ... is not established, such a procedure still leaves the system without any warrant of its rightness or correctness. Partisans of *opposed* cultures, traditions, or social systems may each claim self-evidence

for their own moral principles, and they hold that their respective rules and judgments are the morally right ones. Hence a moral principle's success in justifying . . . any one culture, ideology, or tradition does nothing, of itself, to *prove [its] superiority* over the moral rules or judgments of *opposed* cultures or traditions. (p. x)

Gewirth then goes on to point out that "this fact has supplied one of the strongest intellectual motivations for the various ancient and modern thinkers who have tried to provide a firm, nonrelativist foundation for ethics. By giving a rational justification of one or another supreme moral principle, they have hoped to *disprove or establish the wrongness of rival principles*" (p. x). And Gewirth then notes, no attempt to establish a superior system has been successful; in each case critics have located serious flaws. His challenge, then, is to "present a new version of rational justification" that will give precedence to one moral system over all others.[11]

I have italicized several key words and phrases in these passages in order to reveal a central metaphor underlying much work within the universalist tradition. In effect, it is a metaphor of conflict—of opposition, of rivalry, and the ultimate quest for one system or culture that will achieve superiority over all. Or, to put it in the extreme, it is a quest for universal dominion.

Such hegemonic tendencies often act to disrupt otherwise satisfactory forms of cultural life—forms that often have long histories and operate with a finely balanced sophistication. As the precepts of any group strive toward universality, they operate to discredit ways of life in other groups and to champion as their replacement home customs and folk mores. Thus, as Christian missionaries carry the gospel to other lands, their moral injunctions serve to discredit local customs and justify actions that are disruptive, thus damaging patterns of long-standing utility within the local setting. As Westerners concerned with the liberation of women, we may decry the veiling of the female face in the Islamic world; are the veils not oppressive to women and thus both unjust and inhumane? Yet within traditional Islamic culture the veil plays an important role in constituting and sustaining a large number of interrelated customs and rituals. To remove it on Western ideological grounds would be to threaten Islamic cultural identity itself. (To estimate the effects of removing the veil, consider the results on an expansionary Muslim movement that sought, in the name of a superior morality, to place such veils on the faces of contemporary Western women.) It is not ultimately a matter of ideology or morality that is at stake here, for there is nothing about desiring gender equality that necessarily, and without considerable interpretive work, speaks to matters of facial veiling. Rather, valuational precepts become the justification for undermining congenial and satisfying ways of life in other worlds.[12]

More extreme than the deterioration of cultural traditions are the corrosive hostilities invited by the language of moral superiority. When preferred ways of life are labeled as universally good and deviations as immoral, evil, and inferior, the stage is set for brutalizing conflict. The major problem of arrogating local preferences to the status of universal principles is that the latter brook no compromise, and deviants take on an inhuman demeanor. The number of deaths resulting from claims to superior values is, I suspect, beyond calculation.

The Potentials of a Constructionist Relativism

We now find ourselves sinking into "the morass of moral relativism," or so the condition is often characterized. And, to enmire ourselves more deeply, we also find ourselves rejecting the very psychologistic orientation so long serving as the mainstay of moral accountability. Yet, rather than bemoan this sorry state and use it as the catalyst for yet another ambitious entry into the two-thousand-year-old parade of pufferies, it seems an auspicious time to open inquiry into the positive potentials of relativism. I am not claiming here that all forms of relativism are equal in implication. There are many means to a relativistic end, and each should be considered separately and comparatively. Let us consider, then, the positive potential of a social constructionist view of "the good society."

As we have seen in focusing on the social pragmatics of language, the constructionist de-ontologizes the discourse of both morality and the psychological self. Such discourses, I have proposed, do not inherently describe worlds outside themselves but are used by people in carrying out their various relationships, which, in effect, removes both moral ideals as guides to proper action and selves as intentional agents from the center of concern. They simply cease to be the focus of questions about which deliberation and study should reveal useful or necessary answers. Such a move, however, does not thereby leave us without means to proceed, for this analysis does require that we take seriously processes of relatedness. It is the terrain of human relatedness in which concern with human well-being is rooted. It is only within relationships that persons come to be identified and to be valued.

I would propose that, compared to its psychologistic predecessors, this is a far richer site for exploring means for nurturing "the good society." To the extent that whatever we hold to be "the good" in our culture is achieved through the enhancement of relationships, then it is the process of relating that deserves our closest attention. In this sense, we may confront the pervasive pluralism of contemporary life, not with dismay, but with a sense of reassurance: the very richness of patterns of relationship furnishes a resource, a set of potentials that might be absorbed with advantage into neighboring traditions. In this sense, pluralism and tyranny are antithetical forces. Rather than seek a specifically moral solution to the relativistic ethos—a higher value around which all might coalesce, an abstract universal to which all might agree—constructionism invites a more pragmatic or practice-centered orientation to reconciling contrasting modes of life.[13] Let us consider three particular implications.

FROM IMPERIALISM TO COLLABORATION

We have already touched on the imperialistic potential of universal ethics. Constructionist relativism replaces such absolutist claims with a collaborative search for meaning, and disquisitions on transcendental goods with communal considerations of consequence. Gilligan's (1982) reply to Kohlberg's formulation of ethical decision making provides a useful beginning in this respect. In her research on abortion decisions, she concluded that women were deeply concerned about their responsibilities to others and had a sense of caring for the well-being of others. Their sense of morality could not be disconnected from what they perceived as the web of relationships in which they were engaged. I am not here championing an "ethic of caring," which itself has universalist intimations, but rather focusing on the social process by which solutions are reached. Instead of attempting to work through the implications of abortion as an issue of moral principle, the women engaged in dialogue—which in its idealized form can be seen as a process of expressing, listening, and laboring toward a solution that, while necessarily imperfect, represents a synthesis of the various relationships in which they are engaged. There is little reason to regard this form of collective activity as uniquely feminine. It is a means by which any problem of human conflict, whether or not it is designated a problem of morality, can be approached. In the constructionist frame, it is a way of expanding the number of voices that speak to the issues in question. It enables "the problem" to be refracted through multiple lenses, thus enriching the range of understandings and broadening sensitivity to its manifold consequences. To be sure, such a process of broadened interchange will seldom move toward clear and ineluctable conclusion; however, it is "moral clarity" that endangers the conversation.

FROM RETRIBUTION TO REORGANIZATION

As we have seen, instances of immoral action are traditionally traced to the mental processes of individual actors. According to this view, immoral agents are lacking in common human capacities (for example, a sense of decency, a conscience, a sense of right and wrong, willpower, and so on) or suffering from deficiencies of the mind (such as reason overcome by emotion or temporary insanity). From the constructionist standpoint, however, all such attributions are denatured, and the terms of description reconstructed as relational performatives. We may then ask, how is the language of individual responsibility used? What does it justify? As is soon clear, this language rationalizes and sustains a cultural system of individual blame. But if we step outside the individualist ontology, we open ourselves to the possibility of alternative ways of constructing self and society. Thus, questions of just recrimination, retribution, moral instruction, and the like become secondary. A practical concern with the organization of relationships replaces individual psychology.

Rather than punish the immoral agent, one's concerns move outward to the forms of interaction that render the problematic action intelligible, desirable, or possible. It is not individuals who are ultimately blameworthy, but extended patterns of relationship in which each individual alone can lay claim to moral probity. The legal system moves slowly toward such a dispersion of responsibility. In a recent Philadelphia case, a woman dressed in Army fatigues entered a shopping mall with an automatic rifle and began firing. Several people were killed and many others wounded. From the traditional standpoint, prime attention would be paid to the psychological state of the individual criminal: was the woman emotionally deranged, did she know right from wrong, and so on. The victims of the crime, however, subsequently mounted a suit against an extended array of individuals and institutions: the local police, who were aware of the woman's dangerous condition, the owner of the firearms store where she purchased the weapon, the shopping mall for its lack of protection. Yet, even this expansion in the range of complicity does not go far enough, and it too retains a retributive edge. More effective would be a broadening of the dialogue to include weapons manufacturers, the National Rifle Association, the family and neighbors of the slayer, and so on. What is their contribution to the event and in what ways is retribution reasonable or unreasonable given their various domains of relationship? The challenge in such dialogues should not be that of properly allocating blame, but of attempting to reach an understanding of how the event could occur, what should be done about it now, and what its implications are for future action.

A constructionist standpoint also invites inquiries into the historical roots of developing problems and into the patterns of otherwise unnoticed interdependence. In the former, rather than seek to establish who is right and wrong or who should play the roles of the righteous and the blameworthy, it focuses attention on the ways in which current problems are historically engendered. By viewing issues in a diachronic mode we can often demonstrate that today's taken-for-granted truths or palpable rights and wrongs have only become so by virtue of long and unexamined usage. By exploring their historical contingencies, we can see these truths in a relative context and reexamine our unbridled commitment to them. In addition, inquiry may reveal ways in which otherwise acrimonious groups are locked together in mutually supportive relationships. I think here of the abortion controversy, in which each of the participant parties claims universal right. Compromise within these mutually exclusive frames is impossible. But the roots of both prolife and prochoice ideology have a long and complex history within the Judeo-Christian tradition and the American tradition of individual liberty. They both depend on the same historical resources to justify their commitments. Without their shared traditions they would be unintelligible to each other. They both share traditions that value moral commitment and expression, and this very sharing also establishes a context in which they might begin to see the possibility of some accord—issues about which they might agree, for example, or movements in which they might wish to join forces. In many matters—from local policies on pornography to international policies on environmental protection—prolife and prochoice advocates can walk arm in arm. Further awareness of their shared history and interdependence may soften their absolutist claims.

FROM PRINCIPLES TO PRACTICES

Traditional approaches to moral action have been concerned primarily with establishing universal virtues, and secondarily with installing them in the minds of individuals. From the constructionist perspective, both endeavors are flawed. No amount of debate over the nature of the good and no amount of moral instruction will ensure good acts. Principles of the good do not and cannot dictate concrete actions, and any action at any time may be constructed as good or evil from some vantage point. In a broader sense, hopes for the good society should not ultimately depend on the shaping of persons to principle. The Word will not provide "the way, the truth and the light." This does not mean the abandonment of moral discourse, but it does turn attention from theories or principles of the good to the more concrete processes by which broadly satisfactory outcomes are achieved within relationships. In effect, we shift our concern from the axiological to the practical.

In turning to the practicalities of morality as a social achievement, we confront a new range of questions: for example, under conditions of conflict or distress, what linguistic forms can be employed to bring about satisfactory ends? What linguistic resources do people have at their disposal under such conditions? Can the available range of resources be expanded? It is in this regard that Taylor's attempt to resuscitate the moral languages of the past can be best appreciated. Under certain conditions, and when applied in discriminating ways, moral discourse can be used to achieve social coordination. When used, for example, to affirm a common commitment to a just cause and not as a means of assigning blame or correcting faults, moral discourse can invite lines of mutually agreeable action. Inasmuch as moral discourse is only one way of achieving satisfactory coordination, however, we also need to explore alternative forms of practice. Can new forms of relationship be developed—or fresh rituals for reconciling differences among persons? Communications theorists and family therapists have been highly successful in developing techniques for dealing with interpersonal conflicts: reframing, reconstructing narratives, and shifting from conflict to metareflective postures all contribute in an important way to the repository of cultural resources. These forms of achieving a "sense of the good" within relationships could usefully be incorporated into cultural life more generally.

This emphasis on practices must also move beyond the boundaries of language. We need a way to integrate not only perspectives, ways of framing things, and talk about values, but broader life patterns. There is an important sense in which moral discourse is divisive. When committed to an absolutist language buttressed by a sense of righteousness, those who fail to share that language become "the other." This may be so even when the vast preponderance of one's daily activities is virtually synonymous with that of "the infidel." There is substantial similarity in the quotidian activities of warring Israelis and Palestinians, Irish Protestants and Catholics, Pakistanis and Indians, Greeks and Turks. Yet a commitment to differing absolutes—to alternative formations of sounds and markings—has contributed to enormous conflict and suffering. In addition to an expansion of linguistic forms, then, we need to discover new modes of "breaking bread together."

Constructionism: Peril and Potential

In my view, constructionism does not in itself attempt to establish or institute a code of ethics either on the psychological or the philosophical level. Rather, it brackets "the problem of moral principles," favoring in its place an exploration of those relational practices that enable people to achieve what they take to be a "moral life." The question is not "What is the good?" but instead, given the heterogeneity of the world's peoples, "What are the relational means by which they can move toward mutually satisfactory conditions?" This is not to replace ethics with technology, a common criticism of the social sciences during the heyday of empiricism. Rather, it is to take seriously the patterns of preferred action within various groups and the moral languages by which these patterns are understood and reinforced. It is not to cast out all negotiation of principles, but neither is it to suppose that such negotiation will be the preferred route toward agreeable ends.

These various proposals can and should be subjected to criticism from various standpoints, and two deserve special attention. There is first the problem of moral vacuity. Such relativism, it will be said, offers nowhere to stand, nothing to value, no reason to oppose the worst inhumanities. I have already said a great deal about the failures of past attempts to establish moral grounds for action and the problematic effects on society of "the moral standpoint." But, the critic may venture, without a moral position of some kind, one simply cannot proceed; one is left uncommitted and directionless. To answer this argument I have suggested that principles themselves do not dictate action. There is nothing about commitment to a theory of morality that produces a moral life, and nothing about a decent and fulfilling life that demands a moral language as accompaniment. Moral principles are related to action only by virtue of the social conventions in which one participates.

Still, the critic may continue, the kind of relativism advocated by the constructionist leaves one always floating between moralities, never embedded or committed. But this is mistakenly to presume that constructionist metatheory is itself a "grounds for action" or possibly a "cognitive structure" dictating behavior. As I have argued, constructionism is a form of discursive positioning, an action in itself, and not a causal source of action. Nothing about constructionist relativism denies the possibility of moral commitment. While constructionism may give reasons for reflexive concern, it is not a replacement for normal life. In this sense, I will undoubtedly continue to engage in actions that seem good and right by certain standards—at times I may be strongly committed—but what is removed from the table, according to this view, is the justificatory base for these commitments, the range of "sound reasons" that furnish ultimate sanctions for silencing (or destroying) the opposition.[14] But how did we ever come to believe that we could not act without moral foundations?

It is instructive in this context to consider the case of Nazism—perhaps the ultimate weapon in the anti-relativist arsenal. How can a constructionist justify a stand against Nazism? There is nothing in a constructionist relativism that argues against loathing many of the activities carried out in the name of National Socialism. Given the forms of relatedness in which most of us live, it would be virtually inconceivable to react in any other way. What is removed from use from the constructionist perspective are the kinds of justifications that would invite "eradication of the Nazis" as the policy of preference. The Nazi framework provided a rationale for activities from which we recoil in horror; however, within that system of understanding, such activities had moral sanction. The problem was thus not that the moral fiber of the German people was lacking and that the remainder of the Western world was too slow to detect the evil. Rather, the problem can be traced in large measure to the Western historical context in which groups could come to believe in their own moral superiority (supported by ultimate justifications) and thus render mute all opposing voices. Had the means been available much earlier for an unobstructed interpenetration of meaning systems—Nazi, Jewish, Christian, Marxist, feminist, and the like—one must imagine that the consequences would have been far less disastrous.

There is a second important line of critique, one that is precisely the opposite of the preceding. It is not constructionism's "lack of values" that is at stake, the critic might opine, but its value commitments. While seeming to plump for a form of moral relativism, constructionist arguments in fact belie a deep commitment to an ethical position. I have spoken of human well-being, social harmony, the reduction of conflict, the acceptance of peoples who differ. Are these not, after all, good old-fashioned liberal virtues now operating in a symbiotic relationship with constructionism? Is constructionism not just another foil for status quo conventionalism?

To this accusation there are two replies. Recalling the discussion of the preceding chapter, to attribute any particular value commitment to the present arguments requires an interpretive effort—a replacement of the words themselves with some other, seemingly "more generic," set of words. Yet this otherwise hidden source is neither given transparently in what has been written nor can it be unequivocally derived from the words as given. Are there "hidden values" in the analysis? Yes, but only if one is willing to interpret the text in this way. Second, because of my own immersion in relationships there is no means by which my analysis can escape certain preferences: it favors peace over war, harmony over conflict, and dialogue over monologue. These preferences are not demanded by constructionist arguments; they are congenial, but so are many other advocacies. However, I make no attempt to justify these particular preferences. There is no supportive rationale—no necessity of spirit, no foundational rationality—that favors these particular advocacies over others. In effect, they are groundless entries into conversation, openings to further dialogue, invitations to forms of relationship.

The constructionist quest then is not for solutions to issues of good and evil, but rather for increased problematization. To solve problems of good and evil in any instance is to freeze meaning at a given point and thus to silence voices and segment the social world. The greatest "violence would be to stop the slippage, to erase the ambiguity, to take the play out of events, to put events out of play and into order, to hierarchize them, to erect principal authorities who would give authorized interpretations and definitive solutions and judgments" (Caputo 1993, p. 222). To the extent that the dialogue continues and constructions remain open, local meanings may ramify and people may come to share or absorb each other's modes of life. In this outcome lies perhaps the greatest hope for achieving human well-being.

Part Two

Criticism and Consequence

5   Social Psychology and the Wrong Revolution

Earlier chapters have traced several movements that conspire against traditional commitments to knowledge as an individual possession and have endeavored to replace the individual with the community as the site of knowledge-generation. Ironically, the vast share of contemporary work on the social construction of knowledge is taking place outside the domain of social psychology—the discipline most centrally concerned with processes of everyday interaction—and its absence from the debates is particularly unfortunate, for the discipline stands at once to gain and to lose heavily by the energetic exploration and application of social constructionist thinking. By bringing these issues into the foreground, I want first to extend the critique of the "knowing mind" to the domain of social cognition and then to scan alternative terrains—lines of constructionist inquiry that offer more promising possibilities for a culturally responsible and responsive psychology.

The cognitive revolution in scientific psychology has many faces. Some see it as a shift in emphasis from black-box behaviorism to a neobehaviorist concern with internal processes, others as an alteration from "bottom-up" models of human functioning to "top-down" theories of action, and still others as a shift from an environmentalist to a nativist conception of behavior. Although all these views capture important elements of the transformation, it is now clear that the cognitive revolution has radically reduced inquiry to a restricted range of explanatory constructs. And it is the operation of these constructs (for example, schemas, attention, memory, heuristics, accessibility, and the like) that takes procedural precedence over human activity itself. For the cognitive psychologist, human activity is largely a byproduct of cognitive processes, and it is these that demand focal attention.

Social psychologists have hardly been immune to this revolution in psychology. Indeed, one might say that the work of Kurt Lewin and his protégés (namely, Festinger, Schachter, and Kelley) played a substantial role in its development. How could one resist the strong and insistent message conveyed by this early work, to wit, "It is not the world in itself that determines human action but the way in which the world is perceived." For Festinger (1954) it was not "physical reality" but the individual's "social reality" that determined the course of social comparison. And in his later theory of cognitive dissonance (Festinger 1957), it was a purely cognitive demand for consistency to which broad-ranging (and often aberrant) patterns of behavior were traced. For Schachter (1964) emotions ceased to exist as events *sui generis* and became the result of cognitive labeling. And for Kelley (1972) the attribution of causality was a function of mental heuristics. These themes were central to much of the classic work on person perception (Heider 1958) and attribution theory (see Jones 1990). As texts by Eiser (1980) and Fiske and Taylor (1991) also demonstrate, the cognitive orientation can be successfully extended to include most of the major literature on attitude change, altruism, bargaining, attraction, and equity. To further fortify the revolution, a new and unifying theoretical language (one drawing roughly from the metaphor of the mind as computer) has also emerged in the "glamour areas" of social cognition: prejudice (see Mackie and Hamilton 1993), social schemata (Cantor and Mischel 1979), person memory (Wyer and Srull 1989), category accessibility (Higgins and Bargh 1987), stereotypes (Hamilton and Rose 1980), and social inference (Nisbett and Ross 1990).

To be sure, the cognitive revolution has been a major intellectual achievement. It has succeeded in opening a broad vista of exciting and challenging inquiry, it has raised a host of new and interesting questions, and it has furnished creative solutions to problems of long standing. However, as I hope to demonstrate, the price psychology has paid for these achievements is dear indeed. For social psychologists in particular, this revolution is a self-immolating deviation from its major charge, that of grappling conceptually and practically with the complexities of ongoing social life. As I will argue, psychologists have been all too prone to "get off at the wrong revolution." Not only are there major problems intrinsic to the cognitive perspective, but there is yet another transformation taking place within the intellectual world that is of far greater scope and implication than that embodied in the cognitive foray. Of greater importance, it is a revolution in which social psychology in particular could play a coloratura role.

The Problematics of Cognitive Explanation

As in any major intellectual movement, misgivings have begun to emerge on a variety of fronts: from within, at the borders, and from alternative perspectives. Cognitivists have themselves voiced despair over the lack of cumulative findings or obvious signs of progress in theoretical understanding (Allport 1975). Some have despaired of the representationalist theory of knowledge that underlies most cognitive theory (Maze 1991). Dreyfus and Dreyfus (1986) detail the failure of the cognitive program to make good on its early promises and the fundamental incapacity of rule-based thought to replace intuition. Similarly, Searle (1985) has demonstrated shortcomings in the view that cognitive systems (modeled on the computer) could ever explain human understanding. A serious split has also developed between those holding fast to traditional psychological concepts such as rational process and memory, and those arguing that such misleading "folk ideas" must be eliminated and replaced by fully biological (Churchland 1981) and computational models (Stitch 1983).[1]

At the borders, an increasingly vocal minority are claiming that insufficient attention has been given to the emotions and motivation. Like Freud before them, critics argue that the cognitive system must be motivated if it is to function at all, and thus, cognition must in part be derived from more fundamental psychological wellsprings. The historically oriented have begun to experience a form of *déja vu:* recalcitrant problems from the period of early mentalism have reappeared and remain unsolved within contemporary cognitivism (Graumann and Sommer 1984). Cognitive theories seem primarily based on a metaphor of the intuitive statistician, and many central tenets of cognitive psychology recapitulate deeply flawed theories of statistics (Gigerenzer and Murray 1987). Recent critiques have been even harsher, viewing the cognitive movement as "excessively abstract and implausible," "disengaged," "impersonal," "technological," "intellectualized," "nothing but information that will soon be superseded by more information," and as popular only "because there are powerful cultural and political forces that support it . . . bureaucratic, industrial and military organizations" (Still and Costall 1991).

From outside the cognitive domain, the critiques are sharper still. Ryle's (1949) early arguments about the infinite regress of dualistic explanations of behavior have been extended by contemporary critics (Palmer 1987). Skinner (1989) has shown that cognitive terms are misplaced descriptors of situations or behavior. Using Wittgensteinian critiques of psychologism, Coulter (1983, 1989) has demonstrated a variety of incoherencies in cognitive forms of explanation. Gellatly (1989) has traced the problems in diagnosing cognitive states. Sampson (1981) has taken the cognitive orientation to task for its ideological implications; by placing stress on internal mechanisms, cognitivists suppress the real-world problems in which people are enmeshed. As I argued in Chapter 1, the rational justification for the cognitive venture is sadly depleted.[2]

It is another range of problems I shall address here, however, problems inherited from the Western tradition of understanding itself. For it seems to me that as one extends the logical implications of a cognitive commitment, one confronts a series of inescapable cul-de-sacs. And until we press beyond the tradition in which cognitivism is submerged, the science will not only continue to recycle weary and insoluble enigmas, it will also fail to play any significant role in the future shaping of the culture. Three of these problems deserve special attention: the problem of the vanishing world, of origins, and of the effects of cognition.

COGNITION AND THE VANISHING WORLD

At the outset let us consider a range of topics that a significant social psychology might illuminate. We might hope, for example, that the field would render challenging and constructive accounts of aggression, cooperation, conflict, religious and political commitment, deviance, exploitation, power, irrationality, and the like. In effect, we wish the discipline to speak to major issues confronting the society and to offer insights and possible guidance toward improved social forms. But what is the fate of these various phenomena when they are viewed through the lens of cognitivism? As we have seen, the primary tenet of the cognitivist is that it is not the *world as it is* that determines action but one's *cognition of the world*. Thus, for example, an act of exploitation is not exploitation unless one cognizes it to be such; a hostile attack is not hostile until perceived in this way; groups do not exist unless they are conceptualized by their members as groups. The result of this line of argument, when extended, is that there are no exploitative acts, hostile attacks, groups, and the like in and of themselves. If one lived in a culture where no one perceived anything that counted as exploitation, there simply would be no exploitation in that world. Worldly events, then, are granted existence only by virtue of the perceiver's category system. Or, to put it another way, according to the cognitive perspective, the world is reduced to a projection or a byproduct of the individual cognizer.

At this point, many are inclined to shrug their shoulders and conclude that cognitive reductionism may be unfortunate, but it is simply a fact of life. Who can deny that it is the world as perceived rather than the world as it is to which we respond? Let us examine the logical implications of such a conclusion, for if we continue to reduce the world as it is to the world as mentally represented, the "real world" in which the individual operates ceases to exist. And by implication, a subject matter for the science also ceases, for how can we excuse the scientist from the same argument? Are not scientists, too, locked within their own conceptual or perceptual systems, expressing their own subjectivities, not accurate representations of the way things are? When cognitivism is extended in implication, there is no real world, no science, and essentially nothing that we could call knowledge. The cognitive account lapses into solipsism.[3]

Is there any means of escaping this infelicitous conclusion? I do not believe so insofar as psychology remains committed to a dualistic metaphysics. That is, the discipline has unwittingly fallen heir to a Cartesian world view in which a strong distinction is made between the knowing subject and the object of knowledge, mind reflecting material, consciousness mirroring nature (see Chapter 1). In the past we have taken the distinction more or less for granted; it represents part of the sedimented common sense of the discipline and, indeed, of the culture more generally. Yet what is the warrant for such a distinction? On what grounds is it to be justified? Certainly not on the grounds of objectivity (it is simply and obviously "there" for inspection), since the very concept of objectivity as it is currently used (mind accurately reflecting nature) already grants the distinction. In effect, it is a metaphysical leap; there are no evidential grounds that demand it. And if one is sensitive to a long line of conceptual critiques, from Wittgenstein (1953), Ryle (1949), and Austin (1962), through Rorty (1979), one may wish to escape it altogether. The following arguments give further weight to this alternative.

THE IMPASSE OF ORIGIN

Understandably, most cognitivists have wished to stop short of solipsism. Instead, for research purposes, they have abandoned their theoretical commitment and forged on to describe a real world of experimental particulars (beyond their own cognitive constructions). Then they treat the relation between the real and the cognized world as a problem to be explored empirically. In effect, an empirical challenge replaces (or, let us say, suppresses) the conceptual impasse. In this context the preeminent research question is, of course, how to account for mental representation. How does the real world inform the cognitive world? How is our repository of internal thoughts, concepts, schemata, and the like built up from experience? How is it that they come to reflect the world in a way that allows the organism to adapt? In effect, how are we to account for the origin of cognitive contents? Without answers to these questions, cognition remains isolated from its surrounds and without ostensible survival value.[4]

Let us briefly consider three of the most prominent solutions to the problem of origins, along with their major shortcomings. At the outset, one confronts a variety of *reinforcement* accounts of concept development. Such accounts have been popular within general psychology since the publication of Hull's (1920) classic work on concept attainment. Such theories typically, though not exclusively, cast the concept-learning process as the metaphor of the hypothesis test. Thus, for example, Restle (1962) described a variety of hypothesis-testing strategies of concept attainment, each based on the assumption that concepts are learned through environmental success and failure. Similarly, Bower and Trabosso (1964) proposed that concept development depends, at least in part, on error signals from the environment. In Levine's (1966) work, correct responses are emphasized as opposed to errors. In a model placing greater emphasis on cognitive mediation, Simon and Kotowsky (1963) proposed that one forms a hypothesis about the sequential pattern to which he or she has been exposed and then tests the adequacy of the hypothesis against subsequent exposures. And in more recent social psychology, Epstein (1980) has proposed that the self-concept is developed in much the same manner as scientific theory: it comes to reflect the results of hypothesis testing and is corrected through falsification.

But all such accounts suffer from a major shortcoming. If, as the cognitivist proposes, it is our perception of the world and not the world itself to which we respond, then the theorist faces an impasse in explaining how the process of reinforcement (or hypothesis testing) gets under way. To be more specific, in order for reinforcement (outcomes, errors, or other forms of environmental feedback) to correct or modify one's concept, an individual must already possess an extensive conceptual repertoire. First, he or she would have to be capable of conceptualizing a world of actions and/or entities to which reinforcement or feedback (error signals) would be relevant. For environmental feedback to function as a corrective or a verifying device, the infant must possess some form of hypothesis or conceptual structure enabling her to conclude that "This is a breast, and not some other object; I am an entity and this breast is separate from me; there are temporal units, and this event occurs at a separate time than that event," and so on. Without such a conceptual forestructure, there is nothing the individual would be asking of the environment, no information for which he or she would be searching. The world would essentially be empty of discriminant content. Further, the reinforcement model requires that the individual possess prior concepts of reinforcement classes. If one cannot conceptualize an event as a "success" or an "error," then he or she simply remains uninformed by passing events. If children cannot distinguish between a "parental admonishment" and the remainder of the booming, buzzing confusion of daily life, if they possess no preliminary concepts of what the utterances "good" and "bad" or "yes" and "no" could mean, then environmental feedback would fail to influence or extend their conceptual repertoire.

As we quickly discern, however, it is precisely the origins of these various conceptual forestructures that theories of reinforcement are designed to explain. After all, where do the various concepts making up the world in which reinforcement functions come from, and how does the child actually acquire concepts of admonishment and praise? In effect, reinforcement accounts fail to offer a satisfactory explanation of conceptual development, because reinforcement (or hypothesis testing) cannot function without an already intact conceptual structure.

A major alternative to reinforcement theories in psychology is what we might term *cognitive mapping*. As a class, these accounts generally presume that unconstrained observation of the external world enables the individual to develop conceptual templates, cognitive representations, or other mental systems that capture important features of the real world. This is essentially the position taken by Fiske and Taylor (1991) in their summary of the literature on schema development. As they conclude, "schemata change as they develop out of repeated exposures with instances. Schemata become more abstract, more complex, and often more moderate. They also seem to become more organized and compact, which frees up the capacity to notice discrepancies and to assimilate exceptions without altering the schema" (p. 178). Such views are also implied by most pattern recognition models in psychology. The most well developed theory of this variety is Rosch's (1978) "natural category" formulation. From Rosch's perspective, cognitive categories increasingly accommodate themselves to the contours of reality. Through the observation of objects in the real world, people become acquainted with the structure of real-world attributes. They observe that such attributes are not randomly distributed but appear in recurring combinations. Thus, for example, certain creatures have wings, beaks, feathers, and claws. Continued exposure to such a configuration of commonly associated features lends itself to the formation of the natural category "bird." Ultimately, then, exposure to real-world events produces a cognitive map, an environmentally valid form of mental representation.

The precise way in which mental mapping occurs is as yet forthcoming. The process by which the individual searches the environment, registers certain configurations and disregards others, creates hypotheses about co-occurrences, moves logically from discriminate sensations to general abstractions, and so on—all critical to the ultimate intelligibility of a mapping theory—remain unarticulated. Or, as Sandra Waxman, a cognitive developmentalist, has put it, "we have yet to discover a set of elementary features, to determine the sense in which they are primitive, to understand the mechanisms by which they are acquired, or to derive their rules of combination" (1991, p. 108). Perhaps this lacuna is not surprising. The theorist once again confronts the problem of understanding how the individual comes to recognize the features, objects, or configurations of events in order for mapping to begin. How is it possible to recognize the features of a particular configuration without a preliminary concept of those features?

How does one come to distinguish classes of feathers, beaks, wings, and so on, all of which enter into the generation of the natural category "bird"? Must one not already possess a category system in which such features are rendered sensible and discriminant in order to recognize them? What is the origin of this category system? Or in Waxman's (1991) words, "the assumption is that the [prototype] for a given concept is abstracted from a set of exemplars. However, this argument is circular, for one is left wondering how the child managed to cull the appropriate exemplars in the first place. What keeps the child (or adult) from trying to abstract a summary representation for a 'concept' that includes dogs, sugarbowls, and hailstorms?" (p. 108).

Of course, there is no salvation in arguing that the attributes of the exemplars are built up from exposure to their subfeatures or attributes, for such a rebuttal would simply place the critical question at a further remove. How would these subfeatures be recognized? In effect, to solve the problem of how people come to have concepts of birds and other "natural occurrences," the mapping theorist must ultimately rely on the existence of transparently available or *uncategorized* inputs (such as feathers, beaks, and so on) into the cognitive system. But if inputs only count or are significant to the individual insofar as they are cognized (interpreted, labeled, categorized, and so on) then such entries into the mental system are nonsensical. They simply would not register as identifiable events.[5]

Faced with such stultifying dilemmas, many thinkers are tempted to fall back on some form of *nativist* explanation of category development (see, for example, Markman 1989; Carey 1985; Fodor et al. 1980). Extending a tradition traceable at least to Kant's positing of a priori categories, the nativist argument holds that humans are genetically equipped to make certain basic distinctions. For Kant, human nature enables the individual to comprehend space, time, causality, and other elementary aspects of the world. In neo-Kantian fashion, Chomsky (1968) has proposed that the individual possesses an innate knowledge of language, a semantic knowledge that would enable an infinity of well-formed sentences to be generated. And, as Gibson (1979) and his followers postulate, the individual's categories for understanding the world are in some form correspondent with the world, for if they were not, the human species would have perished long ago. Natural selection has essentially left us with a set of cognitive distinctions that are adapted to the world as it must be. This is also the position to which Harré (1986) is finally driven in his attempt to defend a realist basis for a philosophy of science.

Yet, the nativist orientation to concept origin also presents substantial problems. At the outset, it is very difficult to sustain an argument that genetic preparedness could furnish more than a rudimentary set of conceptual orientations (color, time); as the number of presumed categories begins to approximate the language of a culture, it is hard to avoid an environmentalist alternative. Even if a limited set of distinctions are admitted, however, one is at pains to determine how the further array of concepts typically available to the individual could be derived. Given certain kinds of distinctions, how are others developed? If one is genetically programmed to distinguish between the melody "God Save the King" and "everything else," on what grounds are distinctions within the realm of "everything else" to be made? How is Mozart's Piano Concerto no. 21 to be distinguished from "Yankee Doodle"? Both are efficiently located in the null category; what would provoke a fresh assault on the existing construct system, and how?[6] Correspondingly, it is difficult to square the nativist account with the immense and ever-growing vocabulary of human affairs. New words emerge every day ("the EC," "PMS," "musical sampling"), and if these words enter the conceptual world of the individual, how does this take place? No one would propose that we are genetically prepared to understand, nor does an environmentalist account explain such comprehension.

Faced with the twin dilemmas of a thoroughgoing environmentalism and an equally otiose nativism, many contemporary researchers find themselves drawn to theories that combine both processes: a limited form of "bottom-up" environmentalism and an equally constrained "top-down" computational process. For example, Yale researchers (see Galambos, Abelson, and Black 1986) propose a view in which knowledge structures operate simultaneously on both a bottom-up and a top-down basis. The understanding of the world (and, more specifically, of texts) depends on both input from the environment and the active processing of content-rich mental schemata. For example, when a reader encounters the word *albatross* in a text, it may trigger various schemata, some of which may contain information about birds. These schemata are said to affect the reader's subsequent understanding of the text. Yet one is left to ponder how the schemata were initially developed. If understanding is based on the application of schemata, how would sense be made of *albatross* on the initial (or any subsequent) confrontation? The combination of environmentalist and nativist orientations fails to provide a viable answer to the question of origin; whenever one orientation is confronted with incoherence, it simply passes the enigma to its mate.

THE IMPASSE OF ACTION

Thus far we find that within the cognitive arena there is no viable way of deriving cognitive categories from the nature of the world, no way of building up categories of representation from external inputs. We must now inquire into the relationship between cognition and subsequent behavior. If the preceding problems could somehow be solved, how are we then to comprehend the influence of cognition on human action? It was often said of the early cognitivist Edward Tolman that his theory of cognitive maps was problematic because it left the organism "lost in thought." It provided no means for generating action from cognition. Has this fundamental problem now been solved? With an eye cast toward the history of philosophy, one might suspect that it has not. Philosophers since Descartes have unsuccessfully pondered how mind is able to influence matter or physical movements, how a realm without spatio-temporal coordinates can cause changes in a second realm that does possess these features.[7]

Additional problems surface more distinctly in present-day cognitive inquiry. One concerns the movement from the realm of abstract concepts to the realm of concrete action. Concepts or mental categories are traditionally viewed as abstractions from reality. They are thus not eidetic images of the world but categories into which the individual places events according to a specified range of criteria. As many commentators put it, cognition is that process through which sensory experience is *organized;* often they add that this organization serves as an *abstraction* from or codification of sense data; many maintain that the abstractions are *propositional* in form. Yet, if concepts, schemata, and the like are superordinate, one rapidly confronts the question of how such knowledge might be put to behavioral use. How does the individual employ a system of abstractions for generating concrete or particularized actions? (see also Chapter 3, pp. 101–102). Attempts to answer this question lead us into a conceptual morass parallel to and no less penetrable than that confronted in the case of concept origin.

Consider the individual who cognizes himself as a "friendly person" and wishes to place this concept into action. How can he determine what constitutes a "friendly" action on any particular occasion, since in this respect the concept of "friendly person" is fully mute. In itself, the abstraction does not recommend or specify any particular set of bodily movements (for example, "extend the right hand forward from the body at a velocity of 20 mph . . ."). And to complicate matters further, virtually any movement of the body might be considered friendly or unfriendly depending on the circumstances (there is no eidetic image that the concept of "friendly" necessarily entails). This enigma appears to be solved if one resorts at this point to a second-order construct or rule, namely, one that prescribes the exact character of "friendly actions" on various occasions. This second-order construct (possibly viewed as a hierarchical substructure of the more general class "friendly") might inform the individual, "On occasions when you meet a friend, a smile and a greeting represent friendly behavior." Yet, as is readily discerned, this second-order rule is also in the abstract form; it too leaves important questions of particulars unanswered. It tells us nothing of what counts in a concrete situation as "meeting a friend" or what form of bodily action constitutes a "smile" or a "greeting." What is now required is a third-order construct or rule, one that informs the individual of what these concepts mean in the concrete instance. Such a construct might indicate that a "friend" is one who "gives you support" and that "smiling" is a matter of "turning the corners of the mouth in an upward direction." But how is the individual now to determine what constitutes "support" on any occasion, and what, in terms of bodily movements, does it mean to "turn the corners of the mouth upward"? Such instructions are, once again, abstractions without specified particulars. The problem of applying conceptual knowledge to concrete circumstances thus casts one back upon subsidiary conceptualizations (application rules), which must themselves be defined in terms of still other conceptualizations (rules), and so on in an infinite regress. There is no place at which the conceptual meaning can be defined in other than conceptual terms and thus no exit to a range of unconceptualized particulars. Nowhere does abstract or conceptual thought enable one to make derivations to the realm of concrete action. Contemporary views of cognition essentially leave the actor "roving the dictionary of the mind."

This problem is a companion to the conundrum of concept origin. There we found no way to derive the categories of representation from real-world objects. Real-world particulars do not demand that any particular conceptualization be made of them. In the same way, once within the conceptual realm there is no means of determining what would necessarily count as a concrete realization of the mental category. In effect, there are no relationships of logical necessity between concrete particulars at either the stimulus or the response end of the traditional continuum. And if this is so, of what consequence is cognition in the species' struggle for survival? If observation makes no demands on cognitive representation, and representation has no necessary behavioral consequences, then what role does cognition play in guiding or directing effective action?

The theorist struggling to relate cognition to action faces still further difficulty. Specifically, we must ask how a cognitive category, set of propositions, representational structure, or the like can produce action. Cognitive entities are typically portrayed as machinelike in character, as stable and enduring structures. They are not in themselves originary sources of action. Thus, one may cognize a given situation as "life threatening" and conclude, "I must escape." However, there is nothing within this conceptual state that demands or causes any particular form of action. Even should one conclude, "I must run!" there is nothing in the appraisal itself that would generate movement of the body. Once armed with a particular array of concepts, then, what finally moves the individual to action?

To solve this problem, many theorists have found it necessary to posit additional psychological resources, most typically, energies, motives, or dynamic processes. It is these sources that *move* the individual to action, it is held, while concepts or schemas more properly furnish the direction or criteria for action. Or, in the more popular vernacular, we possess desires, wants, and needs, and we use our knowledge of the world to help us toward their fulfillment. Yet, consider the resulting problems: First, should the theorist admit that cognition is driven by a motivational system, then the centrality of cognition in human makeup is concomitantly reduced. If motives drive the organism, and cognition serves merely as the "map of the terrain," then motives (or other energic sources) become the critical focus of study, replacing cognition as "the originary source" of action. In the extreme case, cognitions become "mere derivatives" or "pawns" to fundamental energies. For the cognitivist to move in the direction of energic sources is to threaten the cognitive enterprise.[8]

Should the motivational source be added to the explanatory compendium, one confronts the new question of how motives and cognitions work together. How, for example, does the conceptual system "know" (register or reflect) the motivational direction, what constitutes the goals of our desires? Would the conceptual system not have to possess a means of identifying the state of the motivational system? Yet, if the conceptual system is top-down in nature—if it is the perception of the desire rather than the desire itself that counts—then is desire not effectively removed from the scene? Desire disappears as an instigating device in the same way that the "real world" was obliterated in the earlier analysis. If cognition is theorized as bottom-up in this case, doesn't the cognitivist reinstigate all the problems of an environmentalist view of knowledge (now at the level of internal process) that the concept of top-down cognition was designed to solve? And if we consider the motivational source and its operation, we confront still further problems. How is it, for example, that motivation can operate without some means of (1) identifying the goal that it is attempting to achieve (knowing what would give it pleasure or satisfaction); and (2) holding this goal in place for a duration sufficient to allow effective action? If we grant to the motivational source these kinds of capabilities—the capacity for "recognition" and "memory"—it rapidly becomes clear that we have created yet a second domain of cognition. That is, we have endowed motivation with the same attributes previously granted to cognition. We now have not one cognitive system within the individual but two, and the theoretical edifice begins to stagger under its weight.

The Second Revolution: Social Epistemology

The preceding arguments amplify the concerns of previous chapters in extending the range of impediments to a cognitive account of human knowledge. As they suggest, the cognitive orientation not only removes from scientific interest the vast share of human concerns, it is also unable to explain either the origin of its structures or the means by which cognition affects action. As I have suggested in earlier chapters, the major difficulties with the cognitive orientation in psychology derive from the more general problems inhering in a dualistic metaphysics.[9] When a real world is to be reflected by a mental world and the only means of determining the match is via the mental world, then the real world will always remain opaque and the relationship between the two inexplicable.

Yet, as we have seen, there is another revolution taking place within the intellectual world, one that not only allows these hoary problems to be abandoned, but invites new forms of inquiry. It is a revolution that extends across the disciplines and which replaces the dualist epistemology of a knowing mind confronting a material world with a *social epistemology*. The locus of knowledge is no longer taken to be the individual mind but rather patterns of social relatedness. To clarify the implications of this shift for a revitalized social psychology, it is useful to underscore several major arguments from the preceding chapters.

If we first suspend concern with the unyielding problems of how mind and world are related, we are free to labor in an orchard where the fruits lie within a more satisfying reach. Rather than puzzle futilely over the "concepts in our heads," we may usefully shift attention to the function of language (in all forms) in daily affairs. We may put aside murky questions about how schemas, prototypes, memories, motives, and the like operate, and focus on the way our words are embedded within our life practices. This move prepares us for yet another, for spoken and written language is inherently an outcome of social interchange. Should an individual possess a language that is solely private, it would not by common standards be considered a language. Should these proposals seem reasonable for the moment, then we are positioned to conclude that what we take to be knowledgeable propositions about the world are essentially the outcome of social relatedness. What we take to be knowledge-bearing propositions ("The world is round and not flat," "People are biologically prepared for emotional expression") are not achievements of the individual mind, but of social relationships.

The critical question posed by a dualist epistemology is how the mind comes to reflect the nature of the real world. Until this question can be answered, there is no means of determining when an individual has acquired accurate knowledge, or deciding which of several competing accounts best approximates the truth. In effect, standards of truth depend on answering what we have seen to be a set of intractable conceptual problems. By shifting our focus from mind to language, however, the nature of our concerns shifts dramatically. We cease to be concerned with foundational issues of truth and objectivity. What we happen to call things on any given occasion is not a matter of fidelity to the world as it is. It is a matter of the particular relationships in which we are participating. This does not render the scientist any more accurate in his judgments than the six-year-old; it is simply to say that each individual uses terms that are more or less adequate to a series of practices in which he or she is engaged.

For the constructionist, concepts of truth and objectivity may largely be viewed in terms of social pragmatics. They are useful, for example, in rendering praise or allocating blame. We reward a child for "telling the truth" not because he has accurately reported on the state of his sensory neurons but because his report accords with our adult conventions. When we prize the medical specialist who discovers the cure for a fatal illness, it is not because she has seen bodily processes for what they are. Rather, she has carried out a series of practices (along with socially agreeable modes of indexing) that eventuate in what we conventionally call "the prolonging of life."

As outlined in preceding chapters, these conclusions generate new domains of concern for the scientist. One of the most promising is that of human values. In the case of dualist epistemology, concern with ethics, morals, and ideology is secondary (and for many, is discarded altogether). The critical problem is whether the scientist is accurately registering the world as it is; whether the scientist happens to like or loathe the object of observation is irrelevant, if not obfuscating, to the process of acquiring knowledge. For the social epistemologist, in contrast, accounts of the world are embedded in social practices. Each account will render support to certain social practices and threaten others with extinction. Thus, a critical question to be put to various accounts of the world is what kinds of practices they support. Do they enable us to live in ways we hold valuable or do they threaten these social patterns? For the social epistemologist, a major question to be asked of, let us say, Skinnerian behavior theory, is not whether it is objectively valid; it is, rather, if we adopt the theoretical language proposed in this domain, in what ways are our lives enriched or impoverished? Do we wish to abandon the various practices in which terms such as "intention," "freedom," and "dignity" are central constituents? If the reply is negative, we can press on to other understandings.

Forms of Constructionist Exploration

What forms of social psychological inquiry are favored by this shift from an individual to a social epistemology? In what fashion is research and practice to proceed? Here it is first necessary to distinguish between an *internal* and an *external* program of inquiry. That is, adopting the assumptions of a constructionist epistemology specifically favors certain lines of inquiry. As endeavors carried out *in terms of* the epistemological stance itself, they extend its presumptions and treat its terms (for all practical purposes) as if they reflected the world as it is. Yet, because a concern with truth has been replaced by issues of intelligibility, social utility, and human value, constructionism does not demand that all inquiry be carried out in its terms. Indeed, it also invites the scholar to explore and extend *any form of intelligibility* that he or she finds significant within ongoing relationships—both in and out of the scholarly world. I will say more about the extended program shortly. However, let us first sample three forms of inquiry that demonstrate the potential of a reconstructed social psychology.

SOCIAL AND REFLEXIVE CRITIQUE

Because the shift to a social epistemology also brings with it a renaissance of concern with values and ideology, the psychologist is invited to speak out on matters that have heretofore bordered on the unprofessional (for science, it is said, "deals in facts, not values"). Value-committed analyses, ideologically based critiques, and ethically informed proposals for alternative modes of social life are now welcomed to the ranks of professional investments. By far the greater share of evaluatively based work in psychology has centered on the science itself. As many believe, in their claims to superiority in matters of objective truth the sciences are dangerously mystifying: the scientist's value commitments are cloaked in the misleading language of objective neutrality. The problem is all the more severe inasmuch as most psychologists themselves seem either disinterested or blind to the social and political implications of simply "telling it like it is" (Ibanez 1983).

To date, the major internalist critiques have primarily been voiced by "critical school" and feminist psychologists. The former, drawing sustenance from Marx's early attack on the seeming value neutrality of capitalist economic theory, and spurred by the later writings of Adorno, Horkheimer, and Habermas, have been vigorous and far-reaching in their criticism. Plon's (1974) critique of conflict research, Newman's (1991) attack on empiricist psychology, Wexler's (1983) proposal for a "critical social psychology," and edited volumes by Armistead (1974), Larsen (1980), and Ingelby (1980) all provide relevant exemplars. Attempts have also been made to move beyond critique alone to build a new form of psychology lodged in neo-Marxist thought. In the mental health sector, the radical psychology movement (Brown 1973; Newman 1991) has been a vital catalyst. In the experimental domain, the work of Klaus Holzkamp and his colleagues has been central to the vision of a new psychology (see Tolman and Maiers 1991).

Even more extensive is the range of critique offered by the feminist movement in psychology. Early attacks focused on the gender bias of psychological research—the excessive use of male samples, theoretical insensitivity to gender differences, and other "within-paradigm" issues (Deaux 1985; Eagly 1987; Parlee 1979). However, within recent years feminist critics have begun to challenge the entire edifice of empirical psychology, including its basic epistemological and methodological assumptions. As it is reasoned, psychology's traditional view of knowledge is saturated with androcentric biases. Its research strives for control over its object, separates the scientist from those "under study," thrives on manipulative methodology, and is insensitive or impervious to the individual's (and particularly the woman's) understanding of his or her own actions (Unger 1983; Belenky et al. 1986; Gilligan 1982; Squire 1989). What these critiques demand, then, are new ways of thinking about knowledge (M. Gergen 1988b; Hare-Mustin and Maracek 1988; Kitzinger 1987), methodology (Roberts 1981; Fonow and Cook 1991), and the ends psychological inquiry is intended to serve. In the latter instance, feminist psychologists are in the process of developing alternative views of psychological inquiry (Hollway 1989; Wilkinson 1986; Morawski 1987; M. Gergen 1988).[10]

Although critical school and feminist analyses are among the most concerted and fully developed forms of critique, the critical impulse now extends across a broad spectrum. Apfelbaum and Lubek (1976) have shown how mainstream research in conflict resolution "renders invisible" the plight of various minorities and the particular forms of injustice to which they are subjected. Both Furby (1979) and Stam (1987) have articulated ideological biases underlying locus of control research. Sampson (1978, 1988) has developed a series of powerful arguments against the ideology of "self-contained individualism" unwittingly furthered by most forms of psychological theory. Deese (1984) has shown how many popular conceptions in contemporary psychology obliterate the presumptions underlying democratic forms of governance. Wallach and Wallach (1983) have argued that much psychological theory sanctions selfishness. Echoing this view, Schwartz (1986, 1990) has shown how theories depicting human action as motivated by a desire for maximal gain and minimal loss foster the very kinds of activities they predict. Other analyses have been focused on the political and ideological functions served by specific theorists, such as Daniel Stern (Cushman 1991), Abraham Maslow (Daniels 1988), and Jean Piaget (Broughton 1981). Bradley (1989, 1993), Vandenberg (1993), Morss (1990), and Walkerdine (1993), along with Broughton's (1987) edited work, have brought common presumptions in developmental research into sharp reflexive question. Both Larsen (1986) and Parker and Shotter (1990) have orchestrated a dozen contributions placing traditional social psychology under critical scrutiny—and giving special attention to its un-examined ideological advocacies.

Because their messages are often painful and their grounds poorly under-stood, such lines of inquiry have hardly been embraced (and scarcely read) by rank and file psychologists. However, the importance of such work can hardly be underestimated, in terms of either the new modes of expression offered to the profession or its sensitizing the discipline to the social and political impact of its "objective reports." The major needs at this point are for further expansion in the range of voices represented in this endeavor and the broadscale institutionalization of self-reflexive inquiry (the devel-opment of courses, journals, networks, and so on). This is not to argue for the cessation of all those activities that are placed under critical scrutiny; it is, however, to favor opening scientific activities up to a far richer array of considerations than heretofore.

Coupled with internal or disciplinary critique, a constructionist episte-mology also encourages evaluative analyses of the culture more generally. What, from the standpoint of the ethically invested scholar, are the short-comings of contemporary society? What alternatives should be considered? Prior to the hegemony of behaviorism and empiricism in this century, psy-chologists could more freely (and unashamedly) participate in cultural di-alogues on values, policies, and goals. Beginning with Freud's *The Future of an Illusion* and continuing with the works of Horney, Fromm, and Mar-cuse, there was a vital participation in discussions of the cultural good. Later contributions by Robert Lifton, Thomas Szasz, Rollo May, Warren Bennis, and Philip Slater have all left significant marks on public conscious-ness.[11] However, such discussions have been largely ignored or viewed with antipathy from within the academy. As empiricistic demands have begun to wither and social considerations rise to consciousness, the way is again opened for broad cultural critique. Dinnerstein's (1976) analysis of gender relations, perhaps a pivotal volume, demonstrates the possibility of bearing a powerful social message without sacrificing scholarly integrity. In *Chang-ing the Subject,* Henriques et al. (1984) attack the individualized forms of understanding common across Western institutions and point to their ill effects on organizational life, politics, education, and gender relationships. Walkerdine (1988) has extended this form of analysis to focus more ex-plicitly on the subjugation of reasoning processes in educational institu-tions. Volumes by Tavris (1989) and by Averill and Nunley (1992) move the dialogue from the academy into the culture as they challenge the broadly accepted view of emotion as biologically fixed and through constructionist analysis open alternatives for everyday action. My own offering, *The Sat-urated Self,* attempts to trace the critical consequences of communication technology for contemporary conceptions of self and relationship.

FORMS OF SOCIAL CONSTRUCTION

A second line of constructionist inquiry is centered on people's constructions of self and world. Such work typically falls under the rubrics of social
construction, discourse analysis, everyday understanding, social accounting, or ethnomethodology. The central attempt of this kind of inquiry is to
document the taken-for-granted realities that are so integral to patterns of
social life—how it is that people characterize (describe, understand, index)
themselves and the world about them so that their actions are intelligible
and justifiable. Illustrative of this burgeoning form of research are inquiries
into the constructed nature of our taken-for-granted conceptions of the
body (Young 1993), sex differences (Laqueur 1990), medical disease (Bury
1987; Wright and Treacher 1982), sexual desire (Stein 1990), pregnancy
(Gardner 1994), childhood (Stainton Rogers and Stainton Rogers 1992),
intelligence (Andersen 1994), wife abuse (Loseke 1992), the life course
(Gubrium, Holstein, and Buckholdt 1993), and world geography (Gregory
1994).

On the surface, this enterprise bears a strong similarity to research in the
areas of social cognition (Semin and Krahe 1987), phenomenology (Giorgi
1985), subjective theory (Groeben 1990), and social representation (Moscovici 1984). In each case research centers on spoken or written language.
However, there are important differences among the ventures, and their
methods and implications. Primary is the difference in the inferences drawn
from the research procedure and the use to which the research is put. For
researchers in social cognition, phenomenology, and subjective theory, language samples are used to draw inferences to mental conditions (schemas,
propositional networks, lifeworlds, argumentation structures). In effect,
the language samples are expressions or emanations of a locus of scientific
interest that lies elsewhere. The language is not in itself socially significant;
it acquires importance in terms of the access it provides to "yet another
world." Further, the theory of science that rationalizes such work is individualist and (except for certain phenomenologists) dualistic in origin. In
each of these respects, such work differs in important ways from social
constructionist inquiry.

The case of social representation is more complicated. In its original
Durkheimian phase, social representation was defined as "the elaborating
of a social object by the *community* for the purpose of behaving and communicating" (Moscovici 1963, p. 251; italics mine). In effect, the emphasis
was noncognitive and in this way it shared much with social constructionism. At the same time, the focus was macrostructural, and constructionist
issues of microsocial relations were of little concern. Later formulations
(see, for example, Moscovici 1984) adopt a distinctly cognitive orientation;
social representations are considered forms of mental makeup and community representations simply a summation of many individual actions. Al-

though the cognitive view has been subject to significant critique (see Parker 1987; McKinlay and Potter 1987), much of the associated research has continued within the initial frame. Thus, for example, inquiry into views of health and illness (Herzlich 1973), images of the body (Jodelet 1984), representations of student-teacher relationships (Gilly 1980), television relationships (Livingstone 1987), and others (see Farr and Moscovici's 1984 summary) all focus on the shared public understandings extant within the culture. Such research bears a close affinity with many constructionist endeavors.

There is, however, one additional emphasis of much constructionist research, which separates it from many social representationist accounts, along with the related inquiry in social cognition, phenomenology, and subjective theory. Most of the research in these various domains favors cultural *stabilization*. That is, its goal is typically to fix or give definitive structure to the mode of thought (or societal pattern) under consideration. The task of social cognitivists, for example, is complete when they have fully delineated the character of the cognitive world. Similarly, phenomenologists may be content when they have grasped the essentials of the individual's phenomenal field, and subjective theory researchers may be pleased when they have fully explicated the individual's subjective theory. The application of this knowledge—should it occur—is usually left to others—to practitioners or those outside the scientific spectrum. In contrast, for those engaged in constructionist or discursive inquiry, the more frequent research aim is *destabilization*. Because people's constructions of self and world are constitutive elements of cultural life, and because they are the implements by which relationships are carried out, documenting them in the service of validating abstract, decontextualized theory holds little appeal. Such documentation would be of no more consequence than documenting people's recitations of the Lord's Prayer, which would simply elucidate common conventions. The more challenging problem is to locate conventions that are not commonly recognized as such (that are "natural" or taken for granted), and are in some way problematic or injurious to the society. The constructionist centers attention on the "ways of putting things" people generally fail to recognize as constructions and which the investigator wishes to challenge.

Some of the earliest illustrations of the destabilizing impulse of much constructionist inquiry were stimulated by Spector and Kitsuse's (1987) volume, *Constructing Social Problems*. Rather than accept social problems as given and race headlong toward solutions, they explore the ways in which such problems come to be defined as they are. For whom is alcoholism, homosexuality, drug abuse, and so on a problem, and why? How can such issues be confronted in terms of the matrices of meaning in which they are embedded? Further examples of destabilization include Kessler and Mc-

Kenna's (1978) analysis of the multiplicity of gender definitions that stand against the traditional binary. Along similar lines, investigators demonstrate the various ways in which gender is constructed (Lorber and Farrell 1990), along with the concepts of hetero- versus homosexuality (Greenberg 1988; Urwin 1985), premenstrual syndrome (Rodin 1992) and, indeed, sexuality itself (Tiefer 1992; Caplan 1989). Others have destabilized traditional forms of organizational theory (Kilduff 1993) and organizational taboos (Martin 1990). Such research is clearly political in implication, unsettling the taken-for-granted and opening new possibilities for action. The destabilizing implications are made especially clear in Kitzinger's (1987) demonstrations of how liberalist constructions of lesbianism undermine the radical implications of lesbian lifestyles and contribute to homophobia. Other research has attempted to reveal the constructed character of various psychological "phenomena." These studies place in jeopardy long-standing beliefs in the existence of cognitive processes (Coulter 1979), hostility (Averill 1982; Tavris 1989), attitudes (Potter and Wetherell 1987), physical pain (Cohen 1993), love (Averill 1985), emotional classifications (Harré 1986; Day 1993), sincerity (Silver and Sabini 1985), intention (Jayyusi 1993), personality structure (Semin and Chassein 1985; Semin and Krahe 1987), child development (Kessen 1990), and adolescence (Hill and Fortenberry 1992). Similarly questioned are the ontological grounding for anxiety (Sarbin 1968; Hallam 1994), schizophrenia (Sarbin and Mancuso 1980), depression (Wiener and Marcus 1994; Nuckells 1992), and anorexia and bulimia (Gordon 1990), and psychiatric classifications more generally (Gaines 1992; Gremillon 1992). By revealing the ways in which we construct ourselves psychologically, it is reasoned, we need no longer be constrained by traditional beliefs, either in our daily affairs or in the psychological laboratory.

Such forms of deconstruction are effectively supplemented by Jan Smedslund's (1988, 1991) important research into the conventions governing the use of psychological discourse. As Smedslund argues, in order to be intelligible, empirical research in psychology must employ these common conventions, because to fail in making conventional sense is to make no sense. Thus, empirical research in psychology is largely pseudo-empirical: it appears to test hypotheses, but if it contradicts the hypotheses it violates common conventions of understanding (such as in *proving* that "when people intend to act, they do not act"). Using similar arguments I have attempted to demonstrate the analytic or definitional basis for all meaningful propositions relating mind to world and action (Gergen 1988a).

In its emphasis on the contingent nature of reality posits, constructionism also invites the researcher to think in terms of politically gauged research. Rather than try to "reflect truth" in a traditional fashion, research itself becomes an instrument for emancipation or intervention. It generates a critical posture toward the taken-for-granted. In this vein, researchers have focused on existing discourse on aging and the life course (Spencer 1992; Gubrium, Holstein, and Buckholt 1993), the cultural representation of AIDS (Treichler 1987), the social negotiation of rape (Wood and Rennie, in press), the construction of problem behavior in schools (Epstein 1991), and the myths and ceremonies that lead welfare policy to affirm stereotypes about the poor (Handler and Hasenfeld 1991). Additional inquiry has been directed at such topics as beliefs about racial equality (Allen and Kuo 1991), conceptions of literacy (Gowen 1991), the media construction of news (Iyengar 1991), and the production of political reality (Edelman 1988).

Traditional empiricist research is largely concerned with establishing general principles, that is, knowledge about cognition, memory, perception, and so on that is uncontaminated by or independent of either culture or history. Other than the light they may shed on universal processes (either extending or delimiting a given hypothesis), it has little interest in other cultures and historical periods. The constructionist, in contrast, has an acute sensitivity to the perspectives of other peoples and times. For one, if the investigator can demonstrate significant variations in people's accounts of self and world, these findings may challenge the commonsense realities of contemporary culture. Such research can be used, then, to deconstruct contemporary ontologies and thereby open a space for considering alternatives. Averill's (1982) research on anger is an excellent example. Currently there is a strong tendency to consider the emotions as biologically fixed—as natural tendencies common to all normal people. Yet, by exposing marked differences in action patterns across cultures, Averill demonstrates that what we take to be biological givens are more plausibly viewed as cultural byproducts. Anger takes the form of a performance; it may be carried out well or poorly, or it may be abandoned altogether as a technique of relating. This conclusion is amplified by and resonant with a steadily expanding literature on the cultural specificity of emotion (see Harré 1986; Lutz 1986a, 1988; Rosaldo 1980), conceptions of knowledge (Salmond 1982), and a variety of other psychological processes (Bruner 1990; Shweder and Miller 1985; Kirkpatrick 1985; Heelas and Lock 1981; Carrithers, Collins, and Lukes 1985; Gergen and Davis 1985).

As we begin to appreciate the local validity of how other cultures construct the world, we are also primed to consider alternative conceptions of human functioning, of knowledge, and of related practices. More specifically, such work challenges the traditional presumption of a unified subject matter of psychology (for example, cognition, emotion, and so on), and a unified methodology (for example, experimentation, correlational methods, and the like). In light of the fact that such traditional presumptions are often seen as creating the remainder of the world in a Western image and as a justification for further colonization, this is an end much to be valued.

Thus favored by comparative constructionist analysis is a sharing of resources across cultures, and a broad enrichment of theories, methods, and practices.

In addition to stimulating interest in other cultures, such analysis also adds a significant new dimension to historical study. In reminding us of the contingent condition of our given realities, demonstrations of historical change operate like cross-cultural comparisons. For example, prompted by the ground-breaking work of van den Berg (1961) and Ariès (1962), investigators have focused extensively on historical variations in the conception of the child (see reviews by Kagan 1983; Borstelman 1983; Goodnow and Collins 1990). As Kessen (1979) concludes, such historical variations demand new ways of conceptualizing research in child development. The view of cumulative empirical study is outmoded. Kessen's perspective is additionally supported by inquiry into the early historical roots of contemporary conceptions of developmental process (Kirschner, in press), and by a variety of studies comparing constructions of the child across cultures (see Goodnow 1984; Harkness and Super 1983; Gergen, Gloger-Tippelt, and Berkowitz 1990). The destabilizing implications of this work are intensified by further inquiry into historical variations in mother love (Badinter 1980; Schutze 1986), passion (Averill 1985; Luhman 1987), jealousy (Stearns 1989), sense of smell (Corbin 1986), and sense of taste (Borg-Laufs and Duda 1991). Particularly important for stimulating the self-reflexive impulse in psychology are works exploring the sociohistorical roots of psychology's concept of the person (Buss 1979), of the subject in psychological research (Danziger 1990), and of the concept of the psychological experiment (Morawski 1988). Such research invites us to reconsider our contemporary professional commitments and to be sensitive to alternative possibilities.

PROCESSES OF CONSTRUCTION

A third form of inquiry invited by a constructionist epistemology centers on social processes themselves. By what processes do people collectively achieve understanding, how do failures in understanding occur, under what conditions are communal constructions likely to change or to resist change, how can contradictory constructions of the world be reconciled? Constructionism opens a new set of questions and offers a range of resources for inquiry. Thus far, such inquiry has benefited greatly from Garfinkel's (1967) pioneering work on ethnomethodology, Goffman's (1959, 1967) many insights into microsocial strategies, and Harré's various contributions (with Secord 1972, 1979) to an ethnogenic social psychology. One compelling feature of this work has been its shift in the locus of interest and explanation from the internal or psychological realm to the domain of interaction. It has replaced interest in psychological processes within single individuals—common fare in experimental social psychology—with a concern for interdependencies, jointly determined outcomes, or "joint action." Although not always breaking with the individualistic perspective, research into self-presentation and impression management (Schlenker 1985; Tseelon 1992a), social accounting (Semin and Manstead 1983; Antaki 1981), close relationships (Hendrick 1989; Duck 1994; Burnett, McGhee, and Clarke 1987), interaction episodes (Marsh, Rosser, and Harré 1978; Forgas 1979), and the management of meaning (Pearce and Cronen 1980; Sigman 1987) has placed a strong emphasis on social interdependence.

Further emphasis on social process *sui generis* is found in the work of Mummendey (1982) and her colleagues on the ways in which aggression emerges not as an expression of an inner impulse but as a product of interaction. Felson (1984) has effectively demonstrated the importance of this view for understanding various criminal offenses. Other vistas have been opened by incursions into discourse processes. Developmentalists such as Youniss (1987) and Berkowitz, Oser, and Althof (1987) have explored the social construction of morality in children. Miller et al. (1990) have researched the means by which narrative practices affect the child's construction of the self. Riger (1992) has similarly focused on gender as a performance born of interaction, and Henwood and Coughlan (1993) have furnished insights on the mutual construction of "closeness" in the mother-daughter relationship. Davies and Harré (1990) have theorized the positioning of self in discourse. Potter and Wetherell (1987) have examined ways in which "conversational objects" are generated through social interchange and various conversational moves are used to warrant or justify various reality posits. In research that poses a significant challenge to the traditional view of persons striving for cognitive consistency, Billig and his colleagues (1988) have demonstrated the inconsistencies in people's ideological discourse. Edwards and Potter (1992) have elucidated how processes of social construction properly replace traditional views of cognitive construction and probed the discursive manner in which self and world are constituted. They develop the rudiments of a "discursive psychology," emphasizing processes of "fact" making, the creation of agency in conversation, and responsibility as a discursive production. Others have explored the construction of meaning within organizations (see, for example, Gray, Bougan, and Donnellon 1985; Cooperrider 1990). Process-oriented inquiry also invites historical or diachronic analysis. In this arena, Rose (1985) has critically analyzed ways in which psychological measurement developed within and lent support to an ethos favoring the societal control of the individual. Both Gergen (1991b) and Parker (1992) have focused on historical changes in psychological discourse from the romantic to the postmodern eras.

Empiricists have often distinguished between knowledge "generation" and "application." The research scientist is responsible for the former, while those outside the scientific establishment are—through a series of systematic deductions—to reap the benefits through application. I outlined problems with this orientation in Chapter 2. From the standpoint of a constructionist epistemology, this distinction between the "knower" and the "doer" is no longer relevant. Because the human sciences generate meaningful discourse and practices, and these discourses and practices affect cultural life, human science inquiry is itself a form of social action. Knowledge and application are not fundamentally separable. It is largely for this reason that research within the constructionist frame is more frequently tied to prominent cultural issues—matters of conflict, gender relations, ideology, power, and the like. Discussions of these matters are themselves entries into cultural dialogues.

Practical challenges have innervated many constructionist endeavors. A variety of studies growing out of ongoing practical settings emphasize this pragmatic stance. Thus, for example, Edwards and Mercer (1987) and Brice Heath (1983) explored the ways in which realities are constructed in the classroom. The implications of constructionist processes for pedagogical practice have been elaborated in Bruffee's (1993) inquiries into collaborative learning and Lather's (1991) explorations into postmodern pedagogy. Constructionist views have been extended to practices of organizational management (Astley 1985) and the means by which organizations form and change realities (Srivastva and Barrett 1988; Deetz 1992). Bhavnani (1991) is concerned with the political views of adolescents and their implications for power arrangements in the society. The political concern is also reflected in a variety of studies on racist discourses (van Dijk 1992), rhetorics of conformity (Nir and Roeh 1992), and street harassment (Kissling 1991). Divorce counselors have begun to understand a couple's problems in terms of gendered discourses (Riesman 1990). Anderson and Goolishian (1988), along with Schnitman and Fuks (1993), have reframed the therapeutic process as one of co-constructing possible worlds. Reiss (1981) has opened research on the family's construction of reality, and with other colleagues McNamee and Gergen (1992) has begun to elaborate the implications for therapeutic practice. We shall return to the problem of therapeutic practice in Chapter 10.

Within the social sphere, particular attention is directed to the textual or rhetorical procedures through which various realities are realized or discredited. In this vein, Leary (1990) has brought scholars together to explore the function of metaphor in constructing psychological reality. Sternberg (1990) has compared metaphors of intelligence, and Brown (1992) has shown how such metaphors have lent rhetorical power to the intelligence-testing movement. Sarbin (1986) has provided a similar service in demonstrating the significance of narrative in both science and everyday life. Kleinman's (1988) work on illness narratives, narrative studies of developmental theory (Gergen and Gergen 1986; Valsiner 1992), and Spence's (1982) discussion of therapeutic narratives furnish rich illustrations of narratives at work (see also Chapters 8–10). A compilation of papers edited by Shotter and Gergen (1989) and works by Kondo (1990) and Eakin (1985) demonstrate the operation of textual and rhetorical processes in identity formation.

One of the most significant developments in studies of social process is the relocation of psychological process within the interpersonal sphere: processes traditionally assigned to the mental world are reconstituted within relationships. Relational conceptualizations will become focal in Part III.

Toward Detente: The External Domain

These various endeavors illustrate some of the potentials of the constructionist revolution. At the same time, it is noteworthy that they are all consistent with the suppositions of a social constructionist epistemology. In their attempt to provoke, clarify, or transform, the suppositions elaborate and extend the constructionist view of social knowledge. The critic will notice that to carry out those tasks, what traditionally pass for empirical research methods are often used. The critic may thus ask, if a social epistemology abandons claims to truth, is it not incoherent to use various empirical methods of research? As I argued in Chapter 3, the response is that in the present range of studies such methods do not function in the traditional sense as warrants for the validity of the propositions they accompany. Endeavors of the kind outlined above are not important because they are true or false; their significance derives from the social and intellectual utility of constructing social life in this way. They offer a significant alternative to many contemporary ways of framing the world and may thereby offer new alternatives for action. In this sense, much "empirical" research is essentially rhetorical in its function. It furnishes an effective way of lending vivifying force to various accounts of reality. It translates abstract theoretical language into the argot of daily life, thus rendering that life anew.

It is this orientation to empirical research that, in the end, opens the way for a detente between social constructionists and social psychologists of a more traditional stripe. It is not the aim of constructionism to obliterate all forms of research that are incoherent with its own suppositions. If the primary function of scientific language is pragmatic, rather than truth bearing, then we may celebrate the traditional metatheories, theories, and methods for what they may contribute to the culture's resources, and properly criticize them when their implications seem injurious. By the same token, however, we may also assess constructionist research and practice in terms of cultural outcomes.

Consider the empiricist alternative. Since the function of theories is to picture the world as it is, competition between theories approximates a zero-sum game: if one theory is accurate, discrepant voices can be eliminated. Framed in this way, the competition between radical behaviorism and cognitivism is a fight to the death: the two theories cannot simultaneously be true. And so the terrain of contemporary psychology is dotted with warring and hostile camps, and dialogue between encampments is minimal. Yet, when one enters the world of constructionist epistemology, such warfare proves irrelevant. The game is not zero-sum with objectivity serving as the arbiter among domains. Rather, each form of theoretical intelligibility—cognitive, behaviorist, phenomenological, psychoanalytic, and the like—provides the culture with discursive vehicles for carrying out social life. As the number of theoretical intelligibilities within the profession expand, so the symbolic resources of the culture are augmented. To rid the world of psychological theory would be to impoverish the landscape of social interchange.

In this sense, the earlier critiques of the cognitive program are not meant to be lethal. They are primarily attempts to curb the otherwise imperious thrust of a highly circumscribed and nonreflexive form of science. As I have indicated, the cognitive movement has had much to offer in the way of new and interesting views of individual action, but to the extent that this view dominates the discursive landscape, the discipline loses its capacity to enrich the culture.

... we multiply distinctions, then
Deem that our puny boundaries are things
That we perceive, and not that which we have made.

      —WILLIAM WORDSWORTH, *The Prelude*, Book III

We cannot have ... psychiatry without names.

      —HENRY BRILL, M.D., *Classification in Psychiatry and Psychopathology*

6   The Cultural Consequences of Deficit Discourse

As I have outlined in preceding chapters social constructionism invites reflexive analysis of cultural life. I wish to explore here what I view as an increasingly significant problem in contemporary culture, one that appears to be both accelerating in magnitude and without obvious perimeters. It is also a problem to which the discursive practices of the mental health professions—most notably psychiatry and clinical psychology—make a substantial contribution. Judging from my many colleagues, students, and friends who are engaged in therapeutic practices, I believe they generally share a strong and genuine commitment to a vision of human betterment. In addition, although research on the effects of therapeutic intervention yields conclusions of interminable equivocality, it is clear that many who have sought help believe that the therapeutic community plays a vital and humane role in contemporary society. Yet, my concern is with the paradoxical consequences of the prevailing vision of human betterment and the pervasive hope that these professions can improve the quality of cultural life. There is reason to believe that in their very effort to furnish effective means of alleviating human suffering, mental health professionals simultaneously generate a network of increasing entanglements for the culture at large. Such entanglements are not only self-serving for the professions, they also add exponentially to the sense of human misery.

Psychological Discourse: Pictorial or Pragmatic?

In order to appreciate the nature and magnitude of the problem, let us extend the preceding discussion of language functions to matters of mental discourse. From this discussion we can draw a distinction between two views of the vocabulary of mind, the pictorial and the pragmatic. Most commonly we employ such terms as "thinking," "feeling," "hoping," "fearing," and the like *pictorially:* that is, in the same way that we give different names to individual persons or different labels to objects distinguished in nature, we use mental terms as if they reflected distinctive conditions within the mind. The statement "I am angry" is intended, by common convention, to describe a state of mind different from other states, such as *joy, embarrassment,* or *ecstasy.* The vast majority of therapeutic specialists also proceed in a similar manner. They listen to their clients for hours to ascertain the quality and character of their "inner life"—their thoughts, emotions, unarticulated fears, conflicts, repressions, and most important, "the world as they experience it." It is commonly presumed that the individual's language provides a vehicle for "inner access"—revealing or setting forth to the professional the character of the not-directly-observed. And, the reasoning goes, revelation is essential to the therapeutic outcome—whether to furnish the therapist with information about the client's mental condition, provoke self-insight, enhance the client's sense of autonomy or self-esteem, induce catharsis, reduce guilt, and so on.

Our earlier discussion of language functions (Chapter 2) brought a variety of criticisms to bear on the picture theory of language and its place in the traditional conception of knowledge. We focused particular attention on the social, ideological, and literary problems inhering in the traditional view. Yet, if language cannot serve as a picture or map of the external world, there is little ground for clinging to this possibility in the case of psychological discourse. If the language of biology, chemistry, art criticism, politics, athletics, and so on is used to construct what we take to be "the facts of the matter," there is little reason to presume that psychological discourse is any less constitutive of its referential field. More significantly, in the case of mental discourse, there is good reason to argue that there are no local referents to which such language *can* be attached. As we have seen, in the case of biology, chemistry, and art criticism, for example, it is possible for communities to develop local agreements about what various "events" or "objects" are to be called. Communities of biologists can come to agree about how terms such as "neuron," and "synapse" index various "states of affairs" (see Chapter 3). Yet, in the case of psychological discourse, such local standards of ostensive reference cannot in principle be established. Consider some of the problems attendant upon attaching psychological terms—"attitudes," "anxiety," "intentions," "feelings," and the like—to an internal state of affairs:[1]

- What are the characteristics of mental states by which we can identify them? By what criteria do we distinguish, let us say, among states of anger, fear, and love? What is their color, size, shape, or weight? Why do none of these attributes seem quite applicable to mental states? Is it because our observations of the states prove to us that they are not?

· Could we identify our mental states through their physiological manifestations—blood pressure, heart rate, and so on? If we were sufficiently sensitive to differing physiological complexes, how would we know to which states each referred? Does an increased pulse rate indicate anger more than love, hope more than despair?

· How can we be certain when we identify such states correctly? Could not other processes (for example, repression or defense) prevent accurate self-appraisal? (Perhaps anger is eros after all.)

· By what criterion could we judge that what we experience as "certain recognition" of a mental state is indeed certain recognition? Wouldn't this recognition ("I am certain in my assessment") require yet another round of self-assessments ("I am certain that what I am experiencing is certainty"), the results of which would require additional processes of internal identification, and so on in an infinite regress?

· Although we may all agree in our use of mental terms (that we experience fear, ecstasy, or joy, for example, on particular occasions), how do we know that our own subjective experiences resemble those of others? By what process could we possibly determine whether my "fear" is equivalent to yours? How then do I know I possess what everyone else calls "fear"?

· How are we to account for the disappearance from the culture of many mental terms popular in previous centuries, along with the passing fashions in mental terminology of the present century? (Whatever happened to *melancholy, sublimity, neuralgia,* and the *inferiority complex?*) Have the words disappeared because such processes no longer exist in mortal minds?

· How are we to account for the substantial variations in psychological vocabulary from one culture to another? Did we once have the same mental events as the primitive tribesman, for example, the emotion of *fago* described by Lutz (1988) in her studies of the Ifaluk? Have we lost the capacity to experience this emotion? Is it lurking somewhere in the core of our being, buried beneath the layers of Western sophistication? By what standards could we decide one way or another?

These problems have long resisted solution and strongly suggest that using mental language in a referential fashion is deeply misleading. Rather, we may properly view the presumption that mental language reflects, depicts, or refers to actual states within the individual as *reificationist*. Such an orientation treats as real (as ontological existants) that to which the language seems to refer. Or, in other terms, by treating the language as if it indexed distinct states of mind, one engages in a *fallacy of misplaced concreteness*. One treats as concrete the putative object of the signifier rather than the signifier itself. This is not to conclude that "nothing is going on" within the individual when he or she is shouting in anger, is locked in an embrace, or hears ominous sounds in the dark. However, there is nothing about these human conditions that demands a distinctly mental vocabulary. Wholly differing "experiential interiors" may take place as one plays the part of King Lear, as opposed to that of Othello or Falstaff. However, the actor requires neither a language of mental states nor physiology to explain his actions—to render them intelligible to others. (It is sufficient for most purposes to know that one is "playing Lear" without adding a description of psychological or physiological "underpinnings.") In effect, to use mental language referentially is to freight it with unwarranted and obfuscating implications.

Let us contrast the pictorial orientation to mental language with another, one we may term *pragmatic*. For this purpose, let us bracket the view of mental language as a referential indicator of inner states and consider such language as a constituent feature of social relationships. That is, following the arguments laid out in earlier chapters, we may venture to say that psychological language obtains its meaning and significance from the way in which it is used in human interaction. Thus, when I say "I am unhappy" about a given state of affairs, the term "unhappy" is not rendered meaningful or appropriate according to its relationship to the state of my neurons or my phenomenological field; rather, it plays a significant social function. It may be used, for example, to call an end to a set of deteriorating conditions, to enlist support and/or encouragement, or to invite further opinion. Both the conditions of the report and the functions it can serve are also circumscribed by social convention. The phrase "I am deeply sad" can be satisfactorily spoken at the death of a close relative but not at the demise of a spring moth. The phrase "I am depressed" can secure the concern and support of others but it cannot easily function as a farewell, an invitation to laughter, or a commendation. In this sense, mental language functions more as a smile, a frown, or a caress than a mirror of the interior; it is more like a strong grip between trapeze artists than a map of inner conditions. In effect, people use mental terms in constituting their relationships.[2]

The Language of Mental Deficit in Cultural Context

The pervasive stance toward psychological discourse in Western culture is decidedly pictorial. We generally accept people's accounts of their subjective states as valid (at least for them). If we are sophisticated, we may wonder if they are fully aware of their feelings, or have been misled in an attempt to protect themselves from what is "really" there. And, if we are of a scientific bent, we may wish to know the distribution of various mental states (such as loneliness or depression) in the society more generally, the conditions under which they occur (such as stress or burnout), and the means by which they can be altered (the comparative efficacy of differing therapies). However, we are unlikely to question the existence of the reality to which such terms seem to refer; and because the prevailing ontology of mental life remains generally unchallenged, we seldom inquire into the utility or desirability of such terms in daily life. If the language exists because the mental states exist, there is little reason for critical appraisal of the language. By common standards, to disapprove of the language of the mind is tantamount to finding the shape of the earth disagreeable.

Yet, if we view psychological discourse from a pragmatic perspective, mental language loses its function as "truth bearing." One cannot claim the right to language use on the grounds that existing terms "name what there is." At the same time, we confront significant questions concerning the existing terminologies, for the "ways we talk" are intimately intertwined with patterns of cultural life. They sustain and support certain ways of doing things and prevent others from emerging. From the pragmatic perspective it is of paramount importance, then, to inquire into the effects of the prevailing vocabularies of the mind on human relationships. Given our goals for human betterment, do these vocabularies facilitate or obstruct? And, most important for our purposes, what kinds of social patterns does the existing vocabulary of psychological deficit facilitate (or prevent)? How do the terms of the mental health professions—terms such as "neurosis," "cognitive dysfunction," "depression," "post-traumatic stress disorder," "character disorder," "repression," "narcissism," and so on—function within the culture more generally? Do they lend themselves to desirable forms of human relationship, should the vocabulary be expanded, and are there more promising alternatives? There are no simple answers to such questions; neither is there widespread discussion. My purpose here is less to develop a final answer than to generate a forum for challenging dialogue.

The grounds for such discussion have been laid in several relevant arenas. In a range of highly critical volumes, Szasz (1961; 1963; 1970) has argued that concepts of mental illness are not demanded by observation. Rather, he proposes, they function much as social myths and are used (or misused, from his perspective) largely as a means of social control. Sarbin and Mancuso (1980) echo these arguments in their focus on the concept of schizophrenia as a social construction. Similarly, Ingelby (1980) has demonstrated the ways in which categories of mental illness are negotiated in order to serve the values or ideological investments of the profession.

Kovel (1980) proposes that the mental health professions are essentially forms of industry that operate largely in the service of existing economic structures. Feminist thinkers have explored the ways in which nosologies of illness, diagnosis, and treatment are biased against women and favor the continuation of the patriarchy (Brodsky and Hare-Mustin 1980; Hare-Mustin and Marecek 1988). And drawing from Foucault's (1978, 1979) analysis of knowledge-power relationships, Rose (1985) and Schacht (1985) have examined various ways in which mental testing, and the realities that it creates, serve the controlling interests of the culture. All these critics question the truth-bearing capacity of mental language and pinpoint some of the oppressive consequences of current language usage.

There is much to be said about the ways in which the language of mental deficit functions within the culture, and not all of it is critical. On the positive side, for example, the vocabulary of the mental health professions does serve to render the alien familiar, and thus less fearsome. Rather than being seen as "the work of the devil" or as "frighteningly strange," for example, nonnormative activities are given standardized labels, signifying that they are indeed natural, fully anticipated, and long familiar to the sciences. At the same time, this process of familiarization invites one to replace repugnance and fear with more humane, sympathetic reactions of the kind appropriate to the physically ill. We can be more nurturing and understanding to someone suffering from a "disease" than to someone who seems intentionally obstructive. Further, because the mental health professions are allied with science, and science is socially represented as a progressive or problem-solving activity, scientific labeling also invites a hopeful attitude toward the future. One need not be burdened with the belief that today's illnesses are forever.

For most of us, current discursive practices represent distinct improvements over many early predecessors (see Rosen 1968). Yet, optimism on such matters is hardly merited. For there is a substantial "down side" to existing intelligibilities, and as I shall hope to demonstrate, these problems are of continuously increasing magnitude. Consider, in particular, the function of mental deficit vocabularies in engendering and facilitating forms of what might be viewed as cultural enfeeblement.

Social Hierarchy

How may I fault thee? Let me count the ways: impulsive personality, malingering, reactive depression, anorexia, mania, attention deficit disorder, psychopathia, external control orientation, low self-esteem, narcissism, bulimia, neurasthenia, hypochondriasis, dependent personality, frigidity, authoritarianism, anti-social personality, exhibitionism, seasonal affective disorder, transvestism, agoraphobia . . .

Although they attempt to occupy a position of scientific neutrality, it has long been recognized that the helping professions are premised on certain assumptions about the cultural good (Hartmann 1960; Masserman 1960). Professional visions of "healthy functioning" are suffused with cultural ideals of personhood (London 1986; Margolis 1966) and associated political ideologies (Leifer 1990). In this context, then, we find that terms of mental deficit operate as evaluative devices, demarking the position of individuals along culturally implicit axes of good and bad. We may often feel a degree of sympathy for the person who complains of incapacitating depression, anxiety, or a Type A personality. However, our sympathies are often tinged with a sense of self-satisfaction, since the complaint simultaneously casts us into a position of superiority. In each case the other is marked by some kind of failure—insufficient buoyancy, levelheadedness, calm, control, and so on. While such results may seem inevitable and even desirable as a means of sustaining cultural values, it is vital to realize that the existence of the terms contributes to the proliferation of subtle but treacherous hierarchies, accompanied as they are by various practices of distancing and degradation (Goffman 1961). In this sense, the existence of a vocabulary of deficit is akin to the availability of weapons—their very presence creates the possibility of targets—and once they are pressed into action, "less than ideal" individuals are encouraged to enter "treatment programs," place themselves under psychopharmacological care, or separate themselves from society by entering institutions. The greater the number of criteria for mental well-being, the greater number of ways in which one can be rendered inferior in comparison to others. And of equal importance, the same actions can be indexed in alternative ways and with far different outcomes. Through skilled language use one might reconstruct depression as "psychic incubation," anxiety as "heightened sensitivity," and Type A freneticism as the "Protestant work ethic," a use of the language that would either reverse or erase the existing hierarchies.

Community Erosion

Differing terminologies invite differing courses of action. To view teenage criminality as a problem of "economic deprivation" has different policy implications than defining it as an outcome of "gang mentality" or a "deteriorated home life." Mental deficit terms, as they function in contemporary society, are shrouded in a medical mystique. They name diseases or afflictions, and, in terms of medical logic, disease or affliction requires professional diagnosis and treatment. Yet, as the "afflicted" enter such programs, the "problem" is removed from its normal context of operation and reconstituted within a professional sphere. In effect, the mental health professions appropriate the process of interpersonal realignment that might otherwise occur in a nonprofessional context. Relations organic to the community are thereby disrupted, communication attenuated, and patterns of interdependency destroyed. In short, there is a deterioration of community life. One may venture that processes of natural realignment are often slow, anguished, brutal, or befuddled, and that life is too short to endure the "fingers that don't fit the glove." But the result is that problems otherwise requiring the participation of communally related persons are removed from their ecological niche. Marriage partners carry out more intimate communication with their therapists than with each other, even saving significant insights for revelation in the therapeutic hour. Parents discuss their children's problems with specialists, or send problem children to treatment centers, and thereby reduce the possibility for authentic (unselfconscious) communication with their offspring or with concerned neighbors. Organizations place alcoholic executives in treatment programs and thereby reduce the kind of self-reflexive discussions that might elucidate their own possible contribution to the problem. Partners of "problem persons" are invited away into "co-dependency support groups" where they discuss the now-objectified partner with strangers. In each case, the tissues of communal interdependency are injured or atrophy.

This point is especially clear to me when I recollect my childhood experiences with Kibby, an older man who often spoke in gibberish, had no job, and sometimes hung around with us kids to play. We were often amused by him, sometimes we avoided him, and in our childish ways we even played jokes on him. My mother and I spoke about him from time to time; she said we should be nice to him but that he was odd and that I shouldn't play with him alone. She talked as well with Kibby's mother about possible dangers and about Kibby's future. Kibby's mother talked with most of the neighbors about her son. At that time we had no vocabulary of "mental illness," no frightening stereotypes from movies and television, and no professionals to name and treat the "illness." Kibby was simply odd, but we all managed to get along in the neighborhood. Today I suspect that Kibby would either be sedated in front of his television or locked in an appropriate institution, no longer a participating member of community life.

Self-Enfeeblement

Mental deficit terms also operate to essentialize the nature of the person being described. They designate a characteristic of the individual perduring across time and situation, which must be confronted if the person's actions are to be properly understood. Mental deficit terms thus inform the recipient that "the problem" is not circumscribed or limited in time and space or to a particular domain of his or her life; it is fully general. He or she carries the deficit from one situation to another, and like a birthmark or a fingerprint, as the textbooks say, the deficit will inevitably manifest itself. In effect, once people understand their actions in terms of mental deficits, they are sensitized to the problematic potential of all their activities and how they are infected or diminished. The weight of the "problem" now expands manyfold; it is as inescapable as their own shadow. At seventeen, Marcia Lovejoy, a woman now working to rehabilitate schizophrenics, was herself diagnosed as schizophrenic. Her doctors informed her at the time that because of her illness, she would never work, finish school, or be able to maintain satisfactory relationships with others. The situation, they said, was hopeless. Lovejoy compared this diagnosis with being told one has cancer. "What would it be like if nobody who got cancer got better, and they were called by their illness? If people said, 'What should we do with these cancers? Isn't it too bad. Let's send these cancers to the hospital since we can't cure them' " (Turkington 1985, p. 52). To be labeled by mental deficit terminology is thus to face a potential lifetime of self-doubt.

These outcomes—social hierarchy, communal fragmentation, and self-enfeeblement—do not exhaust the unfortunate outcomes of mental deficit language. Existentialist theorists have also been concerned with the way in which such language sustains a deterministic view of human action. To have a mental illness, by current standards, is to be driven by forces beyond one's control; it is to be a victim or a pawn. Thus, for the existentialist, people cease to experience their actions as voluntary (Bugental 1965). They feel their actions to be outside the realm of choice, inevitable and unchangeable, unless they place themselves—dependently—in professional hands. Many within the mental health professions are also concerned because the language of individual deficit draws attention away from the social context essential to the creation of such problems. It inhibits the exploration of familial, occupational, and sociostructural factors of possible significance. The person is blamed, while the system remains unexamined. These issues too must remain in focus.

Professional Growth and Mental Illness

Let us consider the problem in historical perspective, particularly the hegemonic tendencies of psychological discourse in general and mental deficit language in particular. As I have already proposed, the discourses of psychology often spring from the natural or everyday languages of the culture. In effect, they are inherited from commonplace cultural traditions. As a result, the referential or realistic quality of such languages is already consensually validated. (Processes of "thought" and "motivation" are worthy of professional attention because their presence within persons is already transparent within the cultural milieu.) Yet, once absorbed by the psychological professions, such languages undergo two major transformations.

First, they are *technologized,* that is, shorn of much of their connotative richness and relocated within a series of technical practices, including theoretical analysis, mensuration, and experimentation. A concept such as rationality is removed from its everyday context, replaced by technical terms such as "cognition" or "information processing," thrust into artificial intelligence formalizations, measured by dichotic listening devices, and submitted to experimental investigation. As the language is technologized, so it is appropriated by the profession. The language of cognition or information processing, for example, becomes the property of the profession, and the professional now lays claim to knowledge that was once in the common realm. The professional becomes the arbiter of what is rational or irrational, intelligent or ignorant, natural or unnatural. As the profession technologizes, labels, and measures people's problems, the layperson is disqualified as a knower. As a consequence, one's normal sense of self as possessing knowledge, insight, and sensitivity is undermined (Farber 1990). In effect, those most intimately acquainted with the "problem" must give way to the dispassionate and delimited voices of an alien authority.

This appropriation of the common languages, and the resulting claims to superior knowledge, are furthered by a second process, one of *self-justification.* The justification for superiority in psychological matters is primarily derived from the alliance of the psychological professions with the scientific tradition more generally, and the broader philosophic heritage through which the sciences are made intelligible. By claiming a position within the sciences (as opposed to, for example, religion or art), technological discourse can acquire the rhetorical weight of disciplines such as physics or chemistry. (How many now doubt the existence of schizophrenia?) Any gains within any sector of the sciences become promissory notes for the potentials within other "scientific" domains. Further, from early Enlightenment thought to twentieth-century empiricist foundationalism, we have been bathed in the rhetoric that science is both rational and progressive. In effect, by claiming themselves to be a science, supported as they are by technological accoutrements, the mental health professions fall heir to a compelling justificatory base.[3]

To illustrate the simultaneous results of both technologizing and self-justification, consider such common terms as "the blues," "sluggishness," "sadness," "punk feelings," and "unhappiness." There is a reasonably high degree of similarity among these terms, but in everyday life each has certain performative or pragmatic capacities not shared by the others. To have "the blues" has certain honorific overtones—one has "seen how it goes," "knows life as it's lived," "has been around." The phrase commands a certain degree of respect. Such overtones are not shared by terms such as "sadness," "punk," or "unhappy." To be "unhappy," for example, often suggests that there is a contrasting state that is more normal and natural and a possible longing or hope for its return. To feel "punk" suggests a possible physical condition—a sleepless night or too much to drink. Each term carries with it a range of implications and offers relational possibilities not fully suggested by the alternatives. In effect, the terms are owned by the populace and serve highly variegated functions in daily life. For the mental health professional, however, these terms are considered "ignorant," merely folk approximations of some essential process lying beneath. The formal term "depression" is offered as a replacement for the more vague and imprecise fumblings of the masses. Technical definitions of depression are developed, case studies described, scales constructed, experimental research conducted, therapeutic strategies instituted, and treatment centers established, all of which reconstitute depression as an object of professional knowledge. Because this technical work takes place within the "scientific region" of the culture, and because science is preeminently justified, the mental health professional becomes the arbiter of knowledge about such matters. The common citizen, now informed that his or her language is "merely colloquial" and scarcely adequate, is moved to silence, and the common language loses its pragmatic potential. As it is devalued it ceases to serve the variegated functions that emerge more organically from the challenges of everyday life.

In other words, the mental health professions approximate *agencies of unbounded transformation* of meaning. They feed from all the cultural sites in which talk about the mind is extant. As these discourses are engorged and reshaped they become the property of the profession—creating "conversational objects" about which the professions are the experts. At present there is no upward boundary to the process. Because of the pictorial orientation of the scientific perspective, there is no means by which one can easily challenge the realities created from within this perspective. In effect, the system operates internally toward full absorption of the common language, and it contains no inherent means of questioning its own premises.

To amplify the argument, let us consider the growth of the mental professions over the past century, a development that can be considered little short of phenomenal. To illustrate, the American Psychiatric Association was founded in 1844 by 13 physicians and hospital administrators. By the end of the century it had grown to 377 members. Today there are over 36,000 members, some ninety-five times the number at the turn of the century. As demonstrated in Figure 6.1, the major expansion has taken place within the last forty years. In every decade since 1940, the membership has grown from between 138 percent to 188 percent. There is no indication of an asymptote.[4]

The increase in the number of practicing psychologists in the United States is similarly dramatic. When the American Psychological Association was founded in 1892 there were only 31 members. By 1906, the number

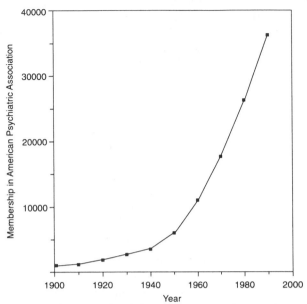

Figure 6.1   The Growth of the American Psychiatric Association

had jumped to 181. Yet, within the thirty-six years that followed, the membership expanded almost a hundredfold to over 3,000. In the following twenty-two years (between 1942 and 1966) the figure increased again almost twenty times over to a total of over 63,000. Of course, not all members of the Association are directly engaged in mental health pursuits, but even those who are not often lend rhetorical force to these professions. Thus, as experimentalists, intelligence testers, organizational consultants, and the like act in ways that reify mental discourse, they add weight to the language of the practitioner. Consider then the number of psychological personnel providing care services per million citizens between 1960 and 1983. Within the first decade, the number of psychological health providers essentially doubled and then trebled between 1972 and 1983. Again, there is no indication of a leveling of numbers.

How are we to explain this expansion in the mental health professions? Let us consider the explanations favored by the two orientations toward mental discourse I outlined above. For the mental realist, using the language referentially, the outlook is an optimistic one. The increment in the number of professionals represents a greater responsivity to cultural needs; existing problems are receiving greater attention. As the professions mature, it may be ventured, there is also an incremental sharpening in our capacity to distinguish among the existing array of psychological states and conditions.

We know increasingly more about psychological distress, and we have sharpened diagnostic distinctions so that we can recognize problems to which we were once insensitive.

As we have also seen, however, the mental realist position is deeply flawed. Mental deficit terminology is not tied referentially to discriminant states of the psyche. There is little to support the view that the professions have burgeoned in response to the deficient state of people's psyche or that over time they have become increasingly sensitive to the failings of the mind. Let us consider, then, a pragmatic account of the trajectory. From this perspective, we find that mental deficit discourse operates to generate and sustain particular ways of life and does so first with respect to the mental health profession. The professions themselves are highly dependent on discursive practices—the sharing of an ontology, a range of values, forms of rational justification, and so on. Professional commitments depend largely on a set of shared understandings about the world and how one is to proceed (see Chapter 3). Thus, the desire of mental health professionals to increase their ranks is a response not to the world as it is, but to a world that is constructed. At the same time, the professions could scarcely succeed in their efforts to "help society" without a public congenial to their perspectives. Sufficient segments of the culture—including prospective clients, lawmakers, the medical profession, and insurance companies—must come to share in the ontology of mental illness and the belief that the professions can and should provide cures. From the pragmatic perspective there is no *pattern of illness* to which the professions are responding; rather, the conception of illness functions in ways that link the professional and the culture in an array of mutually supportive activities.

The Cycle of Progressive Infirmity

As we have seen, mental health professionals exist in a symbiotic relationship with the culture, drawing sustenance from cultural beliefs, altering these beliefs in systematic ways, disseminating these views back to the culture, and relying on their incorporation into the culture for continued sustenance. Yet the effects of this symbiosis seem increasingly substantial. In particular, a cyclical process seems to be operating that, once activated, expands the domain of deficit to an ever-increasing degree. In effect, the process underlying the expansion of the professions is a systematic one that feeds upon itself to engender an exponentially increasing infirmity: hierarchies of discrimination, denaturalized patterns of interdependence, and an expanding arena of self-deprecation. The historical process may be viewed as one of "progressive infirmity."

In exploring this cycle more fully, for analytic purposes it is useful to distinguish among four separate phases. In actual practice, the events in each of these phases may be confounded, the temporal ordering is seldom smooth, and there are exceptions at every turn. For present purposes, the cycle of progressive infirmity may be outlined as follows:

PHASE 1:   DEFICIT TRANSLATION

We begin at the juncture at which the culture accepts both the possibility of "mental illness" and a profession responsible for its diagnosis and cure, a condition increasingly prevalent since the mid-nineteenth century (Peeters in press). Under these conditions the professional confronts clients whose lives are managed in terms of a common or everyday discourse. When life management seems impossible in terms of everyday understandings, the client seeks professional help or, in effect, more "advanced," "objective," or "discerning" forms of understanding. In this context it is incumbent upon the professional first to furnish an alternative discourse (theoretical framework or nosology) for understanding the problem, and then to translate the problem as presented in everyday language into the alternative and uncommon language of the profession. This means that problems understood in the profane or marketplace language of the culture must be translated into the sacred or professional language of mental deficit. A person whose habits of cleanliness are excessive by common standards may be labeled "obsessive compulsive," one who remains in bed for the whole morning becomes "depressive," one who feels he is not liked is redefined as "paranoid," and so on (see Chapter 10). The client may willingly contribute to these reformulations, for they assure him not only that the professional is doing a proper job but that the problem is well recognized and understood within the profession. The final outcome—translation into a professional or mental deficit vocabulary—is inevitable from the outset.

PHASE 2:   CULTURAL DISSEMINATION

The mental health professions, following a nineteenth-century mode of scientific analysis, have placed great importance on establishing inclusive categories for all that exists within a given domain (animal or plant species, tables of chemical elements, and so on). When this penchant for systematic categorization is applied to the domain of mental illness, we find that transforming all problematic activity into a systematic array of mental illnesses not only grants individual illness an ontological status, it removes meanings from their culture and historical contexts. And because there are *illnesses* at stake, there are also public threats to be confronted. Now it becomes a professional responsibility to alert the public to unrecognized or unrealized instances. People must learn to recognize the signals of mental disease so that they might seek early treatment, and they should be informed of possible causes and likely cures.

To some extent, the strong motive to classify and inform may be traced to the mental hygiene movement early in this century. For millions of people, Clifford Beers's famous volume, *A Mind That Found Itself* (which went through thirteen editions within twenty years of its publication in 1908), first served to substantiate mental illness as a phenomenon, to bring the appalling conditions of mental hospitals into the public eye, and by implication, to warn the general public of the existing threat of such illness. Coincident with its publication, the National Committee for Mental Hygiene was founded and by 1917 began publishing its national quarterly, *Mental Hygiene*. This magazine, along with an array of pamphlets on such topics as "childhood, the golden period for mental hygiene," "nervousness, its cause and prevention," "the movement for a mental hygiene of industry," and "the responsibility of the universities in promoting mental hygiene," attempted to bring mental health issues into the public eye and to encourage major institutions (schools, industries, communities) to develop preventative programs. In the same way that the signs of breast cancer, diabetes, or venereal disease should become common knowledge within the culture, it was (and is) argued, citizens should be helped to recognize early symptoms of stress, alcoholism, depression, and the like.

Although the mental hygiene movement has lost its import, its logic has been absorbed by the culture. Today most large-scale institutions do provide services for the mentally disturbed, whether in terms of health services, guidance counselors, clinical social workers, or insurance coverage for therapy. University curricula feature courses on adjustment and abnormality, national magazines and newspapers disseminate news of mental disorders (such as depression and its cure through chemistry), and mental problems are popular fare in television dramas and soap operas. At the same time, the general public has sufficiently absorbed the mental hygienist mentality that books on psychological self-help are now mainstays in the publishing industry. The result is a continuous insinuation of professional language into the sphere of daily relationships.[5]

So sensitized is the culture to possible deficits that in certain quarters professionals are no longer required for the process of "enlightenment." Grass-roots movements dedicated to increasing community awareness of mental deficit, to identifying ways in which the unsuspecting contribute to such deficit, and to developing programs for alleviating the problems have sprung up in dramatically expanding numbers. I recently scanned the pages of a community newspaper from Santa Fe, New Mexico, and found announcements for some fourteen meetings of groups dedicated to overcoming various psychological deficits. One could get help not only for obvious problems with alcohol and other drugs, but for overeating, sexual addiction, being codependent with sex addicts, attitudinal problems, love addiction, gay sexual compulsiveness, and proneness to debt. The same newspaper listed only three meetings for business professionals (such as Rotary or Kiwanis). There are now over one hundred forms of twelve-step, self-help organizations treating people suffering from everything from emotionality to gambling.

PHASE 3:   THE CULTURAL CONSTRUCTION OF ILLNESS

As intelligibilities of deficit are disseminated to the culture, they become absorbed into the common language. They become part of "what everybody knows" about human behavior. In this sense, terms such as "neurosis," "stress," "alcoholism," and "depression" are no longer "professional property." They have been "given away" or returned by the profession to the public. Terms such as "split personality," "identity crisis," "PMS" (premenstrual syndrome), and "midlife crisis" also enjoy a high degree of popularity. And as such terms make their way into the cultural vernacular, they become available for the construction of everyday reality. Shirley is not simply "too fat," she has "obese eating habits"; Fred doesn't simply "hate gays," he is "homophobic"; and so on. As deficit terms increasingly infiltrate everyday intelligibilities, that world becomes increasingly framed by a sense of deficit. Events that once passed unnoticed become candidates for interpretation; actions once viewed as "good and proper" are reconceptualized as problematic. When terms such as "stress" and "occupational burnout" enter the commonsense vernacular, they become lenses through which any working professional can reexamine his or her life and find it wanting. What was valued as "active ambition" can now be reconstructed as "workaholism," the "smart dresser" can be redefined as "narcissistic," and the "autonomous and self-directed man" becomes "defended against his emotions." Furnish the population with the hammers of mental deficit, and the social world is full of nails.

Nor is it simply deficit labeling that is at stake here. For as forms of "illness" are depicted by the media, educational programs, public talks, and the like, their symptoms come to serve as cultural models. In effect, the culture learns *how to be* mentally ill. Consider the spread of "anorexia" and "bulimia," once "eating disorders" became publicly recognized. Similarly, depression has become such a cultural commonplace that it is virtually an invited reaction to failure, frustration, or disappointment. Indeed, if someone were to respond to such situations with equanimity or joy as opposed to depression, he might be viewed with suspicion. In this vein, Szasz (1961) has argued that hysteria, schizophrenia, and other mental disorders represent the "impersonation" of the sick-person stereotype by those confronting the insoluble problems of normal living. Mental illness, in this sense, is a form of deviant role-playing, requiring a form of cultural know-how to break the rules. Scheff (1966) has made a similar case that many disorders serve as forms of social defiance. As Scheff proposes, other people's reactions to rule-breaking behavior are of enormous importance in determining whether it is finally labeled as a "mental disease."

As people's actions are increasingly defined and shaped in terms of the language of mental deficit, the demand for mental health services also increases. Counseling, weekend self-enrichment programs, and regimens of personality refurbishment represent a first line of dependence; all allow people to escape the uneasy sense that they are "not all they should be." Others may seek organized support groups for their "incest victimization," "codependency," or "obsession with gambling." And, of course, many enter organized programs of therapy or are institutionalized. As a result, the prevalence of "mental illness" and the associated expenditures for mental health have been propelled upward. For example, in the twenty-year period between 1957 and 1977 the percentage of the U.S. population using professional mental health services increased from 14 percent to *over a quarter of the population* (Kulka, Veroff, and Douvan 1979; italics mine). When the Chrysler Corporation insured its employees for mental health costs, the annual use of such services rose more than six times in four years ("Califano Speaks," 1984). Although mental health expenditures were minuscule during the first quarter of the century, by 1980 mental illness was the third most expensive category of health disorder in the United States, accounting for more than $20 billion annually (Mechanic 1980). By 1983, the costs for mental illness, exclusive of alcoholism and drug abuse, were estimated to be almost $73 billion (Harwood, Napolitano, and Kristiansen 1983). By 1981, 23 percent of all hospital days in the United States were accounted for by mental disorders (Kiesler and Sibulkin 1987).[6]

PHASE 4:   VOCABULARY EXPANSION

The stage is now set for the final revolution in the cycle of progressive infirmity: a further expansion of the vocabulary of deficit. As people increasingly construct their problems in the professional language and seek help, and as professional ranks expand in response to public demands, more individuals are available to convert everyday language into a professional language of deficit. There is no necessary requirement that such translating be conducted in terms of the existing categories of illness, and, indeed, there are distinct pressures on the professional to expand the vocabulary. These pressures are generated in part from within the profession. To explore a new disorder within the mental health sciences is not unlike discovering a new star in astronomy: considerable honor may accrue to the explorer. In this sense "post-traumatic stress disorder," "identity crisis," and "midlife crisis," for example, are significant products of the "grand narrative" of scientific progress (Lyotard 1984), that is, self-proclaimed "discoveries" of the science of mental health. At the same time, new forms of disorder can be highly profitable for the practitioner, often garnering book royalties, workshop fees, corporate contracts, and/or a wealthier set of clients. In this respect such terms as "codependency," "stress," and "occupational burnout" have come to approximate small growth industries.

On a more subtle level, the client population itself exerts pressure toward the expansion of the professional vocabulary. As the culture absorbs the emerging argot of the profession, the role of the professional is both strengthened and threatened. If the client has already "identified the problem" in the professional language and is sophisticated about therapeutic procedures (as is true in many cases), then the status of the professional is placed in jeopardy. Sacred language has become profane. (The worst case scenario might be when people learn to diagnose and treat themselves within their family and friendship circles, thus rendering the professional redundant.) In this way the professional is under constant pressure to "advance" understanding, to spawn "more sophisticated" terminology, and to generate new insights and new forms of therapy.[7] It is not that a shift in emphasis from classic psychoanalysis to neo-analysis to object relations, for example, is required by an increasingly sensitive understanding of mental dynamics. Indeed, each wave sets the stage for its own recession and replacement; as therapeutic vocabularies become common sense the therapist is propelled into new modes of departure. The ever-shifting sea of therapeutic fads and fashions is no mere defect in the profession. Rapid change is virtually demanded by a public whose discourse is increasingly "psychologized."

When we examine the expansion of deficit terminologies, we find a trajectory that is suspiciously similar to those we encountered in the case of mental health professionals and mental health expenditures. The concept of neurosis did not originate until the mid-eighteenth century. In 1769 William Cullen, a Scottish physician, elucidated four major classes of *morbi nervini:* the *Comota* (reduced voluntary movements, along with drowsiness or loss of consciousness), the *Adynamiae* (diminished involuntary movements), *Spasmi* (abnormal movement of muscles), and *Vesaniae* (altered judgment without coma).[8] Yet, even in the first official attempt in the United States to tabulate mental disorders in 1840, categorization was crude. For some purposes it proved satisfactory, indeed, to use only a single category to separate the ill—including both the idiotic and insane—from the normal (Spitzer and Williams 1985). In Germany both Kahlbaum and Kraepelin developed more extensive systems for classifying mental disease, but these were closely tied to a conception of organic origins.

With the emergence of the psychiatric profession during the early decades of the century, matters changed considerably. In particular, an attempt was made to distinguish between disturbances with a clear organic base, such as syphilis, and those with psychogenic origins. Thus, with the publication in 1929 of Israel Wechsler's *The Neuroses,* a group of approximately a dozen psychological disorders were identified. By the time Rosanoff's *Manual of Psychiatry and Mental Hygiene* was published in 1938, some forty psychogenic disturbances were recognized. Many of the categories remain familiar (hysteria, dementia praecox, paranoia). What is more interesting from the constructionist perspective, however, is that many of these terms have since dropped from common usage (paresthetic hysteria, autonomic hysteria), and some now seem quaint or obviously prejudicial (moral deficiency, vagabondage, misanthropy, masturbation). In 1952, with the American Psychiatric Association's publication of the first *Diagnostic and Statistical Manual of Mental Disorders,* it became possible to identify some fifty to sixty different psychogenic disturbances. By 1987, only twenty years later, the manual had gone through three revisions. With the publication of DSM-IIIR, the line between organic and psychogenic disturbances had become obscured. However, using the standards of the earlier decades, in the thirty-five-year period since the publication of the first manual the number of recognized illnesses *more than tripled* (hovering between 180 and 200 depending on one's choice of definitional boundaries). At the present time, one may be classified as mentally ill by virtue of cocaine intoxication, caffeine intoxication, the use of hallucinogens, voyeurism, transvestism, sexual aversion, the inhibition of orgasm, gambling, academic problems, antisocial behavior, bereavement, and noncompliance with medical treatment. Numerous additions to the standardized nomenclature continue to appear in professional writings for the public—for example, seasonal affective disorder, stress, burnout, erotomania, the harlequin complex, and so on—and again, we find no indication of an upper limit.

Progressive Infirmity: No Exit?

As I am proposing, when the culture is furnished with a professionally rationalized language of mental deficit and people are increasingly understood according to this language, the population of "patients" expands. This population, in turn, forces the profession to extend its vocabulary, and thus the array of mental deficit terms available for cultural use. In this way more problems are constructed within the culture, further help is sought, and the deficit discourse again inflates. One can scarcely view this cycle as smooth and undisrupted. Some schools of therapy remain committed to a single vocabulary, others have little interest in disseminating their language, and some professionals attempt to speak with clients only in the common language of the culture. In addition, many popular concepts within both the culture and the profession lose currency over time (see for example, Hutschemaekers 1990). We are speaking here of a general historical drift—but one without an obvious terminus. I recently received an announcement for a conference on the latest theory and research on addiction, which was called the "number one health and social problem facing our country today." Among the addictions to be discussed were exercise, religion, eating, work, and sex. If all these activities, when pursued with intensity or gusto, are defined as diseases that require cures, it would seem that little can withstand enfeebling translation.

I am in no way attempting to allocate blame for this trajectory—for the most part it is a necessary byproduct of earnest and humane attempts to enhance the quality of people's lives. With certain variations in the logic of the cycle, it is not unlike the trajectories spawned by both the medical and legal professions—toward increased medical needs and expenditures in the first instance and burgeoning litigation in the other. To the extent that the mental health professions are concerned with the quality of cultural life, however, a discussion of progressive infirmity should be initiated. Are there important limitations to the above arguments; are there signs of a leveling effect; are there ways of reducing the proliferation of enfeebling discourse? All are questions of broad significance.

It is to the question of abatement that I wish finally to direct attention. There are many extant critiques of the mental health professions: of the scientific shakiness of its claims, the implicit sexism of its categories, the dehumanizing effect of treatment, the cultural myopia of its prevailing theories, and so on. Among the critics, there are many who simply wish to see the mental health establishment abandoned. In my view, however, this alternative is unrealistic because of the entrenchment of existing institutions, nor is it desirable, since the professions provide better alternatives to earlier, more barbaric reactions to cultural deviance. Short of abandonment, there are many who wish to see the basic biases corrected—to remove prejudices, misclaims, and the resulting inhumanity. But the impulse to correct existing practices remains lodged, for the most part, in the realist view of mental events and the belief that there can be objectively correct accounts of the interior world (we have already considered arguments against this view). Still others wish to *de*stigmatize mental illness, to redraw the nosological categories in ways that are less punitive and dehumanizing. Although this is an attractive alternative in many ways, it is not without its problems. The logic of destigmatization depends on the recognition that there are "badly labeled persons." Without such recognition, it makes little sense to opt for destigmatizing, yet recognition reinstates the negative identification and again draws attention to a problematic group. Individuals must continue to be viewed as ill in order for destigmatization to be intelligible.

I have no deeply compelling palliative at hand for terminating this cycle. To be sure, the most important step is to break the link between deficit language and the institutionalization of medical insurance payments. As long as insurance coverage is dependent on standardized diagnostics modeled on the medical system, deficit labeling will continue to expand. Antidiagnostic mobilization is of highest priority. However, more scholarly inquiry is also warranted, and the same logic that undergirds the present analysis may suggest possible openings for change. As I have proposed, progressive infirmity is favored by the reifying of mental language. The cycle begins when we believe that the words for mental deficit stand in a pictorial relationship to processes or mechanisms in the head. When we believe that people actually possess mental processes such as depression or obsession, for example, we can comfortably characterize them as "ill" and place them in treatment.[9] At the outset, then, some form of generalized reeducation in the functions of language is called for.

Of course, it is cavalier to suppose that either formal or informal educational processes could significantly alter the picture theory of language and the companionate assumption of mind-body dualism, both so central to the Western tradition. More promising is the development of alternative vocabularies within the mental health profession, vocabularies that do not trace problematic behavior to psychological sources within single individuals, and ultimately operate to erase the concept of "problem behavior" itself. At present our cultural history furnishes us with innumerable terms for characterizing single persons. When we confront unacceptable actions, we rapidly and securely fall back on this vocabulary. We can scarcely avoid characterizing these actions as outward signs of inner states, such as happiness, fear, anxiety, and so on; the individualized form of self-accounting is ready at hand. At the same time, there are alternatives to individualizing language. As I suggested in the preceding chapter, one significant challenge originates in relational intelligibilities, modes of construction that place individual acts within more extended units of interdependence. With sufficient dialogue—both within and outside the professions—we should be able to develop a vocabulary of relatedness with the rhetorical power to rival that of individualized language. I shall expand on these possibilities in later chapters (see especially in Chapters 8 to 12).

With the development of relational intelligibilities may ultimately come the demise of the category of "dysfunctional behavior" itself.[10] As we begin to see that human actions are embedded within larger units, are parts of wholes, these actions will cease to be "events in themselves." There are no dysfunctional behaviors independent of arrangements of social interdependency. At the same time, we must be careful to avoid creating a new form of deficit discourse derived from a conception of "problematic" or "dysfunctional relationships." We need not require a diagnostics of relationship, which would simply shift blame from individual to group. Family therapy concepts such as the "dysfunctional family" or the "perverse triangle" set the stage for a new cycle of impairment, now directed toward families instead of individuals. From a relational standpoint, the language of "problems," of "evaluation" and "blame," is also a product of social interchange. This language functions to coordinate the activities of individuals around ends they hold valuable. To label actions as "dysfunctional" is thus itself an outcome of relational processes. In this way we see that there are no intrinsic or essential "goods" or goals to which individuals or groups should necessarily strive. There are only goods and goals (and concomitant failures) within particular systems of understanding. The professional need not be concerned, then, with "improvement" as a generalized or real-world challenge. (What we call depression, for example, is not inherently problematic and from another standpoint may serve to maintain the well-being of a group or a family.) As I shall elaborate further in later chapters, what I am advocating is that we shift our attention to the larger system of interdependencies in which evaluations are generated, and reconsider the place of the therapist in this network. For if the spiral of deficit is itself a result of relationships between the profession and the culture, then its curtailment may properly issue from the same matrix.

Subjectivity is an enchanted glass, full of superstition and imposture.
—FRANCIS BACON, *Advancement of Learning*, Book II

7 Objectivity as Rhetorical Achievement

In large degree scientific reports are distinguished from commonplace accounts by virtue of their objectivity: the scientific text is privileged because, unlike the common argot of the culture, it is not a product of subjective and self-serving biases. But if the scientist is truly objective, as is commonly claimed, how is this objectivity achieved? How can others acquire this skill? As I shall demonstrate, objectivity inheres neither in the scientist's particular mental functioning nor in the scientist's capacity to portray nature accurately; it is primarily a linguistic achievement that draws on the machine metaphor of human functioning. By elaborating on these rhetorical characteristics, I hope to challenge the status of such writing and open discussion on alternatives.

The concept of objectivity has enormous rhetorical power in contemporary affairs. It serves as the keystone in justifying and planning scientific research, educational curricula, economic policies, military budgets, and international programs. When decisions seem to lack objectivity, they are open to a range of unhappy epithets: illusory, subjective, unrealistic. As many believe, the achievement of objectivity is closely linked to the capacity for survival: if one's decisions are not grounded in objective appraisal, they may be ill-adapted to the world's contingencies. In many quarters the demand for objectivity is little short of a moral imperative; to live a life of delusion or false consciousness is to fall short of achieving full humanity. But what is it to achieve objectivity in action? What is it about certain accounts or decisions that grants them the authority of objectivity, while others are held to be deluded or deceived? As I shall propose, the achievement of objectivity is only tangentially related to survival and ill-suited to moral arbitration. Objectivity is primarily a rhetorical achievement, and in relying on this rhetoric we may be threatening both survival and morality.

Objectivity and the Mechanical Self

The concept of objectivity has a long and varied history (see Daston 1992), and the traces of myriad conversations and colloquies now furnish both its meaning and its significance. Its power to drive decisions across many domains of contemporary culture is derivative, lodged within a forestructure of cultural understandings without which its use would be little more than exclamation. To understand objectivity as an achievement, then, we must inspect the cultural presumptions that sustain its credibility. My central purpose in examining these suppositions is to ask whether they are adequate for directing or guiding the forms of action to which objectivity might be attributed: given a set of beliefs about the nature of objectivity, can it be achieved, and if not, how are we to understand its function in science and everyday life?

A full treatment of existing conceptions of objectivity is far beyond the scope of this chapter. Rather, I wish to explore only one significant prefiguration, namely, the particular image of the human being that objectivity commonly presupposes. What image of the self is necessary if we are to make sense of the concept of objectivity in everyday affairs? Although there are numerous ways of characterizing this particular vision of the self, each emphasizing particular features and implications, I have chosen the metaphor of the machine because I wish to draw on the continuing traces of the Enlightenment notion of the cosmos as "one great machine," on the modernist emphasis on the machinelike character of the human being, and on the mechanistic forms of explanation so central to contemporary psychology.[1] At the same time, this choice also allows for a convenient extension of our earlier epistemological discussion (see especially Chapters 1 and 5).

The relationship between the concept of objectivity and the image of the self is revealed in much of our ordinary language. First, consider the way objectivity is defined by its oppositional polarities. By common parlance, to be objective is to be *other* than *deluded, self-deceived, biased, lost in imagination,* or *subjective.* We learn more about the concept by considering its near synonyms: *realistic, accurate, correct.* From this array, it is clear that objectivity is first and foremost a condition of individual human functioning. We do not generally demand that dogs and cats be objective, but we do hold individual persons responsible for being deluded, biased, or lost in imagination. Further, to be objective is to be in possession of a particular psychological state. "Delusion," "self-deception," and "imagination" are states of the individual mind. Language is also implicated as a major device by which objectivity can be assessed. Words, we generally hold, are indicators of an individual's mental condition. The words give expression to one's perceptions ("the way I see the world"), emotions ("the way I feel"), and numerous other states and conditions (such as intentions, ideas, motives). Thus, it is through the individual's words that we can detect whether he or she is "seeing things clearly and accurately" or is being "unrealistic."

What we find, then, is that the appeal to objectivity is closely wedded to a dualistic view of human functioning—one in which the individual's psychological states are contrasted with an external, material world. Most important, an objective mind is one that systematically reflects the character of the external world. It is a mind that is accurately attuned to the nuances and variations in external conditions. One who is objective "sees things for what they are," "is in touch with reality," or "takes a good look at things." The image of the individual as a machine is now apposite, because reinstantiated here is the Enlightenment view of the cosmos as one grand array of mechanistic relations between causes and the resulting effects. From this perspective, the individual achieves objectivity *when each and every alteration in the external or material world produces an equivalent alteration in the individual's state of mind.* Therefore, when no alterations occur within the antecedent conditions of the external world, there should be no consequent effects within the mental sphere. And because words can be accurate reflections of mental states, the machine metaphor extends to the domain of objective reporting. When one speaks objectively, all variations in the mental world (as a reflecting device for the material world) are registered in the linguistic domain, and failures in variation at the mental level should yield no variance in language.

Failure to achieve the status of an efficient and effective input-output machine is indexed by various terms of derision: deluded, self-deceived, and the like. Yet, by linguistic extension, we find that such terms do not simply indicate an absence or a state of nonreflection. They also suggest a variety of powers or processes that interfere with the adaptive operation of the mechanical self. Thus we say, "he's too self-absorbed," "value invested," "emotional," "zealous," "committed," or "conflicted," to be objective. In effect, we presume the existence of a variety of additional mental processes suffused with energy, which operate to disrupt the otherwise adaptive functioning of the self. Strong motives, values, and emotions can all serve in this capacity. And because environmental inputs can trigger these processes (as in "she upset him," "he was overwhelmed by the loss of his brother," or "he is caught up in religious fervor"), objective mental processing depends on maintaining relative independence from the environment. That is, to achieve objectivity one must ideally be uncontaminated by relationships, investments, or other projects in the external world. Other than maintaining an open window to material reality, it is maximally adaptive to remain insulated and self-contained.

The Viability of the Objective Self

Given this mechanical conception of the self, how is one to achieve objectivity? The existing belief system demands a particular set of mental activities, but in what manner are they to be carried out? How is the individual to attune the mind to the exigencies of the material world, suppress interfering effects, and report the results with accuracy? At this point the aspirant to objectivity confronts an array of problems as profound as they are intractable. For the most part, these problems have been well articulated in various sectors of philosophy and psychology over the last century.[2] Some of this work is also represented in earlier critiques of knowledge as an individual possession (Chapter 1), the presumption of mental categories (Chapter 5), and the pictorial theory of mental language (Chapter 6). As these discussions suggest, if objectivity were a mental process within the individual, there are few ways by which it could be achieved. However, to add further weight to these arguments, let us consider three additional enigmas confronting the individual attempting to achieve objectivity.

THE SEPARATION OF THE MATERIAL AND THE MENTAL

At the outset, one confronts the task of differentiating between the *object* of experience and the *experiencing* of the object. The differentiation is a critical one, for if one cannot determine that there is an object that differs or is distinguished from one's mental states, then one cannot transcend the condition of subjectivity. Yet, according to the usual standards, experience is altogether a mental condition, and there are no criteria for isolating certain aspects of this condition and attributing them to yet another world—that of the material realm. How can one determine, then, whether one's mental conditions correspond to an external world when all that is available is an internal world? How can we conclude that there is indeed a material world as distinct from a mental world? On what grounds could we draw such a conclusion? Not from our experience, because experience is itself mental. Or, as philosophers have put the case in its extreme form, if one begins with the presumption that we live only within our mental states, there is no compelling reason to posit a world outside these states.

THE OBSERVATION OF MENTAL STATES

The problem of distinguishing between subject and object is further intensified when one confronts the problem of recognizing, categorizing, or reporting on one's experiences (see also Chapter 3). How is it that one scans experience to draw conclusions about what is the case? How, in effect, can one *experience one's experience,* that is, turn back on the mental representation and recognize that it is, indeed, a representation of a bear, for example, and not a tiger? By what means does experience split itself in this way, holding the object of experience in one register and experiencing this experience in a second one? If one's mind operates as a mirror, then how is the mirror to ascertain its own reflection?[3]

THE MONITORING OF THE MIND

Should some way be discovered for solving these initial problems, there is yet a third impasse to be confronted: determining the accuracy of one's internal identifications. If I conclude that indeed I am experiencing a bear standing before me, how can I know whether I have identified the experience accurately? How can I be sure that I am not existing in a state of false consciousness, that what I am categorizing as a bear is not a tiger? If objectivity is the outcome of individual mental functioning, surely I must be able to distinguish true from false consciousness. Otherwise I would never know that I know. But how is this feat to be achieved? At this point one must presume yet another lamination of the psyche, one that is split apart from, and ascertains the accuracy of, the categorization or recognition process. How is one to separate consciousness yet again? Or if the process takes place at an unconscious level, how is one to trust its messages to the conscious mind? And if this mental feat can somehow be accomplished, on what grounds is one to trust the monitoring process? Could it not also be faulty—processing information, for example, in ways that are personally comforting? Is yet another monitor not essential at this point, determining that one's sense of knowing is truly objective? And if so, are not additional monitors required in an infinite regress of self-assessment?

As these problems suggest, if objectivity were a private mental condition—as common language suggests—there is no evident means by which it could be achieved. People's attempt to separate world from mental representation, to observe their own mental conditions, and to render accurate reports on these internal states are all enigmas without solutions. They simply leave the individual floundering in isolation with no clear procedure for accomplishing the goal of objectivity. And should one consult others for instruction, how should they proceed? They have no access to an individual's mental condition; they are in no way positioned to say, "Your mental condition does (or does not) match reality." In effect, others cannot teach one to distinguish objective from subjective states of mind.

Although the scientific community has generally avoided these challenges, hoping that philosophers would eventually furnish the necessary solutions, they have attempted to build in safeguards to objectivity, and these attempts are significant. While it is generally acceded that objectivity within the single observer may be faulty, by expanding the number of observers, it is reasoned, one may eliminate the biases of a single individual. Or, using the mechanistic metaphor, while the mechanical apparatus of the single individual may be defective, it is unlikely that a population of machines will be so. Of course, this redoubt is more compelling on the practical level than in principle. For, if in principle there is no compelling reason to believe that single individuals can monitor the accuracy of their mental states, then there is little reason to conclude that a population of individuals can correct the biases of the individual. And, in a worst case scenario, should the single individual be endowed with special gifts of sensitivity, the "communal correction" would even operate to subvert objectivity. Throughout the sciences and other domains laying claim to objective reports, there is a pervasive attempt to establish conditions of *public replicability*. Research studies are reported so that others can repeat them; details are reported that enable others to observe the same events or to collect corroborating evidence. Objectivity is thus derived from a multiplication of subjectivities.

This institutionalization of objectivity is of no small moment, for as the monitoring of objectivity becomes a matter of broad social policy, we discover that indeed, some modes of conduct do meet communal criteria for objectivity in action. Although individuals cannot accomplish the task privately, they can behave in ways that will yield imputations of objectivity from a broad community. It is this social achievement that now demands scrutiny.

The Rhetorical Achievement of Objectivity

Within communities of scientists, news writers, policy-makers, and the like, individual objectivity is judged according to public standards. Following the mechanical view of human functioning, these judgments are often based on the individual's words, which are a putative expression of mental process. Objectivity is most typically achieved, then, in one's written and spoken communications to others. To be objective is to "render an accurate or correct representation"; it is a *textual* achievement. If this is so, how is one to speak or write in an objective way? How can one learn to be objective in using language? Earlier in this century logical empiricist philosophers, eager to ground the sciences on rational foundations, attempted to furnish just such guidelines. As generally argued, an *objective* language should be linked to observables;[4] insofar as is possible, terms at the level of theoretical description should be defined with reference to publicly observable entities or processes. In this way, the compendium of terms within an objective science should be an inventory of the world. Or, to put it more metaphorically, an objective description should furnish a map or a picture of the world as it is. Yet, as we have seen, the correspondence view of language is deeply flawed (see Chapter 2). Just as objectivity cannot be an achievement of the individual mind, neither can it be a matter of accurate description.

If objectivity is the achievement of neither reflective mentation nor photographic language, how then is the aspirant to objectivity to proceed? At this juncture it is instructive to consider Raymond Queneau's clever little volume *Exercises in Style,* which exposes the reader to 195 different descriptions of the same incident. The reader's impressions of the incident are vitally altered as Queneau moves through various language styles emphasizing first metaphor, then narrative, notation, comedy, verse, and so on. Consider, for example, the following account:

> In the centre of the day, tossed among the shoals of traveling sardines in a coleopter with a big white carapace, a chicken with a long, featherless neck suddenly harangued one, a peace-abiding one, of their number, and its parlance, moist with protest, was unfolded upon the airs. Then, attracted by a void, the fledgling precipitated itself thereunto.
>
> In a bleak, urban desert, I saw it again that self-same day, drinking the cup of humiliation offered by a lowly button.

Most readers, I suspect, do not feel that this account is adequately objective. It does not tell us what was *really* going on. Consider an alternative:

> In the S bus, in the rush hour. A chap of about 26, felt hat with a cord instead of a ribbon, neck too long, as if someone's been having a tug-of-war with it. People getting off. The chap in question gets annoyed with one of the men standing next to him. He accuses him of jostling him every time anyone goes past. A sniveling tone which is meant to be aggressive. When he sees a vacant seat he throws himself on to it.
>
> Two hours later, I meet him in the Cour de Rome, in front of the gare Saint-Lazare. He's with a friend who's saying: "You ought to get an extra button put on your overcoat." He shows him where (at the lapels) and why.

Now we somehow feel relieved—the veil of obscurity has been lifted and we are beginning to "know" what actually happened. What is it about the second account that provides this enhanced "sense of objectivity"? Is it simply the less metaphoric or more literal use of language that is at stake? Consider a third account which, by common standards, is even more precisely literal:

> In a bus of the S-line, 10 meters long, 3 wide, 6 high, at 3 km. 600 m. from its starting point, loaded with 48 people, at 12:17 P.M., a person of the mas-

culine sex aged 27 years 3 months and 8 days, 1 m. 72 cm. tall and weighing 65 kg. and wearing a hat 35 cm. in height round the crown of which was a ribbon 60 cm. long, interpellated a man aged 48 years 4 months and 3 days, 1 m. 68 cm. tall and weighing 77 kg., by means of 14 words whose enunciation lasted 5 seconds and which alluded to some involuntary displacements of from 15 to 20 mm. Then he went and sat down about 1 m. 10 cm. away.

57 minutes later he was 10 meters away from the suburban entrance to the gare Saint-Lazare and was walking up and down over a distance of 30 m. with a friend aged 28, 1 m. 70 cm. tall and weighing 71 kg. who advised him in 15 words to move by 5 cm. in the direction of the zenith a button which was 3 cm. in diameter.

This account is replete with precise, no-nonsense, literal terminology (by common standards), but somehow the event lapses once again into obscurity. It is a flawed form of objective writing.

The major challenge for the analyst, then, is to identify the particular forms of literary figuration that furnish accounts with the sense of objectivity—and thus give them rhetorical force in science and everyday affairs. It is not my intent to offer a full treatment of these techniques. An enormous range of literature—from the various realms of semiotics, rhetoric, and literary theory—bears on the problem.[5] Particularly apposite are the many and varied accounts of nineteenth- and twentieth-century realism in the novel. Such works make it clear that there are numerous techniques by which realistic effects may be achieved through language, their origins are scattered across several centuries of literary history, and their rhetorical power waxes and wanes. In effect, contemporary writers have available to them a ragbag of disparate and differentially effective resources for achieving a sense of objective reality. As I hope to demonstrate, there is at least one powerful family of such devices that owes its illocutionary power to the metaphor of the mechanical self.

The Mechanical Self and Modes of Objectivity

Let us reconsider the mechanical view of the self that has been so closely associated with objectivity. As we have seen, these interlocking assumptions about human functioning have failed to furnish adequate directives for the individual achievement of objectivity. Yet this does not challenge the contribution of this view to the social achievement of objectivity. In fact, the mechanical metaphor establishes the rationale for a range of specifically rhetorical techniques, which together operate to achieve textual objectivity. I wish to focus on four textual devices that are both sustained and reinforced by the pervading view of the mechanical self. For illustrative purposes I shall draw the major examples from common textual practices in branches of empirical psychology.[6]

SUBJECT-OBJECT INDEPENDENCE

Essential to the mechanistic view is the assumption that there is a real world independent of those seeking knowledge of its character. The world remains essentially as it is, regardless of the disposition of the knowing agent; reality does not perish along with us. At the outset, this premise establishes the necessity for two language forms, one appropriate to objects in the real world, the other indexing states of mental representation. Without ways of making linguistic distinctions, it would be impossible to denote a state of objectivity (or correct mental representation) as opposed to a *misrepresentation,* or an illusion. Yet, in part because of the difficulties involved in observing one's own experience, there can be no distinctive descriptive language for the internal or perceptual world of the individual.[7] Or in Wittgenstein's terms, there is no possibility of a "private language." Because reference to objects "in the world" can only be established by social agreement, we have a single language of public events and no separate language of the "event as represented in the mind." Descriptions of the private or psychological world must necessarily employ many of the same terms used in describing the publicly observable world. Under these conditions, how then is the rhetor to establish that his or her private experience matches the world as it is?

Perhaps the most common way is simply to declare (either directly or by implication) that the "real-world" language of the occasion is the language of individual experience, that one can employ the commonly shared language for external events to describe one's internal perceptions. To illustrate: the common language holds that under certain circumstances (for example, at the zoo or driving in the Rockies) the term "bear" is an objective descriptor; it accurately denotes a material object at hand. Under these circumstances individuals will be judged objective if they rely on the common term to describe "their experience." Should they deviate from the common conventions of real-world talk, their account of their experience will cease to count as objective. To announce that one spies "a carnivorous mammal," "Smokey," or "an *Ursus americanus*" will seem not only less than objective, but also possibly "imaginative," "metaphoric," or "playful." To say that one sees a "turtle" or an "eagle" will seem perverse or a possible sign of mental illness. Objectivity and banality walk hand in hand.[8]

When the language of personal experience largely duplicates the common language of the exterior or objective world, however, the rhetor faces an additional challenge: ensuring that the ostensive referent for the objective language is indeed exterior to experience. Otherwise there is a lack of clarity in using the common language: is one truly reporting on what there is or speaking only of subjective impressions? What we require, then, are *distention devices,* linguistic means of placing the object at a distance from our private experience. At the simplest level, particular words often serve this function: *the, that, those,* or *this* call attention from the agent to events or objects at a seeming distance. Distention devices may be contrasted with *personalizing descriptors,* terms calling attention to the object as a private possession of the mind. "My view," "my perception," "my sense of . . ." all achieve such a result. Objectivity is threatened when one either fails to employ distention devices or resorts to personalizing descriptors. To the extent that inner processes enter the linguistic arena, the putative object of the discourse recedes into subjectivity. As a result, the scientist is likely to speak of "*the* apparatus," as opposed, for example, to "my sense of an apparatus," "*that* experimental chamber" as opposed to "my impression of an experimental chamber," or "*those* questionnaires" and not "my image of questionnaires."

It is important to recognize that such language choices are ontologically arbitrary. There is nothing about what is the case that would demand or require the use of distention devices in any given instance. One might equally well attribute whatever is the case to an "in here" as to an "out there." However, consider the difference in illocutionary impact between a statement such as "After this apparatus was used in the experimental chamber those particular gauges began to function" and a contextually similar statement in which distention devices have been replaced by personalized descriptors: "After what I sensed as an apparatus was used in what impressed me as an experimental chamber, what I imagined to be a particular kind of gauge proved what I felt to be functional." From a scientific point of view, the former statement would stand as creditable, while the latter would arouse deep suspicion.

The distancing of object from observer can also be achieved through the use of distending metaphors, which place the object at a distance from the individual. Consider, for example, the metaphor of the *hidden continent.* The hidden continent in this case is the entity to which one wishes to claim objective access. The scientist-explorer is essentially occupied with the attempt to locate the exact position of the continent, to bring back news of its existence, and to enable others to visit it as well. In many sciences, the discovered land may be given the name of the explorer. Astral bodies, areas of the brain, laboratory effects, and so on all bear the names of their so-called discoverers. Thus, one confronts such phrases as "Smith first *discovered* the effect," "Jones *found* that . . ." "Brown *detected* that . . . ," and so on. Terms such as "unearthed" and "brought to light" are similarly used, suggesting a companionate metaphor of *buried treasure.* Scientific papers will often cite a range of studies that reach similar conclusions—in effect demonstrating that not one but many explorers have visited the exotic land or seen the treasure for themselves. We can appreciate the rhetorical effects of such metaphors more fully if we contrast them with the same accounts in the personalized mode. Instead of "Smith discovered the fact," consider

"Smith labeled his impression"; replace "Jones found that . . ." with "Jones selected new terms for his experience"; for "Brown detected . . ." substitute "Brown strove for prominence in the field and thus sought to produce findings that others would see as unique." In each case, the rhetorical shift obliterates objectivity.

THE CHARACTER OF THE OBJECTIVE WORLD

The image of the mechanical self demands a dual discourse, one suggesting an internal and the other an external world. At the same time, this image furnishes a rationale for more specific characterizations of the external world. At the outset, the vast share of epistemological writing has relied heavily on the modality of vision. One writes of the ideal relationship of the knower to the known as that of a *mirror* to its object, a *picture* to its subject. When functioning soundly, the mind of the mechanical self is a reliable visual record of the world.[9] The pervasive use of the visual metaphor establishes the major means by which objectivity is secured within scientific writing. The language of objectivity is primarily the language of vision. A typical research description in psychology, for example, will speak of subjects, questionnaires, tachistoscopes, chimpanzees, and so on—all objects of the visual world. Descriptions of the same "objects" carried out in terms of any other modality would be doubted. If experimental subjects were described in terms of smell ("ten foul-smelling subjects were compared with fragrantly scented ones"), questionnaires in terms of taste, tachistoscopic devices in terms of touch, and chimps in terms of sound, the descriptions would rapidly be discounted as merely the personal, subjective experience of the investigator and therefore potentially biased and unreplicable. In contemporary science we rely on vision to mirror the world as it is.

The metaphor of the mechanical self also establishes the grounds for the degree and type of details that may be attributed to the objective world. In this case, however, there are two disparate traditions that inform contemporary scientific writing, each fashioning reality in a different way. On the one hand, there is a long-standing view of human vision as furnishing highly differentiated pictures of the world—enormous amounts of sensory stimulation that must be reduced through conceptualization lest experience buckle under its volume. From this perspective, objective writing should feature a high degree of detail, for if language reflects experience as experience reflects the world, then objective language should furnish pictures of sophisticated nuance. Indeed, the demand for elaborate detail was one of the major characteristics of nineteenth-century realistic writing. In contemporary psychology this tradition is best represented in clinical writing, and primarily in reports of single case studies and qualitative research. By furnishing minute detail, much of it irrelevant to his conclusions, the author demonstrates that his observation is unbiased. In Freud's terms, the observer has properly demonstrated "evenly hovering attention."

The technique of microscopic detailing is seldom found in the more scientifically self-conscious sectors of psychology. Here a contrasting aspect of the mechanical self plays a stronger role. The effectively functioning machine will organize inputs into classes, sorting stimuli into units of cause and effect. In the same way, it is the task of objective science to avoid excessive and obfuscating detail and to report only on events within the essential classes. Congenial with this rationale, most experimental journals in psychology furnish only the sparest account of experimental procedures and outcomes. Particular details of the lives of experimental participants, for example, are never included in an objective description of the research. That participants are male as opposed to female may be mentioned, but whether a participant comes from a broken home, uses addictive drugs, or had a sleepless night would be viewed as extraneous, if not the result of a soft-headed humanism. Researchers only document those aspects of the procedure that officially count as "stimuli" (antecedents) from a particular theoretical perspective and only those aspects of the participants' actions that can be indexed as "responses" (consequents) resulting from this perspective. Should a researcher greet experimental participants with howls of ghoulish glee, and should the participants soon find themselves annoyed and anxious to leave, these events would scarcely be included in an objective description of the proceedings.

The presumption of a mechanical relationship between the external world and the experience of the self finally lends itself to attributions made to both world and mind. In particular, environmental events are often imbued with an active power, while observers are characterized as passive victims. If individual perception operates in a machinelike fashion, responding to antecedent conditions in the external world, it follows that internal knowledge of events should largely result from the external forcing its effects on the internal. Such assumptions lend themselves to the pervasive use of the passive voice in research reporting: "Aggression was observed" and not "I observed aggression"; "the results were obtained" and not "I obtained the results." If the researcher strives to see a certain pattern, the result may not be due to the "thing in itself" so much as the striving of the mind. It is also an ode to nature's facticity that one is virtually forced by its very presence to take notice of it. If one speaks of oneself as a "victim of circumstance," the credibility of "circumstance" independent of "victim" is enhanced. Exemplars of the passivity motif include such phrases as "one is *struck* by the fact that . . . ," "the data *spoke* clearly . . . ," "one is *compelled* by these findings to conclude . . . ," "this result *clarifies* . . . ," and so on—all phrases that cast the scientist's senses as victims of the circumstances of nature.

Again the rhetorical power of such phrasing is nicely illustrated by contrasts in which metaphors of passivity are replaced by terms of mental activation. For example, to be "struck" by findings is more objective than to "seek" them; when data "speak for themselves," the conclusion is more trustworthy than when one "prefers the interpretation"; and it is more rhetorically advantageous to be "compelled" by findings than to "search for findings that agree with one's theory." Objectivity is thus secured by portraying oneself as but an impersonal integer in the "one great machine."

EXPERIENTIAL PRESENCE AND THE ESTABLISHMENT OF AUTHORITY

One of the major appeals of Enlightenment thinking—and its allied conception of mental machinery—has been its capacity to wrest the power of the word from authorities of high rank and place it in the hands of the populace. No longer must one trust the pronouncements of popes or kings about what is the case; the privilege of voice is granted to whoever confronts or is exposed to the relevant sector of the world. In effect, whoever has been struck, smitten, or constrained by nature, or whoever has visited that alien land directly, thereby gains authority. Voice is achieved by establishing *experiential presence.*

Thus linguistic forms are invited for establishing one's presence at the site of the putative fact. Experiential presence is often achieved during the initial pages of a scientific report by the use of personal pronouns, such as "I" or "we," or equivalent possessives ("my" or "our"). One might say, for example, "Our attempt was to explore . . ." or "We were concerned with . . ." thus insinuating experiential presence into the scientific activity to follow. Similar effects can be achieved by demonstrating that the research was itself conducted by the author(s) or closely supervised assistants, and that the author was not absent during the major share of the research process. Consider, for example, the effects of scientific writing that violates these presumptions: "I was very busy with my teaching and various conferences during the semester, so I had little time to observe the research process. Smith, my graduate student, actually did most of the work—for which he has duly been rewarded with a junior authorship—though I did discuss the conception of the research with him and checked his statistical calculations." To announce that one did not, in fact, conduct the research, that one is reporting results discovered by another, would deeply discredit the report. Of course, scientists continuously discuss research findings that are conveyed only through written documents; however, in each case they presume that the findings can ultimately be traced to the direct experience of the relevant writers.

Yet the establishment of experiential presence is simultaneously problematic. To assert the I (the "eye") alone is to suggest that the putative object of description is the product of this very presence. If only the investigator has confronted the event, if only he or she has dwelled in the exotic land and observed its denizens, how is the account to be fully trusted? Or is it possible that the so-called "findings" are driven by a biased way of viewing the world? To avoid such threats, the rhetor is invited to adopt a *transcendental shift* in perspective: first it is useful to establish experiential presence, then to shift to the standpoint of an impersonal agent, an evenly hovering, all-seeing presence.[10] Thus, we find that in most scientific reports the prevailing perspective is that of the impersonal collectivity, the perceptual vantage point not of the author but of an "omniscient eye," looking down on all that transpires. This effect is often accomplished through the use of impersonal pronouns. Rather than "I observed . . . ," the phrase "One observed . . ." is used; in preference to "I found that . . . ," the phrasing shifts to "It was found. . . ." Most frequently, no reference whatsoever is made to point of view, thus implying that the point of view is that of everyman and shared by all. It is, in Thomas Nagel's phrase, "the view from nowhere." One writes, "The stimulus was presented" and not "I observed that the stimulus was presented," "The button was pressed" in lieu of "My assistant saw the button pressed. . . ." In effect, the well-wrought reality must simultaneously establish the presence of the author's experience within the scene and subtly substitute a transcendental standpoint.

PURIFICATION OF THE LENS

The mechanical self achieves objectivity when there is no interference with the processes responsible for mirroring the external world and drawing conclusions as to its nature. From Locke's eighteenth-century *Essay on Human Understanding* to psychological studies in the present century, it has been broadly held that consciousness comes to know the world through the sensory system. One is initially conscious of primary sense data. Although this claim is widely debated, it is generally agreed that these sensations are eventually converted or transformed into percepts (or mental categories). If the process is operating without interference, sensations serve as a mirror to the world, and the resulting categories are available for rational thought and communication through language. This set of presumptions suggests, by implication, that any other form of mental activity may potentially interfere with these essential functions of observation and categorization. Particularly suspect are any processes that link the individual to the external world in a way that alters, unsettles, or affects his or her actions. These processes are of the kind that alter the individual's capacity for objective observation. Thus, emotions, motives, values, and desires—as traditionally conceived—are all potentially threatening to objectivity. They are not constituents of the effectively functioning machine. All link the individual to the world in such a way that certain lines of action become imperative and others abhorrent. The resulting clamor toward action may unsettle the sensitive instrument of sensation and the finely tuned process of categorization. It invites biases and distortion; it threatens survival.

The mechanical view of the self thus furnishes the rationale for additional techniques for achieving discursive objectivity. At the outset, the objective report will *suppress affective description* of the self. For the rhetor to describe or explore various emotions, desires, values, or motives possibly at play at the time of observation would denigrate the process and undermine the seeming objectivity of the description. One can say, "We recorded a mean of 5.65 . . . ," "It was observed that the subjects were ill at ease . . . ," or "The results demonstrated . . ." with impunity. Such phrasing suggests that the mirror of the mind was operating with fidelity; it makes no reference to internal states of feeling, motivation, or desire. However, should affective terminology be insinuated into the same phrases, the effects would be debilitating. Consider the outcome of the rephrasing, "My heart was set on finding a mean of over 5.00 and I was overjoyed when I got it . . . ," "Given that the research would be virtually unpublishable if we didn't get positive results, we sought evidence that the subjects were ill at ease. Lo, they proved so to be . . . ," or "The results demonstrated that indeed those actions we investigators find morally reprehensible lead to failure in the experimental setting." To admit one's affective engagement in the research is, by contemporary rhetorical standards, to see through a glass darkly.

These ethnopsychological assumptions for the rhetorical achievement of objectivity have a second important repercussion. Not only is observer affect systematically muted, but there is also a general *suppression of the arousing characteristics* of the object. To the extent that the object of research possesses qualities or characteristics that can stimulate the affect, motives, or desires of the observer, the resulting account becomes less creditable as a reflection of reality and more likely a product of the observer's arousal. It is partly for this reason that research reports in the behavioral sciences are so frequently antiseptic and devoid of human interest—even when the topics might excite broad attention. Little about the "objects" of study can be mentioned save, for example, a range of neutralized demographic characteristics. We learn that the research subjects were college males, for example, or women aged forty to sixty, or black school children from the inner city. In contrast, there is no mention of such matters as sexual attractiveness, off-putting obesity, cloying superficiality, charming manners, stupefying ignorance, enviable clothing, repulsive pimples, and so on. The mention of these features would suggest that the observer's feelings or motives were aroused during the period of observation. To note such redolent features would be to subvert the ostensive objectivity of the report.[11]

In sum, we find that the conception of the mechanical self operates as a rationalizing forestructure for a range of techniques that enable authors to speak with authority. Rhetorical conventions for separating subject and object, characterizing the objective world, establishing authorial presence (and absence), and cleansing the lens of perception are among the most prominent means of generating the sense of objectivity. An author who fails to employ these devices may be judged subjective, overly imaginative, or even mad.

Objectivity and Action

I began this chapter by underscoring the prevailing reverence for the concept of objectivity within the culture. Its achievement is viewed as a key to survival that approximates a moral obligation. To disregard or to fail in this aspiration is to be shunted to the backwaters of society, there to join those who indulge in metaphors, mere rhetoric, and other practices of the effete, romantic, and neurotic. Yet as the argument has unfolded we find little warrant for the hierarchical arrangements invited by the objective-subjective binary, no means for linking the achievement of objectivity to an elevated form of psychological processing or a mimetically superior form of description. Rather, the achievement of objectivity is textual—inhering in historically and culturally situated practices of writing and speaking. But there is little about these particular ways of organizing language that would seem to merit the prestigious position they occupy within society. In the end, this analysis invites critical appraisal of the functions and dysfunctions of the discursive practices of objectivity: Are there reasons for sustaining these linguistic modes, or should concerted attempts be made to break the binary and open the practices of common discourse to more varied possibilities? What is to be said, then, about the politics of objectivity?

This, of course, is yet a new topic, and I wish here to make only two points. In my view, the strongest arguments can be made for dismantling the traditional objective-subjective dichotomy and its discursive practices. Not only does the discourse of objectivity generate and sustain unwarranted hierarchies of privilege—along with an accompanying array of prejudices, hostilities, and conflicts—but it excludes many voices from full participation in the culture's constructions of the good and the real.[12] Objective measurement has long been used to challenge the authority of various elites claiming prescience and clairvoyance, and has thus been placed on the side of democracy (Porter 1992). However, as objective measurements have increasingly become the property of experts (see, for example, Chapter 6), we now confront a new, largely unchallenged technocratic elite. The discourse of objectivity fails to reveal the problematics of its own origins and wages war on all nonobjective languages. It thus threatens the rich and varied array of alternative linguistic forms—pragmatic resources garnered from the culture's history. Further, those captured by the language of objectivity are resultingly demeaned. As they are transformed into objects of scrutiny, they lose both their humanity and right to voice (MacKinnon 1987; Schott 1988). And as they become increasingly "countable," so do they become subject to increasing control (Rose 1990). As I have suggested, broad agreement is now emerging within poststructuralist, post-empiricist, and postmodern domains of scholarship that the Western conception of the individual self has run its course. The view of the private self as the source of art and literature, practical decisions, moral deliberation, emotional activity, and the like is no longer viable—not only on conceptual grounds but in terms of the societal patterns it invites. For many, the present challenge is how to replace the self as the critical unit of social life. Accounts that emphasize contextual embeddedness, relational formations, and dialogic process are under development. And, as we saw in Chapter 2, there are concurrent disruptions in the traditional conventions of scientific writing. Bold experiments with new forms of discourse are slowly taking place and beginning to offer alternatives to the traditional modes of objectification. There is reason, then, to anticipate a slow displacement of the prevailing rhetoric, and with it an expansion in the range of voices empowered within the cultural dialogue.[13]

Yet, as these avenues are pursued, reflexive moments are also essential. In *Varieties of Realism*, Rom Harré writes that "science is not only the major intellectual achievement of mankind but also its most remarkable moral order" (1988, p. 8). The latter is largely owing, he argues, to the sense of mutual trust enjoyed within scientific enclaves. Provided that one remains within the language games of the scientific community and goes along with their localized forms of indexing, the scientific account is estimably trustworthy. Harré continues, "The product of these communities, scientific knowledge, is itself defined in moral terms. It is that knowledge upon which one can rely. That reliance might be existential, concerning what there is or might be, or it might be practical, concerning what can and cannot be done, or both" (p. 11). Given the central place of the discourse of objectivity in scientific communication, we need to question its contribution to communities of trust. Within this context the dispassionate and unremarkable language of objectivity may operate as a performative—like the clasp of a handshake—indicating that the words may be cashed out in usable action. The language of subjectivity, in contrast, may suggest a relaxing of restrictions, an invitation to pleasure or play. Further, as I proposed in Chapter 3, the banal language of the objective world may be required for communities of scientists to realize their collective goals. Without repetitive and unremarkable agreements within the sciences about "what things are to be called," the hurdles to technological accomplishments would be enormous. In this sense the discourse of objectivity may be useful to achieve what Megill (1991) calls *disciplinary* and *procedural* objectivity. It is perhaps dysfunctional, then, to suggest a full-scale abandonment of these conventions of trust.

At the same time, there is much to be said for exploring alternatives to these conventions, so that we might signal trust without simultaneously denigrating alternative forms of declaration. Umberto Maturana (1988) proposes that all so-called "objective" writing be placed in brackets, thus symbolizing its local or parochial character. More is to be gained, however, by giving expression to a multiplicity of rhetorical forms. Although objectivist or realist discourse is prevalent, it is scarcely the only form of effective rhetoric. Further, by juxtaposing several different forms of writing within the same text, the effect is both to reduce the totalizing impact of the singular voice, and to broaden the number of dialogues in which the reader (and writer) can subsequently participate. Thus, the text moves not to diminish the dialogic spectrum but to expand it. Such possibilities are encouraged by Van Maanen's (1988) elucidation of the multiple forms of ethnographic writing. Here, realist ethnographies are contrasted with the powerful potential of what Van Maanen calls "confessional" (first person revelations) and "impressionist" (imaginative narration) writing. For pedagogical purposes, Lather (1991) challenges her students to write in multiple voices. Thus, after carrying out a standard empirical analysis, a second writing might assess the ideological implications of the first; still a third analysis could explore the constructed character of the initial text. In effect, there is a three-tiered expansion of intelligibilities. For the human sciences, these are indeed promising beginnings to a more responsible and creative future.

Part Three

From Self to Relationship

8   Self-Narration in Social Life

Enriching the range of theoretical discourse with the particular hope of expanding the potential for human practices is one of the central challenges for constructionist scholarship. One of the most inviting theoretical departures, because of its affinity with constructionist metatheory, arises from relational theory, the attempt to account for human action in terms of relational process. It attempts to move beyond the single individual to acknowledge the reality of relationship. Here, I want to propose a relational view of self-conception, one that views self-conception not as an individual's personal and private cognitive structure but as *discourse* about the self—the performance of languages available in the public sphere. I replace the traditional concern with conceptual categories (self-concepts, schemas, self-esteem), with the self as a narration rendered intelligible within ongoing relationships.

This, then, is a story about stories—and most particularly, stories of the self. Most of us begin our encounters with stories in childhood. Through fairy tales, folktales, and family stories we receive our first organized accounts of human action. Stories continue to absorb us as we read novels, biography, and history; they occupy us at the movies, at the theater, and before the television set. And, possibly because of this intimate and long-standing acquaintanceship, stories also serve as a critical means by which we make ourselves intelligible within the social world. We tell extended stories about our childhoods, our relations with family members, our years at school, our first love affair, the development of our thinking on a given subject, and so on. We also tell stories about last night's party, this morning's crisis, or lunch with a companion. We may even create a story about a near collision on the way to work or about scorching last night's dinner. In each case, we use the story form to identify ourselves to others and to ourselves. So prevalent is the story process in Western culture that Bruner (1986) has gone as far as suggesting a genetic proclivity for narrative understanding. Whether it is biologically prepared or not, we can scarcely underestimate the importance of stories in our lives and the extent to which they serve as vehicles for rendering ourselves intelligible.

Yet, to say that we use stories to make ourselves comprehensible does not go far enough. Not only do we tell our lives as stories; there is also a significant sense in which our relationships with each other are lived out in narrative form. For White and Epston (1990), "persons give meaning to their lives and relationships by *storying* their experience" (p. 13). The ideal life, Nietzsche proposed, is one that corresponds to the ideal story; each act is coherently related to all others with nothing to spare (Nehamas 1985). More cogently, Hardy (1968) has written that "we dream in narrative, daydream in narrative, remember, anticipate, hope, despair, believe, doubt, plan, revise, criticize, construct, gossip, learn, hate and love by narrative" (p. 5). Elaborating on this view, MacIntyre (1981) proposes that enacted narratives form the basis of moral character. My analysis will stop short of saying that lives *are* narrative events (in agreement with Mink 1969). Stories are, after all, forms of accounting, and it seems misleading to equate the account with its putative object. However, narrative accounts are embedded within social action; they render events socially visible and typically establish expectations for future events. Because the events of daily life are immersed in narrative, they become laden with a storied sense: they acquire the reality of "a beginning," "a low point," "a climax," "an ending," and so on. People live out the events in this way and, along with others, they index them in just this way. This is not to say that life copies art, but rather, that art becomes the vehicle through which the reality of life is made manifest. In a significant sense, then, we live by stories—both in the telling and the realizing of the self.

In this chapter I shall explore the nature of stories, both as they are told and as they are lived in social life. I shall begin with an examination of story form or, more formally, the structure of narrative accounts. I shall then consider the manner in which narratives of the self are constructed within social life and the uses to which they are put. As my account unfolds it will become increasingly clear that narratives of the self are not fundamentally possessions of the individual but possessions of relationships—products of social interchange. In effect, to be a self with a past and potential future is not to be an independent agent, unique and autonomous, but to be immersed in interdependency.

The Character of Self-Narrative

Writers of fiction, philosophy, and psychology have frequently portrayed human consciousness as a continuous flow. We do not confront a series of segmented snapshots, it is said, but an ongoing process. Similarly, in our experience of self and others we seem to encounter not a series of discrete, endlessly juxtaposed moments, but coherent, goal-directed sequences. As many historiographers have suggested, accounts of human action can scarcely proceed without temporal embedding. To understand an action is indeed to place it within a context of preceding and subsequent events. To bring the matter home, our view of the self in any given moment is fundamentally nonsensical unless it can be linked in some fashion with our own past. Suddenly and momentarily to see oneself as "aggressive," "poetic," or "out of control," for example, might seem whimsical or puzzling. When aggression follows a long-standing and intensifying antagonism, however, it is rendered sensible. In the same way, being poetic or out of control is comprehensible when placed in the context of our own personal history. This particular point has led a number of commentators to conclude that an understanding of human action can scarcely proceed on other than narrative grounds (MacIntyre 1981; Mink 1969; Sarbin 1986). For our purposes here, the term "self-narrative" will refer to an individual's account of the relationship among self-relevant events across time.[1] In developing a self-narrative we establish coherent connections among life events (Cohler 1982; Kohli 1981). Rather than see our life as simply "one damned thing after another," we formulate a story in which life events are systematically related, rendered intelligible by their place in a sequence or "unfolding process" (de Waele and Harré 1976). Our present identity is thus not a sudden and mysterious event but a sensible result of a life story. As Bettelheim (1976) has argued, such creations of narrative order may be essential in giving life a sense of meaning and direction.

Before embarking on this analysis I must say a word about the relationship between the concept of self-narrative and related theoretical notions. The concept of self-narrative in particular bears an affinity with a variety of constructs developed in other domains. First, in *cognitive psychology* the concepts of scripts (Schank and Abelson 1977), story schema (Mandler 1984), predictability tree (Kelly and Keil 1985), and narrative thought (Britton and Pellegrini 1990) have all been used to account for the psychological basis for understanding and/or directing sequences of action across time. In contrast to the cognitive program, with its search for universal cognitive processes, *rule-role* theorists (such as Harré and Secord 1972) and *constructivists* (see, for example, Mancuso and Sarbin's [1983] treatment of "narrative grammar") tend to emphasize the cultural contingency

188 REALITIES AND RELATIONSHIPS

of various psychological states. Thus, the cognitivist's presumption of a narrative base of personal action is retained but with a greater sensitivity to the sociocultural basis of such narratives. Bruner's (1986, 1990) work on narratives falls somewhere between these two orientations, holding to a view of universal cognitive function while simultaneously placing strong emphasis on cultural meaning systems. *Phenomenologists* (see Polkinghorne 1988; Carr 1984; Josselson and Lieblich 1993), *existentialists* (see Charme's [1984] analysis of Sartre), and *personologists* (McAdams 1993) are also concerned with individual internal process (often indexed as "experience") but typically eschew the cognitivist search for predication and control of individual behavior and replace the emphasis on cultural determination with a more humanistic investment in the self as author or agent.

In contrast to all these approaches, which place their major emphasis on the individual, I wish to consider self-narratives as forms of social accounting or public discourse. In this sense, narratives are conversational resources, constructions open to continuous alteration as interaction progresses. Persons in this case do not consult an internal script, cognitive structure, or apperceptive mass for information or guidance; they do not interpret or "read the world" through narrative lenses; they do not author their own lives. Rather, the self-narrative is a linguistic implement embedded within conventional sequences of action and employed in relationships in such a way as to sustain, enhance, or impede various forms of action. As linguistic devices, narratives may be used to indicate future actions, but they are not themselves the cause or determinant basis for such actions. In this sense, self-narratives function much like oral histories or morality tales within a society. They are cultural resources that serve such social purposes as self-identification, self-justification, self-criticism, and social solidification.[2] This approach joins with those that emphasize the sociocultural origins of narrative construction, though it is not intended to endorse a cultural determinism—it is through *interacting* with others that we acquire narrative skills, not through being acted upon. It also agrees with those concerned with personal engagement in narrative, but it replaces the emphasis on the self-determining ego with social interchange.

Scholars concerned with narratives are sharply divided on the issue of truth value: many hold that narratives have the potential to bear truth, while others argue that narratives do not reflect but construct reality. The former view sees narrative as fact-driven, while the latter generally holds narrative to be fact-organizing or even fact-producing. Most historians, biographers, and empiricists understandably emphasize the truth-bearing possibilities of narrative. Because this assumption grants to cognition an adaptive function, many cognitive theorists also plump for narrative verisimilitude. To possess a "restaurant script" in the Schank and Abelson (1977) formulation, for example, is to be prepared to function adequately in this locale. As should be clear from the arguments of preceding chapters, the social constructionist approach stands at odds with this view. There are indeed limits on our accounts of events across time, but they are not to be traced either to minds in action or to events in themselves. Rather, both in science and in daily life, the stories serve as communal resources that people use in ongoing relationships. From this standpoint, narratives do not reflect so much as they create the sense of "what is true." Indeed, it is largely because of existing narrative forms that "telling the truth" is an intelligible act. The special ways in which this is so will be further amplified in the following pages.

The Structuring of Narrative Accounts

If narratives are demanded neither by cognition nor the world as it is, then what account can be given of their properties or forms? From the constructionist standpoint, the properties of well-formed narratives are culturally and historically situated. They are byproducts of people's attempts to relate through discourse, in much the same way that styles of painting serve as a means of mutual coordination within communities of artists or specific tactics and countertactics become fashionable within various sports. In this regard, White's (1973) analysis of the literary character of historical writing is informative. As he demonstrates, at least four different forms of narrative realism shaped early nineteenth-century historical writing. In the late nineteenth century, however, these rhetorical forms were repudiated and largely replaced by a different array of conceptual strategies for interpreting the past. This means that narrative form is, in effect, historically contingent.

It is interesting in this context to inquire into contemporary narrative conventions. What are the requirements for telling an intelligible story within the present-day culture of the West? The question is particularly significant, since an elucidation of these conventions for structuring stories sensitizes us to the limits of self-identity. To understand how narratives must be structured within the culture is to press against the edges of identity's envelope—to discover the limits to identifying oneself as a human agent in good standing; it is also to determine what forms must be maintained in order to acquire credibility as a teller of truth. The structure of proper story telling precedes the events about which "truth is told"; to go beyond the conventions is to engage in an idiot's tale. If the narrative fails to approximate conventional forms, the telling becomes nonsensical. Thus, rather than being driven by facts truth telling is largely governed by a forestructure of narrative conventions.

There have been many attempts to identify the characteristics of the well-formed narrative. They have occurred within the domains of literary theory (Frye 1957; Scholes and Kellogg 1966; Martin 1987), semiotics (Propp

1968; Rimmon-Kenan 1983), historiography (Mink 1969; Gallie 1964), and certain sectors of social science (Labov 1982; Sutton-Smith 1979; Mandler 1984). My attempt draws on these various analyses. It synthesizes a variety of common agreements, excludes certain distinctions central to other analytic tasks (such as point of view, the function of characters and actions, poetic tropes), and adds ingredients necessary for understanding why stories possess a sense of direction and drama. It differs from a number of these accounts, however, in its avoidance of universalist assumptions. Theorists frequently make claims for a foundational or fundamental set of rules or characteristics of the well-formed narrative. This analysis, however, sees narrative constructions as historically and culturally contingent. The following criteria in particular appear to be central in constructing a narrative intelligible to significant segments of contemporary culture:

Establishing a valued endpoint. An acceptable story must first establish a goal, an event to be explained, a state to be reached or avoided, an outcome of significance or, more informally, a "point." To relate that one walked north for two blocks, east for three, and then turned left on Pine Street would constitute an impoverished story, but if this description were a prelude to finding an affordable apartment, it would approximate an acceptable story. The selected endpoint is typically saturated with value: it is understood to be desirable or undesirable. The endpoint may, for example, be the protagonist's well-being ("how I narrowly escaped death"), the discovery of something precious ("how he discovered his biological father"), personal loss ("how she lost her job"), and so on. Thus, if the story terminated on finding 404 Pine Street, it would lapse into insignificance. It is only when the search for a much-desired apartment is successful that we have a good story. In a related vein, MacIntyre (1981) proposes that "narrative requires an evaluative framework in which good or bad character helps to produce unfortunate or happy outcomes" (p. 456). It is also clear that this demand for a valued endpoint introduces a strong cultural component (traditionally called "subjective bias") into the story. Life itself could hardly be said to be composed of separable events, a subpopulation of which constitute endpoints. Rather, the articulation of an event and its position as an endpoint are derived from the culture's ontology and construction of value. Through verbal artistry, "the brushing of her fingers on my sleeve" emerges as an event, and depending on the story, may serve as the beginning of or the conclusion to a romance. In addition, events as we define them do not contain intrinsic value. Fire in itself is neither good nor bad; we invest it with value depending generally on whether it serves what we take to be valuable functions (cooking food) or not (destroying the kitchen). Only within a cultural perspective can "valued events" be made intelligible.

Selecting events relevant to the endpoint. Once an endpoint has been established it more or less dictates the kinds of events that can figure in the account, thus greatly reducing the myriad candidates for "eventhood." An intelligible story is one in which events serve to make the goal more or less probable, accessible, important, or vivid. Thus, if a story is about winning a soccer match ("how we won the game"), the most relevant events are those that bring that goal closer or make it more distant ("Tom's first kick bounced off the goal, but on the next attack he deflected the ball into the net with the twist of his head"). Only at the risk of inanity would one introduce a note on fifteenth-century monastic life or a hope for future space travel unless it could be shown that such matters were significantly related to winning the match ("Juan got his inspiration for the tactic from reading about fifteenth-century religious practices"). An account of the day ("It was crisp and sunny") would be acceptable in the narrative, since it makes the events more vivid, but a description of the weather in some remote country would seem idiosyncratic. Again we find that narrative demands have ontological consequences. One is not free to include all that takes place, but only that which is relevant to the story's conclusion.

The ordering of events. Once a goal has been established and relevant events selected, the events are usually placed in an ordered arrangement. As Ong (1982) indicates, the bases for such order (importance, interest value, timeliness, and so on) may change with history. The most widely used contemporary convention is perhaps that of a linear, temporal sequence. Certain events, for example, are said to occur at the beginning of the football match, and these precede the events that are said to take place toward the middle and at the end. It is tempting to say that the sequence of related events should match the actual sequence in which the events occurred, but this would be to confuse the rules of an intelligible rendering with what is indeed the case. Linear temporal ordering is, after all, a convention that employs an internally coherent system of signs; its features are not required by the world as it is. It may be applied to what is the case or not depending on one's purposes. Clock time may not be effective if one wishes to speak of one's "experience of time passing in the dentist's chair," nor is it adequate if one wishes to describe relativity theory in physics or the circular rotation of seasons. In Bakhtin's (1981) terms, we may view temporal accounts as *chronotopes*—literary conventions governing space-time relationships or "the ground essential for the ... representability of events" (p. 250). That yesterday preceded today is a conclusion demanded only by a culturally specific chronotope.

Stability of identity. The well-formed narrative is typically one in which the characters (or objects) in the story possess a continuous or coherent identity across time. A given protagonist cannot felicitously serve as a villain at one moment and a hero in the next or demonstrate powers of genius unpredictably interspersed with moronic actions. Once defined by the storyteller, the individual (or object) will tend to retain its identity or function within the story. There are obvious exceptions to this general tendency, but most are cases in which the story attempts to explain the change itself—how the frog became a prince or the impoverished young man achieved financial success. Causal forces (such as war, poverty, education) may be introduced that bring about change in an individual (or object), and for dramatic effect a putative identity may give way to "the real" (a trustworthy professor may turn out to be an arsonist). In general, however, the well-formed story does not tolerate protean personalities.

Causal linkages. By contemporary standards the ideal narrative is one that provides an explanation for the outcome. As it is said, "The king died and then the queen died" is but a rudimentary story; "The king died and then the queen died of grief" is the beginning of a veritable plot. As Ricoeur (1981) puts it, "Explanations must . . . be woven into the narrative tissue" (p. 278). Explanation is typically achieved by selecting events that are by common standards causally linked. Each event should be a product of that which has preceded it ("Because the rain came we fled indoors"; "As a result of his operation he couldn't meet his class"). This is not to presume that a universal conception of causality is insinuated into all well-formed stories: what may be included within the acceptable range of causal forms is historically and culturally dependent. Many scientists thus wish to limit discussions of causality to the Humean variety; social philosophers often prefer to see reason as the cause of human action; botanists often find it more convenient to employ teleological forms of causality. Regardless of one's preference in causal models, when events within a narrative are related in an interdependent fashion, the outcome approximates more closely the well-formed story.

Demarcation signs. Most properly formed stories employ signals to indicate the beginning and the end. As Young (1982) has proposed, the narrative is "framed" by various rule-governed devices that indicate when one is entering the "tale world," or the world of the story. "Once upon a time . . . ," "Did you hear the one about . . . ," "You can't imagine what happened to me on the way over here . . . ," or "Let me tell you why I'm so happy . . ." would all signal the audience that a narrative is to follow. Endings may also be signaled by phrases ("That's it . . . ," "So now you know . . .") but need not be. Laughter at the end of a joke may indicate the exit from the tale world, and often the description of the story's point is sufficient to indicate that the tale world is terminated.

While in many contexts these criteria are essential to the well-formed narrative, it is important to note their cultural and historical contingency. As Mary Gergen's (1992) explorations of autobiography suggest, men are far more likely to accommodate themselves to the prevailing criteria for "proper story telling" than women. Women's autobiographies are more likely to be structured around multiple endpoints and to include materials unrelated to any particular endpoint. With the modernist explosion in literary experimentation, the demand for well-formed narratives in serious fiction has also diminished. In postmodern writing narratives may turn ironically self-referential, demonstrating their own artifice as texts and the ways in which their efficacy depends on still other narratives (Dipple 1988).

Does it matter whether narratives are well formed in matters of daily living? As we have seen, the use of narrative components would appear to be vital in creating a sense of reality in accounts of self. As Rosenwald and Ochberg (1992) put it, "How individuals recount their histories—what they emphasize and omit, their stance as protagonists or victims, the relationship the story establishes between teller and audience—all shape what individuals can claim of their own lives. Personal stories are not merely a way of telling someone (or oneself) about one's life; they are the means by which identities may be fashioned" (p. 1). The social utility of well-formed narrative is more concretely revealed in research on courtroom testimony. In *Reconstructing Reality in the Courtroom,* Bennett and Feldman (1981) subjected research participants to forty-seven testimonies that either attempted to recall actual events or were fictional contrivances. Although ratings of the stories revealed that the participants were unable to discriminate between the genuine and fictional accounts, an analysis of those accounts believed to be genuine as opposed to false proved interesting: participants made their judgments largely according to the approximation of the stories to well-formed narratives. Stories believed to be genuine were those in which events relevant to the endpoint were dominant and causal linkages among elements more numerous. In further research, Lippman (1986) experimentally varied the extent to which courtroom testimonies demonstrated the selection of events relevant to an endpoint, the causal linkages between one event and another, and the diachronic ordering of events. Testimonies that approximated the well-formed narrative in these ways were consistently found to be more intelligible and the witnesses to be more rational. Thus, the self-narratives of daily life may not always be well formed, but under certain circumstances their structure may be essential.

Varieties of Narrative Form

By using these narrative conventions we generate a sense of coherence and direction in our lives. They acquire meaning, and what happens is suffused with significance. Certain forms of narrative are broadly shared within the culture; they are frequently used, easily identified, and highly functional. In a sense, they constitute a syllabary of possible selves. What account can be given of these more stereotypic narratives? The question here is similar to that concerning fundamental plot lines. Since Aristotelian times philosophers and literary theorists, among others, have attempted to develop a formal vocabulary of plot. As is sometimes argued, there may be a foundational set of plots from which all stories are derived. To the extent that people live through narrative, a foundational family of plots would place a limit on the range of life trajectories.

One of the most extensive accounts of plot within the present century, which relies heavily on the Aristotelian view, is that of Northrop Frye (1957). Frye proposed four basic forms of narrative, each rooted in the human experience with nature and, more particularly, in the evolution of the seasons. Thus, the experience of spring and the blossoming forth of nature gives rise to the *comedy*. In the classic tradition comedy typically involves a challenge or a threat, which is overcome to yield social harmony. A comedy need not be humorous, even though its ending is a happy one. In contrast, the freedom and calm of summer days inspire the *romance* as a dramatic form. The romance in this case consists of a series of episodes in which the major protagonist experiences challenges or threats and through a series of struggles emerges victorious. The romance need not be concerned with attraction between people; in its harmonious ending, however, it is similar to the comedy. During the autumn, when we experience the contrast between the life of summer and the death of oncoming winter, the *tragedy* is born; and in winter, with our increasing awareness of unrealized expectations and the failure of our dreams, the *satire* becomes the relevant expressive form.

In contrast to Frye's four master narratives, Joseph Campbell has proposed a single "monomyth," from which myriad variations can be found across the centuries. The monomyth, which is rooted in unconscious psychodynamics, concerns a hero who has been able to overcome personal and historical limitations to reach a transcendent understanding of the human condition. For Campbell, heroic narratives in their many local guises serve the vital function of psychic education. For our purposes, we might note that the monomyth has a form similar to that of the romance: negative events (trials, terrors, tribulations) are followed by a positive outcome (enlightenment).

Yet, although they possess a certain aesthetic appeal, such quests after foundational plots are unsatisfying. There is simply no compelling rationale to explain why there should be a limited number of narratives. And, given the successful experiments of modernist writers (such as James Joyce and Alain Robbe-Grillet) and postmodernists (such as Milan Kundera and

Georges Perec) in disrupting the traditional narrative, there is good reason to suspect narrative forms, just as the criteria for story telling, are subject to shifting conventions. Rather than seek a definitive account, the culturally based view I am presenting here suggests that there is a virtual infinity of possible story forms, but due to the exigencies of social coordination, certain modalities are favored over others in various historical periods. In the same way that the fashions in facial expression, dress, and professional aspirations shift with time, so do modal forms of self-narration. If we extend the earlier arguments for narrative characteristics, it is also possible to appreciate existing norms and variations.

As we have seen, a story's endpoint is weighted with value. Thus a victory, a consummated affair, a discovered fortune, or a prizewinning paper can all serve as proper story endings, while on the opposite pole of the evaluative continuum would fall a defeat, a lost love, and a squandered fortune, or a professional failure. We can view the various events that lead up to the story's end (the selection and ordering of events) as moving through two-dimensional, evaluative space. As one approaches the valued goal over time the story line becomes more positive; as one approaches failure or disillusionment one moves in a negative direction. All plots, then, can be converted to a linear form in terms of their evaluative shifts over time. This allows us to isolate three rudimentary forms of narrative.

The first may be described as a *stability narrative,* that is, one that links events so that the individual's trajectory remains essentially unchanged in relation to a goal or outcome; life simply goes on, neither better nor worse. As depicted in Figure 8.1, it is clear that the stability narrative could be developed at any level along the evaluative continuum. At the upper end an individual might conclude, for example, "I am still as attractive as I used to be," or at the lower end, "I continue to be haunted by feelings of failure." As we can also see, each of these narrative summaries possesses inherent implications for the future: in the former, the individual might conclude that he or she will continue to be attractive for the foreseeable future, and in the latter, that feelings of failure will persist regardless of circumstance.

The stability narrative may be contrasted with two others, the *progressive narrative,* which links together events so that the movement along the evaluative dimension over time is incremental, and the *regressive narrative,* in which movement is decremental. The progressive narrative is the Panglossian account of life—ever better in every way. It could be represented by the statement, "I am really learning to overcome my shyness and be more open and friendly with people." The regressive narrative, in contrast, depicts a continued downward slide: "I can't seem to control the events in my life anymore. It's been one series of catastrophes after another." Each of these narratives also implies directionality, the former anticipating further increments and the latter further decrements.

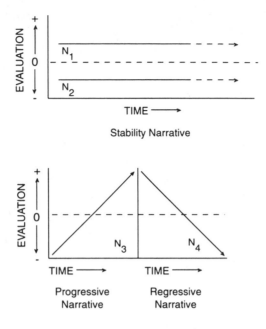

Figure 8.1   Rudimentary Forms of Narrative

As should be clear, these three narrative forms, stability, progressive, and regressive, exhaust the fundamental options for the direction of movement in evaluative space. As such, they may be considered rudimentary bases for other more complex variants.[3] Theoretically one may envision a potential infinity of variations on these simple forms. However, as I have suggested, in various historical conditions the culture may limit itself to a truncated repertoire of possibilities. Let us consider several prominent narrative forms in contemporary culture. There is first the *tragic narrative,* which in the present framework would adopt the structure depicted in Figure 8.2. The tragedy, in this sense, would tell the story of the rapid downfall of one who had achieved high position: a progressive narrative is followed by a rapid regressive narrative. In contrast, in the *comedy-romance,* a regressive narrative is followed by a progressive narrative. Life events become increasingly problematic until the denouement, when happiness is restored to the major protagonists. This narrative is labeled comedy-romance because it conflates the Aristotelian forms. If a progressive narrative is followed by a stability narrative (see Figure 8.3), we have what is commonly known as the *happily-ever-after myth,* which is widely exemplified in traditional courtship. And we also recognize the *heroic saga* as a series of progressive-regressive phases. In this case, the individual may characterize his or her

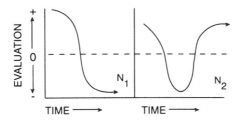

Figure 8.2 Tragic and Comedy-Romance Narratives

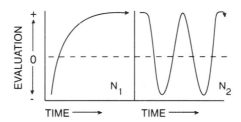

Figure 8.3 The Happily-ever-after Narrative and the Heroic Saga

past as a continuous array of battles against the powers of darkness. Other narrative forms, including unification myths, communion narratives, and dialectic theory, are considered elsewhere.[4]

Narrative Form and the Generation of Drama

Nietzsche once counseled, "Live dangerously, it is the only time you live at all." These words carry with them an important sense of validity. Moments of high drama are often those which most crystallize our sense of identity. It is the major victory, the danger withstood, the return of a lost love, and so on that provide us with our most acute sense of self. Maslow's (1961) studies of peak experiences as identity markers illustrate this point. Similarly, Scheibe (1986) has proposed that "people require adventures in order for satisfactory life stories to be constructed and maintained" (p. 131). But what imbues an event with drama? No event is dramatic in itself, irrespective of its context. A film depicting a continuous but random juxtaposition of startling events (a gunshot, a waving sword, a horse jumping a wall, a low-flying aircraft) would soon become tedious. The capacity of an event to produce a sense of drama is largely a function of its place within a narrative: it is the relationship among events, not the events themselves. What characteristics of narrative form are necessary, then, to generate a sense of dramatic engagement?

The dramatic arts offer a source of insight. It is interesting that one can scarcely locate a theatrical exemplar of the three rudimentary narratives illustrated in Figure 8.1. A drama in which all events were evaluatively equivalent (stability narrative) would scarcely be considered drama.[5] Even a steady but moderate enhancement (progressive narrative) or decrement (regressive narrative) in a protagonist's life conditions would be soporific. However, when we consider the slope line of the tragedy, a drama par excellence (see Figure 8.2), it bears a strong resemblance to the simpler, unarousing regressive narrative, but it also differs in two significant ways. First, the relative decline in events is far less rapid in the prototypical regressive narrative than it is in the tragic narrative. Whereas the former is characterized by a moderate decline over time, in the latter the decline is precipitous. It seems, then, that the rapidity with which events deteriorate in such classic tragedies as *Antigone, Oedipus Rex,* and *Romeo and Juliet* may be an essential aspect of their dramatic impact. More formally, we might say that *the rapid acceleration (or deceleration) of the narrative slope* constitutes one of the chief components of dramatic engagement.

The contrast between the regressive and the tragic narratives also suggests a second major component. In the former (see Figure 8.1) there is unidirectionality in the slope line; its direction does not change over time. In contrast, the tragic narrative (Figure 8.2) features a progressive narrative (sometimes implied) followed by a regressive narrative. Romeo and Juliet are on their way to culminating their romance when tragedy befalls them. It would appear that this "turn of events," this change in the evaluative relationship among events, contributes to a high degree of dramatic engagement. It is when the hero has almost attained the goal—found his sweetheart, won the crown—and then is brought low that drama is created. In more formal terms, the second major component of dramatic engagement is *alteration in the narrative slope* (a shift in evaluative direction). A story in which there were many closely interspersed "ups" and "downs" would constitute high drama by common standards.

A final word about suspense and danger—the sense of intense drama that is sometimes experienced during a mystery story, an athletic contest, or while gambling—must be added to this discussion. Such cases seem to elude the foregoing analysis, since they entail neither acceleration nor alteration in the narrative slope. One is deeply engaged although there are no major changes in the story line. However, on closer inspection it is clear that suspense and danger are special cases of the two preceding rules. In both, the sense of drama depends on the impending *possibility* of acceleration or change. One is in suspense, for example, when a victory, an award, a jackpot, or the like might suddenly be awarded. One is in danger when confronting the potential for sudden loss, destruction, or death. All such events could propel one momentarily toward or away from a valued goal or endpoint in the narrative sequence. Suspense and danger thus result from these implicit alterations in narrative slope.

If we look at prime-time television drama in this context, we see that it typically approximates the comedy-romance (Figure 8.2). A stable condition is interrupted, challenged, or unsettled, and the remainder of the program centers on the restoration of that stability. Such narratives contain a high degree of dramatic engagement, since the slope line alters direction on at least two occasions, and accelerations (or decelerations) can be rapid. In more inventive programming (such as "Hill Street Blues," "Northern Exposure," "NYPD," and many soap operas), multiple narratives may unfold simultaneously. Any incident (a kiss, a threat, a death) may feature in more than one narrative, preventing certain goals while facilitating others. In this way, the dramatic impact of any turn in the plot is intensified. The viewer is set loose on a dramatic roller coaster, with each event now figuring pivotally in multiple narratives.

Narrative Form in Two Populations: An Application

With this rudimentary vocabulary for describing forms of narrative and their attendant drama, we can turn to the issue of potential selves. As I pointed out, in order to maintain intelligibility in the culture, the story one tells about oneself must employ the commonly accepted rules of narrative construction. Narrative constructions of broad cultural usage form a set of ready-made intelligibilities; in effect, they offer a range of discursive resources for the social construction of the self. At first glance it would appear that narrative forms do not impose such constraints. Theoretically, as our analysis makes clear, the number of potential story forms approaches infinity. Attempts such as those of Frye and Campbell unnecessarily delimit the range of potential story forms. At the same time, it is also clear that there is a certain degree of agreement among analysts in Western culture, from Aristotle to the present, suggesting that certain story forms are more readily employed than others; in this sense, forms of self-narrative may likewise be constrained. Consider the person who characterizes him or herself by means of a stability narrative: life is directionless; it is merely moving in a steady, monotonous fashion neither toward nor away from a goal. Such a person would seem an apt candidate for psychotherapy. Similarly, one who characterizes his or her life as a repetitive pattern in which each positive occurrence is immediately followed by a negative one, and vice versa, would be regarded with suspicion. We simply do not accept such life stories as approximating reality. In contrast, if one could make sense of one's life today as the result of "a long struggle upward," a "tragic decline," or a continuing saga in which one suffers defeats but rises from the ashes to achieve success, we are fully prepared to believe. One is not free to have simply any form of personal history. Narrative conventions do not, then, command identity, but they do invite certain actions and discourage others.

In this light it is interesting to explore how various American subcultures characterize their life histories. Let us consider two contrasting populations: adolescents and the elderly. In the former case, twenty-nine youths between the ages of nineteen and twenty-one were asked to chart their life history along a general evaluative dimension (Gergen and Gergen, 1988). Drawing on recollections from their earliest years to the present, how would they characterize their state of general well-being? The characterizations were to be made with a single "life line" in a two-dimensional space. The most positive periods of their history were to be represented by an upward displacement of the line, the negative periods by a downward displacement. What graphic forms might these self-characterizations take? Do young adults generally portray themselves as part of a happily-ever-after story, a heroic saga in which they overcome one peril after another? More pessimistically, does life appear to be growing ever bleaker after the initially happy years of childhood? To explore such matters, an attempt was made to derive the average life trajectory from the data. To this end, the mean displacement of each individual's life line from a neutral midpoint was computed at each five-year interval. By interpolation these means could then be connected graphically to yield an overall life trajectory. As the results of this analysis show (see panel a of Figure 8.4), the general narrative form employed by this group of young adults is unlike any of those conjectured above; it is, rather, that of the comedy-romance. On the average, these young adults tended to view their lives as happy at an early age, beset with

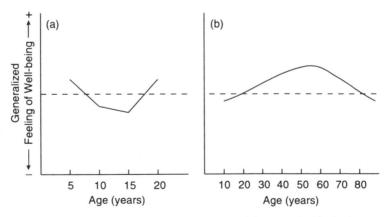

Figure 8.4 Narratives of Well-being for Young Adult (a) and Elderly (b) Samples

difficulty during the adolescent years, but now on an upward swing that bodes well for the future. They have confronted the tribulations of adolescence and emerged victorious.

In these accounts there is a sense in which the narrative form largely dictates memory. Life events don't seem to influence the selection of the story form; to a large degree it is the narrative form that sets the grounds for which events count as important. Let us consider the content through which these adolescents justified the use of the comedy-romance. They were asked to describe the events occurring at the most positive and the most negative periods on their life line. The content of these events proved highly diverse. The positive events included success in a school play, experiences with friends, owning a pet, and discovering music, while low periods resulted from such wide-ranging experiences as moving to a new town, failing at school, having parents with marital problems, and losing a friend. In effect, the "adolescent crisis" does not appear to reflect any single objective factor. Instead, the participants seem to have used the available narrative form and employed whatever "facts" they could to justify and vivify their selection.

More generally, it seems that when the typical young adult describes his or her life history in brief for an anonymous audience, it approximates the narrative form of what I described as the typical television drama (comedy-romance). An informative contrast to this preference is supplied by a sample of seventy-two persons ranging in age from sixty-three to ninety-three years (M. Gergen 1980). In this case, each respondent was interviewed about his or her life experiences. Respondents were asked to describe their general sense of well-being during various periods of life: when were the happiest days, why did things change, in what direction is life now progressing, and so on. These responses were coded so that the results were comparable to the young adult sample (see panel b in Figure 8.4). The typical narrative of the older person follows the shape of a rainbow: the young adult years were difficult, but a progressive narrative enabled the achievement of a peak of well-being somewhere between the ages of fifty and sixty. Life since these "golden years," however, has been on a downward trajectory. Aging is depicted as a regressive narrative.

Such results may seem reasonable, reflecting the natural physical decline in aging. But narratives are not the products of life itself, they are constructions of life—and they could be otherwise. "Aging as decline" is but a cultural convention and so is subject to change. It is at this point that we must also question the role of the social sciences in fostering the view that the life course is a rainbow. The psychological literature is replete with factual accounts of early "development" and late "decline" (Gergen and Gergen 1988). To the extent that such views make their way into public consciousness, they give the elderly little sense of hope or optimism. Different views of what is important in aging—such as those that have been adopted in many Asian cultures—would allow social scientists to articulate far more positive and enabling possibilities. As Coupland and Nussbaum (1993) rightfully propose, the human sciences must critically address the discourses of the life span; are these resources adequate for the challenges of a changing world?

Micro, Macro, and Multiplicity in Narration

So far, we have explored various conventions of narration and their potential for drama. I have argued specifically for replacing a private self-conception with a social process that generates mutual intelligibility. Forms of intelligibility, in turn, are not the byproduct of life events in themselves, but derive largely from available narrative conventions. We now move from narrative resources to the ongoing practices of self-narration—from structure to process. As a transitional concern, it is useful to consider the issue of narrative multiplicity and its byproducts.

The traditional view of self-conception presumes a core identity, an integrally coherent view of the self against which one can gauge whether actions are authentic or artificial. As it is said, an individual without a sense of core identity is without direction, without a sense of position or place, lacking the fundamental assurance that he or she is a worthy person. My argument here, however, throws all such assumptions into question. How often does one compare actions with some core image, for example, and why should we believe that there is but a single and enduring core? Why must one value a fixed sense of position or place and how often does one question one's worthiness? By shifting the emphasis from internal self-perceptions to the process of social intelligibility we can open new theoretical domains with different consequences for cultural life. Thus, even though it is common practice to view each person as possessing "a life story," if selves are realized within social encounters there is good reason to believe that there is no *one* story to tell. Our common participation in the culture will typically expose us to a wide variety of narrative forms, from the rudimentary to the complex. We enter relationships with the potential to use any of a wide number of forms. Just as an experienced skier approaching an incline has a variety of techniques for an effective descent, so we can construct the relationship among our life experiences in a variety of ways. At a minimum, effective socialization should equip us to interpret our lives as stable, as improving, or as in decline. And with a little additional training, we can develop the capacity to envision our lives as tragedy, comedy, or heroic saga (see also Mancuso and Sarbin [1983] on "second-order selves" and Gubrium, Holstein, and Buckholdt [1994] on multiple constructions of the life course). The more capable we are in constructing and reconstructing our self-narrative, the more broadly capable we are in effective relationships.

To illustrate this multiplicity, research participants were asked to draw graphs indicating their feelings of satisfaction in their relationships with their mother, their father, and their academic work over the years. These graph lines pose a striking contrast to the "generalized well-being" account depicted earlier in Figure 8.4. There, the students portrayed their general life course as a comedy-romance—a positive childhood followed by an adolescent fall from grace and capped by a positive ascent. However, in the case of their father and their mother, participants tended most frequently to select progressive narratives—slow and continuous for the father but more sharply accelerated more recently for the mother. For both parents, they portrayed their relationships as steadily improving. Yet, although they were attending a highly competitive college, the students tended to depict their feeling of satisfaction with their academic work as one of steady decline—a regressive narrative that left them on the brink of despair in the present.

Not only do people enter social relationships with a variety of narratives at their disposal, but there are in principle no necessary temporal parameters within which a personal narrative must be constructed. One may relate events occurring over vast periods of time or tell a story of brief duration. One may see his or her life as part of a historical movement commencing centuries ago, or at birth, or in early adolescence. We may use the terms "macro" and "micro" to refer to the hypothetical or idealized ends of the temporal continuum. *Macronarratives* refer to accounts in which events span broad periods of time, while *micronarratives* relate events of brief duration. The autobiographer generally excels in macronarrative, while the comedian, who relies on sight gags, strives to master micronarrative. The former asks that his or her present actions be understood against the backdrop of history; the latter achieves success by removing him or herself from history.

Given our capacity to relate events within different temporal perspectives, it becomes apparent that narratives may also be *nested,* one within another (see also Mandler 1984). Thus, individuals may account for themselves as the bearers of a long cultural history, but nested within this narrative may be an independent account of their development since childhood, and within this account a change of heart experienced moments ago. A person may view himself as bearing the contemporary standard of a race that has struggled for centuries (a progressive narrative), while at the same time seeing himself as one long favored by his parents who disappointed them as he grew older (the tragic narrative), and as one who managed to rekindle the waning ardor of a woman friend the preceding evening (the comedy-romance).

The concept of nested narratives raises a variety of interesting issues. To what extent can we anticipate coherence among nested narratives? As Ortega y Gasset (1941) proposed in his analysis of historical systems, "the plurality of beliefs in which an individual, or a people, or an age is grounded never possesses a completely logical articulation" (p. 166). Yet, there are many social advantages to "having one's stories agree." To the extent that the culture prizes consistency among narratives, macronarratives acquire preeminent importance. They seem to lay the foundations upon which we construct other narratives. An account of an evening with a friend would not seem to dictate an account of one's life history; however, that life history does constitute grounds for understanding the trajectory of the evening. To extrapolate, people with an extended sense of their own history may strive for more coherence between one narrative and another than those with a superficial sense of the past. Or, in a different light, people from a newly developing culture or nation may experience a greater sense of freedom in momentary action than those from cultures or nations with long and prominent historical narratives. For the former there is less necessity to behave in ways that are coherent with the past.

Let us consider the case of terrorist activity in this light. Terrorists have been viewed as disturbed, irrational, or potentially psychotic on the one hand, or as politically motivated activists on the other. However, having examined Armenian terrorist activity, Tololyan (1989) argues that the terrorist is simply carrying out the implications of a culturally shared narrative of long-standing significance. That narrative begins in 450 A.D. and describes many valorous attempts to protect Armenian national identity. Similar stories of courage, martyrdom, and the pursuit of justice continue to accumulate over the centuries and are now embedded within common Armenian folk culture. As Tololyan reasons, to become a terrorist is to live out the implications of one's place in cultural history—or, more aptly, to live out one's life course nested within the broader history of one's people. Failing to possess a past in this way makes political participation optional.

The Pragmatics of Self-Narrative

From a constructionist standpoint, narrative multiplicity is important primarily because of its social implications. Multiplicity is favored by the variegated range of relationships in which people are enmeshed and the differing demands of various relational contexts. As Wittgenstein (1953) advised, "Think of the tools in a tool-box: there is a hammer, pliers, a screw-driver, a rule, a glue-pot, glue, nails and screws. The functions of words are as diverse as the functions of these objects" (p. 6). In this sense, narrative constructions are essentially linguistic tools with important social functions. Mastering various forms of narrative enhances one's capacity for relatedness. Let us consider a selected number of functions self-narration fulfills.

Consider first the primitive narrative of stability. Although generally devoid of dramatic value, people's capacity to identify themselves as stable units has great utility within a culture. In important respects most relationships tend toward stable patterns, and indeed, it is stabilization that enables us to speak of cultural patterns, institutions, and individual identities at all. Often such patterns become saturated with value; to rationalize them in this way is to sustain them over time. The societal demand for stability finds its functional counterpart in the ready accessibility of the stability narrative. To successfully negotiate social life one must be capable of making him or herself intelligible as an enduring, integral, or coherent identity. In certain political arenas, for example, it is essential to demonstrate that in spite of extended absences, one is "truly rooted" in the local culture and part of its future. Or to be able to show on the more personal level that one's love, parental commitment, honesty, moral ideals, and so on have been unfailing over time, even when their outward appearance is suspicious, may be essential to continuing a relationship. In close relationships people often wish to know that others *"are* what they seem," that certain characteristics endure across time. A major way of conveying such assurance is the stability narrative. In this sense, personality traits, moral character, and personal identity are not so much the givens of social life, the building blocks of relationship, but the outcomes of relationship itself. "To be" a person of any special kind is a social achievement and requires continual conversational attention.

It is important to note at this point a major way in which this analysis conflicts with more traditional accounts of personal identity. Theorists such as Prescott Lecky, Erik Erikson, Carl Rogers, and Seymour Epstein have viewed personal identity as something akin to an *achieved condition* of the mind. According to this account, the mature individual is one who has "found," "crystallized," or "realized" a firm sense of self or personal identity. In general this condition is viewed as a highly positive one and, once achieved, it minimizes variance or inconsistency in one's conduct. Much the same idea is advanced by McAdams (1985) in his life story theory of personal identity. For McAdams, "identity is *a life story* which individuals begin constructing, consciously and unconsciously, in late adolescence . . . Like stories, identities may assume a 'good' form—a narrative coherence and consistency—or they may be ill-formed—like the story of the fox and the bear with its cul-de-sacs and loose ends" (p. 57; italics mine).

In contrast, from a constructionist vantage point there is no inherent demand for identity coherence and stability. The constructionist view does not consider identity, for one, as an achievement of mind, but rather, of relationship. And because one stands in shifting relationships to a multiplicity of others, one may or may not achieve stability in any given relationship, nor is there reason across relationships to suspect a high degree of coherence. In terms of narratives, this underscores the previous emphasis on variety in self-accounts. People may portray themselves in many different ways depending on the relational context. One acquires not a deep and enduring "true self" but a potential for communicating and performing a self.

This latter position is fortified when we consider the social functions that are served by the progressive narrative. Society places strong value on change as well as on stability. For example, every stabilization may also be characterized—from alternative perspectives—as problematic, oppressive, or odious. For many, the possibility of progressive change is a raison d'être. Careers are selected, hardships endured, and personal resources (including one's most intimate relations) sacrificed in the belief that one is participating in positive change—a great progressive narrative. In addition, the success of many relationships depends a great deal on people's ability to demonstrate that their undesirable characteristics (such as unfaithfulness, quarreling, and self-centeredness) have diminished over time—even when there are many reasons to doubt it. As Kitwood's (1980) research suggests, people make special use of the progressive narrative in the early stages of a relationship, seemingly to invest the relationship with increased value and promise for the future. In effect, the progressive narrative plays a variety of useful functions in social life.

As should be evident, one must be prepared in most relationships to account for oneself as both inherently stable and undergoing change at the same time. One must be able to show that one has always been the same and will continue to be so, although continuing to improve. Achieving such diverse ends is primarily a matter of negotiating the meaning of events in relationship to each other. Thus, with sufficient conversational work, one and the same event may figure in both a stability and a progressive narrative. Graduation from medical school, for example, may show that one has always been intelligent and at the same time demonstrate that one is en route to high professional status.

Can a case be made for the social value of regressive narratives? There is reason to believe so. Consider the effects of tales of woe in soliciting attention, sympathy, and intimacy. To relate one's story of depression is not to describe the onset of a mental state, but to engage in a particular kind of relationship. The narrative may simultaneously solicit pity and concern, excuse one from failure, and deliver punishment. Within Western culture regressive narratives can also serve a *compensatory function*. When people learn of steadily worsening conditions, the description often operates, by convention, as a challenge to compensate or seek improvement. The decline is to be offset or reversed through renewed vigor; intensification of effort is to turn a potential tragedy into a comedy-romance. Thus, regressive narratives serve as an important means for motivating people (including oneself) toward achieving positive ends. The compensatory function operates on a national level when a government demonstrates that the steady decline in the balance of payments can be offset by a grass-roots commitment to locally manufactured products, and on the individual level when one bolsters one's enthusiasm for a given project: "I am failing at this, I've got to try harder."

The Interknitting of Identities

In this chapter I have attempted to develop a view of narration as a discursive resource and of its richness and potentials as constituting a historical legacy available in varying degree to all within the culture. To possess an intelligible self—a recognizable being with both a past and a future, requires a borrowing from the cultural repository. In Bakhtin's (1981) sense, to be an intelligible person requires an act of *ventriloquation*. However, as developed here, there is also a strong emphasis on ongoing interchange. Narration may appear to be monologic, but its success in establishing identity will inevitably rely on dialogue. It is in this context that I wish finally to draw attention to ways in which narrated identities are interwoven within the culture. It is particularly useful to touch on self-narration and moral community, interminable negotiation, and reciprocal identities.

As I have suggested, self-narratives are immersed within processes of ongoing interchange. In a broad sense they serve to unite the past with the present and to signify future trajectories (Csikszentmihalyi and Beattie 1979). It is their significance for the future that is of special interest here, because it sets the stage for moral evaluation. To maintain that one has always been an honest person (stability narrative) suggests that one can be trusted. To construct one's past as a success story (progressive narrative) implies a future of continued advancement. On the other hand, to portray oneself as losing one's abilities because of increasing age (regressive narrative) generates the expectation that one will be less energetic in the future. The important point here is that as these implications are realized in action they become subject to social appraisal. Others may find the actions and outcomes implied by these narratives (according to current conventions) coherent with or contradictory to the tellings. To the extent that such actions conflict with these accounts, they cast doubt on their validity, and social censure may result. In MacIntyre's (1981) terms, in matters of moral deliberation, "I can only answer the question 'What am I to do?' if I can answer the prior question 'Of what story or stories do I find myself a part?' " (p. 201). What this means is that self-narrative is not simply a derivative of past encounters, reassembled within ongoing relationships; once used, it establishes the grounds for moral being within the community. It establishes reputation, and it is the community of reputations that form the core of a moral tradition. In effect, the performance of self-narrative secures a relational future.

Narrative performance also sets the stage for further interdependence. Because the relationship between our actions and our accounts of them depends on social conventions and because conventions of reference are seldom univocal, there is an inherent ambiguity in how actions are to be understood. Because narratives generate expectations, there is the inevitable question about whether actions measure up to expectations. Does the tax audit contradict the individual's claim to continuing honesty; does the professor's year without publications indicate that the progressive narrative is no longer operative; does the third-set tennis victory indicate that the complaints of aging were only a ruse? In order to sustain identity, successful negotiation is required at every turn. More broadly, it may be said that maintaining identity—narrative validity within a community—is an interminable challenge (see also de Waele and Harré 1976; Hankiss 1981). One's moral being is never a completed project so long as the conversations of the culture continue.

This continuing negotiation of narrative identity is complicated by a final relational feature. So far I have treated narratives as if they were solely concerned with the temporal trajectory of the protagonist alone. This conception must be expanded. The incidents typically woven into a narrative are the actions not only of the protagonist but of others as well. In most instances the actions of others contribute vitally to the events linked in narrative sequence. For example, to justify his account of continuing honesty, an individual might describe how a friend unsuccessfully tempted him to cheat; to illustrate achievement, he might show how another person was vanquished in a competition; in speaking of lost capabilities he might point to the alacrity of a younger person's performance. In all cases, the actions of others become an integral part of narrative intelligibility. In this sense, constructions of the self require a supporting cast.

The implications of this need for context are broad indeed. First, in the same way that individuals usually command the privilege of self-definition ("I know myself better than others know me"), others also demand rights in defining their own actions. Thus, as one uses the actions of others to make oneself intelligible, one becomes reliant on their accord. In the simplest case, if the other is present, no account of one's actions can stand without the agreement that "Yes, that's how it was." If others are not willing to accede to their assigned parts, then one cannot rely on their actions within a narrative. If others fail to see their actions as "offering temptation," the actor can scarcely boast of continued strong character; if others can show that they were not really vanquished in a competition, the actor can scarcely use the episode as a stepping-stone in a success story. Narrative validity, then, depends strongly on the affirmation of others.

This reliance on others places the actor in a position of precarious inter-dependence, for in the same way that self-intelligibility depends on whether others agree about their own place in the story, so their own identity de-pends on the actor's affirmation of them. An actor's success in sustaining a given self-narrative is fundamentally dependent on the willingness of others to play out certain pasts in relationship to him. In Schapp's (1976) terms, each of us is "knitted into" the historical constructions of others just as they are into ours. As this delicate interdependence of constructed narratives suggests, a fundamental aspect of social life is the *network of reciprocating identities*. Because one's identity can be maintained for only so long as others play their proper supporting role, and because one is required in turn to play supporting roles in their constructions, the moment any participant chooses to renege, he or she threatens the array of interdependent construc-tions.

An adolescent may tell his mother that she has been a "bad mother," thus potentially destroying her stability narrative as a "good mother." At the same time, however, he risks having his mother reply that she always felt his character was so inferior, he never merited her love; his continuing narra-tive of "self as good" is thus in jeopardy. A lover may announce to her male partner that he no longer interests her as he once did, thus potentially crush-ing his stability narrative; however, he may reply that he has long been bored with her and is happy to be relieved of his lover's role. In such in-stances, when the parties in the relationship pull out of their supporting roles, the result is a general degeneration of identities. Identities, in this sense, are never individual; each is suspended in an array of precariously situated relationships. The reverberations of what takes place here and now—between us—may be infinite.

9   Emotion as Relationship

Narratives of the self are not personal impulses made social, but social processes realized on the site of the personal. In this chapter I will extend this theme significantly on the way to articulating a relational conception of self. Western tradition is deeply committed to a view of the self as an independent or self-contained unit. As long as this view is sustained, traditional problems of epistemology and social knowledge will remain unsolved (and insoluble), and the broad social practices in which this conception is lodged will remain unchallenged. I do not intend here to develop an entirely new vocabulary, unanchored to cultural practices, but to reconstitute existing conceptualizations. In particular, I intend to demonstrate how the traditional conception of emotion can be redrawn—how the emotions can be viewed as constitutive features not of individuals but of relationships.

We now have at our disposal over two thousand years of accumulated discourse on the self. We share with Plato the concept of abstract ideas (now refigured as prototypes), with Aristotle the concept of logical forms (emerging as cognitive heuristics), with Machiavelli conceptions of social strategy (now impression management), with Augustine, Hobbes, and Pascal the concept of self-love (now self-esteem), and with Locke a concept of the empirical basis of abstract ideas (now mental representation). These are only a few constituents of the rich and finely nuanced discourse of the self available to us. Indeed, contemporary inquiry into the self continues an honored tradition of scholarship, of which these concepts are but a few important artifacts. In our current dialogue our forebears stand as silent interlocutors. Scholars concerned with the nature of individual selves now range across the social sciences and the humanities. They represent the most conceptually advanced, methodologically sophisticated, and politically and economically unencumbered group ever to engage in concentrated consideration of the self. While scholars of earlier centuries were scattered historically and geographically, and often ignorant of each other's work, the contemporary research community is in continuous communication that cuts across geographic, ethnic, religious, and political domains. One may be justifiably awed at the intellectual power brought to the contemporary study of self and deeply concerned with its outcomes.

The consequences of such inquiry could be enormous. Theories of the self are, after all, nothing less than definitions of what it is to be human. Such theories inform society about what the individual can or cannot do, what limits can be placed on human functioning, and what hopes can be nurtured for future change. Further, they inform society about rights and duties, designate those activities to be viewed with suspicion or approbation, and indicate who or what is to be held responsible for our present condition. To define the self is thus to sit in implicit judgment of society.

Conceptions of the self have played and continue to play an immensely important role in human affairs. In the case of psychology, for example, the increasing articulation of the concepts of unconscious forces and self-deception has significantly altered legal proceedings. In important respects the insanity defense is their offspring, and many individuals virtually owe their lives to this conceptual implement. Similarly, the legalization of abortion depended strongly on the elaboration of the concepts of "individual choice" and "mental suffering." The concept of self-esteem, as nurtured and developed by psychologists, was pivotal in American civil rights legislation. The placement of self-esteem at the forefront of personal well-being set the stage for the argument against "separate but equal"—injurious, it was held, to the self-esteem of those held separate. The concept has made its way into the educational sphere, where student self-esteem now figures centrally in curriculum planning. Similarly, the related concepts of intelligence level and personal traits have fired the growth of the mental measurement industry. Assessment procedures are now used across the spectrum of institutional life to sort, constrain, and guide individual lives.[1] These maneuvers of competing intelligibilities on the cultural field are of no small consequence.

More generally, scholarly accounts of individual minds play a powerful role in justifying and sustaining patterns of cultural life. When economists base their predictions on assumptions of individual rationality; anthropologists explore the personalities, subjectivities, or mentalities of other groups; historians elucidate the prevailing values and motives of other times; political scientists document the attitudes and opinions of the populace; and psychologists conduct experiments on perception, cognition, or emotion, they all inform the public that the mind of the single individual is crucial to cultural well-being. And in placing the individual mind at center stage, these pursuits add subtle force to many of our prevailing institutions. They favor a conception of democracy, for example, in which each individual possesses the right to vote; a system of free enterprise in which the individual can exercise the power of rational choice; educational practices devoted to the training of individual minds; and institutions of justice and daily practices of moral adjudication in which individuals are held morally responsible for their actions.

There is much to be said on behalf of these institutions and the supporting intelligibilities so richly supplemented by the argot of the academy. For many psychologists the insanity defense, the concept of self-esteem, and measures of intelligence and personal traits contribute to a humane society. And if scholarly study lends itself to public institutions of democracy, free enterprise, justice, and moral responsibility, so much the better. Much of what we in Western culture hold to be worthwhile can be traced in important respects to our rich and compelling vocabulary of individual minds. Should we simply continue, then, with business as usual, progressively elaborating and extending the discourses of the individual self? It is at this point that we should pause, for in recent decades a once quiet murmur of dissent has given way to a full-scale chorus of critique.

At the outset, the belief in the self-contained individual—to which a commitment to individual knowing minds makes a substantial contribution— lends itself to giving the self priority in daily affairs. This emphasis legitimates a preeminent concern with one's own private condition—beginning with one's state of knowledge and proceeding through the related issues of one's own goals, needs, pleasures, and rights. Buttressed by Darwin's theory of species survival, what we might ask of any project is how the self is affected: "How do *I* gain or lose?" Other individuals should be considered, to be sure, but only insofar as their actions affect our own well-being. Thus, the enlightened individual may favor altruism, but only insofar as there is a positive payoff for oneself. Christopher Lasch's (1979) *The Culture of Narcissism* contains perhaps the most condemning statement of the "me-first" attitude engendered by the individualist impulse. For Lasch, this orientation reduces to trivia emotional relationships and sexual intimacy (carried out to "make me feel good"), scholarly research (conducted to "help my career"), and political discourse (chosen to "help me win").

Closely related to this trivialization, the ideology of individualism also generates a sense of fundamental independence or isolation. For the individualist, people are bounded entities leading separate lives on independent trajectories: we can never be certain that anyone else understands us, and thus, that they can care deeply about us. By the same token, the self-contained individual can never be certain that he or she understands the mind (thoughts, needs, feelings) of others, and is thereby restrained from investing too heavily in their lives. And why should such investments be pursued when they may curtail one's individual freedom? Bellah and his colleagues (1985), along with the psychologists Sarnoff and Sarnoff (1989), have come to the conclusion that institutions such as community and marriage are deeply threatened by the individualist perspective. If one believes that the central unit of society is the individual self, then relationships are by definition artificial contrivances, unnatural and alien. By implication they must be constructed, nurtured, or "worked at." If such efforts prove personally arduous or disagreeable, then one is invited to abandon them and return to the native state of isolation.

On a societal level analysts are also concerned with the effects of individualist ideology on collective well-being. Classic is Hardin's (1968) analysis of the hidden costs of individual rationality. As he demonstrates, if each individual acts to maximize gains and minimize costs, the overall consequences for society may be disastrous. Current environmental crises provide a convenient illustration: the sum of individual gains is collective impoverishment. Sennett's (1977) *The Fall of Public Man* traces the decline of civic life over the centuries. He argues that our individualist preoccupation, and concomitant fear of sincerity and self-revelation, militate against the kind of public life in which people mingle freely on the streets, in parks, or at public gatherings and speak with civil constraint, without embarrassment, and with a sense of the common good. As he sees it, public life has given way to privatized, claustrophobic, and defensive modes of living. Others point to the systematic inattention to broad social configurations favored by the individualist worldview (Sampson 1978, 1981). In higher education there is little consciousness of cooperative modes of learning; business training emphasizes individual as opposed to group performance; courts of law seek to allocate individual blame while remaining blind to the broader social processes in which crime is embedded.

Finally, we must ask whether an individualist ideology can guide us safely into the future. As MacIntyre (1981) argues, there is no reason why one who is committed to individualism should pay heed to the "good reasons" of others. If the individual should "choose what he or she believes is good and right"—as the individualist perspective favors—then any opposing views constitute frustrations or interferences. To pay heed to "the opposition" is to relinquish one's integrity.[2] In effect, individualism promotes interminable conflict among incommensurable moral or ideological commitments. Today the cultures of the world are thrown into ever-increasing contact with each other, problems of international cooperation are ever expanding, and the tools for massive destruction are increasingly effective. In such a world the individualist mentality—each against each—poses a substantial danger.

Toward Relational Realities

If substantial problems inhere in the individualist worldview, and inquiry presuming the reality of the individual mind sustains this view, there is good reason for a reflexive pause. Must we add still further to the enormous vocabulary of psychological states? If we hope that our work might contribute to the common good—to say nothing of the richness of the scholarly tradition—we have strong reason to doubt. Further, constructionist views offer strong theoretical justification for developing alternatives to individualistic forms of description and explanation. As I have proposed, conceptions of the individual—including what we take to be the substance and content of individual minds—derive from social process. For the constructionist, relatedness precedes individuality. The constructionist challenge, then, is to fashion a reality of relatedness, linguistic intelligibilities, and associated practices that offer new potential for cultural life. If successful, such relational constructions should acquire a lived validity at least equal to the language of individual minds. At present we possess a staggering vocabulary for characterizing individual selves but stand virtually mute in the discourse of relatedness. It is as if we have at our disposal an enormously elaborated language for describing rooks, pawns, and bishops but are unable to characterize the game of chess. Can we develop a language of understanding in which individual characteristics are derivatives of more essential forms of relationship? Can we elucidate the reality of the relationships in which the sense of self is rooted?

At this juncture we find that constructionism itself offers no clear account of relational selves. Its discourse does not contain an implicit language of relatedness simply awaiting articulation. If relatedness is to be made real, the theorist must dip into the cultural resources for metaphors, narratives, and other rhetorical devices. There are indeed many such resources, but they vary substantially in promise. For example, in *The Fiction of Relationship,* Weinstein (1988) discusses the many ways in which relationships are given visceral palpability in the novels of the past three centuries. At the same time, it is interesting to note the extent to which relationships in these works are predicated on the more fundamental presumption of the individual self. Thus, among the central concerns of this literary tradition, according to Weinstein, are "how the self longs for union but is blind to the reality of the other; how the self evolves over time while remaining linked to another; how the self is involved in 'breaking-and-entering' schemes, be they erotic, chemical, or ideological; how the self comes to adequate knowledge of the other only by becoming that other, and the cost of such transformation; how the self may apprehend—with joy or with misery, as heaven or as hell—the larger configuration of which it is a part" (p. 308). In effect, although relatedness has lived a robust life in Western fiction, it is a relatedness between otherwise alienated identities.

It is this view of the individual self working outward toward relatedness that dominates much of the literature in social psychology—that discipline most centrally concerned with conceptualizing relationships. The concept of the group *qua* group virtually disappeared from social psychology with the advent of methodological individualism in the 1930s. Among the thirty chapters of the 1985 edition of the *Handbook of Social Psychology* there is no single chapter on the psychology of groups. There is a chapter on "intergroup relations," but here the "perspective consists of the systematic study of relations between individuals as they are affected by group membership" (Stephan 1985, p. 599). Although concerned with patterns of relationship across time, social exchange theory (Thibaut and Kelley 1959) was based on an account of individual strategies for maximizing gain. Relationships, then, are the artifactual outcomes of individuals making their own private decisions. More promising in this regard is more recent work on personal relationships (Gilmour and Duck 1986). Here one finds significant discontent with the individualistic conception of relatedness (see, for example, Berscheid 1986). With notable exceptions, however, most of this work remains committed to the individual as the cornerstone of the relationship—thus emphasizing how individuals conceptualize relationships, how they are equipped for successful relationships, or how various factors influence individuals in relationship. Feminist psychologists have demonstrated significant concern with relationships. Yet, even here it has been difficult to break with the explanatory fulcrum of the individual mind (see, for example, Chodorow 1978; Gilligan, Lyons, and Hanmer 1989).

For alternatives to the view that relationships are a byproduct of individual selves we must look elsewhere. In much nineteenth-century writing, the self is viewed *as a constituent of the whole*. According to this view, the society as a monolithic structure of relatedness precedes the individual, and the self is only realized through participation in the whole. This account is foreshadowed by Hegel's conception of *Folkgeist*—literally, "spirit of the people." For Hegel (1979) this overarching spirit of community was fundamental to the human condition; the individual was a secondary derivative. As Hegel envisioned, "the individual is an individual in this substance (which characterizes a community) . . . No individual can step beyond [it]." Or again, "for the single individual as such is true only as a universal multiplicity of single individuals. Cut off from the multiplicity, the solitary self is, in fact, an unreal, impotent self." The writings of both Durkheim and Marx resonate with this romance of the whole—yet nostalgically. In earlier times, they propose, when society was either less complex (Durkheim) or less governed by capitalist domination (Marx), the self was an integral part of the whole. However, with the increasing complexity of the modern state, "organic solidarity" has given way to "mechanistic" relations (Durkheim); "personal dependence" has been replaced by "objective dependency relations" (Marx). This theme of the self in interactive relationship to a social whole continues through the more recent work of Parsons (1964) and Giddens (1984).

Yet most theorists occupied with selves in relationship find concepts of social structure (the community of the whole) remote from their concerns. Such all-encompassing units seem removed from the more immediate exigencies of daily life. The structures are always "off stage," immanent but never transparent. How, then, is it possible to conceptualize relationships neither as the interchange of autonomous individuals nor as manifestations of the whole? At least one promising possibility is that of viewing relationships in terms of *intersubjective interdependency,* or coordinated mentalities. Mead's (1934) work stands as a major contribution to this view. As Mead saw it, human beings can instinctively coordinate their actions. As development proceeds, however, they acquire the capacity for self-reflection—consciousness of themselves and the effects of their actions. Self-consciousness, in turn, is influenced by adopting the standpoint of the other toward the self. Thus, one's conception of self and one's actions are essentially dependent upon the attitudes and actions of others; there is no self and no meaningful action without dependency. This theme is also echoed in the late writings of Vygotsky (1978). Like Mead, Vygotsky argued for certain biological prerequisites to human interchange. However, as the child begins to coordinate with others in language, new developments occur. Over time, the child internalizes language and begins to use it privately and autonomously. Here is the beginning of the higher mental functions of thought, voluntary attention, logical memory, and self-consciousness. For Vygotsky, every process in the development of higher mental functions occurs twice, "first, on the social level, and later, on the individual level; first *between* people *(interpsychological)* and then *inside* the child *(intrapsychological)*" (p. 57). This emphasis on intersubjective relatedness continues to lead a healthy life in symbolic interactionist and child development research (Kaye 1982; Youniss 1980). It is also reflected in the symbolic anthropology movement (Geertz 1973; Shweder 1991), cultural psychology (Bruner 1990), and theory and research on organizational culture (Frost et al. 1991).[3]

Although rich in implication and a significant move away from the individualistic basis of much previous theory, theories of intersubjectivity are not without problems. It is difficult to reconcile the epistemology implied by this position with the claim that we can know about anyone outside our own culture; if we only know from within our culture, we can never recognize or know the subjectivity of anyone who is alien to that culture. There are also intractable conceptual difficulties inhering in the problem of socialization—how the unthinking child becomes mindful (see Chapters 5 and 11). With these reservations at hand, we are prepared to address a final orientation toward relatedness, one that shifts concern from the remote realms of social structure and individual subjectivity to the domain of *microsocial pattern*. Here the forms of interdependent action—the realm of the *between*—becomes focal. Goffman's (1959, 1967, 1969) many writings have played a central role in developing this possibility. In his explorations of self-presentation, "face work," degradation ceremonies, conversational framing, and the like, he has illustrated the rich potential of addressing social interdependency without psychological explanation.[4] Also of landmark significance is the work of Garfinkel (1967) and his colleagues on ethnomethodology. The early work is of particular importance in demonstrating how rationality can be viewed as a social, as opposed to an individual, achievement. Its implications are now born out in a rich range of inquiry into conversational forms and strategies (see, for example, Craig and Tracy 1982; McLaughlin 1984). The implications of the microsocial perspective for emotions are effectively drawn by Hochschild's (1983) inquiry into emotional management.

A similar emphasis on microsocial processes has emerged in the therapeutic domain. Neo-Freudians, and most especially object relations theorists, have long been concerned with the intimate relationship between the ego and the social world. However, this work continues to place a strong emphasis on internal or individual psychological processes (see, for example, Curtis 1990). The possibilities for microsocial understanding were foreshadowed in Sullivan's (1953) attempts to trace aberrant symptoms to interpersonal as opposed to interpsychic processes. However, it was not until the pioneering efforts of Bateson (1972) and his colleagues to embed pathology in systems of human communication that the potential of the interpersonal began to be realized.[5] This work, emphasizing patterns of communication, their effects on the individual (for example, the double bind theory of schizophrenia), and the constitutive part played by the individual within the system as a whole, virtually gave birth to modern practices of family therapy (see Hoffman's 1981 review). Influenced by the cybernetic metaphor pervasive at the time, subsequent work was largely built around such physical concepts as homeostasis, family structure, hierarchy, and systems. Therapeutic practices were aimed at altering family structure or communication systems through specialized strategies.

Gradually, however, the conception of physical systems has given way to a more human view of communication, one placing emphasis on the negotiation of meaning within therapy (Hoffman 1992). In place of physical metaphors, this view emphasizes the co-construction of meaning (Goolishian and Anderson 1987; Selman and Schultz 1990), narratives of the self (Epston and White 1992), and reflexive constructions of reality (Andersen 1991). This work is highly congenial with constructionism, and as I will propose in Chapter 10, favors a radical recentering of the therapeutic effort.

A Socially Reconstituted Psychology

If microsocial process moves to the center of concern, what are the implications for understanding the emotions and other psychological processes? Traditionally we have viewed the emotions as inherent possessions of the single individual, genetically prepared, biologically based, and experientially grounded. From this perspective, the individual emotions could have *effects* on microsocial process, or the reverse. Yet emotions in themselves are not microsocial events. Can this array of commonsense assumptions be challenged, and more specifically, how can microsocial theory replace the individualist account? It does seem essential that the microsocial account not obliterate the existing vernacular of the emotions. To simply abandon such terms as "anger" and "fear" in favor of a new vocabulary, unsullied by cultural traditions, would not only ask the reader to suspend the lived realities of daily life. It would also result in an unusable language, abstracted from any context and without illocutionary potential.

If we commit our theory to the traditional vernacular, the challenge is then to reconstitute the meaning of mental terms. This may be accomplished in part by removing the referential locus for such terms from the head of the individual actor and placing it within the sphere of relationship. Rather than hammer out a new argot of understanding—descriptive and explanatory terms without currency in the marketplace of daily life—we can leave the psychological vocabulary intact but alter the way in which we understand such terms. To illustrate: The term "liberal" once had strong rhetorical appeal in the United States. To be liberal was to be flexible and forward looking, to be concerned with social justice and the plight of the downtrodden. However, thinkers on both the far left and the far right have since altered the context of understanding so that for many the term now approaches epithet. For the politically left, the term connotes rightist individualism; for the right, left-wing sentimentalism. The term remains in use, but its pragmatic implications have been significantly altered. In the present case, by reconstituting mental predicates as relational, I hope to blunt the impact of self-contained individualism and to engender a fuller appreciation of interdependence.

In an important sense, ethnomethodological inquiry opened the door to this social relocation of the mental. If rationality is not a product of individual minds but of participation in local routines of interchange, then we may begin to consider a major relocation of the cognitive. This same possibility is manifest in Douglas's (1986) *How Institutions Think*. Rather than trace decisions to the minds of individual managers, Douglas demonstrates that rationality within organizations is socially distributed, with various individuals or units contributing to an overall outcome that may be judged as rational or irrational. A similar conclusion is reached by Engestrom, Middleton, and their colleagues (1992) in their analysis of the ways in which groups generate legal opinions, determine health decisions, pilot airliners, produce scientific conclusions, and so on. They have coined the term "communal cognition" to refer to the ways in which individuals collaborate to achieve rational outcomes for the group as a whole. This work is closely related as well to various explorations of "collective remembering" (Middleton and Edwards 1990). Here, investigators demonstrate ways in which accounts of the past are products of continuing negotiation—in families, communities, professions, and the culture at large.[6] Billig's (1987) reconstruction of reasoning as participation in a rhetorical tradition is also apposite. Reasoning, according to this account, is not an inherently private act; it is rather to engage in the traditional practices of argumentation. It is not the individual who thinks and then argues but the social forms of argumentation that "think the individual." A similar transformation of the concept of attitude is proposed by Potter and Wetherell (1987). They argue that the traditional view that attitudes are located within the mind of the individual and propel action is deeply problematic. To possess an attitude is, rather, to adopt a position within a conversation.[7]

In the remainder of this chapter I wish to press this reconstructive project forward to encompass the emotions, to refigure the emotions as events within relational patterns—as social actions that derive their meaning and significance from their placement within rituals of relationship. There is good reason for doing so. As we have seen, emotions within Western culture are regarded as individual possessions par excellence. We may be willing to admit that our thoughts are derived from their social surrounds and that our memory reports are biased by the demands of social context. But emotions, we generally hold, are lodged deep within the psyche; they are not the product of social rules, and we can be little mistaken about their presence within the psyche. Thus, the challenge to social refiguration is substantial. To further prepare the way, I will first consider the shortcomings of traditional inquiry into the emotions.

In Search of Emotion: From Individual to Relationship

In recent years, the scientific literature on emotions has reached enormous proportions. We have already considered a number of the ideological reasons for challenging the prevailing conception of emotion. But to appreciate the force of my argument, it is also useful to consider some of the substantial problems inherent in this body of literature. For it is precisely these problems that invite an alternative formulation, and it is specifically a relational account that enables us to abandon the enigmas. Let us begin with the most elementary question: How are we to identify the phenomena under investigation, that is, to establish that emotions exist, and that they are of several different kinds? Without an answer at this most basic level, an attempt at scientific study can scarcely be justified. If we cannot identify the phenomena of concern and differentiate them from other existing things, how can we study them? Would we not be equally justified in launching a full-scale research program on the human spirit? Of course, in Western culture we readily presume that there are emotions; indeed, it is this conviction that prompts such an enormous investigatory undertaking. But then again, we were once convinced of the factuality of human spirit, and we should not wish to be misled at this juncture by founding our scientific studies on mere folk belief. How, then, are we to identify the phenomena?

Contemporary science offers two major answers to the question of identification. The first belongs to the more humanistic, phenomenological, and subjectively oriented schools: personal experience. We may justifiably study the human emotions, it is proposed, because of their transparent existence in human experience. And it is experience that also enables us to differentiate among emotions: "I know that love, fear, and anger are different because I experience the differences clearly and distinctly." Yet, while compelling in its intuitive appeal, in the end this form of answer proves inconsequential. Rather than answer the challenge, it triggers a new and more extensive array of impenetrables. For example, are we not unquestioningly presuming a Western metaphysics of dualism with a knowing subject as against an independent object of knowledge? How is this presumption to be justified? And if we do make this leap, do we truly experience *interior* objects in the same way we claim to perceive *exterior* or "real-world" objects? How is experience to serve simultaneously as subject (the perceiver) and object (the perceived)? Further, what is the object in this case? What is the size, the shape, the color, or the form of an emotion, let us say, as compared to an intention, an attitude, or a value? By what means can we differentiate among all the mental events to which we make explicit claims? These problems have already been elaborated in Chapters 6 and 7.

If we were able to perform the feat of interior identification, how would we know what to label the events or how to describe them? We couldn't model ourselves after others in this regard, for we have no access to their emotional experiences (when Jill says she feels angry, we don't know what "object" she is describing). Thus, even if we were sure we were "feeling something" on a given occasion, and all our friends agreed they were feeling sad, we could not be certain (1) that they were indeed feeling "an emotion" (as opposed, let's say, to a "taste," a "value," or an "urge"); (2) that they were all indeed experiencing the same feeling; or (3) that what we were experiencing was identical to any of their feelings. More broadly, there is little doubt that we are born into a culture with a finely differentiated vocabulary of the emotions. However, we have no viable means of understanding how we could ever learn that we are applying the vocabulary correctly to our internal world.

For these and other reasons, most scientists are not content to rely on personal experience as the basis for identifying the emotions. Rather, it is argued, we must replace the vagaries of introspective folk reports with the dispassionate observations of ongoing behavior. We must develop rigorous measures of emotions, measures that are precise and reliable, and which enable the community of scientists to reach univocal agreement about what is and what is not the case. It is thus that an enormous array of emotional indicators have been developed—biological measures of heart rate, GSR, blood pressure, and penile erection; behavioral measures of facial expressions, motor movements, molar activities; verbal measures of emotional expressions, and so on. Although precise and unambiguous readings are achieved through these means, and the findings are often replicable, this focus on observable manifestations of emotions fully suppresses the vulnerability of the fundamental premises, first, that emotions do exist, and second, that they are manifest in these measures. That we observe increased pulse rate, grimacing behavior, and the verbal declaration "I am fearful," is not in doubt here; it is the conclusions that "fear exists" and that "these are its expressions" for which the research provides no justification.[8] To re-admit our initial question: how are the phenomena of investigation to be identified? The rudimentary questions—essential to the rationale for conducting the investigation in the first place—are never addressed. The presumptions that emotions are *there* and that they somehow *manifest* themselves are embraced a priori. They constitute a leap into metaphysical space.

Not only does empirical research fail to address the fundamental question on which it is premised, but such research procedures employ a circular form of reasoning that further suppresses the myth upon which it is based. The research first draws from the reservoir of commonsense assumptions. It is an unchallenged truism in Western culture that there are emotions such as love, fear, anger, and so on, and that they are indicated or expressed in facial expressions, bodily movements, tone of voice, and the like. That an investigator would study love versus liking, and claim that intensity of gaze differentiates the former from the latter raises virtually no questions. Common folk beliefs attest to a special state of "being in love," which is *ex*pressed in one's gaze on the beloved. Thus buttressed by convention, the research can proceed to demonstrate, for example, that the state of attraction is produced or stimulated by a variety of factors (such as arousal, the other's attraction to the self, profitability), and that the state of attraction predicts many different actions (altruism, attitude change, agreement, maintaining close proximity).[9] In short, the research gains initial credibility by virtue of cultural truisms, and with the aid of controlled research and technical measurement proceeds to draw conclusions about the causes and the effects of the emotion. These conclusions serve to objectify the conventional constructions; they give a sense of warrantable palpability to a folk myth. Once the game of research is underway, there is no turning back to ask whether there is, in fact, anything there.[10]

Let us contrast these realist approaches to emotion with that of the constructionist. For the constructionist the very attempt to identify the emotions is obfuscating. Emotional discourse gains its meaning not by virtue of its relationship to an inner world (of experience, disposition, or biology), but by the way it figures in patterns of cultural relationship. Communities generate conventional modes of relating; patterns of action within these relationships are often given labels. Some forms of action—by current Western standards—are said to indicate emotions. Following Averill (1982), the actions themselves are properly viewed as performances, or "transient social roles." In this sense one isn't "motivated" or "incited to action" by emotions; rather, one *does* emotions, or participates in them much as he or she would on stage.[11] To perform the emotions properly (so that the actions are identifiable by cultural standards) may require a substantial biological contribution (heart rate, blood pressure, and so on). In the same way, we could scarcely run a one-hundred-meter race without substantial bodily engagement. From the constructionist standpoint, to ask how many emotions there are would be similar to asking a theater critic to enumerate the number of roles there are in the theater; to explore the physiology of different emotions would be to compare the heart rate, adrenalin surges, or neural activity of actors who play Hamlet as opposed to King Lear. Emotions do not "have an *impact* on social life"; they *constitute* social life itself.

This view not only eliminates the thorny problems besetting the traditional search for emotions, it also allows us to place the emotions within the broader networks of cultural meaning. For example, as variously reasoned by Bedford (1957), Harré (1986), and Armon-Jones (1986), the emotions cannot be extricated from the arena of moral evaluation. People can be blamed for feeling angry, jealous, or envious, for example, or praised for their love or their sadness (as in the case of mourning). If emotions were simply biological events triggered by hormones or neural excitation, they would figure little in these rituals of sanction. One can scarcely be blamed for one's heart rate or vaginal secretions, or praised for one's digestive processes. To extract all social meaning from the emotion would reduce the person to automaton status, personlike but not fundamentally human (De-Rivera 1984).

Further, the constructionist position is highly congenial with much anthropological and historical inquiry. As such inquiry suggests, both the vocabulary of the emotions and the patterns of what Westerners call "emotional expression" vary dramatically from one culture or historical period to another (Lutz 1985; Harkness and Super 1983; Heelas and Lock 1981; Shweder 1991; Lutz and Abu-Lughod 1990). For example, as Averill (1982) has demonstrated, patterns of what Westerners call "hostility" are scarcely found in many cultures, and bizarre patterns (such as "running amok") are wholly unknown in Western culture. Lutz (1985) has shown that these unique forms of performance (what we in the West would label emotional) have specialized meanings within their own cultural setting. In addition, the vocabulary of the emotions (along with their allied performances) is subject to historical creation and erosion. We no longer speak extensively of our *melancholy* or *acedia,* excusing ourselves from work or social obligations on their account, but we could meaningfully have done so in the sixteenth century.[12] We effortlessly extemporize on our *depression, anxiety,* feelings of *burnout,* and *stress,* none of which would have registered significantly even a century ago. Such sociohistorical variations are difficult to square with the individualist presumption of universal, biologically fixed propensities.

Given a view of emotions as cultural constructions, it is then important to realize the ways in which emotional performances are circumscribed by or embedded within broader patterns of relationship. We tend to view emotional performances as events *sui generis,* primarily because they are frequently more "colorful" (more or less animated or voluble) than actions in their surrounds. In the same way, the football fan fastens on the quarterback's pass while failing to regard the extensive efforts of his teammates to protect him. Yet without the actions of others—preceding, simultaneous to, and following—there would effectively be no performance. If cut away from ongoing relationships, emotional performances would either not occur or be nonsensical. For example, if the hostess at a dinner party suddenly bolted from her seat in rage or began loudly sobbing, guests would undoubtedly be unsettled or abashed. If she could not make it clear that such outbursts were related to a series of preceding and/or anticipated events (essentially a narrative account)—if she announced that she was moved to such outbursts for no particular reason—they might consider her a candidate for serious diagnostic work. To achieve intelligibility the emotional performance must be a recognizable component of an ongoing chain of actions. There is good reason, then, to view emotional performances as constituents of larger or more extended patterns of interaction.

Scholars have taken significant steps toward placing emotion performances within the broader social network. For example, Armon-Jones (1986), Lutz and Abu-Lughod (1990), and Bailey (1983), among others, have explored the various cultural and political functions served by emotional expressions, giving special attention to the pragmatic importance of such expressions in adjudicating moral claims, aligning or realigning relationships, distributing power, and establishing identities. Ancillary inquiry has explored the kinds of social contexts appropriate to various emotional expressions (Scherer 1984). Although such attempts are both interesting and illuminating, my analysis moves in a different direction. Rather than inquire into broad social functions or specific eliciting conditions, I hope to give an account of relational life in which emotional expressions are a constituent part.

This attempt grows directly from the soil of the narrative formulations developed in the preceding chapter. Narratives are forms of intelligibility that furnish accounts of events across time. Individual actions, it was proposed, gain their significance from the way in which they are embedded within the narrative. In the same way, emotional expressions are meaningful (indeed, succeed in counting as legitimate emotions) only when inserted into particular, cross-time sequences of interchange. In effect, they are constituents of lived narratives.

To illustrate: In order to count as legitimate by contemporary standards, expressions of jealousy must be preceded by certain conditions. One cannot properly express jealousy at the sight of a sunset or a traffic light, but jealousy is appropriate if one's lover shows signs of affection toward another. Further, if the jealousy is expressed to the lover, he or she is not free (by current cultural standards) to begin a conversation about the weather or to express deep joy. The lover may apologize or attempt to explain why jealousy is unwarranted, but the range of options is limited. And if the apology is offered, the jealous agent is, again, constrained in the kinds of reactions that may intelligibly follow. In effect, the two participants are engaged in a form of cultural ritual or game. The expression of jealousy is but a single integer within the sequence—the ritual would be unrecognizable without it—but without the remainder of the ritual, jealousy would be nonsensical. These patterns of relationship can be viewed as *emotional scenarios*—informally scripted patterns of interchange. From this standpoint, the emotional expression is only the possession of the single individual in the sense that he or she is the performer of a given act within the broader relational scenario; however, the emotional act is more fundamentally a creation of the relationship and even more broadly, of a particular cultural history.[13]

Emotional Scenarios: The Case of Escalating Hostility

Let us first consider acts of hostility. Rather than view them as outer expressions of inner feelings, we can more properly cast them as modes of cultural performance—"doing the right thing at the right time." And, rather than see them as individual actions, we may usefully consider the part they play in broader scenarios of interchange. How can research help to bring these scenarios to life and give them a sense of "the real"? Traditional experimental methodology offers little assistance in this task, since such methods focus only on the immediate effects of a given stimulus. Experiments are ill-equipped to make sense of patterns of action that unfold or emerge over longer periods of time.[14] However, recall the study by Felson (1984) outlined in Chapter 4. Felson interviewed 380 ex-criminal male offenders and mental patients for whom violence had been a problem. Among other things, the respondents were asked to describe an incident in which violence had occurred and the circumstances preceding the violent act. In analyzing these narratives Felson reached the conclusion that violent actions were not spontaneous, uncontrollable eruptions triggered by an immediate stimulus. Rather, violence was typically embedded in a reliable pattern of interchange. The typical pattern of interaction was one in which person *A* violated a social rule or norm (such as tuning the radio too loud, stepping to the front of a line, interrupting another's privacy). A verbal exchange followed in which person *B* typically reproached *A*, blaming and ordering him or her to cease or correct the offensive behavior. When *A* refused to accept the blame or obey the order, *B* threatened; *A* continued the undesirable action, and *B* then attacked *A*. In effect, Felson succeeded in revealing a common interaction scenario or lived narrative in which physical aggression is a reliable part.

By common standards, the relationship between violence and the emotions is an intimate one; violence is typically viewed as an expression of hostile feelings. In this sense Felson's research provides a significant illustration of emotional performances as components of more extended relationships. The present work attempts to explore possible scenarios of hostility and violence in normal populations. This exploration was further inspired by an interesting argument put forward by Pearce and Cronen (1980). As they pointed out, there are many recurring patterns of interchange that are unwanted by the participants and yet are willingly and frequently repeated. Domestic violence may be a significant exemplar of such *unwanted repetitive patterns*: neither husband nor wife may want physical violence, but once the pattern (or scenario) has begun, they may feel little choice but to bear on toward its normative conclusion—physical abuse. This view also suggests that under certain conditions hostility and physical violence may be viewed as appropriate, if not desirable, by one or more of the participants in a relationship. Although hostility and violence are typically abhorred in our textbooks and treated as abnormal if not bizarre, these treatments fail to appreciate the contexts of their occurrence. To the participants, violence may seem at a given moment in lived history not only appropriate but morally required.

In what way are people caught up in a relational pattern leading to violent outcomes? To answer this requires an intelligibility that would render immediate actions and reactions reasonable in themselves, but simultaneously propel the pattern of exchange toward an ever more extreme outcome. Such a possibility seems to derive from two cultural rules of broad consequence: First is the *imperative of reciprocity*. As an enormous literature in the social sciences makes clear, persons have a right, indeed almost a moral obligation, to return actions in kind.[15] Thus, by common cultural standards, kindness should be reciprocated with kindness and hostility with hostility. To respond to kindness with hostility would be shameful; and while a loving reaction to another's bestiality is admirable, such acts are reserved for the spiritually transcendent. The second imperative is that of *retribution*. While it is appropriate by virtue of the reciprocity imperative to return negative acts in kind, when another's hostility is unprovoked or wanton a second imperative becomes salient—that of punishing the provocateur. It is insufficient that a thief apprehended with stolen goods be forced to reciprocate, that is, to return to the owner what was taken. The thief should also be punished for the crime. By the same token, if someone gratuitously attacks another's work, the reciprocity norm invites counterattack; the retribution norm furnishes the right—if not the duty—to add punitive weight to the effort.

With these normative demands in place, it is possible to understand the widespread participation in scenarios of escalating hostility. In ordinary terms, if one believes another's actions are wrong and inflicts punishment, the victim will feel it appropriate—by virtue of the reciprocity convention—to return the punishment. Yet, because the victim can seldom appreciate the rationale for the punishment, it will often be seen as gratuitous hostility. Thus, simple reciprocity is insufficient; the victim has the right to inflict punitive damage. When confronting such reactions, the punitive agent may be justifiably shocked: his or her well-intentioned and appropriate delivery of punishment is yielding wanton retaliation. Such aggression should be both reciprocated and punished. And so the escalating pattern of aggression continues until a point at which physical violence may seem fully appropriate.

To illustrate these possibilities, my colleagues Linda Harris, Jack Lannamann, and I designed a research study.[16] Research participants responded to a series of vignettes describing an ongoing relationship between two people.

In the initial vignette one protagonist mildly criticized the other. The story was interrupted at this point, and the participants asked to rate the *probability, desirability,* and *advisability* of each of a series of possible reactions. The list of options ranged from highly conciliatory actions, on the one extreme, to physical violence on the other. Thus, for example, the participants read about a young married couple. In the first scene the husband mildly criticized his wife's cooking. The participants then rated each of a series of options (from embracing and kissing her husband to physically striking him) in terms of their likelihood, desirability, and advisability. After they had made their evaluations the participants turned the page to read that the reaction of the wife had been to escalate the hostility—she responded by criticizing her husband. Again, the story was halted and ratings made of the husband's probable reactions to his wife, along with their desirability and advisability. In the next episode the participants found that the husband became harsher in his comments to his wife, and so on. Eight instances of escalation were thus furnished to participants, who made evaluations after each.

The results depicted in Figure 9.1 are exemplary of the general pattern of evaluations for each of the stories and all three measures. The figure displays the average probability ratings for the most hostile options (combined) and the most conciliatory options (combined). As is shown, the rated probability of hostile options increased over the eight intervals, while the probability of conciliatory options decreased. The results proved highly

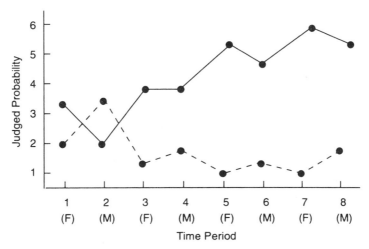

Figure 9.1 Judged Probability of Aggression *(solid line)* and Conciliation *(broken line)* for Male and Female Protagonists

reliable on a statistical basis and suggest that we are tapping a highly conventionalized scenario within the culture.

Most interesting, however, is that this same pattern of mounting hostility and decreasing conciliation was revealed in the ratings of both desirability and advisability. That is, the research participants not only saw the increasing hostility as probable, they also saw it as appropriate and praiseworthy. Although at the outset of the scenario the participants would never recommend that the husband or wife throw the dinner on the floor, by the end of four exchanges they were quite willing to endorse this option. The sawtooth trajectory featured in the figure is the result of the participants' ratings of the husband versus the wife in the story. Interestingly the sample generally endorsed more hostility for the female than the male. None of them advised that the husband strike the wife, but many were willing to endorse the wife's use of physical violence.

As this research suggests, when mild hostility is expressed, it seems both appropriate and desirable for the target to respond with hostility as well. And, although neither participant may lean toward an embittered antagonism, this early exchange invites the participants to engage in a widely shared cultural scenario. Each may righteously attack the other with slightly increasing intensity, and as the scenario unfolds there is little that either can do—at least within the currently available rituals of hostility—to change the direction of events.

Of course, this illustration is highly delimited and artificial.[17] Its purpose is not to furnish a basis for generalization and prediction, but to offer a way of understanding social activity. On this level, the pattern generates a resonance with myriad other circumstances, from the domestic to the international. In the same way that husband and wife engage in hostilities that often mount in cumulative fashion between them, governments often enter a struggle of mutual threat and counterthreat, verbal attack and counterattack, armed assault and counterassault, until major loss of life and property result. The inability of either the United States or its many antagonists of recent decades (for example, Korea, Vietnam, Cuba, the USSR, Libya, Iraq) to leave the field of mutual hostility voluntarily suggests that the ritual is broadly shared. The norms of reciprocity and retribution may leave nation states no less than individuals with few alternative courses of action.[18]

According to traditional empiricist standards, the scientist's task is complete when research has "carved nature at the joint." In contrast, the constructionist aim here is transformative—to generate alternatives to existing patterns of action. The shift is from *carving* nature to *enriching* it. Thus, explicating patterns of escalating hostility is only a beginning. Should this particular construction seem plausible and compelling, and should one find the pattern disturbing and thus worthy of change, then the challenge is to generate alternative possibilities. Are there other moves that can be made by participants in the traditional scenario, perhaps during its early stages, that might avert disastrous outcomes? Can the scientist or the practitioner locate or invent actions that could plausibly be inserted into the unfolding pattern, thus enabling combatant couples or hostile nations to transcend or abandon the all too "logical" sequence? I will explore these possibilities in what follows.

Emotional Scenarios: Expanding the Spectrum

In more recent work we have broadened and enriched the relational view by exploring a variety of different emotions—including anger, depression, and happiness—as lived narratives. We have attempted to locate emotional performances ("expressions") within the broader relational scenarios from which they derive their intelligibility. In this case the research strategy has been more open-ended than in the foregoing.[19] Rather than vivify a single pattern, as in the case of escalating hostility, we explored the possibility of multiple scenarios. It seemed plausible that any given emotional expression might be embedded in a variety of common sequences or scenarios, just as a given move of the torso might figure in a variety of gymnastic routines. An emotion such as anger, for example, may be an intelligible reaction to a variety of circumstances (such as frustration, attack, disappointment) and may simultaneously offer others a variety of possible reactions. In effect, there may be multiple scenarios, of which the emotion is an integral part. This exploratory technique also seemed fruitful in underscoring the differences between effective or desirable scenarios and ineffectual or failing ones. As in the case of escalating hostility, some conventional patterns of interchange lead people in unwanted directions. However, by broadening the range of possible routines, it seemed possible to isolate promising as opposed to failing forms of interchange. In effect, by using open-ended procedures we may be sensitized to various "grass-roots" means of avoiding undesirable, repetitive patterns. We may discover little-used but potentially valuable sequences that might be shared more broadly within the culture.

The procedure employed in these various cases was identical. An initial group of some twenty undergraduate participants was presented with a vignette in which they were told of a friend who expressed to them one of several emotions. Typically, the friend was a roommate who entered the room and expressed a given emotion (such as "I am really angry at you," "I'm feeling so depressed," or "I'm so happy"). In each case the research participants were asked how they would respond to the expression. As a result of preliminary analysis it became apparent that such expressions would engender only a *single* form of reply: an inquiry into the cause. In effect, people are scarcely free to reply to a friend's expression of emotion in a random way. To remain intelligible by cultural standards, one must inquire into the source. And given the framework of lived narratives, it is also possible to determine the function of this inquiry. Far from being a cultural formality, it enables the actor to establish the grounds for the ensuing scenario. To put it another way, the other's emotional expression is itself without sense, merely a random occurrence, until it is placed within a narrative context—that is, supplied with antecedents that render it appropriate. The answer to the question "Why are you feeling . . . ?" furnishes the listener with an indication of what story is being played out. More metaphorically, the answer serves as an invitation to the listener to participate in a specific game or dance; the answer "names the game" and invites one to play. Without this information it is impossible for the recipient to respond in a sensible or appropriate way.

The research participants were then furnished with a prepared reply: the roommate was angry because the target (the research participant) had revealed a failing grade to a mutual friend after pledging confidentiality; depressed because of a general feeling that nothing was going right, classes were going badly, there had been a recent breakup of a close relationship, the roommate got no sleep, and so on; happy because everything was going well, including classes and a close relationship. The research participants were then asked to indicate how they would reply to this explanation. At this point in the research two rounds of turn taking (or interacts) had thus been achieved:

A's expression of emotion

B's query as to cause

A's establishment of context

B's reaction

This array of partially completed scenarios was then used as the sample pool to explore a third round of turn taking. Sample protocols were selected at random from the initial pool of interchanges and presented to a new group of research participants. This group was asked to take the part of the roommate (A) who had initially engaged in the emotional expression, explained why he or she felt this way, and was then confronted by the roommate's response. How would they now respond; what would they now say? (Participants were also told—both here and later—to indicate whether or not they felt the sequence had reached an end, that is, whether there was nothing more to be said, or, if they felt puzzled, about what might be added. Such indications were taken as signals of scenario closure, and no further inquiries were made.)

Responses at each phase of these scenario samples were then categorized. Could we, as cultural participants, locate categories into which the various responses at the various junctures could easily be placed? With such simplification we hoped that it would be possible to locate broadly conventional or generic scenario forms. As this categorization proceeded it became apparent that at any stage of any interchange more than 90 percent of the responses could be reliably and effortlessly placed into one of three categories. In effect, it appears that at each choice point in the unfolding scenarios, participants generally faced at least three intelligible alternatives. The generality and limits of this pattern remain to be explored.

In order to appreciate the character findings, let us consider the anger scenarios depicted in Figure 9.2. The case is particularly interesting in light of the results of the earlier study of escalating hostility. As the schematic makes clear, we see first that the initial interact is composed of the familiar pair: the expression of anger and the resulting inquiry into its reason. In the second interact the explanation for the anger is given (as described above), and the research participants generate three major options. The most commonly selected option was *remorse* ("I'm very sorry I hurt your feelings"). The second most frequent reaction was that of *reframing*. The reframing response is one in which the interlocutor attempts to redefine the precipitating event in such a way that anger is no longer appropriate. In the present case two forms of reframing dominated, the first a plea of ignorance about the wish that the information remain secret ("I didn't know you wanted the grade to remain secret"), and the second, a claim of positive intent ("I only did it because I thought it would help you"). Ranking third in frequency of

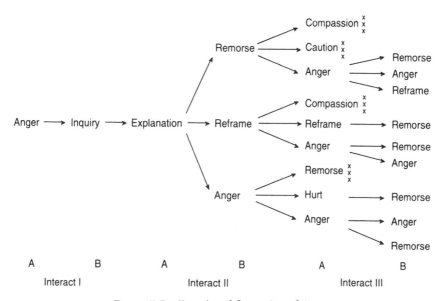

Figure 9.2   Emotional Scenarios of Anger

selection is the response of *anger* ("Don't you think you're overreacting a bit? It's not such a big deal"). This latter pattern points up an important limitation on the earlier study of escalating hostility. Although escalation of hostility is a common scenario in our culture, it is neither essential nor necessary (that is, required biologically). Rather, it is one possible option among several, but at least in the present case, not one that is typically preferred.

As the figure also demonstrates, by the third interact, a natural break in the interchange is sensed, and the participants find it possible to terminate the scenario. The most favored antecedent of the ending is the expression of remorse in the second interact. If remorse is expressed in this instance, two of the three replies (and the most favored two) lead to the end of the narrative. Remorse is likely to be followed by *compassion* ("That's okay. It really doesn't matter so much, I guess") or by *caution* ("Well, I hope you will never do that kind of thing again"). The reframing reply in the second interact is somewhat less successful in bringing the scenario to an end. Of the three options selected by participants, only the least preferred reaction (that of compassion) succeeds in bringing the scenario to rapid conclusion.

The most frequent reaction to reframing, however, is an attempt on the part of the emotional performer to reframe yet again, usually in order to reinstate the validity of the initial claim to anger ("You knew very well it wouldn't help me"). However, a very common reaction to this reframing response is simply more anger. Reframing may be viewed as an insult as it challenges the actor's capacity for understanding the situation. Thus, to reframe simultaneously delegitimizes the anger, avoids admitting one's guilt, and denigrates the actor for his or her poor comprehension. In any case, if reframing engenders anger, the scenario fails to reach a conclusion. A similar picture emerges when we consider the angry reaction to anger. When this occurs, the most common reply is that of still more anger. In effect, these latter results furnish a partial replication of the study of escalating hostility.

We can derive a fuller understanding of these relational patterns from a brief comparison of the anger scenarios with those involving depression and happiness (Figures 9.3 and 9.4). In the case of depression, *reframing* ("Oh, things aren't as bad as you see them"), *advice* ("If you would just work harder, I'm sure you would succeed"), and *commiseration* ("I know exactly how you feel") are the most common reactions. And of the subsequent reactions to these moves all but two options lead to a story ending. Apparently, offering advice is not a very effective reply to expressions of depression; in fact, there is at least a small possibility that it precipitates anger. Whether or not the introduction of anger into a depression scenario then serves as the overture to a new array of scenarios (now involving the performance of anger as in Figure 9.2) remains to be explored. Further, if

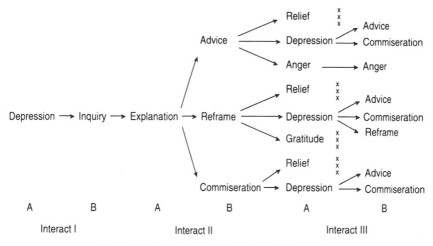

Figure 9.3   Emotional Scenarios of Depression

one commiserates with depression there is a high probability that even more intense expressions of depression will result. At this juncture, the reframing option seems most promising for bringing the depression scenario to a conclusion.

With regard to expressions of happiness, the most common reaction by far (70 percent of the participants) is that of *empathy* ("That makes me

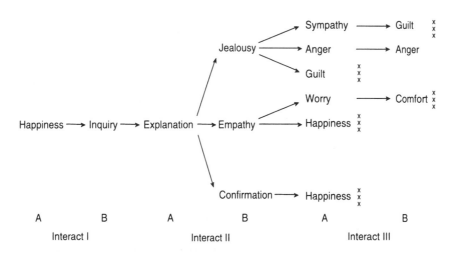

Figure 9.4   Emotional Scenarios of Happiness

happy too"). This reply also circumscribes the subsequent reactions of the initiator; another expression of happiness on his or her part typically brings the scenario to a conclusion. Much the same result occurs if one responds to happiness with *confirmation* ("That's really great for you"). The scenario rapidly ends with the initiator's further expression of happiness. However, as the figure demonstrates, scenarios of happiness are not always so rapidly completed. In particular, a friend's expression of happiness may, with a slight degree of probability, lead to an expression of *jealousy*. If this reaction occurs, a range of possible reactions, including guilt, anger, and hurt may be triggered in the actor, and the scenario remains open to further iterations.

To be sure, these explorations are only illustrative. However, within the present framework they do suggest that:

- Conversational markers (or other opening cues) are required in order for participants to coordinate their actions within a single scenario.

- Once a scenario is underway, there are multiple options for transformation; any particular fragment or sequence of fragments may be used within more than one intelligible scenario. The opening of a scenario does not necessarily dictate either its subsequent form or its termination. At the same time, this latitude is not infinite; cultural tradition vastly truncates the possibilities for intelligible action.

- Emotional scenarios almost invariably conclude with the expression of neutral to happy sentiments. It appears to be difficult in contemporary culture to complete a scenario with a performance of anger, jealousy, depression, fear, or the like.

- Scenarios commencing with a positive emotional performance appear to be less extended than those in which a negative emotion is focal. Given the difficulty of concluding a scenario with a negative emotion, it appears that in contemporary culture negative emotions are indexed either as a "problem to be solved" ("How can we reduce Harry's depression?") or as an indicator of some other problem ("What is it about my behavior that makes you so angry?"). In this sense, the typical scenario involving a negative emotion approximates the Aristotelian romance or the comedy. Both these narrative forms commence on a positive level, the protagonists are then propelled along a descending narrative slope, and the remainder of the story is occupied with reestablishing a positive level (harmony, success).

More broadly, emotional scenarios approximate forms of cultural dance; the available forms may be limited, but the conventions are subject to historical erosion and accretion. It would be useful at this juncture to explore variations on the common scenarios, as well as people's common ways of subverting or escaping their demands. Therapeutic implications must also be elaborated. Emotional problems, from this perspective, may stem from poor skills or poor training in the common scenarios of the culture, or from an inability to locate alternatives to those that propel relationships toward disaster. Finally, consideration must be given to the broader relational patterns in which emotional scenarios are embedded. Just as focusing on individual emotions was found disabling, the exploration of microsocial scenarios also has important limitations. Such scenarios do not simply materialize within the dyad; each scenario may play a significant role in a larger complex of interrelations. The horizons of theory and practice are again extended.

10 Transcending Narrative in the Therapeutic Context

Traditional therapy has centered on the problems of individual minds; family therapists struggle toward understanding broader social processes; both remain largely committed to the twin concepts of a dysfunctional unit and therapeutic cure. From a constructionist standpoint, the emphasis shifts from individual mind to the joint-negotiation of reality, and from cure to the pragmatics of meaning in social context. A chief vehicle for generating meaning is the narrative. However, constructionist therapy must finally press beyond the task of reconstructing narratives. The problem is not to locate a new narrative, but to transcend narrative lodgment.

When people seek psychotherapy they have a story to tell. It is frequently the troubled, hurt, or angry story of a life or a relationship now spoiled. For many it is a story of calamitous events that conspire against a sense of well-being, self-satisfaction, or efficacy. For others the story may concern unseen and mysterious forces that have insinuated themselves into life's organized sequences, disrupting and destroying. And for still others it is as if, under the illusion that they know how the world is or ought to be, they have somehow bumped up against trouble for which their favored account has left them unprepared. They have discovered an awful reality that now drains all past understandings of cogency. Whatever its form, the therapist confronts a narrative, often persuasive and gripping, that may terminate within a brief period or extend over weeks or months. At some juncture, however, the therapist must inevitably respond to this account, and whatever follows within the therapeutic procedure will draw its significance in response to it.

What options are available to the therapist as he or she now contributes to the relational scenario? At least one option is pervasive within the culture and is sometimes used as well within counseling, social work, and short-term therapies: the *advisory option*. The client's story remains relatively inviolate; its terms of description and forms of explanation remain unchallenged in any significant way. What the advisor attempts to do is to locate forms of effective action "under the circumstances" as narrated. Thus, for example, if the individual speaks of being depressed because of failure, the advisor seeks ways to reestablish efficacy. If the client is rendered ineffectual because of grief, the advisor may suggest a program of action for overcoming the problem. In effect, the advisor accepts the client's life story as fundamentally accurate for him or her, and defines the problem as one of locating ameliorative forms of action within the story's terms.

There is much to be said on behalf of the advisory option. Within the realm of the relatively ordinary, it is "reasonable" and probably effective. Here is the vital stuff of quotidian coping. Yet, for the more seriously chronic or deeply disturbed client, the advisory option harbors serious limitations. At the outset, it does little to confront the extended origins of the problem or the complex ways in which it is sustained; the advisor is primarily concerned with locating a new course of action. Whatever the chain of antecedents, they simply remain the same—often continuing to operate as threats to the future. In addition, the advisory option makes little attempt to probe the contours of the story, to determine its relative utility or viability. Could the client be socially out of sync or defining things in a less than optimal way? Such questions often remain unexplored. Accepting "the story as told" ensures that the definition of the problem also remains fixed, thus limiting the range of options for action. If the problem is said to be failure, for example, the relevant options are geared toward reestablishing success, and other possibilities are thrust to the margins of plausibility. In the chronic or severe case, locating action alternatives too often seems a superficial palliative. For one who has been frustrated, struggling, and desperate for a period of years, simple advice for living may seem little more than whispering in the wind.

In this chapter I want to explore two more substantial alternatives to the advisory option. The first is represented by most traditional forms of psychotherapy and psychoanalytic practice. In its reliance on various neo-Enlightenment assumptions dominant in the sciences of the present century, this orientation toward client narratives may be viewed as *modernist* (see also Chapter 4). In contrast, much thinking within the *postmodern* arena—and more specifically, that of the postmodern constructionist view—forms a powerful challenge to the modernist conception of the narrative.

Therapeutic Narratives in a Modernist Context

Much has been written about modernism in the sciences, literature, and the arts, and this is scarcely the context for a thorough review.[1] Yet it is useful to consider briefly a set of assumptions that have guided activities in the sciences and the allied professions of mental health, for it is this array of assumptions that have largely informed the therapeutic treatment of client narratives. The modernist era in the sciences has been one committed, first of all, to the empirical *elucidation of essences*. Whether it be the character of the atom, the gene, or the synapse in the natural sciences, or the processes of perception, economic decision making, or organizational development in the social sciences, the primary aim has been to establish bodies of systematic and objective knowledge. As should be clear, both empiricist metatheory and cognitive psychology of the kind I have discussed in earlier chapters are quintessentially modernist.

From the modernist standpoint, empirical knowledge is communicated through scientific languages. Narratives are essentially structures of language, and insofar as they are generated within the scientific milieu they can, according to the modernist account, function as conveyors of objective knowledge. Thus, the narratives of the novelist are labeled as "fiction" and considered of little consequence for serious scientific purposes. People's narratives of their lives, what has happened to them and why, are not necessarily fictions, but, as the behavioral scientist proclaims, they are notoriously inaccurate and unreliable. Thus, they are considered of limited value in understanding the individual's life and far less preferable than the empirically based accounts of the trained scientist. As a result, the narrative accounts of the scientist are accorded the highest credibility and are set apart from and above the homespun stories of everyday life and the markets of public entertainment.

The mental health profession today is largely an outgrowth of the modernist context and shares deeply in its assumptions. Thus, from Freud to contemporary cognitive therapists, the general belief has been that the professional therapist functions (or ideally should function) as a scientist (see also Chapter 6). By virtue of scientific training, research experience, knowledge of the scientific literature, and countless hours of systematic observation and thought within the therapeutic situation, the professional is armed with knowledge. To be sure, contemporary knowledge is incomplete, and more research is ever required. But the knowledge of the contemporary professional is far superior to that of the turn-of-the-century therapist, so it is said, and the future can only bring further improvements. Thus, with few exceptions, therapeutic theories (whether behavioral, systemic, psychodynamic, or experiential/humanist) contain explicit assumptions regarding (1) the underlying cause or basis of pathology; (2) the location of this cause within the client or his or her relationships; (3) the means by which such problems can be diagnosed; and (4) the means by which the pathology can be eliminated. In effect, the trained professional enters the therapeutic arena with a well-developed narrative for which there is abundant support within the community of scientific peers.

It is this background that establishes the therapist's posture toward the client's narrative, for the client's narrative is, after all, made of the flimsy stuff of daily stories—replete with whimsy, metaphor, wishful thinking, and distorted memories. The scientific narrative, by contrast, has the seal of professional approval. From this vantage point it is clear that the therapeutic process must inevitably result in the slow but inevitable replacement of the client's story with the therapist's. The client's story does not remain a free-standing reflection of truth, but rather, as questions are asked and answered, descriptions and explanations reframed, and affirmation and doubt disseminated by the therapist, the client's narrative is either destroyed or incorporated—but in any event replaced—by the professional account. The client's account is transformed by the psychoanalyst into a tale of family romance, by the Rogerian into a struggle against conditional regard, and so on. It is this process of replacing the client's story with the professional's story that is so deftly described in Spence's (1982) *Narrative Truth and Historical Truth.* As Spence surmises,

> [the therapist] is constantly making decisions about the form and status of the patient's material. Specific listening conventions . . . help to guide these decisions. If, for example, the analyst assumes that contiguity indicates causality, then he will hear a sequence of disconnected statements as a causal chain; at some later time, he might make an interpretation that would make this assumption explicit. If he assumes that transference predominates and that the patient is always talking, in more or less disguised fashion, about the analyst, then he will "hear" the material in that way and make some kind of ongoing evaluation of the state of the transference. (p. 129)

Such replacement procedures do have certain therapeutic advantages. For one, as the client gains "real insight" into his or her problems, the problematic narrative is removed. The client is thus furnished with an alternative reality that holds promise for future well-being. In effect, the failure story with which the client entered therapy is swapped for an invitation to a success story. And, like the advisory option I outlined earlier, the new story will probably suggest alternative lines of action, such as forming or dissolving relationships, operating under a daily regimen, submitting to therapeutic procedures, and so on. Within the professional story there are new and more hopeful things to do. And by providing the client with a scientific formulation, the therapist has played his or her appointed role in the family of cultural rituals in which the ignorant, the failing, and the weak seek counsel from the wise, the superior, and the strong. It is indeed a comforting ritual for all who will submit.

Yet in spite of these advantages, there is substantial reason for concern. Major shortcomings in the modernist orientation to therapy have been pointed out. As outlined in previous chapters, the traditional approach favors a form of person blame, is often blind to the social conditions in which problems develop, is frequently insensitive or oppressive in its treatment of women and minorities, presumes an unwarranted empiricist view of mental knowledge, and in reifying mental disorder may generate and sustain cultural deficit. Over and above these problems, there are specific shortcomings in the modernist orientation to client narrative. There is, for one, a substantial imperious thrust to the modernist approach. Not only is the therapist's narrative never placed under threat, but the therapeutic procedure virtually ensures that it is the one that will be vindicated. In Spence's terms, "the search space [within therapeutic interaction] can be infinitely expanded until the (therapist's) answer is discovered and . . . there is no possibility of finding a negative solution, of deciding that the (therapist's) search has failed" (p. 108). Thus, regardless of the complexity, sophistication, or value of the client's account, it is eventually to be replaced by a narrative created before his or her entry into therapy and according to contours over which he or she has no control.

It is not simply that therapists from a given school will ensure that their clients come away believing in their particular account. By virtue of the bounded ontologies, the ultimate aim of most schools of therapy is hegemonic. All other schools of thought, and their associated narratives, should succumb. In general, psychoanalysts wish to eradicate behavior modification, cognitive-behavioral therapists see systems therapy as misguided, and so on. Yet the most immediate and potentially injurious consequences are reserved for the client, for in the end, the structure of the procedure furnishes the client with a lesson in inferiority. The client is indirectly informed that he or she is ignorant, insensitive, or emotionally incapable of comprehending reality. In contrast, the therapist is positioned as all-knowing and wise, a model to which the client might aspire. The situation is all the more lamentable owing to the fact that in occupying the superior role, the therapist fails to reveal its weaknesses. Almost nowhere are wobbly foundations of the therapist's account made known; almost nowhere do the therapist's personal doubts, foibles, and failings come to light. And the client is thus confronted with a vision of human possibility that is as unattainable as the heroism of a Hollywood film.

The modernist orientation also suffers from the fixedness of the narrative formulations. As we have seen, modernist approaches to therapy begin with an a priori narrative justified by claims to a scientific base. Because it is sanctioned as scientific, this narrative is relatively closed to alteration. Minor modifications can be entertained, but the system itself bears the weight of established doctrine. To the extent that such narratives become the client's reality and guide his or her actions, life options are severely truncated. Of all possible modes of acting in the world, one is set on a course that emphasizes ego autonomy, self-actualization, rational appraisal, emotional expressiveness, and so on depending on the particular brand of therapy selected. Or to put it another way, each form of modernist therapy carries with it an image of the "fully functioning" or "good" individual; like a fashion plate, this image serves as the guiding model for the therapeutic outcome.

This constriction of life possibilities is all the more problematic because it is decontextualized. The therapist's narrative is an abstract formalization cut away from particular cultural and historical circumstances. Modernist narratives do not deal with the specific conditions of living in inner-city poverty, with a brother who has AIDS, with a child who has Down's syndrome, with an attractive boss who is sexually solicitous, and so on. In contrast to the complex details that crowd the corners of daily life—which are indeed life itself—modernist narratives are nonspecific. They aspire toward universality and say very little about particular circumstances. As a result, these narratives are precariously insinuated into an individual's life circumstances. They are, in this sense, clumsy and insensitive, and fail to register the particularities of the client's life engagements. To emphasize self-fulfillment to a woman living in a household with three small children and a mother-in-law with Alzheimer's disease is not likely to be beneficial. To press a Park Avenue attorney for increased emotional expressiveness in his daily routines is of doubtful assistance.[2]

Therapeutic Realities in a Postmodern Context

As described in the opening chapters, the arguments leading toward constructionism pose a major challenge to the modernist view of knowledge and science. In an important sense, constructionism is a child of the "postmodern turn" in cultural life.[3] Such arguments also extend the critique of psychotherapy in the modernist frame. As increasing attention is devoted to the problem of representation, or the means by which "reality" is set forth in writing, the arts, television, and so on, the criteria for accurate or objective representations are placed in question. As I argued in the case of writing, for example, each style or genre of literature operates according to local rules or conventions, and these conventions largely determine the way we understand the putative object of representation. As we saw in Chapter 7, the sense of objectivity is largely a literary achievement. And as I outlined in Chapter 8, narrative accounts are not replicas of reality but the devices from which reality is constructed. Scientific writing, then, furnishes a picture of reality that is no more *accurate* than fiction. All accounts of the world—mythical, scientific, mysterious—are guided by historically and culturally based conventions.

Such arguments form a major challenge to the modernist orientation to therapy. At the outset they remove the factual justification of the modernist narratives of pathology and cure, transforming these accounts into forms of cultural mythology. They undermine the unquestioned status of the therapist as a scientific authority with privileged knowledge of cause and cure. The therapist's narratives thus take their place alongside the myriad other possibilities available in the culture, not transcendentally superior but different in pragmatic implications. By the same token, significant questions must be raised about the traditional practice of replacing the client's stories with the fixed and narrow alternatives of the modernist therapist. There is no justification outside the small community of like-minded therapists for hammering the client's complex and richly detailed life into a single, preformulated narrative, a narrative that may be of little relevance or promise for the client's subsequent life conditions. And finally, there is no broad justification for the traditional status hierarchy that both demeans and frustrates the client. Therapist and client together form a community to which both bring resources and from which the contours of the future may be shaped.

Although these various critiques cast a pall over the modernist adventure and deflate its accompanying optimism, from the ashes of deconstruction a new conception of therapy is slowly taking form. Its early stages drew strong sustenance from constructivist writings of various sorts—from Kelly, Maturana, and von Glasersfeld. As I outlined in Chapter 3, each placed a strong emphasis on the world as constructed by the individual subject; each thereby challenged the modernist view of knowledge as an accurate picture of the world. The work of Bateson and his colleagues also emphasized holistic conceptions of human action, challenging the modernist view of individuals as isolated essences harboring diseases that are theirs and theirs alone. These conceptions were further bolstered by cybernetic views of self-organizing systems and their strong invitation to therapists to search for patterns of relationship—especially within families—of which the individual's problems are but a localized symptom. This work has become multifaceted and richly laminated (see Hoffman 1992; Olds 1992).

Constructionism—one of the more challenging outcomes of postmodern thought—now brings to these ventures new forms of consciousness that place certain lines of reasoning in question and introduce new conceptions and practices. The constructionist concurs with the constructivist in both the rejection of subject-object dualism and the related presumption that knowledge is an accurate representation of the world. However, while constructivists tend to replace the dualism with a form of cognitive monism, constructionists move from the mental world to the domain of the social (see Chapter 3). World construction takes place not within the mind of the observer but within forms of relationship. This shift is of major consequence in its implications for therapy.

From mental to social process. Both the modernist and constructivist therapist work at plumbing the depths of client subjectivity—for example, the client's cognition, construals, meanings. For the constructionist, in contrast, the emphasis shifts to the more accessible domain of client discourse. The pioneering work of Watzlawick, Beavin, and Jackson (1967) on the pragmatics of therapeutic language has had a major impact on the therapeutic field. However, this work, like many of its grandchildren (see, for example, Reiss 1981; Efran, Lukens, and Lukens 1990) has also placed a strong emphasis on individual conceptual or cognitive processes. Constructionist writings, in contrast, deemphasize or bracket concern with individual construals and focus on language as a microsocial process. How is life being framed, what words are selected, what is their impact? New analytic concepts now make their way into the therapeutic arena—concepts of metaphor, metonomy, narrative form, and the like. Such concepts invite new questions and new modes of therapeutic departure. Concern shifts to "the ways in which a plurality of perspectives are coordinated into coherent patterns of interaction, each potentiating and simultaneously constraining particular forms of action" (McNamee 1992, p. 191). A therapist may ask whether elements of a given self-description can be incorporated via metaphor or metonomy into a new form of account. Are there alternative narratives that make equally good sense of the facts of life as given? Can a voice that has been marginalized within the discourse be given room for greater articulation? Can the content of a couple's arguments be bracketed ("ineffective ways of putting things") and their attention directed to the conditions or cues that invite argument as opposed to cooperation? What are the means of effectively deconstructing and reconstructing client reality? For extended discussions of such issues see Andersen (1991), White and Epston (1990), Goolishian and Anderson (1987), and Lax (1992).

Toward equalization and coconstruction. The modernist view of the therapist as superior knower has been challenged by constructivist writings (Mahoney 1991). Yet for most constructivists, the therapist remains independent of the client's subjectivity and from this remote and implicitly superior standpoint attempts to "perturb the system" of the client. From the constructionist standpoint, however, the therapist's loss of authority is primary; the traditional hierarchy is dismantled. Instead, the therapist enters the arena not with superior truth about the world, but with various modes of being—including a range of languages. Nor are these modes of being inherently superior to those of the client. They are not model ways of life. Rather, they are forms of life that, together with the client's actions, may engender useful alternatives. As commentators increasingly put the case, the therapist becomes a collaborator, a coconstructor of meaning.

From diagnostics and cure to cultural responsibility. Within the modernist view the therapist typically attempts to locate the illness and destroy it: the process is diagnosis and cure. The medical model of disease remains robust. Although constructivists offered an important challenge to this view, a pervasive concern with "problems" that require "solutions" remained. For Kelly (1955) there were problematic construals, for systemic structuralists there are dysfunctional family patterns, and so on. But as the emphasis shifts to the linguistic construction of reality, illnesses and problems lose ontological privilege. They cease to be "there" as constituents of an independent reality and take their place among the array of cultural constructions (see Chapter 6). Thus, one may speak of problems, suffering, and alleviation, but such terms are always considered to index reality only from a particular perspective. There are no problems beyond a culture's way of constituting them as such. On the one hand, this conclusion suggests first that the process of diagnosis, or "locating the problem," is unnecessary. Indeed, the arguments developed in Chapter 6 suggest that the very existence of nosological categories and illness labeling adds incrementally to the cultural sense of enfeeblement.

Equally problematic is the related concept of "cure." If there are no "illnesses" in nature, then what counts as "cure"? Yet questioning at this level sends ripples of anguish across the profession. For if the concept of cure is sacrificed, the function of therapy is also placed in question. If there are no problems in reality and no solutions, then how is therapy to be justified? Why should people seek therapeutic help, why should one enter the profession, and why should people be charged for these services? Surely, in principle, discussion of such questions is unbounded (why, after all, should one do anything ... only because there is adequate justification?). However, in the final analysis we cannot escape culture; we cannot remove ourselves to ask how we should act in a world that is unconstructed. We can continue to play out the rituals in which we accept others as having real pain for which there are real cures, or we can locate or develop alternative realities. But we cannot live outside any constitution of the real. There is, then, no knockdown argument against "treating problems" and making claims for "cure" and therapeutic "progress." What the constructionist perspective adds, however, are reflexive and creative dimensions—it acknowledges the contingent nature of one's constructions, it is sensitive to their possible effects, and it demonstrates an openness to generating alternatives. In effect, one is thus encouraged to consider the implications of one's choices, their outcomes and their implications from a variety of standpoints, and the potential of alternative endeavors. In the broader sense this is to acknowledge one's membership in the culture, one's continuing participation in the multiplicitous enclaves of meaning.

The full implications of a constructionist approach are far from clear. We stand at a critical juncture, a point of radical departure from traditional assumptions about knowledge, persons, and the nature of illness and cure. We now require substantial deliberation and exploration, and even then we shall have only additional fuel for a conversation that, ideally, should have no end. It is in this spirit that I offer the remaining arguments. In certain respects, current discussions of narrative meaning in therapy still retain significant vestiges of the modernist worldview. But if the potential of postmodernist constructionism is to be fully realized, we must press beyond narrative construction. The ultimate challenge for therapy, I would venture, is not so much to replace an unworkable narrative with a serviceable one, but to enable clients to participate in the continuous process of creating and transforming meaning. To appreciate this possibility, we must first explore the pragmatic dimension of narrative meaning.

The Pragmatics of Narration

Narrative accounts in a modernist frame serve as potential representations of reality—they are true or false insofar as they match events as they occur. If the accounts are accurate, they also serve as blueprints for adaptive action. Thus, in therapy, if the narrative reflects a recurring pattern of maladaptive action, one begins to explore alternative ways of behaving. Or, if it captures the formative processes for a given pathology, one prescribes palliatives. Within the modernist view, the therapist's narrative has a privileged status in prescribing an optimal way of life. In contrast, for most therapists informed by postmodern perspectives, the modernist concern with narrative accuracy is uncompelling. Narrative truth cannot be distinguished from historical truth, and when closely examined, even the latter concept is found to be problematic. What, then, is the function of narrative reconstruction? Most existing accounts now point to the potential of such reconstructions to reorient the individual, to open new courses of action that are more fulfilling and more adequately suited to the individual's capacities and proclivities. Thus, the client may alter or dispose of earlier narratives not because they are inaccurate but because they are dysfunctional in his or her particular circumstances.

A question must now be raised: In precisely what way or ways is a narrative "useful"? How does a language of self-understanding guide, direct, or inform lines of action? What does the story do for (or to) the client? Two answers to this question pervade postempiricist camps at present, and both are flawed in important ways. On one side is the metaphor of *language as a lens*. According to this account, a narrative construction is a vehicle through which the world is *seen*. It is through the lens of narrative that the individual identifies objects, persons, actions, and so on. And many argue that it is on the basis of the world as seen, not of the world as it is, that the individual determines a course of action. Thus, one who sees life as a tragic fall would perceive its unfolding events in these terms. Yet, as I outlined in Chapter 3, to take this position is to view the individual as isolated and solipsistic—as simply stewing in the juices of his or her own constructions. The possibilities for survival are minimal, for there is no way to escape encapsulation in the internal system of construals. Further, as we saw in Chapter 5, such an account generates a range of notorious epistemological problems. How, for example, does the individual develop this lens? From whence comes the first construction? For if there is no world outside that which is internally constructed, there would be no means of understanding and thus of developing or fashioning the lens. How can we defend the view that the sounds and markings employed in human interchange are somehow transported into the mind to impose order on the perceptual world? This was indeed Whorf's (1956) proposal, but it is a view that never succeeded in being more than controversial. The argument for language as lens seems poorly taken.

The major alternative to this view holds that narrative constructions are *internal models,* forms of story that can be interrogated by the individual as guides to action. Again, no argument is made for the truth of the model; the narrative operates simply as an enduring structure that informs and directs action. Thus, for example, a person who features himself as a hero whose feats of bravery and intelligence will prevail against all odds finds life unworkable. Through therapy he realizes that such a view not only places him in impossible circumstances, it works against close feelings of intimacy and interdependence with his wife and children. He works out a new story in which he comes to see himself as a champion not for himself but for his family. His heroism will be achieved through their feelings of happiness and will thus depend in a major way on their assessments of his actions. It is this transformed image that is to guide his subsequent actions.

Although there is a certain wisdom to this position, it too is problematic. Stories of this variety are in themselves both idealized and abstract. As such, they can seldom dictate behavior in complex, ongoing interaction. What does the new story of self say, for example, about the best reaction to his wife's desire that he spend fewer hours at work and more at home with the family; how should he respond to a new job offer, challenging and profitable, but replete with risk? Stories as internal models are not only lacking specific directives or implications, they remain static. The individual moves through numerous situations and relationships—a parent dies, a son is tempted by drugs, an attractive neighbor acts seductively, and so on. Yet, the narrative model remains inflexible—unbending and of obscure relevance. The "model in the head" is largely useless.

There is still a third way of understanding narrative utility, one that grows out of the constructionist emphasis on the pragmatics of language (it is detailed more fully in the discussion of self-narratives in Chapter 8). As I have proposed, narratives gain their utility primarily within social interchange. They are constitutive components of ongoing relationships, essential for maintaining the intelligibility and coherence of social life, useful in drawing people together, creating distance, and so on. Stories of the self enable us to establish public identities, to render the past acceptable, and to follow the rituals of relationship with ease. The utility of these stories derives from their success as moves within these relational arenas in terms of their adequacy as reactions to previous moves or as instigators of what follows.

Consider, for example, a story of failure—how someone tried his best to pass a professional exam but failed. As we have seen, the story is neither true nor false in itself; it is simply one construction of events among many. However, as this story is inserted into various forms of relationship—into the games or dances of the culture—its effects are strikingly varied. If a friend has just related a story of great personal achievement, one's story of failure is likely to act as a repressive force and alienate the friend who otherwise anticipated a congratulatory reaction. If, in contrast, the friend had just revealed a personal failure, to share one's own failings is likely to be reassuring and to solidify the friendship. Similarly, to relate one's story of failure to one's mother may elicit a warm and sympathetic reaction, in effect, enabling her to be a "mother"; but to share it with a wife who worries each month over making ends meet may produce both frustration and anger.

To put it another way, a story is not simply a story. It is itself a situated action, a performance with illocutionary effects. It acts to create, sustain, or alter worlds of social relationship. In these terms, it is insufficient that the client and therapist negotiate a new form of self-understanding that seems realistic, aesthetic, and uplifting within the dyad. It is not the dance of meaning within the therapeutic context that is primarily at stake but whether the new shape of meaning is serviceable in the social arena outside these confines. How, for example, does the story of oneself as "hero of the family group" play for a wife who dislikes her dependent status, a boss who is a "self-made woman," or a rebellious son? What forms of action does the story invite in each of these situations; what kinds of dances are engendered, facilitated, or sustained as a result? It is evaluation at this level that therapist and client should confront.

Transcending Narrative

The focus on narrative pragmatics sets the stage for what may be the most critical argument. Many therapists making the postmodern turn in therapy continue to view the narrative as either a form of internal lens, determining the way life is seen, or an internal model for guiding action. In light of our discussion of pragmatics, these conceptions are lacking in three important respects. First, each retains the *individualist* cast of modernism, in that the final resting place of the narrative construction is within the mind of the single individual. But as we have reconsidered the utility of the narrative, we have moved outward from the individual's mind to the relationships constituted by the narrative in action. Narratives exist in the telling, and tellings, for good or ill, are constituents of relational forms. Second, the metaphors of the lens and the internal model both favor *singularity in narrative;* both tend to presume the functionality of a single formulation of self-understanding. The individual possesses "a lens" for comprehending the world, it is said, not a *repository* of lenses; and through therapy one comes to possess "a new narrative truth," as it is often put, not a *multiplicity* of truths. From the pragmatic standpoint, the presumption of singularity operates against functional adequacy. Each narrative of the self may function well in certain circumstances but lead to miserable outcomes in others. To have only a single means of making the self intelligible, then, is to limit the range of relationships or situations in which one can function satisfactorily. Thus, for example, it may be very useful to be able to "do" anger scenarios effectively and to formulate accounts to justify such activity. There are certain times and places in which anger is the most effective move in the dance. At the same time, to be overskilled or overprepared in this regard so that anger is virtually the only means of moving relationships along will vastly reduce these relationships. From the present perspective, narrative multiplicity is vastly to be preferred.

Finally, both the lens and the internal model conceptions favor a *belief in* or a *commitment to* narrative. Both suggest that the individual lives *within* the narrative as a system of understanding: one "sees the world in this way," and the narrative is thus "true for the individual." Or the transformed story of self is "the new reality"; it constitutes a "new belief about the self" that can support and sustain the individual. Again, however, as we consider the social utility of narrative, belief and commitment become suspect. To be committed to a given story of self, to adopt it as "true for me," is vastly to limit one's possible relationships. To believe that one *is a success* is thus as debilitating in its own way as believing that one *is a failure.* Both are only stories after all, and each may bear fruit within a particular range of contexts and relationships. To crawl inside one and put down roots is to forego the other and thus to reduce the range of contexts and relationships in which adequacy is achieved.

To frame the issue in another way, postmodern consciousness favors a thoroughgoing relativism in expressions of identity. On the metatheoretical level it invites a multiplicity of accounts of reality, while recognizing the historically and culturally situated contingency of each. There are only accounts of truth within differing conversations, and no conversation is transcendentally privileged. Thus, for the postmodern practitioner a multiplicity of self-accounts is invited, but no commitment need be made to any of them. From this standpoint, the client should be encouraged to explore a variety of narrative formulations but discouraged from commitment to any particular "truth of self." The narrative constructions thus remain fluid—open to the shifting tides of relationship.

Can we tolerate such a conclusion? Is the individual thus reduced to being a social con artist, adopting whatever posture of identity garners the highest payoff? Certainly the constructionist emphasis is on flexibility in self-identification, but this does not simultaneously imply that the individual is either duplicitous or scheming. To speak of duplicity is to presume that a "true telling" is otherwise available. We have found this view to be deeply problematic. One may interpret one's actions as duplicitous or sincere, but these ascriptions are, after all, simply components of different stories. Similarly, to presume that the individual possesses private motives, including a rational calculus of self-presentation (the psychological basis of a "con"), is again to sustain the modernist view of the self-contained individual. From the constructionist standpoint, relationship takes priority over the individual self: selves are only realized as a byproduct of relatedness. Thus, to shift the form and content of self-narration from one relationship to another is neither deceitful nor self-serving in the traditional sense. Rather, it is to honor the various modes of relationship in which one is enmeshed. It is to take seriously the multiple and varied forms of human connectedness that make up a life. Adequate and fulfilling actions are only so in terms of the criteria generated within the various forms of relationship themselves.[4]

Therapeutic Moves

As we have found, therapy as a means toward narrative reconstruction or replacement fails either to realize the full implications of constructionist theory or to facilitate the full range of possibilities for human functioning. A thoroughgoing constructionism emphasizes narrative within the broader social process of generating meaning. This involves an appreciation of the contextual relativity of meaning, an acceptance of indeterminacy, the generative exploration of a multiplicity of meanings, and the understanding that it is unnecessary to adhere to an invariant story or search for a definitive identity. "Re-authoring" or "re-storying" seems, then, but a first-order therapeutic approach, one which implies the replacement of a dysfunctional master narrative with a more functional one. At the same time, this result carries the seeds of a prescriptive rigidity—one which might also serve to confirm the illusion that it is possible to develop a set of principles or codes that can be invariantly applied, irrespective of relational context.

From a certain standpoint, one may also venture that this very rigidity is constitutive of the difficulties people often bring to the therapeutic situation. This possibility is worthy of attention. Just as psychotherapists may be restrained by a limiting code, so people who describe their lives as problematic often seem trapped within a limiting vocabulary, behavioral codes, and constitutive conventions from which the contours of their lives are molded. Acting in terms of a singular narrative and its associated actions, one is not only restrained from exploring alternative possibilities but can become imprisoned in painful transactional patterns with others.[5]

If language provides the matrix from which human understanding derives, then psychotherapy can be aptly construed as "linguistic activity in which conversation about a problem generates the development of new meanings" (Goolishian and Winderman 1988, p. 139). Put differently, psychotherapy may be thought of as a process of *semiosis*—the forging of meaning in the context of collaborative discourse. It is a process in which the meaning of events is transformed through a fusion of the horizons of the participants, alternative ways of narrating events are developed, and new stances toward self and others evolve. A crucial component of this process may inhere not only in the alternative ways of accounting generated by the discourse but also in the different conception of meaning that emerges concurrently.

A transformation in discourse may frequently provide a release from the tyranny of the implied authority of governing beliefs. Such release may be facilitated by a transformative dialogue in which new understandings are negotiated together with a new set of premises *about* meaning. In terms of Bateson's (1972) distinctions between levels of learning, it is a move beyond learning to replace one punctuation of a situation with another (Level 1), to learn new modes of punctuation (Level 2), to evolve what Keeney calls "a change of the premises underlying an entire system of punctuation habits" (1983, p. 159) (Level 3). It is a progression from learning new meanings to developing new categories of meaning to transforming one's premises about the nature of meaning itself.

These transformations also demand a facilitating context. At the outset there is much to be said for Goolishian and Anderson's (1987) emphasis on creating a climate in which clients have the experience of being heard, of having both their point of view and their feelings understood, of feeling themselves confirmed and accepted. Yet, while helping the therapist to understand the premises from which the client's viewpoint arises, interested listening does not simultaneously imply a commitment to the client's premises. Rather, it serves as a contextual validation for a particular account, a validation that enables client and therapist to reconstitute this reality as a conversational object, now vulnerable to a new infusion of meaning. How is this process to proceed? There is no single answer to this question, just as there can be no principled constraint over the number of possible conversations. However, therapists sensitive to postmodern dialogues have been highly creative in developing conceptually congenial practices. Hoffman (1985) sets the contours for "an art of lenses." Goolishian and Anderson (1992) employ a form of *interested inquiry,* asking questions that simultaneously credit the client's reality while pressing it toward evolution. Andersen and his colleagues (1991) have developed the practice of the *reflecting team,* individuals who observe the therapeutic encounter and then share their opinions with both therapist and client. The reflecting team reduces authority (the therapist), generates an appreciation for multiple realities, and furnishes the client with a variety of resources for proceeding. White and Epston (1990) employ letters (and other written documents) to help clients to *re-author* their lives. These letters may be written by both client and therapist. Penn and Frankfurt (in press) also rely on client letter writing, generating a dialogic process within the clients' stories in order to forge new openings for conversations with others. O'Hanlon and Wilk (1987) lay out an array of conversational means by which client-therapist *negotiation* may proceed toward a dissolution of the putative problem. De Shazer (1991) encourages conversation about *solutions* (as opposed to problems), and Friedman and Fanger (1991) about *positive possibilities.* Lipchik (1993) emphasizes client talk about *balancing* the various goods and bads in existing alternatives to replace an either/or orientation with a both/and. Many therapists place a strong emphasis on *positive construction* of self and life circumstances (see, for example, Durrant and Kowalski 1993). Fruggeri (1992) encourages different descriptions of given events, new ways of connecting behaviors and events, and a process of continuous reflexivity. Coelho de Amorim and Cavalcante (1992) help disabled adolescents to produce puppet shows through which they narrate their life conditions and their possibilities.

Yet simply because these therapeutic forms grow from the soil of a postmodern constructionism does not mean that all other therapies are outmoded or must be abandoned. On the contrary, as I have outlined in preceding chapters, a constructionist standpoint—unlike its metatheoretical predecessors—does not attempt to eradicate alternative languages of understanding and their associated practices. Such prefixes as "is true," "is objective," and "is more successful in producing cures" may be removed from the process of critical comparison. However, all theories of therapy, all forms of therapeutic practice, must be considered in terms of what they add (or subtract) from the conversational matrix we call therapy and its ramifications for cultural life more generally. Couches, dream analyses, positive regard, strategic interventions, circular questioning—all are entries into the broader vocabulary of the profession. They invite certain lines of interchange and action and suppress others.

By the same token, we must view the modernist attempt to replace lay languages (of "ignorance") with scientific languages—typically, a univocal language of the true—as unnecessarily and detrimentally constraining. The common languages by which people live their daily lives have enormous pragmatic potential. Living-room languages, street languages, spiritual languages, New Age languages—these and others are prime movers in the culture. To restrict their entry into the therapeutic setting is to reduce the possibilities for conversation. Belief is not in question here, for the concept of belief (as indexing a mental state) is itself deeply suspect. Rather, the major challenge concerns the potential of the therapeutic conversation to be carried into relationships outside this context.

More generally, we can ask whether our therapeutic languages and practices can liberate participants from static and delimiting conventions and enable a full flexibility of relationship. Can those turning to the therapist in times of trouble transcend the restraints imposed by their erstwhile reliance on a determinate set of meanings? Can they be freed from the struggle that ensues from imposing their beliefs on self and others? For some, new solutions to problems will become apparent, while for others, a richer set of narrative meanings will emerge. For still others, a stance toward meaning itself can perhaps evolve, one which betokens that tolerance of uncertainty, that freeing of self that comes from acceptance of the unbounded relativity of meaning. For those who adopt it, this stance offers the prospect of a creative participation in the unending and unfolding meaning of life.

11   The Communal Origins of Meaning

In the preceding chapters I have argued that conceptions of the self and others are derived from and sustained by patterns of relationship. Through relational coordination, language is born, and through language we acquire the capacity to render ourselves intelligible. Relationship thus replaces the individual as the fundamental unit of social life. Yet, we are left with the problem of meaning: How do words and gestures come to have meaning for people? How is it that we reach common understandings or often fail in our attempts to understand? Traditional psychological approaches are incapable of solving these essential problems. How can they be solved from a relational perspective?

Scholarly problems are invariably wedded to particular perspectives—languages that frame them as "problems" and demand something we call "solutions." Likewise, the way in which problems are articulated simultaneously circumscribes the range of possible outcomes. A problem stated within a given system of understanding will limit itself to solutions born of that system, and assertions from alternative systems will remain unrecognized. In large measure, the problem of meaning within the human sciences has been framed within a particular tradition of Western epistemology (see Overton 1993). Yet, in my view, this venerable tradition frames the issue of meaning in a way that precludes a viable answer; the tools of the tradition are ill formed to solve the question as posed. If the problem of meaning is structured by an alternative system of suppositions, however, we gain not only in terms of intellectual coherence but in terms of broadened research vistas and societal promise as well.

Although the concept of "meaning" forms a promontory in a variety of intellectual landscapes, for many scholars—psychologists included—it is preeminently defined in terms of *individual signification,* or the internal symbolization (representation, conceptualization) of the external world. From this grounding supposition scholars derive not simply one "problem of meaning" but a set of interrelated and profoundly challenging enigmas. Among the more prominent: How is it that the external world comes to have meaning for the individual (the problem of epistemology)? How can we account for what appear to be differences among people in the meaning of events (cultural psychology)? How does individual meaning come to be expressed in language (psycholinguistics)? Yet it is to none of these daunting problems that I direct the present arguments. Rather, I raise a derivative but equally significant issue, namely that of *meaning with others.* Here the chief question is how we can apprehend each other's meanings, successfully communicate, or understand each other. Whatever solutions are offered for the initial variants on "the problem of meaning," they must finally be able to render an account of meaning with others. Any theory of individual meaning that cannot be squared with the possibility of shared meaning would not only leave us with the unsatisfactory conclusion that social understanding is impossible, it would also leave us with the unhappy paradox that we could not understand the theory itself.

If we focus, then, on the problem of meaning with others, we can distinguish two orientations, one with a rich and venerable tradition and the other of recent and more humble origin. Because of its stronger intuitive appeal, its regnant command over contemporary psychology, and its critical role in the developmental sphere, I shall first consider the traditional orientation. As the inadequacy of this outlook becomes clear, we open the way for consideration of the alternative. The traditional orientation in this case derives from a fundamental belief in individual signification—or more directly, a belief in a phenomenal "I," an Archimedian point of individual agency, or the private authorship of ideas. It is the conscious "I" who can mean, and it is the "I" who conveys meaning through words and deeds. To "know another's meanings" from this standpoint is to gain access to the other's subjectivity or symbol system. To understand another is to press past the visible surface to the other's interior, to comprehend what he or she subjectively "means" or intends by words and deeds. If we are to communicate successfully, according to this account, we must acquire a state of intersubjective transparency.

The problem of intersubjective understanding has had an uneven history over the past century. For nineteenth-century German scholars it was critical for separating the natural sciences *(Naturwissenschaften),* which focus on the physical world, from the human sciences *(Geisteswissenschaften),* which are concerned with the meaningful activity of human beings. As has often been argued, the processes necessary for understanding physical objects (nonmeaningful entities) must necessarily differ from those involved in understanding intentional agents. In Dilthey's (1984) terms, "in the human studies . . . the nexus of psychic life constitutes the originally primitive and fundamental datum. We explain nature, but we understand psychic life . . . Just as the system of culture—economy, law, religion, art and science—and the external organization of society in the ties of family, community, church and state, arise from the living nexus of the human mind *(Menschenseele),* so can they be understood only by reference to it" (p. 76).

Although psychology's concern with intersubjectivity has continued into the present century, the hegemony of American behaviorism largely cast such issues to the margins of interest. For the behaviorist, the individual's overt responses serve as stimuli to the actions of others, and vice versa. From this standpoint, there simply is no problem of intersubjectivity, and thus of meaning as we have generally understood the term. It was not until the cognitive movement gradually reinstated the domain of mental life that the problem of intersubjectivity could again enter the scholarly agenda. Yet, attempts to solve the problem of how one "cognitive system" can convey its contents to another are rare (see, for example, Johnson-Laird 1988). However, as Bruner argues in *Acts of Meaning,* the dominant metaphor of the individual as "information processor" has continued to obscure the problem, for this metaphor places the individual's psychological processes on center stage while shunting interpersonal concerns to the wings. One of the major exceptions to this tendency is to be found, interestingly enough, not in social psychology but in the developmental domain, in the works of Jean Piaget. For unlike modern cognitivists Piaget was concerned with how meaning can be transmitted from one subjectivity to another. The following passage from Piaget's *The Language and Thought of the Child* provides a clear framing of the issue:

> understanding between children occurs only in so far as there is contact between two identical mental schemas already existing in each child. In other words, when the explainer and his listener have had . . . common preoccupations and ideas, then each word of the explainer is understood, because it fits into a schema already existing and well defined within the listener's mind. (p. 133)

Yet, in spite of the historical significance of this work and the richness of the tradition that it represents, I fear that its elaboration ends in impasse. So long as the problem of interpersonal meaning is derived from a belief in the individual as the center of meaning, it will remain resistant to solution. In effect, to begin with the assumption of meaning as individual signification will lead us to the untenable conclusion that interpersonal understanding is impossible. Let me fortify this contention with two troublesome lines of critique.

The Hermeneutic Impasse

There are many grounds for doubting the intersubjective view of human meaning, some as old as the tradition itself. This view grows from the soil of dualism—from distinguishing a mind (logos, soul, consciousness) separated from material, a "within here" from an "out there." It has long been a nettlesome problem for philosophers that if we begin with human consciousness (an "in here") we have no way of being certain of an external reality—which also includes the possible existence of other minds. We have no way to transcend subjectivity, to locate an extrasubjective vantage point from which we can view the relation between the subjective and the objective (or between two isolated subjectivities) to determine when and how the one is related to the other. These were Piaget's problems as well, as he attempted to compensate for the debilitating consequences of his rationalist commitment with large doses of pragmatism and functionalism (Kitchener 1986). As we have seen, so severe are the problems of dualist epistemology that materialists, phenomenologists, and Wittgensteinians alike have since opted (albeit on differing grounds) for its abandonment.

Although these and other problems of epistemology have long plagued the dualist tradition, it is to other arguments that I now turn. These discussions are of more recent vintage and more distinctly tied to issues of human meaning. The first derives from the hermeneutic tradition and, more specifically, from theories concerning the proper or valid interpretation of texts. Hermeneutic theory is pivotal to the issue of human meaning, for a proper theory of textual interpretation should, in principle, furnish insight into the means by which intersubjective communion is achieved. That is, hermeneutic theory should furnish the directions by which the individual can press past the phonemic surface to grasp the intentional impulse of the speaker. And if hermeneutic theory cannot answer this challenge, we have reason to suspect the very presumption of intersubjective transparency.

There are at least two important strands of hermeneutic thought that lend strong support to the intersubjective account of human meaning. On the one hand, romanticist hermeneutics, reaching its apex within the preceding century, was centrally concerned with the means by which the individual can "inhabit" or "ingest" the experience of the other. From the romanticist standpoint, to understand another is to experience in some manner the other's subjectivity. It is in this vein, for example, that Dilthey (1894) proposed a process of *Verstehen* by which the individual prereflexively transposes him or herself into the other, empathizing with or apprehending some aspect of the "lived experience" of the other. Yet, in spite of their intuitive appeal, romanticist views of shared subjectivities could not be sustained, in part because theorists could not render a compelling account of how a process such as *Verstehen* could take place. By what faculty does such mental transposition occur? How does one experiential field grasp the essence of the other? How can accuracy be determined? The answers to these questions remain clouded in mystery.

With the waning of romanticism in the twentieth century and its replacement by a modernist mentality, belief in the empathic grasping of others' subjectivities was pushed aside in favor of reason and observation. For the modernist, the task of the reader is not to "feel with" but to use systematic analytic procedures in moving toward the central meaning behind the text. Emblematic of modernist hermeneutics is the work of Hirsch. In his widely debated *Validity in Interpretation,* Hirsch (1967) proposed that authors are privileged with respect to the meaning of their words, that, in effect, "the meaning of a text is the author's meaning" (p. 25). It is the task of readers or interpreting agents to deploy processes of careful observation, combined with logical inference and hypothesis testing, to move from the text as given to increasingly more accurate interpretations of the author's intent. For the modernist, understanding is achieved by individual minds searching for meaning within the other; a logical means replaces a romantic one.

Yet modernist views of rationality and hypothesis testing have been abandoned in contemporary debate, and at least one significant reason for their demise is the extension of Heideggerian arguments by his disciple, Hans-Georg Gadamer. As Gadamer proposed (1975), we confront the text (and by analogy each other) with a "forestructure of understanding"—an array of prejudgments or prejudices—questions that we put to the text and assumptions about the array of possible answers. This array of prejudices is historically contingent; its character has evolved over the course of time and circumstance. In Gadamer's terms, we approach the text with a given *horizon of understanding* that will influence the way in which we interpret its meaning. Thus, for Gadamer there is no meaning *in itself,* an authorial impulse that we must necessarily grasp in order to derive the correct interpretation of the text. Meaning cannot but be informed by the interpreting agent's forestructure of understandings.

Although compelling, this conclusion propels Gadamer into a new problem, that of solipsism. Does the reader simply recapitulate his or her own biases in each new confrontation with a text? How would the horizon then change across time? How could one ever escape the prison of prejudice? To answer, Gadamer proposes that one's horizons may be expanded by joining with the text in a dialogic relationship. The text is thus allowed to influence one's prejudices and its meaning is simultaneously influenced by these prejudices. This *fusion of horizons* is achieved when the voice of the text is allowed to ask questions of the reader and thereby enables him or her to become aware of the array of prejudgments. Interpretation, according to this view, does not take place in the head of the reader but grows out of the dialogic interplay between text and prejudices. Or, as Gadamer would have it, the fusion of horizons takes place *between* reader and text; the result is not a correct or accurate reading, but one that represents a fusion of text and reader. For Gadamer, "understanding is always more than the mere recreation of someone else's meaning" (p. 338).

In my view, however, Gadamer does not succeed in solving either his self-imposed problem of solipsism or the more general problem of social meaning. For if the individual can only understand in terms of a system of meaning that is brought to a text, there is no obvious means by which he or she can stand outside this system to allow the text to ask its own questions or to generate a consciousness of his or her own biases. How would the "questions of the text" be understood if there were no forestructure in place? How indeed would one become aware of his or her own biases except in terms of an already existing set of understandings? In answer, Gadamer proposes that all those within a culture share similar experiences; the cultural heritage in which the text is embedded will ensure that its members transcend the contemporary horizon and invite the interpreter into new forms of understanding. But this conclusion fails to be compelling, first because it subtly reintroduces the presumption of intersubjective transparency. That is, Gadamer presumes that the reader can somehow make contact with an essence lying behind the text, a meaning that can ask questions or inform a consciousness without biases. Further, he fails to offer a means by which anyone could understand someone who did not participate in the same cultural heritage or whose experiences in the culture were at variance with those of his or her predecessors. There would be precious little possibility for cross-cultural understanding. Thus, while it raises significant questions about the assumption of intersubjective connection, I do not believe Gadamer's theory provides a viable replacement.

Piaget (1955) himself labored with the hermeneutic problem. As he puzzled in *The Language and Thought of the Child,* how could he be certain that his own mental structures corresponded with those of his subjects. "It is impossible," he admitted, "by direct observation to be sure whether they [the children] are understanding each other. The child has a hundred and one ways of pretending to understand, and often complicates things still further by pretending not to understand" (p. 93). Piaget never solves the problem, and for my own part, I believe that principled difficulties underlie the intersubjectivist attempt to establish validity in interpretation. The problem commences when one treats the text (or another social action) as opaque and presumes a second level (an internal language) that must be located in order to render the covert transparent. But all we have at our disposal in the process of understanding is a domain of public discourse (or action). We suppose there is a domain of private mentation of which the public discourse is an expression, yet we possess access neither to the private domain itself nor to the rules by which it is translated into the public domain. Therefore, any attempt to translate (or locate meaning) must be based on an a priori set of suppositions and must thereby draw conclusions both limited to and determined by these suppositions: first, a priori agreements as to the ontology of the mental world (what can possibly be "on people's minds"), and second, how such states are related to forms of expression (which states produce what words or actions). It follows that the sense of accurate reading or translation can only proceed through a circular process of self-verification ("the hermeneutic circle" in vicious form).

We would face a similar problem if we attempted to read the mind of God through weather conditions. Without an array of presuppositions we could scarcely proceed; weather variations would stand mute as to God's mind. However, if we could commit ourselves first to a mental ontology of the Holy One (God is a being who "wishes," "desires," "wills," and so on) and second to a set of rules for linking states of the mental vernacular to weather conditions (when God is "angry" the sky is dark), we might proceed with efficacy. Once the imagined suppositions were in place, God's thoughts would be transparent. However, they would be so only by virtue of the system of suppositions we have constructed to carry out the task. If there is no "inner impulse" to which we can gain access, then all attempts to interpret the "inner" by virtue of the "outer" must be inherently circular. In this same vein Charles Taylor (1981) concludes that, "making sense . . . [of another's actions] cannot but move in a hermeneutical circle. Our conviction that an account makes sense is contingent on our reading of action and situation. But these readings cannot be explained or justified except by reference to other such readings, and their relation to the whole. If an interlocutor does not understand this kind of reading, or will not accept it as valid, there is nowhere else the argument can go" (p. 127).

From Interpretation to Textuality

Let us consider a second and related line of discussion, derived in this case from literary criticism. As we saw in Chapter 2, literary theory of the past two decades represents a major disjunction from its preceding forms, and the unfolding dialogue is of critical relevance to the problem of meaning. A central concern is the standards for textual criticism: by what criteria is a literary work to be judged; or, resonating with hermeneutic concerns, are there any rational or foundational standards for privileging certain interpretations over others? Traditionally, literary criticism has shared in the intersubjective view of meaning. The analyst's concern is to locate the "inner meaning" of the literary work, that is, the private meaning the author was attempting to express publicly. However, with the advent of the New Criticism in the 1950s, authorial intention began to wane in significance. As the New Critics compellingly argued, a literary work is a unity unto itself. Interpretation should properly focus on its structure, internal workings, coherence, and the like. For example, a poem is itself a self-contained and self-sustaining entity (Krieger 1956). What the author happens to think or feel about the work is of scant interest.

With the waning of the authorial standpoint in the modernist period, the stage was set for the more radical move of the postmodern. Consider the recently emerging emphasis on reader response (Sulieman and Crossman 1980). Reflecting Gadamer's concern with the reader's participation in the process of generating meaning, theorists focus on the presumptions, heuristics, ideologies, feelings, or cognitive dispositions that determine the reader's interpretation of texts. As reader dispositions come to dominate the meaning derived from the text, authorial intention recedes into insignificance. There is an important sense in which reader response theorists such as Fish (1980) also began to furnish an alternative to the subjectivism that haunted (and ultimately subverted) the Gadamerian orientation. For Gadamer the reader brought to the text a horizon or *forestructure of understanding* that could, without intervention, wholly appropriate the text. For Fish this individualized sensitivity is replaced by a *community of interpreters*. It is the standards of interpretation embedded within the community that determine how the text is read. Although Fish, along with most reader response analysts, stops short of a fully social account (imbuing the reader, as he does, with processes of reason, intention, and the like), it would be but a short step to eradicate the individual mind altogether. One could account for the actions of the individual reader without recourse to his or her "mind" and simply place the full explanatory weight on the communally generated criteria. In this sense, the individual mind of the interpreter would join the individual subjectivity of the author in vanishing from the analytic spectrum. I shall return to this possibility shortly.

Even with this more extended departure from intersubjectivist assumptions, however, reader response accounts fail to take us far enough. In the end we are left without a viable account of human meaning, and in place of the impenetrable isolation of individual subjectivity—invited by the traditional account—with a form of *social solipsism*. Each community of readers shares standards of interpretation through which the meaning of texts is appropriated. Thus, texts based on the communal criteria of other groups would fail to be understood on their own terms, and intergroup understanding would be impossible to achieve. In neocybernetic terms, the texts of the "other" would simply trigger the internally determined self-organizing processes of the community of readers. Few would be satisfied with such a view of human communication.

More radical in its subversion of the intersubjectivist account of meaning is deconstructionist literary theory. The chief villain in Derrida's writings (1976, 1978) is essentially the *logocentric* view of human functioning, the view that individual actors possess reasoning powers capable of fixing meaning and generating language. In a sense, his writings press toward the eradication of individual subjectivity in the process of communication, which he accomplishes in part by demonstrating the fatal incoherence of texts that sustain the logocentric tradition. More critically, however, Derrida demonstrates the futility of the search for the signified—the meaning behind or within the text. We have traditionally proceeded as if others present us with spoken or written language (an array of *signifiers*) and this language informs us about the state of the communicator's mind (for example, intentions, meanings, and so on) and of the world (objects, structures, and the like)—that is, the realms of the *signified*. However, as I outlined in Chapter 2, when we probe the domain of the signifiers to locate the signified, we find that each signifier is in itself empty. It tells us nothing; its meaning (or signified) is displaced. We are forever led to other signifiers—those that inform us of the precise nature of the signifier in question. But this deferral of meaning is again only temporary, for the signifiers purporting to clarify or elucidate the signified are found, on closer inspection, to lie empty also—unless supplemented by still further signifiers. Ultimately, then, meaning cannot be fixed; each choice leaves us in a state of indecision. The realms of the signified are lost and we are left with text only.

If there is nothing outside of text, how are we then to understand the process by which humans communicate with words? In what manner do we achieve what passes for understanding? Why is the endless search for the signified commonly terminated in everyday affairs? At present, deconstruction theorists fail to furnish answers to such questions. Of course the deconstructionist could reply by questioning the concept of human meaning altogether. From the deconstructionist standpoint, theories of meaning are not about the world; they are essentially arrays of signifiers within a body of interrelated texts. Their meaning is not derived from their relationship to an *actual* process of meaningful interchange (even the term "actual" is defeasible), but from their relationship to other signifiers. In this sense, we are invited to abandon the present theoretical quest as simply one more textually determined (or merely academic) exercise.

As I proposed in Chapter 2, however, even by deconstructionist standards one is also free to reject such an invitation—not for any reason (merely another textual gesture, from the deconstructionist standpoint) but as an ungrounded action in itself. Such rejection is compelling, not only because of the immobile and self-ingurgitating end reached through deconstructionist analysis, but also because if we foreground certain premises, we find that the deconstructionist argument itself contains the nucleus for a theory of meaning. Deconstructionists tend to confine their analysis to the world of texts, but if we extend the implications of such analyses, we open new alternatives in the social domain. Consider first that there are no fixed entities within the deconstructionist frame. Each single signifier is found, on close inspection, to be an imposter, a stand-in for another signifier. When we approach the real entity behind the signifier, it too shows itself as a dissembler. Yet although entities dissolve, there is a constant within the analysis on the level of relationship. No signifier itself is informative, but the process of deferral generates meaning. When the signifier is encountered in the reflected light of other signifiers—a reflection of which it is indeed a constituent element—we gain momentary clarity. The "interstice" effectively gives shape to its boundaries; in a symbiotic transfer, meaning is born.

Let us press the analysis outward to a "world" beyond texts. Why should we so circumscribe the concept of "the text"? Are texts necessarily forms of writing (or uttered sounds)? What prevents us from introducing what we call "actions" or "objects" into the domain of textuality (as signifiers)? This possibility was indeed demonstrated in the discussion of reference in the natural sciences in Chapter 3. In effect, if we extend the "play of signifiers" in this manner, it converges first with Wittgenstein's concept of "language games" and, what is more important, with his more generalized concept of "forms of life." The play of signifiers is essentially a play within language, and this play is embedded within patterns of human action in what we call material contexts. We may then abandon the text in its traditional sense and consider the manner in which a process of relatedness is continuously at work in generating a world of palpable particulars.

Meaning in Relationship

Recent developments in hermeneutic and literary theory leave us in the following condition: the traditional view that meaning originates within the individual mind, is expressed within words (and other actions), and is deciphered within the minds of other agents is deeply problematic. If meaning were preeminently a process of establishing intersubjectivity, we would be unable to communicate. There appears to be no way of inferentially or intuitively moving past another's words (or actions) to the subjective source; nor would it be possible to understand anything outside one's pre-existing system of meanings. In short, to begin solving the problem of human meaning with the assumption of individual subjectivity leaves no avenue to solution.

Yet to echo the theme of preceding chapters, the question of meaning need not be framed within the individualist tradition. There is an alternative way of approaching the problem of social meaning: removing the individual as the starting point opens a range of promising possibilities. Rather than commence with individual subjectivity and work deductively toward an account of human understanding through language, we may begin our analysis at the level of the *human relationship* as it generates both language and understanding. Such an approach is given impetus, for one, by the semiotics movement pioneered by Peirce and Saussure and significantly extended by Barthes, Eco, Greimas, and many others. Attention in this case is more often directed to the system of language or signs common to a given culture. Society is, in effect, held together through common participation in a system of signification. With the system of signs thus foregrounded, we may view social understanding as a byproduct of participation within the common system. In this sense, it is not the individual who preexists the relationship and initiates the process of communication, but the conventions of relationship that enable understanding to be achieved.

In important respects, the literary theory just discussed is congenial with, or draws heavily from, the semiotic tradition. Reader response theory abandons the problem of meaning within the mind of the author, concentrating instead on the shared sign systems of the interpretive community. In effect, the community generates the meaning of the text by appropriating it into its system of signs. Similarly, for Derrida the meaning of any given signifier is both evanescent and contingent, since meaning is ever deferred to other signifiers and ultimately diffused throughout the entire system of signification. Yet, as we have also seen, in their present form such theories fail to provide a satisfactory account of the means by which humans generate or sustain meaning, nor within the semiotic tradition more generally are there unequivocal accounts of this process. As one commentator (Sless 1986) observes, "nowhere in semiotics is the sense of uncertainty more obvious and profound than in relation to meaning" (p. 88).

It would be premature at this juncture to offer a fully articulated account of social meaning from a relational perspective. It is useful, however, to sketch out a range of rudimentary suppositions, thus extending existing dialogue and foreshadowing a possible future. To do so, I will make use of the semiological tradition and its near relatives, but with one major departure. Semiotic tradition focuses chiefly on the properties of language (and more typically, the text); it attributes the production of meaning to linguistic (or textual) patterning. However, to extend the arguments of Chapter 2, this focus obscures the site from which meaning derives. Words (or texts) within themselves bear no meaning; they fail to communicate. They only appear to generate meaning by virtue of their place within the realm of human interaction. It is human interchange that gives language its capacity to mean, and it must stand as the critical locus of concern. I wish then to replace *textuality* with *communality*. This shift allows us to restructure much that has been said about meaning within texts as a commentary on forms of relatedness.[1] At the same time, it allows significant linkages to be made between textual traditions and social analysis. Let us consider, then, several rudimentary stipulations for a relational theory of human meaning.

An individual's utterances in themselves possess no meaning. In the intersubjective account of meaning, the mind of the individual serves as an originary source. Meaning is generated within the mind and transmitted via words or gestures. In the relational case, however, there is no proper beginning, no originary source, no specific region in which meaning takes wing, for we are always already in a relational standing with others and the world. Therefore to speak of origins we must generate a hypothetical space in which there is an utterance (marking, gesture, and so on) without relational embedding. Granting this idealized case, we find that the single utterance of an individual itself fails to possess meaning. This is most obvious in the case of any selected morpheme (such as *the, ed, too*). Standing alone, the morpheme fails to be anything but itself. It operates, as in the textual case, as a free-standing signifier, opaque and indeterminate. One may generate a variety of apparent exceptions to this initial assumption—a shout of "help" on a dark night, or more extended word sequences, such as "Eat at Joe's." But the communicative value of such exceptions will inevitably prove to depend on a prior history of relationships, one in which shouts and billboards, for example, play a role in coordinating human affairs. In Bakhtin's (1981) terms, "utterances are not indifferent to one another, are not self-sufficient; they are aware of and mutually reflect one another" (p. 91). Consider the sound "woo" issued from the lips of a damsel in a nearby glade. Although the utterance drips with significatory potential, it is ultimately obscure. Even in context, it remains untranslatable.

The potential for meaning is realized through supplementary action. Lone utterances begin to acquire meaning when an other or others coordinate themselves to the utterance, that is, when they add some form of supplementary action (whether linguistic or otherwise). The supplement may be as simple as an affirmation ("yes," "right") that indeed the initial utterance has succeeded in communicating. It may take the form of an action (shifting the line of gaze upon hearing the word "look!"). Or it may extend the utterance in some way (when "the" uttered by one interlocutor is followed by "end!" uttered by a second). In the case of the damsel, meaning is generated when we hear a voice that responds to "Woo" with, "Yes, dear," which furnishes the sound with meaning as the calling of a name.

We thus find that an individual alone can never "mean"; an other is required to supplement the action and thus give it a function within the relationship. To communicate is thus to be granted the privilege of meaning by others. If others do not treat one's utterances as communication, if they fail to coordinate themselves around the offering, such utterances are reduced to nonsense. In this regard, virtually any form of utterance may be granted the privilege of being meaningful or, conversely, serve as a candidate for nonsense. Kosinski's *Being There* furnishes numerous puckish examples of how the words of Chauncy Gardner, a seeming idiot, are turned into profundity by surrounding believers. Garfinkel's (1967) exercises in questioning the routine rituals of everyday conversation—"exactly what do you mean by 'flat tire'?"—demonstrate the possibility of aborting even the most obvious and the most sophisticated candidates for meaning.

In semiotic terms, I am attempting to remove meaning both from the impersonal structures of the text and the "system of language" and to place it within the process of relationship. For many semioticians, the fundamental unit of meaning is contained in the relationship between signifier and signified; it is not located within either unit individually but within the linkage between the two. Here, however, I am removing linkage from its textual location and placing it within the social realm. Thus, we may view an individual's actions as a primitive "signifier," while the responses of another person now take the place of the "signified." This "sign" relationship—signifier-linked-to-signified in semiotic terms—is now replaced by action-and-supplement. It is only by virtue of supplementary signifiers that signified actions gain their capacity to mean, and it is only within the relationship of action-and-supplement that meaning is to be located at all. In Shotter's (1993b) terms, meaning is not born of action and reaction but of *joint action*.

Supplements act both to create and to constrain meaning. The initial action of the individual (utterance, gesture, and so on) does not, in the hypothetical space I have developed thus far, demand any particular form of supplementation. Standing alone it possesses no *logical force* (Pearce and Cronen 1980). The act of supplementation thus operates in two opposing ways. First, it grants a specific *potential* to the meaning of the utterance. It treats it as meaning this and not that, as inviting one form of action as opposed to another, as placing certain demands as opposed to some others. Thus, if you ask me "Do you have a light," I can react by staring at you in puzzlement (thus negating what you have said as meaningful action). Or, conversely, I can react in a variety of different ways, each bestowing a different meaning on the utterance. For example, I can busily search through my pockets and answer "no," I can answer "yes" and walk away, I can tell you "I am not serving beer," I can ask you what it is you really want, or I can even shriek and fall into a fetal crouch.

At the same time, as I create your meaning in one of these various ways I simultaneously act to *curtail* its potential in many others. Because I have created it as meaning this, it cannot mean that. In this sense, while I invite you into existence as a bearer of meaning (an "intentional agent"), I also act so as to negate your potential. From the enormous array of possibilities, I thus create direction and temporarily narrow the possibilities of your identity and agency. But this curtailment must not be viewed as unidirectional, the supplement both creating and delimiting what has preceded. In the roughly ordered state of ordinary cultural life, action-supplement coordinations are already in place. Actions appear to have a logical force—to demand certain supplements as opposed to others—because only these supplements are considered sensible or meaningful. Thus, although falling into a fetal position is possible in principle, it risks abrogating the very possibilities of meaning within the relationship. In this way, the action-supplement relationship is more properly viewed as *reciprocal*: supplements operate to determine the meaning of actions, while actions create and constrain the possibility of supplementation.

Any supplement (or action-and-supplement) is a candidate for further supplementation. The supplement once executed now comes to stand in the same position as the initial action or utterance. It is open to further specification, clarification, or obliteration through subsequent actions of the initial actor (or others). Its function as supplement, then, is both transient and contingent on what follows. Thus, the supplement does not finally affix meaning but serves only as a temporary and defeasible functionary. This is not to say that the supplement is an isolated event similar to the hypothetical "action" with which we began—an action that has no meaning until clarified by further supplementation. Rather, because the supplement occurs within the context of the initial action, and has been created and constrained by that action, we see that it is the relationship between action *and* supplement that becomes subject to future revision and clarification. Thus, for example, if you ask me if I have a light, and I say "yes" and walk away, we have formed a unit that stands to be resignified by you. If you stare after me in amazement, you fail to grant to our interchange (action-and-supplement) the status of a meaningful interchange. If, however, you hurl an oath in the direction of my retreat, you affirm that the action and supplement had meaning (in this case, my supplement serving as a calloused and spiteful reaction to your question). In the same way, you could stand puzzled at my comments about serving beer, thus negating the act-and-supplement as communication; or you might react with laughter (granting my act allusionary reference to light beer commercials), and thereby restore the interchange to a meaningful status.

Simultaneous with the instigation of the second-order supplement, the relationship between the interlocutors has been expanded in its potential and again constrained. Of all possible meanings that might be made of your question and my response in terms of serving beer, your laughter constitutes us as having brought off a joke together. In this sense, your laughter grants us a particular form of potential, one not furnished, for example, by a scowl or a curt rejoinder. And as it invites one future, so it temporarily closes the door on others.

Meanings are subject to continuous reconstitution via the expanding domain of supplementation. In light of these considerations we find that "what is meant" and what is communicated between persons are inherently undecidable. That is, meaning stands as a temporary achievement subject to continuous accretion and alteration through supplementary significations. All that is fixed and settled in one instance may be cast into ambiguity or undone in the next. Sarah and Steve may find themselves frequently laughing together, until Steve announces that Sarah's laughter is "unnatural and forced," that it is just her attempt to present herself as an "easy-going person" (in which case the definition of the previous actions would be altered). Or Sarah announces, "You are so superficial, Steve, that we really don't communicate" (thus negating the interchange altogether as a form of meaningful activity). At the same time, these latter moves within the ongoing sequence are subject to negation ("Steve, that's a crazy statement") and alteration ("You are only saying that, Sarah, because you find Bill so attractive"). Such instances of negation and alteration are subject to continuous change through interaction with and among others (friends, relatives, therapists, the media, and so on). They may also be temporally removed from the interchange itself (consider a divorcing pair who retrospectively redefine their entire marital trajectory or Supreme Court deliberations on the meaning of the Bill of Rights).

It is also the fundamentally open character of "what is meant" that lends itself to an exploration of the social management of meaning. Garfinkel's (1967) early work on the indexicality of meaning and the ad hoc character of making sense within a relationship are classic contributions to this domain. Studies of the ways in which communities of scientists work out mutually acceptable views of "the facts" (Latour and Woolgar 1979), psychologists collectively hammer out a vision of the human subject (Danziger 1990), families establish mutually acceptable views of the past (Middleton and Edwards 1990), acquaintances structure each other's identities (Shotter 1984), and political figures renegotiate the meaning of their public speeches (Edwards and Potter 1992) all serve to fill out the picture of meaning in the making.

At this point, however, we find that the exclusive focus on microsocial relationships is far too narrow. Whether "I make sense" is not ultimately under my control, but neither is it determined by you or the dyadic process in which meaning struggles toward realization. We derive our potential for meaning in the dyad from our previous immersion in a range of other relationships. The relationship is an extension of previous patterns of meaning making. And, as we move outward from our relationship to communicate with others, they also serve as supplements to our relational pattern, thus potentially altering the sense we have achieved; these interchanges may be supplemented and transformed in their meaning by still others. In effect, meaningful communication in any given interchange ultimately depends on a protracted array of relationships, extending, one may say, to the relational conditions of society as a whole. We are all in this way interdependently interlinked without the capacity to mean anything, to possess an "I," except for the existence of a potentially assenting world of relationships.

As relationships are increasingly coordinated (ordered), so do ontologies and their instantiations develop. There is a close relationship between meaning and order. If the interchange between two individuals is random, so that any action on the part of one can serve as the prelude to any reaction of another, we could scarcely call the interchange meaningful. It is only when interchange develops order so that the range of contingencies is constrained that we move toward meaning.[2] If I throw you a ball and you cast it away, I throw you another and you place it in your pocket, and I throw you still another and you crush it under foot, we have failed by common standards to generate meaning. However, if I throw you a ball and you catch it and throw it back, and on each succeeding throw you do the same, then you have given my throw the meaning of an invitation for you to return the throw, and vice versa. Actions thus come to have meaning within relatively structured sequences.[3]

This also means that participants in a relationship will tend to develop a *positive ontology,* or an array of mutually shared "callings" creating the world as "this" and not "that," which enable interaction to proceed unproblematically. Thus, researchers in astrophysics do not shift their theoretical vocabulary from moment to moment, for this would destroy the group's capacity to achieve what they term "productive research results." The effective functioning of the group depends on maintaining a relatively stable language of description and explanation (see Chapter 3). In broader terms, the positive ontology becomes the culture's array of sedimented or commonsense understandings. It is precisely this reiterative patterning that enables scholars to treat language as a "system," or a fixed structure with logical implicature and/or as governed by rules.[4]

As consensus is established, so are the grounds for both understanding and misunderstanding. As we find, relationships tend toward ordered and recursive sequences in which meaning becomes transparent to the various participants. Yet, these suppositions in themselves leave us with no account of mis-meaning—instances in which persons claim they do not understand or fail to comprehend each other. Given the earlier analysis, it is clear that problems of incomprehension cannot be solved by recourse to individual subjectivities. Individuals do not misunderstand by virtue of the inaccessibility of others' mentation, or a failure in their own mental functioning. However, the relational account developed here does suggest far different but related answers. First and most simply, there are multiple contexts in which relationships are formed and local ontologies develop. Participation in one such set of coordinated activities is no necessary preparation for others. Training in the English language and associated patterns of coordination is little preparation for making meaning in rural China. Both infants and students must be absorbed into the conventions of coordination before "proper understanding" can occur.

This latter point is directly related to a second ground for misunderstanding. Thus far I have emphasized the achievement of coordination within dyads or groups. However, it is important to point out that the concept of "understanding" is itself a Western indexical. By tradition we mark various forms of coordination in terms of whether "understanding" has occurred, and we do so for various social purposes. Thus, a couple might achieve a perfectly coordinated routine of arguing, but by cultural standards we might say that they "misunderstood" each other. But if we were directing a play in which a couple was to quarrel, we might conclude that the actors achieved perfect understanding when the quarrel was most intense. Thus, in many cases, failures in understanding may be constituted as such by the particular labeling processes of the culture. This point is especially important in cases where individuals are blamed for misunderstanding. According to the present account, to punish a student who "fails to understand arithmetic" is no more warranted than holding the teacher responsible for his or her failure in teaching. In either case, the "failure to understand" is born of a problem in mutual coordination.

Let us consider a third source of misunderstanding, relevant to persons sharing similar cultural backgrounds. Here people employ a common language but find the process of generating understanding (mutual coordination) fraught with difficulty. From our perspective, such disharmonies may in part be understood as a result of the continuously unfolding character of human relatedness. As people move through life, the domain of relationships typically expands and the context of any given relationship typically changes. In effect, we are continuously confronted with some degree of novelty—new contexts and new challenges. Yet our actions in each passing moment will necessarily represent some simulacrum of the past; we borrow, reformulate, and patch together various pieces of preceding relationships in order to achieve local coordination of the moment. Meaning at the moment is always a rough reconstitution of the past, a ripping of words from familiar contexts and their precarious insertion into the emerging realization of the present. More personally, in each new relationship one's identity bears a metaphoric relation to one's past identity—a translocation of the self from a previous (or literal) context to a novel context in which earlier actions, now repeated, acquire new meanings. In this sense, every cultural implement for engendering meaning (words, gestures, pictures, and so on) is subject to multiple recontextualization. Each term in the language becomes polysemous, multiply meaningful. We thus confront the following condition: each move within a coordinated sequence is simultaneously a move in other possible sequences; each action is thus a possible invitation to a multiplicity of intelligible sequences, each meaning is potentially some other, and the possibility for misunderstanding is permanently and pervasively at hand.

There is a fourth significant source of misunderstanding within cultures, and in many ways it is the most challenging in implication. The Russian literary theorist Mikhail Bakhtin (1981) recognized two major tendencies in the linguistic patterns of a culture, the one *centripetal* (moving toward a centralization or unification of meaning) and the other *centrifugal* (decentering and unsettling the existing unity). Thus, linguistic tendencies toward stabilization are forever competing with those moving away from it. "Every utterance participates in the 'unitary language' . . . and at the same time partakes of social and historical heteroglossia" (p. 272). In the present context we can frame this oppositional dynamic in terms of competing discursive domains: the centripetal thrust is manifested as a domain of *positive* ontology, and the centrifugal in a constant generation of marginality—meanings set against or disruptive to the positive ontology. As the positive ontology is constituted, so does it generate the grounds for the *negative*—or oppositional—ontology. As proposed in Chapter 1, agreements about "what there is" are always made against the backdrop of "what there is not." Thus, in a broad sense, every community of meaning unleashes the potential for its own destruction.

The existence of the negative ontology has significant implications for the problem of understanding. The initiating dyad or community of meaning makers confronts the lingering possibility of negation—that their premises may be replaced by opposing premises—and thus the threat of relational extermination. As communities sustain themselves by virtue of concepts such as God, democracy, equality, and so on, they must be forever watchful of negating discourses such as atheism, fascism, racism. This antagonistic posture would not exist save for the initial articulation of the positive ontology. Simultaneously, however, surveillance and defensiveness generate grounds for systematic misunderstanding. For those within the positive ontology, an "understanding of the other"—a coordination with the negative ontology—would threaten their reality and thus their relational life. To discuss, to deliberate, or to argue with the opposition is, in this sense, not likely to yield understanding, for each side will locate a means to sustain the "evil" of the other.

Meaning in the Context of Developmental Study

By weaving together and extending various recent lines of inquiry, I have tried to set out the rudiments of a relational account of meaning. The formulation envisions the generation of meaning as a tenuous and dynamic process, in which the understanding of another's language (or actions) is the achievement of successful coordination—in terms of local standards of judgment. Understanding is thus not a mental act originating within the mind but a social achievement taking place within the public domain. At the same time, each localized coordination is dependent on the vicissitudes of the broader social processes in which it is embedded—and is therefore vulnerable to reconstitution as a failed project. The achievement of understanding is thus not the result of my personal deliberation but of coordinated action; and it is *our* achievement primarily by virtue of the cultural processes in which we are embedded. In addition, each achievement of meaning within a group sets in motion forces that will work toward destabilization and misunderstanding. In effect, we find a close, interdependent relationship between consensus and conflict: generating social understanding lays the groundwork for its potential dissolution.

My argument in this chapter sustains the critique of cognitivism pervasive throughout this volume. It also stands against theories of meaning based on assumptions of intersubjectivity. The traditional view of meaning as a product of individual minds generates a set of intractable problems regarding social understanding. By beginning with communal coordination rather than individual subjectivity, however, we avoid the critiques posed by contemporary hermeneutic and deconstructionist theory. Yet, critics may respond that just as the traditional account leaves the individual unable to enter into relationships, so the communal approach leaves one with the problem of how the individual acquires sociolinguistic capabilities. How does the child acquire language capabilities? How does he or she achieve coordination? Surely some account of this process is necessary. And, as critics might argue, answers to such questions would seem to require a theory of individual psychology. This is indeed Nelson's (1985) view, as set out in *Making Sense: The Acquisition of Shared Meaning*. "The study of the development of meaning," she avers, "depends upon determining how internal systematicity emerges from the external experience of meaning in context" (p. 9). Yet, to echo my beginning argument, it may be unprofitable to set the problem out in these terms. The problem of how the "outer" seeps its way into the "inner" is as intractable as the companionate enigma of how the inner is transformed into sounds and markings for the other's consumption. Both problems fall out of an individualist tradition, and as I have tried to demonstrate, neither is soluble in principle.

At the same time, a relational view of meaning allows us to pose the question of acquisition in a different way. The descriptive and explanatory vocabularies of the relational theorist should, if fully expanded, furnish a full account of human action—including the socialization of the individual. "Doesn't something happen *within* the individual when exposed to another's actions," critics may rejoin, "and isn't this something vital in determining what the person does?" To be sure, something does happen, but a uniquely psychological or cognitive account of this something is no more essential than a neurological explanation or even one framed in terms of atomic physics. All are ways of characterizing the individual in motion, but none of them is fundamental to generating a sense of understanding. None is required in order to make the individual's actions comprehensible. A description of the "inner essence" of the individual seems no more necessary for getting on in the kinds of relationship in which understanding is achieved than an account of the atomic properties of an individual tennis ball is to winning at Wimbledon.

This is not to foreclose on all future "psychologizing." As we have seen, psychological accounts are essential to Western cultural life, not because of their descriptive accuracy, but because they are constitutive features of relational patterns. If I cannot speak of "my thoughts, intentions, hopes, feelings, desires," and the like, there are many forms of cultural life in which I can scarcely participate. The profession of psychology is—for good or ill—a major contributor to the culture's repository of symbolic resources. And there may indeed be a place for a specifically "cognitive" vocabulary within the relational framework I have outlined. In particular, with a reconceptualization of "cognition," such terms could be used to account for *implicit social actions:* private rehearsal, play, or anticipatory activity that otherwise gains its meaning and significance from its placement within relational sequences. Such a view is coherent with the work of Shotter (1993a), Harré (1986), and Wertsch (1991), among others.

This leads us, at last, to the implications of a relational approach to meaning for developmental theory and research. Three issues are of special significance. First, my arguments press strongly toward relational accounts of human development. That is, rather than view development in terms of either ontogenetic unfolding (nature) or environmental impact (nurture), analysis can more profitably center on relational units and processes. Neither formal nor efficient causality is necessary for explanatory purposes in such cases: all elements within the relational process can be related as pieces in a puzzle or instruments in a string quartet. The relations can be adequately described and explained without reference to concepts of cause and effect. There are, of course, related and significant departures already at hand within the developmental sphere. Works by Kurtines and Gewirtz (1987) on the social dimensions of moral development, Rogoff (1989) on child apprenticeship, Youniss and Smollar (1985) on adolescent relations, Corsaro (1985) on friendship in the early years, and Hinde (1988) on relationships within families are among the most visible. The recent renaissance of Vygotskian theory is also testimony to the "shift toward the social." However, in my view, most of this work remains timidly poised at the entrance to the relational domain. For in most such instances, a concern for the social is secondary to an interest in the individual. The social world is said to influence the cognitive or emotional development of the individual child, or vice versa, but the psyche of the individual child remains of pivotal concern. So long as individual functioning continues to be the grounds for understanding the child's relationships, then relationships will remain secondary and synthetic.

In my view, inquiry in human development may usefully be expanded to the broader spheres of sociality. The mother-child relationship is surely a significant starting point, but it tends to have the same engulfing quality as "the mind of the infant." That is, the mother-child relation tends to be viewed in isolation from the remainder of the cultural sphere. It is also insufficient to extend concern to the full set of family relationships, or to friends and community. Human development may be more fruitfully considered a constitutive feature of broadscale social process—fully enmeshed in the economic, political, educational, technological, and other practices of the culture. In effect, parent-child relations are seldom self-contained; they are constituted by and function importantly within surrounding patterns of cultural life (in the community, workplace, leisure settings, and so on). An adolescent's exercises in moral decision making, for example, are only in the most limited sense possessions of the adolescent mind. They can more usefully be viewed as outcomes of an extended pattern of relationships that immediately connect the adolescent with friends and family, but also with the economy (the availability of jobs), politics (family planning policies), the media (dramas of abortion), and so on. At the same time, a local decision can have a cultural ripple effect of broad implication. To champion abortion serves as a model to others, enables clinics to function, and galvanizes anti-abortion resistance. In this sense, individual decisions about abortion are inherently collective—both in their origins and in their reverberations. A relational approach favors a significant expansion of developmental study.

Finally, reiterating concerns in Chapter 2, the focus on relational accounting draws the professional into a posture of self-reflection. Extending the implications of Wittgenstein's proposals for linguistic meaning as a product of social use calls attention to the manner in which developmental theory and research are themselves embedded within broader patterns of relationship. Developmental psychology has occupied a position of pivotal importance in informing the culture about the nature of the child. Developmental theory often leaps the boundaries of professional circles and enters into the broader practices of the society. (Consider, for example, the insinuation of Piagetian theory into educational practices and child-rearing manuals.) It is a matter of serious ethical and social importance, then, to consider how we in the profession choose to characterize human lives. As I have tried to argue, there is much to be said for moving beyond the individualized view of human functioning.

12 Deceit: From Conscience to Community

Deception, hypocrisy, fraud—all seem increasingly prevalent in our everyday lives, in spite of the severe penalties that often result. Is the moral fiber of the culture eroding? For the constructionist, deceit, as a concept and as a cultural phenomenon, must be scrutinized carefully. The assumption of deceit is dependent upon a companionate belief in "true and honest tellings." If the latter presumption is thrown into question, as preceding chapters have suggested, then deceit too becomes problematic, and an alternative conception of what we commonly take to be deception is demanded. We have considered the rudiments of a relational view of self, emotion, and communication. Now I want to extend this reasoning to the realm of deceit and, with this reformulation, return to this societal problem with a fresh view of its origins and its consequences.

There are few terms in the English language that carry the critical force of "deceit" or its variations—"fraud," "mendacity," "cheating," "duplicity." The curiously unconstrained scolding directed at children who lie to their parents, the expulsion from the profession of scientists who falsify their data, the impeachment of political figures who deceive the public—all suggest an enormous and pervasive animosity toward the perpetrator. At the same time, the ritual castigation of the deceitful forms a dramatic realization of the ideology of individualism. An individual is deceitful when he or she (1) *is cognizant* of the truth; and (2) *intentionally* conceals or distorts this knowledge in communicating with others. In effect, the major defining characteristics of deceit are essentially psychological. Because duplicity is considered an immoral action, its occurrence is typically attributed to an underdeveloped or deteriorated condition of conscience. It is the individual who deceives, it is the individual who must be held responsible, and ultimately it is the individual who must be subject to correction and punishment. The simple concept of deceit, then, is embedded in an enormous network of discursive and nondiscursive actions. The common usage of the term implies nothing less than a view of the social order as derived from and dependent on the minds and hearts of single individuals.

From the time of Aristotle to the present, scholars have done much to reinforce this view. For Kant lying was immoral in large measure because it violates the individual's duty to self. The individual expresses his or her full moral nature through moral action, and deceiving others violates standards of moral action. To deceive is thus cowardly, a weakness in character, a capitulation to base inclinations, for it is effectively a betrayal of one's deepest nature.[1] Others maintain that lying is the individual's offense against others. It undermines the trust or common faith necessary for the good society and destroys the very basis for human connection, including the possibility of both justice and love.[2] In addition, deceit is a form of domination. It undermines the possibility of equality in relationship, giving the liar unfair advantage over others.

In light of the arguments developed in earlier chapters, however, we must pause. We have already found that enormous problems inhere in distinctly psychological forms of explanation. There are neither conceptual nor empirical means that warrant claims about the mind; attempts to cast the mental world as a mirror of the physical world and to see mental acts as causing physical acts are deeply flawed. Assumptions about mental functioning can most convincingly be traced to processes of social interchange, and are thus subject to cultural and historical influences. Moreover, the ideology of the self-contained individual favored by psychological explanation, which views persons as fundamentally alone and incapable of understanding others, is problematic. When these arguments are brought to bear on the concept of deceit, we see that its central psychological ingredients, self-cognizance and intention, are both thrown into question. Both appear to be constructions peculiar to the Western conception of the mind, both are defeasible, and neither is subject to foundational justification.

What I am suggesting, then, is that to question the psychological basis of deceit demands a reconsideration of its character—along with the enmity in which it is held. For the constructionist this demand is all the more pressing since the concept of falsehood also depends for its intelligibility on a concept of truth. Without a firm presumption of "telling the truth," how could we identify what it is "to tell a lie"? Yet, as previous chapters have made clear, the concept of objective truth is problematic. There is little support for the assumption that language can reflect or mirror independent states of affairs. If language does not depict what is the case—either accurately or inaccurately—the traditional view of language as truth bearing suffers. And if language does not bear truth, then what does it mean to tell a lie? How can one deceive or mislead if there is no viable account of accurate representation?

At the same time, terms such as "deceit" are used in daily affairs with some degree of reliability. There are public events that can be indexed in these terms and command broad agreement. Rather than argue for the abandonment of such terms, then, the wiser course is that of reconstitution: to reconceptualize deceit and, more specifically, to cast its meaning in terms of relational practices. In this sense, my account extends the arguments of preceding chapters for a microsocial reconstruction of psychological predicates. In the process, I shall also argue that we may anticipate an acceleration of deceit in coming decades. Technological changes are affecting social life in ways that will make deceit an increasingly possible outcome. Finally, in confronting deceit, I hope to show that the tradition of moral approbation is of limited and problematic utility. From a relational perspective, our attention may usefully shift from issues of conscience and correction to matters of conflicting social allegiance.

Multiple Realities and the Emergence of Deceit

An analysis of deceit depends first on having an account of *truth*—proper standards against which deviations or falsehoods can be contrasted. Much has already been said against traditional views of truth as the mind's accurate reflection of the world or as words that hold a mirror to what is the case. I have made a case instead for truth as a cultural construction, the byproduct of relations among persons. As developed in preceding chapters, we may say that as persons interact over time they will tend to generate a local ontology, a language of representation that enables them to carry out their relations in satisfactory ways. Communities will expend great effort—including both public censure and physical punishment—to sustain the true and the real, for what is at stake is nothing less than the continued vitality of a way of life. Drawing from the Chapter 1 concern with integral forms of intelligibility, let us view this initial unit of reality making as a *relational nucleus*. Within any nucleus, then, the participants may be able to identify what is "true," that is, index conventional or agreeable modes of representation. Thus, if we agree that "it is a beautiful, sunny day" and I continue to make such reports at the times we have agreed I should make them, I will remain for a you a truthful reporter of the weather. This is not because such days truly are beautiful and sunny (from other standpoints they might be "aggressively bright," "bourgeois idealizations," or "burdened with the guilt of unfulfilled desires"), but because we agree on how to talk "weather."

Given the absence of universal truth criteria, how are we then to understand the nature of deceit? If truth is achieved by matching neither mind nor words to world, if it is instead a product of microsocial coordination, then a reconceptualization is required. At the outset, it is important to see that under conditions of ontological unanimity, where there is complete consensus in what is the case, deceit is a virtual impossibility. Or in other terms, deceit could never occur within an isolated relational nucleus. This is so primarily because for people who fully agree about the nature of the world it would make no sense to tell a falsehood. Any description that was not integral to the existing standards of the nucleus would be meaningless. For example, if we completely agree that certain kinds of days are "warm and sunny," and there is no other way of describing them, I possess no private description discrepant with this account. I could scarcely harbor the view that they are actually "rangible," as opposed to warm and sunny, because rangible is not a meaningful term within the relational nucleus. I could not possess a private account that was any other than the public one.

To extend the example, we might consider the case of theft. In a culture in which it is always and everywhere agreed that each individual is entitled to certain goods and no others,[3] there would be no way to understand how anyone could take such goods from someone else. Under these conditions, there would simply be no theft because no individual could make sense of such an act. To take another's goods in such a society would be equivalent to, let us say, a European eating his dog for breakfast. It is physically possible to indulge in such a meal, but it is also nonsensical. On the other hand, should we develop a cultural rationale for such behavior, people might pay for the privilege.[4]

It follows that in order for deceit to occur, there must first be multiple nuclei possessing discrepant accounts of reality, and second, the possibility of simultaneous membership in multiple nuclei. If there were only local understandings of reality, deceit would remain impossible. If one group of people were fixed to a belief in private property and a second group could only conceptualize property as communal, they would be capable of violating each other's conventions but not of deception. In the former group I might retain property for myself, thus acting in a way incomprehensible to the latter group. However, I would not (and indeed could not) do so surreptitiously unless I also possessed knowledge of the alternative set of conventions. If I failed to comply with local conventions, I might be branded ignorant or unobservant, but I could not be blamed for being deceitful. To deceive, one must be immersed in at least two forms of intelligibility—one in which an act is comprehensible and another one in which it is not.

To put the matter another way, the existence of multiple nuclei sets the stage for mutually exclusive but equally "true" accounts of the same "events." The possibility of deceit arises when an individual shares membership in at least two relational nuclei—one in which an act is intelligible and another in which it is not. In relationship A, for example, it may be commonly agreed that people have certain rights of ownership, that to take another's goods is a violation of these rights, and that such actions should be punished. As we have seen, if all participants in the relationship shared these and only these views, theft would never occur. However, if one of the participants in relationship A is also a member of a second nucleus, B, the possibility exists for negating the ontology specific to A. In particular, if participants in B believe that the system of private ownership is unfair or oppressive and that relieving the "haves" of their possessions is an honorific act, then there is good reason in relationship B to do that which would be loathsome in A. The possibility of deceit arises when an individual who is a member of both groups is called into account by group A for just such acts. Let us survey the major possibilities open to the individual suspected of "theft" in system A.

1. *Confession:* The suspect may confess his or her crime ("Yes, I stole the car"), and thus agree solely with the view of reality shared in system A. The result will be not only punishment but the negation of an alternative reality, B ("This car belongs to me because the wealthy are greedy and leave me no chance of gain"), and the associated relationships upon which this reality rests.

2. *Explication:* The suspect may attempt to educate his or her accusers in the alternative system of intelligibility. He or she may demonstrate why there was "good and valid reason" to engage in the action. If the suspect is fully successful in teaching this new ontology, the act will thereby be discounted as a "crime": "Yes, you are right to take the car," the accusers might conclude, "you have been unfairly treated and we shall change our ways and our laws." Of course, such an outcome is improbable, and so it normally will be. For the reality nucleus A is a lived intelligibility—a specification of the true and the good intricately woven into the patterns of everyday life. Immersion in this reality disadvantages any alternative. If the alternative were fully intelligible, the shared understandings within community A would no longer be the same: the alternative understanding and its accompanying practices would replace them. So long as members of A wish to remain in their system of understanding, there is no means by which an alternative view can be justified.

3. *Deceit:* As is clear, neither of these options is optimal for the accused. The first brings punishment and the negation of an alternative community in which one holds membership. The second is unlikely to succeed. The invited option, then, is to deny to those in

the accusing group that the action took place in the terms by which they understand it—in effect, to deceive them. If the deception is a success, the individual will not only avoid punishment and sustain ties to the alternative group, he or she will continue to enjoy "membership in good standing" in the community of accusers.

In a highly complex society in which individuals participate in multiple relationships, each with its potentially unique form of constructing reality, deceit will be strongly invited. Of course, much deceit will be petty in nature (the "white lies" of daily life). However, because of the high costs of confession (punishment and the denial of alternative forms of relatedness) and the difficulty of explication (groups will, for example, typically protect their realities in order to sustain their lifeways), deceit becomes attractive. In these terms there is strong reason to believe that occasions of deceit will multiply in succeeding years. As I have detailed elsewhere (Gergen 1991b), the technologies of the present century have brought about an exponential increase in our capacity for relatedness. Beginning with the telephone, the automobile, and the radio early in the century, carrying through the jet plane and the television in more recent decades, and now adding computers, satellite transmission, transistor-based information processing, and the like, we have become saturated by others—by their values, their attitudes, their opinions, and their personalities. This is so not only in the arena of daily life, where friendships, intimacies, and family ties can be generated and sustained around the globe; in the institutional sphere—business, government, education, the military, and so on—global interconnection is becoming a necessity. To these impulses toward interdependence we must add the thousands of grass-roots organizations—religious groups, political and ethnic groups, athletic leagues, environmental organizations, and the like—which increasingly bring people from disparate locales together.[5]

This expansion in the realms of human connection essentially multiplies the range of relational nuclei in which we participate—the possible senses of the real and the right. It expands the range of justifiable actions and thus the number of ways we can be "caught out," acting rationally and rightly by the standards of one relationship but impropitiously by those of another. The increase in our capacity for relatedness lends itself to secrecy and deceit. It is thus that we are now besieged with instances of duplicity, spying, double-dealing, infiltration, organizational leaks, insider trading, falsification of documents, and plagiarism. Are we not, then, facing the possibility of a major erosion in public trust? Many believe that the erosion is already profound.

Although I can offer no grand solutions to the societal expansion of deceit, the relational view developed here opens new vistas of dialogue. Before exploring these possibilities, however, I wish to consider a single case of political scandal from the relational perspective and in this way clarify the issues and their possible implications.

Deceit and the Iran-Contra Controversy

During the spring of 1987 the capacity of the United States government to carry out its various missions was severely compromised, primarily because of attempts by both the Congress and the press to assess the dimensions of deceit within the executive branch of government (including President Reagan, his staff, the cabinet, and associated agencies). It was alleged that the Congress, the populace, and the nation's allies were gravely misled about the actions of the executive branch. While President Reagan advised other nations against "making deals" with the hostage-taking Iranians and made public vows on behalf of the U.S. government, he and his colleagues were doing precisely that. At the same time, after Congress enacted laws against further military support of the Nicaraguan Contras, a counterinsurgency army designed to overthrow the socialist government of Nicaragua, the president and his associates proceeded privately and surreptitiously to raise monies and arms for exactly such insurgency. To compound the subterfuge, it became apparent that monies gained from weapons sold to Iran for hostage favors were later sent on to support Contra military activities. Finally, when accusations about Contra aid were made, the executive branch firmly denied all such activities. In effect, the words and deeds of those in highest office did not appear trustworthy. Because of this broken trust, the process of governance was severely impeded.

In its revelation of governmental deceit, the Iran-Contra scandal is hardly a novel event, either in American politics or elsewhere. Since the Watergate debacle of the Nixon years, the American press has been acutely sensitive to the possibility of duplicity in high office. Deceit is a highly profitable commodity in the world of news making. Nor are these periodic bloodlettings limited to American culture. The French have long been deeply suspicious of the activities of their government officials; public revelations of interior treachery are frequent in their press. The British press has been unswerving in its attempt to locate mendacity, double-dealing, and spying on the government level. Similarly, since the reunification of the Germanies, revelations of deceit among East German Communists have become a journalistic mainstay. In some degree, this pervasive concern with duplicity in governance can be traced to what many believe is a generalized delegitimation of authority in Western culture. As scholars such as Habermas (1979) and Lyotard (1984) have argued, the traditional legitimations of authority have become deeply eroded, on both moral and logical grounds. In effect, those in power are no longer trusted to "call the ontology" in their relations with the populace. Their "invitations to reality" seem increasingly self-serving. Public trust seems in decay.

Yet the preceding analysis gives us good reason to believe that the pervasive misgivings of the present era are likely to continue, if not intensify. In spite of the character of those holding office, the establishment of penalties and safeguards, and the prevailing sensitivity to the bitter lessons of the past, deceit is likely to do a brisk business for some time to come. Periodic bloodlettings may become a common feature of the political landscape, and public trust in governance may continue to deteriorate. I have attempted to explain this shift in terms of technology and the proliferation of realities. However, the Iran-Contra scandal adds an important dimension to the discussion by elucidating the multiple realities of organizational life.

First, let us consider what might be termed the *laminations of reality* within the organization—the layers of nucleic relationships within a complex bureaucracy. An unlaminated relationship exists between only two interlocutors; this is the condition of the relational nucleus. As we have seen, activities within the nucleus should work toward the development of a set of beliefs beyond local question. If there were no competing realities, deceit, as I have also argued, would be an unintelligible option. Such a condition might exist if the president worked out all his policies with, let us say, a single member of the press. If the two participants had no frame of reference outside of what they shared, deceit would be a logical impossibility.

But let us add an element of realism to this hypothetical situation by "laminating" the president's field of relationships. Let us treat his relationship with presidential advisors as a second nucleus. At this point, the conditions are established for the emergence of a second ontology (see Figure 12.1). There may be a discrepancy between the reality negotiated in the president's relationship with the press and that hammered out in the inner chambers of the White House. At precisely this point the possibility of deceit is created: that which is said in the company of a journalist is not necessarily that which is uttered in the inner chambers. Actions condoned in one domain may be censored in the other.

The possibility of deceit is further extended in this case by virtue of the fact that the press is engaged in at least one additional nucleus—that formed by their own relationship with the consumers of media. This additional lamination means that the president cannot trust that negotiations of reality developed with a journalist will remain unchanged as they are recreated for the media consumer. In effect, the media representative is also capable of deceit—securing views in good faith but exploiting ("distorting") them for his or her group's purposes (creating controversy, winning prizes, selling papers) in addressing the public.

With the possibility of systematic deceit thus multiplied, a further com-

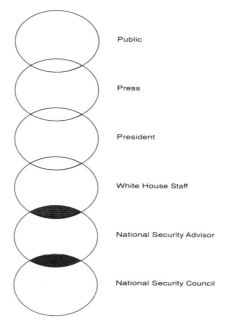

Figure 12.1   Laminations of Political Reality

plication sets in. The fact that the president cannot trust the press ensures that the president's public presentations (in this case, his meetings with the press) will receive preliminary attention within his advisory group. That is, the reality that he is allowed to negotiate within the public domain will be the calculated outcome of private deliberations within the White House. The public address is thus no longer an authentic outcome of the president's relationship with the press (or public) but an artificial contrivance designed for maximum impact within the fields of public reality. Should the deliberations in the White House be made available to the public, the authenticity of the president's words would be undermined. And, as the press and the public become progressively aware of such deliberation (as in the Watergate revelations) the public presentations become increasingly suspect.

Let us further consider the effects of extending the laminations of reality at the various levels of government. Members of the cabinet, for example, all preside over sizable organizations of their own—the Department of State, the Department of Defense, and so on. One critical member of the White House staff is the National Security Advisor. In turn, the National Security Advisor heads a large organization (which increased steadily during the Reagan years) whose members do not generally meet with either the staff or the president. In effect, the National Security Advisor is simultaneously committed to at least two relational nuclei, in which at least two competing realities are made possible (see Figure 12.2).

At this point the possibility of deceit within the executive office increases still further, for the ontology generated within the National Security Council may differ from that generated with the White House staff, which again may differ from that generated in the staff's relationship with the president, and in turn, the president's relationship to the press. This complex array of possibilities indeed consumed American interest for many months. The activities of the National Security Council—both in trading arms for hostages and in illegally providing support for the Contras—came under close scrutiny. The apparent duplicity of this group also threatened the credibility of the president and his advisors.

Thus far we have seen how laminations in relational nuclei within the government lend themselves to deceit and distrust. Yet each nucleus in a governmental system is attached not only in a vertical direction, but horizontally as well. The president carries on a relationship with his staff, but he is also tied interdependently to members of the cabinet, the Congress, the Supreme Court, his political party, the business community, and so on. This process is repeated within every governmental lamination. Further, each of these individuals (or groups) is tied still further to other relationships, both vertically and horizontally. This *multiplicity in interdependency* greatly exacerbates the potential for deceit, because each member of any nucleus can potentially renege on the reality of that nucleus in his or her alternative relationships. That which is negotiably "real" and sensible in one relationship may be reformulated within an alternative reality system to seem sim-

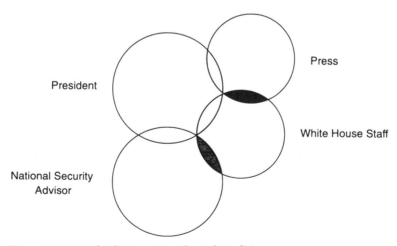

Figure 12.2   Multiplicity in Presidential Realities

plistic, naive, mistaken, immoral, or even treacherous. Within any given relationship only "good sense" is made; the world is constructed in ways that seem appropriate and correct. However, once this reality is transposed into alternative contexts of understanding, the potential for "deceit" is rampant.

The most obvious instances of systematically engendered subterfuge take the form of "leaks" and "confessions." Individuals at any given level of governance will reveal to the press the secret realities from within the sanctuary. A White House aide reveals the deliberations of other staff members, a pilot tells of secret missions to deliver arms to the Contras, a secretary to Oliver North of the National Security Council speaks of the frenzied attempt to destroy documents before an investigation, and so on. Within the internal nuclei, participants carry out activities that seem reasonable and right. Faith Hall is a conscientious secretary doing the right thing by hiding documents in her clothing as she passes through security checks. However, when the same words and deeds are transformed into the reality of the press, they become evidence of a grand cover-up.

As I would also suggest, charges of duplicity are invited even when those in government fully believe themselves to be serving the will of the people. That is, accusations of deceit may be anticipated even when those in power are committed to the common good. How is this so? In large measure this outcome may be traced to subtle *transformations of ontology* occurring as one moves through various laminations or across the horizontal array of relationships. Ontological transformations are alterations in meaning that occur as differing domains of discourse (or ontological systems) are brought into contact with each other. Thus, if an individual participates in two systems with different conceptions of reality, he or she is likely to develop an amalgam of the two systems, one that borrows from each but duplicates neither. For example, what was "essential for national security" in one reality and "a gross infringement on the rights of others" in another may become "a wise but imperfect policy." In this way the individual may not experience a sharp disjunction between the competing ontologies; they will overlap enough so that one can feel that he or she dwells within a single reality.

As we move through successive laminations of an organization (or a complex society), however, the intelligibility in the initial nucleus is further dissipated. Words that meant one thing in one context come to mean another in a second, and shift their meaning still further in a third. Suppositions become increasingly abstruse and flexible; crucial commitments may be unobtrusively abandoned. At some point, that which is held to be "real" at the public level cannot be reconciled with the reality at the level of the deeper or more remote nuclei. Consider again Reagan's request that his allies avoid negotiating with terrorists and his subsequent denial that he was engaged in doing so. Yet, as evidence strongly suggested, this public reality was only partially replicated within the interior of the White House. In meetings with his staff, the president also declared that he wished to secure the freedom of hostages held by Iranian terrorists and that, if necessary, strong measures were to be taken. As documents further indicate, this abstract message at the level of the White House staff was transformed again at the level of the Security Council. Here the message was translated as an invitation to seek negotiation with the Iranian government. In particular, the Security Council believed that if arms could be supplied to Iran it might reduce Iranian dependency on Soviet support, secure a more lasting relationship with moderate factions, and indirectly induce the Iranians to free the hostages.

Another domain of ontological transformation must be added, one merging with the international negotiation process itself. As American and Iranian representatives met, it became increasingly clear that there was to be a *quid pro quo*: arms for hostages. In spite of commitments made at another level of exchange, the public reality had now become completely dissipated. As news reports also suggest, reality brokers at these alterior levels took steps to ensure that this conceptualization was not translated in its raw form back through the system. In effect, they had become aware of the discrepancy in ontologies, which invited subsequent deceit. As a general surmise, however, at each level of organization we find decisions that were both "reasonable and good" according to some local standard, and in a sense, all were decisions of persons who consider themselves righteous and dedicated. Yet, as the realities were multiplied and transformed through the system, the result was an "appalling duplicity."

Deceit and the Place of Moral Judgment

Readers may object to this microsocial account of deceit as it stands. After all, isn't there something abhorrent about this analysis, a suggestion that since deceit is inevitable, we must simply resign ourselves to it? Why should we pursue a theory that seems to forgive those who mislead or break the public trust? How can organized society continue if we fail to hold people morally responsible for deceitful actions? Such concern is surely merited. However, my analysis should in no way be read as approval of, let us say, the various parties to the Iran-Contra charade. Nor do I wish to furnish indirect support to the deceptions of Hitler, Stalin, and their like. Let us instead consider the contrasting implications of taking a moral stance toward these various forms of deceit, as opposed to the relational perspective developed both here and in earlier chapters. Following the reasoning developed in Chapter 4, we might suppose that, in the long run, a moral judgmental reaction to instances of deceit will be less effective in improving our social lot than pursuing the implications of a relational perspective.

To explore, let us consider significant problems attending the moral reaction to deceitful acts. At the outset, such judgments rest on problematic assumptions about the mind and language—that the mind serves as an originary source of action and that language can furnish an accurate picture of the real. As I have demonstrated, both lines of reasoning prove faulty on a variety of counts. In addition, moral judgments form an alienating wedge between the agent of judgment and the perpetrator. The judge establishes him or herself as a moral superior to whom the target must submit for punishment and scorn. At the same time, because the perpetrator typically remains committed to the view that justified his or her actions, he or she often finds punishment and scorn unwarranted. Rather than contrite resolve to do the moralist's will, the frequent reaction is resentment, hostility, alienation, and a desire for revenge—grim prospects for future relationships.

Finally, moral sanctimony also lacks the kind of foundations necessary to give broad justification. There is currently no system of ethical principles that demands general agreement.[6] Nor from the constructionist perspective is there any reason to suppose that a universal ethics can ever be locked in place. There are few means by which the moral rationality developed within one community or relational nucleus can be made intelligible or binding within an alternative community of understanding. Even within Western tradition, the committed moralist is seldom dedicated to a universal principle of honesty.[7] To punish in the name of the principle of honesty is in this sense hypocritical, for who would wish to demand honesty under all conditions? Even the strict moralist will be prepared to honor those who lied to protect Jews from Nazi concentration camps. Most of us uphold "dishonesty" if it is carried out for a just cause. It is not deceit in general that is unsettling; rather, its importance seems to depend on the outcomes of specific instances. It is this final point that prepares the way for reconsidering the implications of deceit from a relational perspective.

Let us consider first the possibility that vindictive cries of "deception" are uttered primarily when participants in a given relational nucleus find they are suffering losses as a result of a dishonest (from their standpoint) account. In the Iran-Contra case, members of the Congress condemned the executive branch because the "false" reports undermined their power and violated what they felt was wise and/or fair policy. If, in contrast, the executive branch inflates budget estimates for military spending, we seldom hear accusations of deception. It is more or less expected that the executive branch will feign the figures. Most important, however, is the fact that such deception does not threaten the array of understandings extant in Congress.

Members continue to see themselves as having control over the budget and exercising their duties in a rational and effective manner. It should also be clear here that "loss" for any group depends on a set of shared interpretations within the group. Losses are not real-world existants but depend on negotiations of reality within a social sphere. Thus, for Congress to see the Iran-Contra swap as a violation of their power, members had to share a broad array of assumptions about what constitutes power, the national good, the rights of the executive branch, and so on. All are defeasible, subject to reconstruction from other standpoints.

When viewed in this light, we see that actions counting as "deception" and subject to punishment within a group are those that violate the common understandings of that group. They are accounts carried out in the group's system of intelligibility, and thus by someone ostensibly participating in that ontology. (The thief understands perfectly what is meant by "I didn't steal the car.") However, they are accounts that are fallacious according to the group's standards. As a result, they reveal that the deceiver is not "one of us," does not honor our codes, does not believe as we do, and may destroy our relationships and institutions. In the Western tradition, these failures are attributed to the individual perpetrator—his or her poor judgment, deteriorated moral condition, or evil character. Seldom do we consider the social or relational context that would render the immoral action, and the subsequent necessity for deception, intelligible. Or, in broader terms, what we fail to appreciate is that deceit is the outcome of *conflicting relational allegiances,* of being located within the interstice of at least two incompatible forms of intelligibility. We may punish the deceiver for a moral (psychological) failing; however, this is to obscure the chief source of both the faulty action and the reason for falsehood.

Although punishing individuals may discourage others from similar actions, we have also glimpsed its potential for provoking deep hostility. In contrast, the present account invites the agents of judgment into a more dialogic posture. Rather than view their taken-for-granted worldview as "a true and accurate reflection of the way things are," and their accompanying views of right and wrong as "fundamental," the judging parties are invited to see their understanding within a comparative frame, as one among many. Further, as the locally constructed character of this reality becomes clear, alternative constructions may be opened for consideration. What this makes possible is an extension of comprehension, an opening to systems of understanding in which otherwise "villainous actions" become intelligible. In the case of the Iran-Contra conflict, for example, investigatory panels, litigation, and personal defamation might be replaced with forms of dialogue. How could the actions of the National Security Council, the CIA, and other governmental organizations be made intelligible to Congress and the public? In what senses were these actions decent and honorable? With such increments in intelligibility, we can also understand the inviting character of deceit.

Of course, this shift toward a relational perspective should scarcely be limited to the agents of judgment. We need to develop forms of dialogue in which those whose actions necessitate deceit come to a deeper understanding of those whose realities are being threatened and their place within these realities. Consider the wife who is drawn by the intelligibility of an extramarital affair. When caught in her lies she may be subject to sharp condemnation. The result may be a lifelong relationship of alienation between the spouses. However, if husband and wife were fully immersed in the other's intelligibility—its local validity and suasive force—the invitation to a love affair would be less appealing, and its potentials more fully appreciated. Lying would be less necessary and moral remonstrance would abate. This is not to eradicate the conflicts among opposing realities but to render them less agonistic. In a more promising light, such understanding might simultaneously promote greater flexibility and commitment or, let us say, new forms of relationship in which committed companionship endorses the multiple relationships that contribute to its existence.

From this standpoint, the problem with the National Security Council was inherent not in its acting on its local reality but in its failure to appreciate fully the reality of Congress and that of vast segments of the public. Should members of the council acknowledge the rationality of alternative perspectives and, indeed, their reliance on and commitment to these perspectives, their local realities would have been altered. If they allowed their own membership in other relationships—beyond the walls of the Executive Office Building—to enter more fully into their proceedings, then heinous actions (by congressional and public standards) would be far less inviting. In principle, if all parties participate in all systems of intelligibility, then actions for which deceit is an attractive option become less reasonable.

In most domains of daily life it is probably idealistic to anticipate the kind of multirelational reflexivity necessary to reduce the temptation either to deceive or to blame. When we are immersed in the reality making of the moment, alternative discourses—even those held dear—are easily shunted to the margins. When engulfed by the tango, one is ill equipped to waltz. Much needed, then, are concrete and continuous means by which salient realities can be placed in motion. This is strongly to endorse the many efforts at increasing the number of alien voices entering contexts of decision making—in government, business, the university, the military, the police, and the like. Such attempts reduce the totalizing potential of any particular reality and its accompanying forms of moral justification. However, such dialogues have limited potential when the identity of the participants is circumscribed—one representing "the female view," another "the black," another "the poor," and so on. Not only does the dialogue tend to freeze people into alien categories, it also denies the manifold intelligibilities of which most people are a part. What is required is creative attention to means by which persons can undefensibly share the multirelational character of their social existence.

Notes

1. The Impasse of Individual Knowledge

1. For an elaboration of developments linking scientific psychology and logical empiricism see Koch (1963) and Toulmin and Leary (1985).
2. Clearly there are many other processes operating to determine the degree of support in any given case. Support may depend, for example, not only on shared suppositions, but on similarities in derivatives. That is, if the similar outcomes (implicatures) are favored by two otherwise independent (or opposing) systems, they may operate in a mutually supporting way.
3. Parapsychology is perhaps the most obvious case of expulsion in psychology. The psychology of religion, existential psychology, humanistic psychology, and phenomenological psychology have also hovered at the margins of acceptability. And increasingly, as its links to the dominant supports of metatheory and method are severed, clinical psychology is also becoming suspect as a constituent of "proper psychology."
4. For attempts to lay out the rules for such exchange see van Eemeren and Grootendorst (1983).
5. It is an interesting question as to whether all discursive modalities are potentially contentious, such that an account, for example, of Malaysian history could discredit a theory of stellar movement. What may be required for a meaningful argument is a range of mutually acceptable or overlapping assumptions. For example, empiricists and rationalist philosophers may have engaged in centuries of contention primarily because of their shared belief in individual knowledge and its importance in cultural affairs. Should there not be substantial agreement in ontology and/or values, argumentation would largely be prohibited. More generally, then, difference may depend for its sustenance on similarity, negation on affirmation.

6. Similarly problematic in Kuhn's account is the mysterious metaphor of the "Gestalt shift" in understanding. The metaphor is taken from studies of visual illusions in which a single figure yields to two mutually exclusive senses of reality (figure becomes ground or ground becomes figure). Yet theories are inherently linguistic constructions. The difficult question thus arises: How do shifts at the perceptual level affect language (or vice versa)? Do changes in visual perception necessitate alterations in one's accounts of the world? Do shifts in the sounds and markings we call language change our sense perceptions? These are indeed difficult proposals to justify. Nor am I sanguine about Kuhn's (1977) later revisions of his social account, in which he replaces empiricist foundationalism with an appeal to an array of so-called "epistemic values." As Kuhn proposes, in evaluating theory such traditional criteria as predictive accuracy, explanatory comprehensiveness, and internal consistency may be justified in terms of the value placed on the outcomes, namely improvement in explanation and prediction. Although stopping short of reasserting rational foundations for science, this account still remains open to criticism on grounds of its individualist base (the individual agent as chooser of values), and its lodgment in a view of reference in which descriptive accuracy is possible.

7. To appreciate the mutually supporting effects of the theoretical, metatheoretical, and methodological discourses of the time, it is useful to contrast the prevailing account of what occurs in an experimental procedure with other possibilities. For example, it is a metaphysical commitment of some magnitude to say that "independent variables" have "causal" effects. One might equally view "stimulus conditions" as "affordances," "perceived" as opposed to "real conditions," or "invitations to a ritual dance." To say that experiments "demonstrate causal relations" is little more than a rhetorical convenience.

8. In a certain sense, Feyerabend's (1976) critique of empiricism, while powerful, also served to sustain its foundation. In basing his critique—designed to inform the reader of how scientific progress is "really" achieved—on what were purported to be a range of historical facts, he implicitly undermined his attack on the use of observation as scientific justification.

9. As I will explore in the following chapter, a broad array of methodological alternatives has emerged within the past decade—feminist, dialogic, reflexive, and so on. However, these are not offerings within the existing binary schema. Rather, they are attempts to realize an alternative conception of both persons and science, thus abandoning the traditional binary altogether.

10. The focus on active (as opposed to passive) or determinative cognitive processes, possessing their own inherent tendencies or requirements, has been a hallmark of the cognitive movement from its earliest beginnings. In Miller, Galanter, and Pribram (1960), for example, individual behavior was traced to internal *plans*, which hierarchically ordered the structure of activity. Processes of *matching* templates, *detecting* features, *attending* selectively, *constructing* mental models, and *processing* information have all played a central role in cognitive formulations since this time; all such processes are treated as originary, in the sense that they themselves are not required by the contours of the world as it is. The widely used concept of the cognitive schema typically functions in this same way. A schema has been equated with "a plan, an outline, a

structure, a framework, a program, etc. In all these meanings the assumption is that schemas are cognitive, mental plans that are abstract and that they serve as guides for actions, as structures for interpreting information, as organized frameworks for solving problems, etc." (Reber 1985).

2. Crisis in Representation and the Emergence of Social Construction

1. Classic contributions include Adorno (1970), Horkheimer and Adorno (1972), and Marcuse (1964). For extensions of this perspective into contemporary scholarship see, for example, Parker (1992), Sullivan (1984), and Thomas (1993).
2. See, for example, Butler (1990), Fine (1993), Harding (1986), and Haraway (1988).
3. See, for example, Clifford and Marcus (1986), Fabian (1983), Mitchell (1982), Rosen (1987), Said (1979, 1993), Schwartz (1986), and Stam (1987).
4. This connection is made explicit by Althusser and Balibar (1970).
5. See Pinder and Bourgeois (1982) for an exemplary expression of this view.
6. For further treatments of the distinction between modernism and postmodern-ism, see Lyotard (1984), Harvey (1989), and Turner (1990). For discussions of the postmodern turn in the social sciences see Rosenau (1992), Kvale (1992), and Seidman and Wagner (1992). For a treatment of the relationship between postmodern scholarship and transformations in cultural life see Connor (1989) and Gergen (1991b).
7. Nencel and Pels's (1991) edited volume *Constructing Knowledge: Authority and Critique in Social Science* demonstrates the intensity of these disputes. For example, in reply to the emerging textual emphasis in anthropology, the neo-Marxist anthropologist Jonathan Friedman (1991) writes, "Textual experi-mentation is the luxury of the postmodern minority . . . all of whom are in positions of 'institutional power,' or at least, who belong to groups controlling such positions, that is men, and people of no color . . . We have here the voice of the tired and bored occupants of an ivory tower of power . . . an elitist cynicism evidencing the compounding of personal and disciplinary narcissism" (p. 98). In the feminist voice of Annelies Moors (1991), "What is at stake for women is whether postmodernism's acceptance of difference has as its hidden agenda, and ultimate consequence, an indifference on the part of those in power towards women's claims for justice" (p. 127).
8. In certain respects this is the same conclusion that would be reached from a specifically psychological (or cognitive) view of communication, one holding that understanding of the other must proceed on the basis of one's internal processes. A constructionist alternative to the textual and psychological ap-proaches is outlined in Chapter 11.
9. Although there is now an enormous corpus of literature congenial with the preceding account, and a phalanx of scholars contributing to "social construc-tionist scholarship," discussions of the "constructionist successor" to tradi-tional science have been less frequent. Especially useful for this project, however, are the works of Astley (1985), Edwards and Potter (1992), Lincoln (1985), Longino (1990), Shotter (1993b), and Stam (1990).

10. It is for this reason that the hypothesis-testing research in the behavioral sciences is so barren of practical utility. The research itself is oriented around a range of "objective particulars," unique confluences of questionnaire ratings, button pressings, photographic stimuli, and the like. Yet the conclusions reached from these culturally and temporally contingent microprocesses are of the broadest scope. The scientific literature speaks of "aggression," "psychopathology," "reasoning ability," "perception," "memory," and the like as general and universal. However, conclusions of this abstract variety are tied to particulars of no consequence to the culture. How these concepts are to be cashed out in cultural life is indeterminant. For further discussion see also Sandelands (1990).

11. See Benson (1993) for a compilation of recent attempts by anthropologists to bridge the gap between subject and object and to expand the forms of ethnographic writing.

12. A similar argument applies to the case of syntactics. In this sense, the search for a foundational body of syntactic rules, principles, or logics within individual minds is misplaced. It is to relational process that syntactical conventions may properly be traced.

13. See Kukla (1989) for an elaboration of the significance of theoretical work—over and above empirical demonstrations—in psychology.

14. See also Astley and Zammuto's (1992) arguments against the traditional view of organizational scientists as social engineers offering policy applications from a foundational knowledge base. Concurring with my proposals, they see such scientists as generating symbolic resources (language) for use in organizational settings. New languages will constitute reality in different ways, and with such reconstructions new forms of action become intelligible.

15. Specific attempts to place constructionist views into practice now emerge in fields of pedagogy (Bruffee 1993; Lather 1991), sex and marital therapy (Atwood and Dershowitz 1992), mediation and grievance proceedings (Shailor 1994; Salipante and Bouwen 1990), television and press analysis (Carey 1988), and legal proceedings (Frug 1992). A discussion of constructionist contributions to therapy will be taken up in Chapter 10.

3. Constructionism in Question

1. See Stam (1990) for a useful companion to the present account.

2. The terms "constructivism" and "constructionism" are often used interchangeably. Fortunately, there is no tribunal governing concept usage. However, for purposes of coherence and clarity, much can be said for maintaining a distinction. There is a profoundly important difference in the intellectual contexts in which these terms have been nurtured and in their epistemological and practical implications. For a useful clarification of the concepts in contemporary usage see Pearce (1992); for an analysis of their differential implications for therapy see Leppington (1991). For a critical comparison of constructionist versus constructivist premises, see Frindte (1991).

3. As I have discussed elsewhere (Gergen, in press a), von Glasersfeld is forced in the end to retreat from the solipsism attendant in this formulation. By propos-

ing that constructivist processes are ultimately "adaptive," he reinstates the significance of an "external world."

4. See especially von Glasersfeld (1988) and Steier's (1991) edited volume, *Research and Reflexivity*. Arbib and Hesse's *The Construction of Reality* represents perhaps the most extensive attempt to integrate a cognitivist (constructivist) orientation with a social conception of language. However, its cognitivist (dualist, individualist) base also fastens the account to an unworkable and ideologically problematic metaphysics. More will be said about the problems of a "cognitive starting point" in Chapter 5.

5. Raymond Williams (1976) points out that the term "experience" was not used to refer to a specifically mental state (that is, something "felt" or independently sensed) until the nineteenth century. In earlier times, and not infrequently today, it was used to refer to objective circumstances to which the individual had been exposed or which he had undergone ("That was quite an experience").

6. See also Edwards, Ashmore, and Potter (in press) for an account of how attempts to thump tables and kick stones—in refutation of the constructionist standpoint—are themselves rhetorically crafted. As they point out, given a variety of convincing intelligibilities, it is surprisingly easy to question the table's reality. Physicists, for example, very effectively demonstrate "the falsity" of the everyday assumption that tables are solid objects.

7. From a constructionist standpoint one is also encouraged to take a critical look at what we call "medical success" in Western culture. Whether it is a "success" to sustain life indefinitely, regardless of one's physical condition, is surely debatable.

8. Even transcendental realists argue among themselves concerning these possibilities. For example, Harré (1992) brands Greenwood's (1992) account of realism "indefensible" because "the bivalence doctrine, that the propositions of scientific theory are true or false by virtue of the way the world is, cannot fruitfully be used to characterize a defensible realism" (p. 153). Greenwood's is a most unusual case, for unlike physical realists, Greenwood (1991) asserts that psychological states are real and subject to empirical evaluation. At the same time, he holds that such states are socially constituted—that is, they are cultural constructions. In effect, he argues for the possibility of verifying or falsifying—from a standpoint beyond culture—a nonobservable object world implied by various cultural meaning systems. On this account he should, then, be able to prove or disprove whether people's souls have an influence on their actions.

9. For an account of the various realisms as discursive forms see my 1990 paper, "Realities and Their Relationships."

10. As Edwards, Ashmore, and Potter (in press) argue, realists are prepared to declare in advance what is real or true (physics as opposed to witchcraft; matter as opposed to spirit), and in this way deny further intellectual exchange. For example, for materialist realists there is no point in debating the existence of spirit. For constructionist relativists, on the contrary, "the advantage . . . is that we *can* take positions and argue."

11. Perhaps the classic statement of this argument is supplied by Albert (1985). For a discussion of the untestability of realist doctrines, see Trigg (1980). As he argues, there is no observational evidence that can affect the truth of realism:

"The fate of realism cannot be decided by 'success' or 'failure' in science, since the normal sense of these terms presupposes realism" (p. 188). Realism rests its case for "foundations," then, on a speculative metaphysics.

12. It is this potential for reflexivity that separates the kind of constructionism I would favor from that of those such as Guerin (1992), who would wish to establish it as a new and empirically grounded foundation for science. Similarly, Harré (1992) attempts to ground constructionism in a set of basic postulates, such as "the existence of persons." There is, of course, no particular warrant for such a claim; and in this sense it operates to terminate dialogue. It establishes a boundary beyond which discussion cannot proceed—a move that at best is anti-intellectual and at worst imperialistic. Haraway's (1988) attempt is superior in this respect, since she argues for the multiplicity of situated knowledges and the placement of these knowledges into "communities, not isolated individuals" (p. 590). However, when she argues for the "embodied objectivity" of these knowledges over and against "gross error and false knowledge," she again seems to favor a termination of conversation.

13. Apposite is Critchley's (1992) attempt to demonstrate the ethical potential inherent in Derridian deconstructionism.

14. In Edwards, Ashmore, and Potter's (in press) terms, "There is no contradiction between being a relativist and being *some*body, a member of a particular culture, having commitments, beliefs, and a commonsense notion of reality. These are the very things to be argued for, questioned, defended, decided, without the comfort of just being, already and before thought, real and true."

15. Harré (1992) has recently voiced objections of this same variety, primarily as a means of staving off what he sees as a constructionist "slide into relativism." As he points out, constructionists will argue that differing observers will construct the same circumstance in contrasting ways, making it therefore impossible to establish a "correct" account. However, the force of this argument depends on the constructionist's asserting the reality of "the same circumstances," a reality that is not itself constructed. In my view no such assertion is necessary; my previous remarks on ontological relativism apply. The conceptual relativism arguments are often used, as well, to argue that constructionism can give no account of cross-cultural communication. If we have no means of understanding another culture save through our own conceptual schemas, then we should never achieve understanding. Since we do seem to understand other cultures (translations do prove effective), constructionism must be wrong (see Jennings 1988). As I will demonstrate in Chapter 11, the very idea of understanding through conceptual schemas is misconceived, and a relational account of communication provides the needed antidote.

16. Some philosophers have responded to the ball in their court by attempting to justify universal standards of rationality. For example, after detailing the anti-relativist argument outlined here, Katz (1989) proposes that while the content of rational argumentation is relative, the form of argumentation (or "systematic nature") can be universal. For example, the law on noncontradiction, or consistency, would constitute a universal standard. As he concludes, however, "adherence to (such laws) is not as straightforwardly determinable (unfortunately for my argument) as I would like. Minimally, it would require some measure of

semantic 'sameness,' or synonymy" (p. 269). How this can be achieved he never demonstrates. Presumably it would rely on the very standard of noncontradiction he wishes to defend, not only introducing a vicious circularity into the argument but subtly universalizing Western rules of academic rhetoric.

17. Austin himself realized the problems inherent in a strong distinction between the constative and performative, and was inclined in the end to see the former as a species of the latter. For a thorough analysis of why this must be so, see Petrey (1990).

18. I have great admiration for Margolis's (1991) defense of relativism; but Margolis wants to grant the traditional critics the validity of the incoherence critique and to propose an alternative form of relativism (termed "robust relativism") in which the bivalent values of truth and falsity are replaced by many-valued truth values (that is, the possibility for differing criteria of truth under differing conditions). From the present standpoint, Margolis's analysis suffers from its attempt to replace one form of foundationalism with another (albeit a less restrictive one). His emphasis on many-valued truth values is congenial with the arguments I have put forward here. According to the present account, differing communities might well have different standards for evaluating what they call truth. Here, however, I would substitute the term "felicity" for truth to avoid the enigmas of representation provoked by the academic manner of framing the term. More consistent with my analysis is Longino's (1990) conception of "contextual empiricism." As she proposes, "evidential reasoning is always context-dependent, [and] data are evidence for a hypothesis only in light of background assumptions that assert a connection between the sorts of thing or event the data are and the processes or states of affairs described by the hypotheses . . . Social interactions determine what values remain encoded in inquiry and which are eliminated, and thus which values remain encoded in the theories and propositions taken as expressing scientific knowledge at any given time" (pp. 215–216).

4. Social Construction and Moral Orders

1. For further elaboration, see Abrams (1971), Furst (1969), and Schenk (1966).
2. P. B. Shelley (1967, p. 79).
3. In the present century sociobiologists have proposed that moral dispositions are biologically prepared, thus reinstating Darwinism as a theory of morality. However, by valorizing common dispositions in this way, sociobiologists have a difficult time avoiding the equally plausible argument for a biological basis for evil (in aggression, for example, or exploitation). In the end, a sociobiological explanation is little explanation at all, for in the hands of the biologist the very concept of morality disappears from view. If all behavior is essentially biological (the action of neurons, hormones, muscle fibers, and so on), there is nothing left over to be called "moral." Biological reductionism thus thrusts "moral talk" into the realm of the mystical.
4. The arguments against the romanticist tradition, along with the emerging emphasis on reason and observation, have led to a general erosion of moral phi-

losophy. As Regis (1984) describes the situation, "of the several different features that distinguish twentieth-century moral philosophy from that of previous decades, probably none is more important and portentous than its skepticism about whether any moral principles at all can be known or proved to be true. This skepticism has taken many forms: emotivism and other noncognitivisms, intuitionism, subjectivism, prescriptivism, and the more recent practice of laying down ultimate moral principles by fiat or mere say-so . . . moral theorizing [has been reduced] to the level of assertion and counterassertion: to the battle of competing intuitions, 'considered moral convictions,' and different conceptions of 'what we would want to say' " (p. 1).

5. There are exceptions to the general attempt to separate knowledge from moral principle. For example, Goldman (1988) makes a case for a specifically "moral knowledge" grounded in a coherence view of truth. Flanagan (1991) attempts to use the scientific knowledge of human psychology as the basis for developing a philosophy of ethics. A seemingly "well-grounded" intelligibility is thus used to lend force to a more hypothetical one, the problems of which were outlined in Chapters 1 and 2.

6. See also Donagan's (1977) *The Theory of Morality,* which argues for a theory of morality, the violation of which would be "a violation of one's own rationality."

7. The close link between individualism and traditional moral theory is made clear in both Taylor (1991) and Fisher (in press).

8. In his volume *Against Ethics* (1993) Caputo similarly argues that ethical principles are of little guidance in the everyday immersion in obligations. In his elegant words, "ethics flourishes in the element of beauty, universality, legitimacy, autonomy, immanence, intelligibility. Ethics abhors the abyss of singularity and ugly incomprehensibility . . . Obligation is embedded in the density of particularity and transcendence, in a dark groundlessness on which ethics can only gag" (p. 14).

9. See also supportive work by Shweder and Much (1987) and Packer (1987) on the development of moral discourse.

10. In his subsequent work, *The Ethics of Authenticity* (1991), Taylor argues more forthrightly for the moral potential of an individualized discourse. As he avers, "I think that authenticity should be taken seriously as a moral ideal" (p. 22), where authenticity is taken to be "a certain way of being human that is *my* way. I am called upon to live my life in this way, and not in imitation of anyone else's . . . If I am not, I miss the point of my life, I miss what being human is for *me*" (p. 29).

11. Gewirth's own theory is based on what he takes as a transparent truth of human action: that it is voluntary, purposive, and under the individual agent's conscious control. Thus, at its core it is committed to a particular ontology of the person and a particular ideology of individualism—neither of which is shared across cultures and history.

12. See also Said's (1993) critique.

13. The present emphasis on social practices as opposed to ideal moral imperatives is resonant with a variety of other offerings. For example, Habermas (1979) explores the possibility of subverting totalitarian oppression through establish-

ing the pragmatic conditions of communication necessary for full understanding. However, his resolution to this problem presumes an individualistic conception of communication (see Chapter 11), and itself aspires toward universalization. In his volume *Ethics after Babel* (1988), Stout responds to the prevailing pluralism by championing forms of social critique that might represent the range of people's investments but simultaneously enable them to move toward a sense of moral community. However, whether critique is itself an enabling pragmatic for the creation of community (as opposed to conflict) remains an open question. In confronting the problem of plural religions, theologian David Tracey (1987) also favors an action orientation. Rather than search for new or integrative ideals, Tracey opts for "heuristic and pluralistic" hermeneutic strategies, modes of conversing that enable participants to be mutually transformed in light of the other's views. As in the present case, each of these orientations thrusts us into problems of practice as opposed to abstract contemplation.

14. Two recent attempts to confront the moral relativism of postmodern constructionism are noteworthy. With such relativism having "undermined our sense of taboo," Heller and Feher (1988) see a dangerous "irrationality" creeping into international (intercultural) politics. "If total moral relativism . . . gains the upper hand, even the assessment of mass deportation and genocide becomes a matter of taste" (p. 9). They propose countering this tendency by establishing "universal normative ideas of 'equal freedom for all' and 'equal life-chances for all' as standards of judgement" (p. 131), with differences between groups settled by rational argument. In *Postmodernism and Its Critics,* McGowan (1991) also grants the significance of the various arguments against foundational presumptions—regarding both morality and epistemology. However, to combat a full-blown relativism, he proposes "an ethical imperative of democracy" (p. 212). This "Postliberal democracy," as he calls it, "does not base the civil liberties on any notion of natural rights or the inviolability of autonomous individuals but justifies them as necessary means to the desired end of democracy" (p. 213). While both these analyses are critical of modernist foundationalism and deeply concerned with the honoring of multiple voices, in the end they propose yet another set of abstract universals on which to build a future. From the present perspective, not only are such abstractions removed from practical context, but they can lend themselves to reinstating the kinds of hierarchies the postmodern constructionist arguments are at pains to remove.

5. Social Psychology and the Wrong Revolution

1. For a useful discussion of the problems of mental propositions from the eliminative materialist standpoint see Garfield (1988).
2. For additional critiques of cognitive psychology see also Lopes (1991), Shotter (1991), and Bowers (1991) on the rhetorical production of "cognitive facts" and "irrationality" in cognitive research, Graumann (1988) on the ill effects of the cognitive movement on social psychology, Sahlin (1991) on the reliance of cognitive research on an outmoded inductivism, Tetlock (1991) on the limita-

tions of viewing "cognitive misjudgment" as error, and Valsiner (1991) on the limitations of cognitive assumptions for developmental theory.

3. Can these same arguments be turned against the social constructionist views outlined in preceding chapters? Does social constructionism not replace a cognitive solipsism with a linguistic or social solipsism? The answer is no, because constructionism does not yield the conclusion that there is no world outside of its representation. Constructionism is simply mute on matters of ontology. One may participate in cultural meaning systems in which "war," "the body," or "love" are treated as ontological givens. One may, within a local perspective, take up the study of aggression, emotion, and the like. However, the reflexive moment in the constructionist process then serves as a safeguard against reification and universalization.

4. In several of his writings, the quintessential cognitivist Jerry Fodor worries about the problem of solipsism. As he reasons in his 1981 essay "Methodological Solipsism Considered as a Research Strategy in Cognitive Psychology," any attempt to generate laws about the relationship between physical events and mental representations will require a "physical specification of the stimulus," that is, a natural science account of the stimulus and those particular properties that determine its causal relations with mental representations. Yet, such specification requires a richly developed natural science account, thus postponing indefinitely the psychologist's attempt to map the relationship to mental representation. His ironic conclusion: "Heaven only knows what relationship between me and Robin Roberts makes it possible for me to think of him (refer to him, etc.), and I've been doubting the practical possibility of a science whose generalizations that relationship instantiates. But I *don't* doubt that there *is* such a relation or that I do sometimes think of him" (pp. 252–253).

5. An alternative to the reinforcement and mapping accounts is championed by Vygotsky. In particular, Vygotsky (1978) emphasizes the priority of the social over the cognitive. For him, higher-level thought is an internalized form of social process. Yet, this places him at risk in attempting to account for those processes that enable the child to understand social processes, clearly a necessity if the child is to incorporate them. As Cole (1985) concludes in his discussion of Vygotsky, "the process of transformation of independent features of culture into individual cognitive processes is as yet unspecified" (p. 147).

6. As Johnson-Laird (1988) summarizes, the problem of concept acquisition has driven Jerry Fodor to the extreme conclusion that all concepts are innate. Fodor demonstrates that children who understand a simple logic could never derive a more complex logic from its premises, because they would first have to understand a new set of expressions. For Fodor, "there literally isn't such a thing as the notion of learning a conceptual system richer than the one one already has" (quoted in Johnson-Laird, p. 135). To combat what he sees as the untenability of Fodor's conclusion, Johnson-Laird replaces innate categories with an innate process of maturation. This still leaves the problem of concept acquisition unanswered.

7. Although contemporary psychology is largely premised on a dualist metaphysics dating from at least Descartes, dualistic assumptions have never reached broad acceptability within philosophy. And, as Smythies and Beloff (1989)

note in their recent attempt to defend this "discredited" position, "the most common objection to the Cartesian position (indeed, it worried Descartes himself) was, and still is, that once we have defined mind and matter so that they have nothing in common, it is hard to understand how they can interact as they appear to do in life" (p. vii).

8. Freudian theory represents a good example of the way in which an emphasis on motivational sources (the id) reduces the importance of cognition (the ego) in understanding human action. Contemporary cognitivists are well aware of the potential threat of the "energic world." There is a vital movement within the cognitive camp to develop theoretical means of either converting motivation to a form of cognition (see, for example, Kruglanski 1992), or viewing emotions as cognized energies (Schachter 1964), thus subverting the energic world and sustaining the cognitivist hegemony. However, in all such cases the theorist then recapitulates the present problem (even if now hidden beneath the table): how do abstractions, concepts, ideas, or internal propositions in themselves *produce* action?

9. Elsewhere I have used the term "socio-rationalist," thus forming a useful contrast between empiricist epistemology on the one hand and rationalist on the other (Gergen 1994). The term suggests that what we term rationality is a derivative not of individual minds but of social interchange. Social epistemology is chosen in the present context to emphasize the replacement of the classical subject-object account of knowledge with a specifically social view. Although not fully relinquishing the ties to cognition, Fuller's (1988) elaborate formulation of a social epistemology—extending the sociology of knowledge to its epistemological limits—is resonant with the present account.

10. There is no necessary agreement between those "alternative psychologies" favored by either the critical school or the feminists and social constructionism. Although there is a potential affinity between much feminist writing and a constructionist standpoint, most writers of the critical school see their program as realist and materialist. The major point, however, is that a constructionist view favors both ideological critique and expanding the vocabularies of social life. It does not require that the outcomes of such critical work should be consistent with a constructionist perspective.

11. In other social science domains, where the empiricist commitment was less intense, social critique continued to flourish. Hannah Arendt, Robert Bellah, Allan Bloom, Barbara Ehrenreich, Ivan Illich, Christopher Lasch, and David Riesman are only a few of those stimulating cultural consciousness in the present century.

6. The Cultural Consequences of Deficit Discourse

1. See Mary Boyle's (1991) careful critique of diagnoses of schizophrenia. As she shows, such diagnoses are not evidentially based, but highly interpretive and rife with conceptual confusion. See also Wiener's (1991) critique of the concept of schizophrenia.

2. This is not to say that certain states of the body, along with various forms of

behavior, are not significant in giving meaning to mental terms—especially the vocabulary of the emotions. Psychological discourse is typically but one aspect of a more fully embodied performance, and without the full performance (perhaps involving tears, shouting, heart acceleration, and so on) the words would not be intelligible. More will be said about mental terminology in general, and the emotions in particular, in Chapter 9.

3. Foucault's (1978, 1979) discussions of the early development of scientific rationality and the effects of these developments on power relations in society are apposite. Also compelling is Murray Edelman's (1974) discussion of the "professional imperialism" of the helping professions. For a more baldly stated case against psychiatry's appropriation of power in the present century, see Gross (1978).

4. For an extended account of the expansion of psychiatry in the United States and the accompanying "psychiatrization of difference" see Castel, Castel, and Lovell (1982).

5. See also Gordon's (1990) analysis of the function of the media in the generation of what we index as anorexia and bulimia.

6. Not fully represented in these figures is the enormous growth in expenditures for psychopharmaceuticals. Consider the major antidepressant, Prozac. According to a *Newsweek* (March 26, 1990) report, a year after the drug was introduced to the market, sales reached $125 million. One year later (1989) the sales had almost tripled, to $350 million. Sales are expected to reach $1 billion by 1995.

7. See also Kovel (1988) on psychiatry as a market economy.

8. See Lopez-Pinero's (1983) more extended account.

9. It is in this respect that we may celebrate the mental patients' liberation movement (Chamberlin 1990), an attempt by ex-mental patients to join together in reclaiming the power of self-definition.

10. Also relevant is Sarbin and Mancuso's (1980) argument for the "transvaluation of social identity," an attempt to recognize the broader set of relationships in which judgments of normality and abnormality are embedded.

7. Objectivity as Rhetorical Achievement

1. For more extended accounts of the mechanistic self, see Hollis's (1977) *Models of Man,* Overton and Reese's (1973) essay "Models of Development: Methodological Implications," and my volume (1991b) *The Saturated Self.*

2. Wittgenstein's *Philosophical Investigations* is among the richest critiques of the dualist tradition in psychology. See also William Lyons's *The Disappearance of Introspection,* Richard Rorty's *Philosophy and the Mirror of Nature,* Gilbert Ryle's *The Concept of Mind,* and J. L. Austin's *Sense and Sensibilia.*

3. For an elaboration of this point see Lyons's *The Disappearance of Introspection.* Also see the discussion of labeling mental states in Chapter 6.

4. For further elaboration, see Chapter 2.

5. Particularly useful here are Roland Barthes's *S/Z,* Wayne C. Booth's *The Rhetoric of Fiction,* Kathryn Hume's *Fantasy and Mimesis,* Georg Lukacs's *Studies in European Realism,* and Wallace Martin's *Recent Theories of Narrative.*

6. A variety of prominent contributions to the rhetorical analysis of social science writings were cited in the preceding chapter. Additional entries of importance include Bazerman's *Shaping Written Knowledge,* Nelson, Megill, and McCloskey's *The Rhetoric of the Human Sciences,* Prelli's *A Rhetoric of Science,* Simons's *Rhetoric in the Human Sciences* and *Case Studies in the Rhetoric of the Human Sciences,* Spence's *The Freudian Metaphor,* Edmondson's *Rhetoric in Sociology,* and Green's *Literary Methods and Sociological Theory.* Lang's (1990) rhetorical analysis of philosophical writing is also apposite.

7. For a more extended account of the splitting of subject and object languages and their implications for scientific epistemology, see my paper, "Knowledge and Social Process," in Bar-Tal and Kruglanski's (1988) *The Social Psychology of Knowledge.*

8. Relevant here is the preceding chapter's discussion of the means by which the empirical psychologist attempts to circumvent the problem of repeating "what everybody knows."

9. For an elaboration of this argument, see Richard Rorty's *Philosophy and the Mirror of Nature.*

10. I am indebted here to Vincent Crapanzano's essay, "Hermes' Dilemma: The Masking of Subversion in Ethnographic Description," in *Writing Culture.*

11. For an extensive account of the effects of scientific methodology on psychology's construction of the experimental subject, see Danziger (1991).

12. In order to escape the stranglehold of the objective-subjective binary, Donald McClosky (personal communication) has coined the term "conjective." Scientific accounts are neither objective nor subjective according to this view, but fundamentally consensual.

13. See Ibanez (1991) for further discussion of this point, and Hawkesworth (1992) for a discussion of feminist criticism of the concept of objectivity.

8. Self-Narration in Social Life

1. The initial elaboration of the concept of self-narrative is contained in Gergen and Gergen (1983).

2. See also Labov's (1982) analysis of narratives as vehicles for requests and responses to requests, Mischler's (1986) analysis of narratives functioning within relational power structures, and the work of Tappan (1991) and Day (1991) on the function of narration in moral decision making.

3. Here it is interesting to compare the present analysis with similar attempts by others. In 1863 Gustav Freytag proposed that there was but one "normal" plot, which could be represented by a rising and falling line divided by points labeled A, B, C, and D. Here, the rising section AB represents the exposition of a situation, B the introduction of the conflict, BC the "rising action" or increasing complication, the high point at C the climax or turn of the action, and the downward slope CD, the denouement or resolution of the conflict. As my analysis indicates, by more fully delineating the criteria of the narrative and altering the form of configuration, a richer set of emplotments is revealed. Although Freytag recognized only one prevailing narrative, he did believe that he was

confronting a social convention and not a logical or biological necessity. More recently, Elsbree (1982) has attempted to delineate a series of fundamental narrative forms. He pinpoints five "generic plots," which include *establishing or consecrating a home, engaging in a contest or battle,* and *taking a journey.* Yet, Elsbree's analysis is not lodged in the assumption of cultural convention; for him the generic plots are fundamental to human existence.

4. See Gergen and Gergen (1983) and Gergen and Gergen (1987).
5. There are exceptions to this general surmise. Drama is also intertextual in the sense that any given presentation depends for its intelligibility (and thus for its emotional impact) on familiarity with other members of the genre and on contrasting genres. Thus, if one is exposed only to the genre of tragedy, a stability narrative may gain in dramatic engagement by virtue of its contrast. In the same way, understated advertisements often capture increased interest by their placement in a context of hyperstimulating enticements.

9. Emotion as Relationship

1. See Rose (1985, 1990) for a critical analysis of the ways in which the psychological establishment contributes to an increasing control over the citizenry.
2. Charles Taylor's (1991) *The Ethics of Authenticity* is interesting by contrast. Taylor agrees that individualism in contemporary society has been justifiably discredited. But rather than attempt to open new horizons, Taylor attempts to argue toward a more responsible and viable form of individual agency.
3. See Burkitt (1993) for an interesting attempt to synthesize various theories in this domain.
4. As Tseelon (1992b) points out, many scholars do see in Goffman an implied theory of subjectivity. Her careful analysis leads her to conclude that "in dramaturgical analysis the meaning of the human organism is established by its activity and the activity of others with respect to it . . . selves are outcomes not antecedents of human interaction" (p. 3).
5. Olds's (1992) *Metaphors of Interrelatedness* usefully extends Batesonian thinking into present discussions.
6. For an extension of this line of argument to the level of biographical memory see Gergen (in press b).
7. Le Fevre's (1987) work on invention as a social act is also apposite. As she demonstrates, there are significant limitations to the view that literary or scientific creativity is the product of the single, socially insulated mind. Invention, for Le Fevre, is saturated with social history and requires ongoing negotiation to constitute it as a "real" invention.
8. There is an instrumentalist rejoinder to this form of skepticism, one that apologizes for speaking so boldly about what is the case and adds, "Of course, it goes without saying that we are really speaking of *hypothetical constructs.* Yet, if our hypothetical model can account for enough predictions, we are satisfied in treating it as objectively true for all practical purposes." But the instrumentalist reply is multiply flawed. Not only does it provide no safeguards against wholesale reification (as amply evidenced in contemporary cognitivism) and misconstrue the function of theory (see Chapter 3); it also suppresses discussion

of theoretical choice. That is, it removes from the table the vital questions of how theory, once reified, will function in cultural life. In the present case, for example, what gains and losses to cultural life are served by rendering emotional terms *objective?*

9. There are investigations of emotions that do not rely on such commonsense assumptions. For example, Pribram (1980) makes claims for the relationship between dopamine and depression, and the enkephalins and feelings of comfort. However, the rhetorical efficacy of such research depends, in the final analysis, on subjects' reports of their depression and comfort levels—in effect, a reinstantiation of "the folk." Ironically, while attempting to avoid the methodological nightmare of introspective reports, such research would be of marginal significance to the understanding of emotions without just this kind of folk support. If people did not report that they experienced emotion, the study of dopamine and enkephalin effects would be of little interest to emotion researchers. It also follows from these arguments that the study of emotion can never be reduced to biology. The biological study of emotions is ultimately a derivative of cultural folklore. If one commenced the study of emotion with biology alone, there would be no means of identifying the emotions. From a relentless assay of neurological structures, synapses, dopamine production, and the like one could never induce a differentiated vocabulary of the emotions. In effect, emotions are not elements in the ontology of biology. For biologists to speak of emotions at all they must fall back on the commonplace assumptions of the culture.

10. In this light it is interesting to consider Lazarus's (1991) "progress report" on emotion theory. In spite of virtually a century of scientific research into the emotions, Lazarus acknowledges that "there has never been any agreement about which emotions should be distinguished" (p. 821), and that most questions about the definition of an emotion "remain unresolved."

11. See Fivush (1989) for a demonstration of the way children learn accounts of their emotions through relationships with parents.

12. See, for example, Burton's (1989) sixteenth-century account of melancholy.

13. Useful insights into the microsocial functioning of emotional performances can be found in treatments of belief (Day 1993), apology (Schlenker and Darby 1981), teasing (Pawluk 1989), and passion (Bailey 1983) and in transactional approaches to "mental illness" (Marcus and Wiener 1989). Conversational analyses also suggest useful ways of approaching the problem of emotional patterning (for example, Schlegoff and Sacks 1973; Auer 1990).

14. For a more complete discussion of the limitations of the experimental method in a diachronically sensitive science, see Gergen (1984).

15. See for example, Simmel (1950) and Gouldner (1960).

16. For a full description of the research see Harris, Gergen, and Lannamann (1986).

17. In a more extensive study of naturally occurring conflict in families, Vuchinich (1984) has demonstrated remarkably stable relational sequences.

18. It is interesting to note that in further research using a hostile exchange between two males, respondents came to recommending and condoning physical violence as an outcome of their heated exchange, but when asked for alternative

means of solving their difference, could think of none—save through outside intervention.

19. I am indebted to Wendy Davidson for her assistance in this research.

10. Transcending Narrative in the Therapeutic Context

1. For additional discussions of modernism see Berman (1982), Frisby (1985), Giddens (1991), and Gergen (1991b).
2. For an extensive account of the problems of the modernist (or empiricist foundationalist) orientation to psychotherapy, see Ryder (1987).
3. More extended references to the postmodern turn are provided in Chapter 2. For discussion of the particular relationship between postmodernism and therapeutic practice, see Gergen (1991b), Ibanez (1992), and Lax (1992).
4. My chief emphasis in this chapter is on change and flexibility in narrative construction. However, this is in no way intended to make a principled argument for these ends. I stress change primarily because those seeking therapy are typically discontent with the status quo. For those leading fulfilling lives within a stable and delimited set of narratives, the emphasis may indeed shift to means of holding tight in a world that constantly threatens disruption.
5. Relevant are Shotter's (1993a, pp. 83–86) descriptions of ex post facto fallacies, although it would be a mistake to trace all difficulties to a self-reinforcing construction of life. Attention must also shift outward to the way in which such constructions function within existing relationships, and the possibility that aberrant rigidity may itself develop as relationships drop away and others no longer challenge or furnish alternatives to an existing construction.

11. The Communal Origins of Meaning

1. Piaget was fully aware of the possibility of a social invasion of the mental. In *The Psychology of the Child,* he and Inhelder warn of the threat posed by the "sociological school of Durkheim" and the argument that "language constitutes not only an essential . . . factor in the learning of logic, . . . but is in fact the source of all logic for the whole of humanity" (p. 87). They then put forward evidence to dispute this possibility and reinstantiate the individualist conclusion that "language does not constitute the source of logic, but is, on the contrary, structured by it" (p. 90). However, the "evidence" in this case depends on problematic assumptions of an interior mind, which assumptions also work circularly to ensure the conclusion.
2. To put it another way, demonstrating what we call understanding in a relationship is achieved not by accessing the other's subjectivity but by carrying out an appropriate action within an established sequence.
3. Although the present analysis suggests considerable latitude in one's capacity to create and constrain meaning, the existence of long-standing patterns of interchange within the culture virtually ensures that not "anything goes."
4. It should not be concluded that we are therefore locked into more or less permanent and necessarily conflicting systems of meaning. New forms of relationship are always possible; one is not prevented by past commitments from

entering new or alien forms of intelligibility—no more than a lifetime of playing chess prevents one from being socialized into croquet.

12. Deceit: From Conscience to Community

1. See especially Kant's (1971) *The Doctrine of Virtue.*
2. Sissela Bok (1978) embodies this view in her general "principle of veracity" (p. 32), and traces it from the writings of Cicero through twentieth-century philosophies of morality.
3. For amplification, see Cooperrider and Pasmore (1991) and Gergen (1991b).
4. For a useful discussion of subcultural realities, see Carbaugh (1990).
5. The present diagrams are intended only as analytic aids. A more adequate formalization could be rendered in three-dimensional space with clusterings of interrelated nuclei. However, for the purposes of the present argument, two dimensions are sufficient.
6. See Chapter 4 for elaboration.
7. The present analysis emphasizes membership in diverse nuclei, thus tracing deceit to membership in multiple groups. However, because members of any group inherit the sense-making devices of a heterogenous cultural past, membership itself may not be a requirement for deceit. Thus, one may understand the advantages of theft not because one belongs to another group in which theft is honored but because even within mainstream culture the intelligibility of theft is carried through history. Spy and detective stories, war stories, and even romance novels glorify theft for good ends. In this sense most of us carry with us multiple and often antithetical intelligibilities (see also Billig et al. 1988).

References

Abrams, M. H. 1971. *Natural supernaturalism: Tradition and revolution in romantic literature*. New York: Norton.

Adoni, H., and S. Mane. 1984. Media and the social construction of reality. *Communication Research*, 11: 323–340.

Adorno, T. 1970. *The authoritarian personality*. New York: Norton.

Ajzen, I., and M. Fishbein. 1980. *Understanding attitudes and predicting social behavior*. Englewood Cliffs, N.J.: Prentice-Hall.

Albert, H. 1985. *A treatise on critical reason*. Princeton: Princeton University Press.

Allen, B. 1993. *Truth in philosophy*. Cambridge: Harvard University Press.

Allen, R. L., and C. Kuo. 1991. Communications and beliefs about racial equality. *Discourse and Society*, 1: 259–279.

Allport, C. A. 1975. The state of cognitive psychology. *Quarterly Journal of Experimental Psychology*, 27: 141–152.

Althusser, L., and E. Balibar. 1970. *Reading capital*. New York: Pantheon.

American Psychiatric Association. 1987. *Diagnostic and statistical manual of mental disorders*, 3rd ed. revised. Washington, D.C.

Andersen, M. L. 1994. The many and varied social constructions of intelligence. In T. R. Sarbin and J. I. Kitsuse, eds. *Constructing the social*. London: Sage.

Andersen, T. 1991. *The reflecting team: Dialogues and dialogues about the dialogues*. New York: Norton.

Anderson, H., and H. Goolishian. 1988. Human systems as linguistic systems: Evolving ideas about the implications for theory and practice. *Family Process*, 27:371–393.

Anscombe, G. E. M. 1976. *Intention*. Oxford: Basil Blackwell. Originally published in 1953.

Antaki, C. 1981. *The psychology of ordinary explanations*. London: Academic Press.

Apfelbaum, E., and I. Lubek. 1976. Resolution vs. revolution? The theory of conflicts in question. In L. Strickland, F. Aboud, and K. J. Gergen, eds. *Social psychology in transition*. New York: Plenum Press.

Arbib, M. A., and M. B. Hesse. 1986. *The construction of reality*. Cambridge: Cambridge University Press.

Argyris, C. 1980. *Inner contradictions of rigorous research*. New York: Academic Press.

Ariès, P. 1962. *Centuries of childhood: A social history of family life*. Trans. R. Baldick. New York: Vintage.

Armistead, N. 1974. *Reconstructing social psychology*. Baltimore, Md.: Penguin.

Armon-Jones, C. 1986. The social functions of emotion. In R. Harré, ed. *The social construction of emotions*. Oxford: Blackwell.

Astley, G. 1985. Administrative science as socially constructed truth. *Administrative Science Quarterly*, 30: 497–513.

Astley, W. G., and R. Zammuto. 1992. Organization science, managers, and language games. *Organization Science*, 3: 443–459.

Atkinson, J. M. 1977. *Discovering suicide: Studies in the social organization of sudden death*. London: Macmillan Press.

Atwood, J. D., and S. Dershowitz. 1992. Constructing a sex and marital therapy frame: Ways to help couples deconstruct sexual problems. *Journal of Sex and Marital Therapy*, 18: 196–217.

Auer, P. 1990. Rhythm in telephone closings. *Human Studies*, 13: 361–392.

Austin, J. L. 1962a. *How to do things with words*. New York: Oxford University Press.

——— 1962b. *Sense and sensibilia*. London: Oxford University Press.

Averill, J. R. 1982. *Anger and aggression: An essay on emotion*. New York: Springer-Verlag.

——— 1985. The social construction of emotion: With special reference to love. In K. J. Gergen and K. E. Davis, eds. *The social construction of the person*. New York: Springer-Verlag.

Averill, J. R., and E. P. Nunley. 1992. *Voyages of the heart*. New York: Free Press.

Baars, B. J. 1981. *The cognitive revolution in psychology*. New York: Guilford Press.

Badinter, E. 1980. *Mother love: Myth and reality*. New York: Macmillan.

Bailey, F. G. 1983. *The tactical uses of passion*. New York: Cornell University Press.

Bakhtin, M. 1981. *The dialogic imagination*. Austin: University of Texas Press.

Bandura, A. 1977. *Social learning theory*. Englewood Cliffs, N.J.: Prentice-Hall.

Barnes, B. 1974. *Scientific knowledge and sociological theory*. London: Routledge and Kegan Paul.

——— 1992. How not to do the sociology of knowledge. *Annals of Scholarship*, 8: 321–337.

Barratt, B. B. 1984. *Psychic reality and psychoanalytic knowing*. Hillsdale, N.J.: Erlbaum.

Barrett, W. 1979. *The illusion of technique*. Garden City, N.Y.: Anchor.

Barthes, R. 1964. *Elements of semiology*. Paris: Jonathan Cape.

——— 1974. *S/Z*. New York: Hill and Wang.

Bateson, G. 1972. *Steps to an ecology of mind.* New York: Ballantine.

———— 1979. *Mind and nature.* New York: E. P. Dutton.

Baudrillard, J. 1988. *The ecstasy of communication.* New York: Semiotext(e).

Bazerman, C. 1988. *Shaping written knowledge.* Madison: University of Wisconsin Press.

Bedford, E. 1957. Emotions and statements about them. *Proceedings of the Aristotelian Society, 57.*

Belenky, M., B. M. Clinchy, N. R. Goldberger, J. M. Tarule. 1986. *Women's ways of knowing.* New York: Basic Books.

Bellah, R. N., et al. 1985. *Habits of the heart.* Berkeley: University of California Press.

Bennett, W. L., and M. S. Feldman. 1981. *Reconstructing reality in the courtroom.* New Brunswick, N.J.: Rutgers University Press.

Benson, P. 1993. *Anthropology and literature.* Urbana: University of Illinois Press.

Berg, D., and K. Smith, eds. 1985. *Exploring clinical methods for social research.* Beverly Hills, Calif.: Sage.

Berg, I. K., and S. de Shazer. 1993. Making numbers talk: Language in therapy. In S. Friedman, ed. *The new language of change.* New York: Guilford Press.

Berger, P., and T. Luckmann. 1966. *The social construction of reality.* New York: Doubleday/Anchor.

Berkowitz, M., F. Oser, and W. Althof. 1987. The development of sociomoral discourse. In W. Kurtines and J. Gewirtz, eds. *Moral development through social interaction.* New York: John Wiley and Sons.

Berman, M. 1982. *All that's solid melts into air: The experience of modernity.* New York: Simon and Schuster.

Berscheid, E. 1986. Mea culpa and lamentations: Sir Francis, Sir Isaac, and the slow progress of soft psychology. In R. Gilmour and S. Duck, eds. *The emerging field of personal relationships.* Hillsdale, N.J.: Erlbaum.

Bertaux, D., ed. 1984. *Biography and society: The life history approach in the social sciences.* London: Sage.

Bettelheim, B. 1976. *The uses of enchantment.* New York: Knopf.

Betti, E. 1980. Hermeneutics as the general methodology of the *Geisteswissenschaften.* In J. Bleicher, *Contemporary hermeneutics.* Boston: Routledge and Kegan Paul.

Bhagat, R. 1983. Intellectual performance and utilization in a two-paradigm administrative and organizational science: A philosophy of science-based assessment. In R. H. Kilmann and K. Thomas and Associates, eds. *Producing useful knowledge for organizations.* New York: Praeger.

Bhaskar, R. 1978. *A realist theory of science,* 2nd ed. Atlantic Highlands, N.J.: Humanities Press.

———— 1989. *Reclaiming reality.* London: Verso.

———— 1991. *Philosophy and the idea of freedom.* Cambridge: Blackwell.

Bhavnani, K. 1991. *Talking politics: A psychological framing of views from youth in Britain.* Cambridge: Cambridge University Press.

Billig, M. 1987. *Arguing and thinking.* London: Cambridge University Press.

Billig, M., et al. 1988. *Ideological dilemmas: A social psychology of everyday thinking.* London: Sage.

Bleier, R. 1984. *Science and gender: A critique of biology and its theories on women.* New York: Pergamon.

Bloom, A. 1987. *The closing of the American mind.* New York: Simon and Schuster.

Bloor, D. 1976. *Knowledge and social imagery.* London: Routledge Kegan Paul.

Bogen, D., and M. Lynch. 1989. Taking account of the hostile native: Plausible deniability and the production of conventional history in the Iran-Contra hearings. *Social Problems,* 36: 197–224.

Bohme, G. 1977. Cognitive norms, knowledge interests and the constitution of the scientific object. In E. Mendelsohn and P. Weingart, eds. *The social production of scientific knowledge.* Dordrecht: Reidel.

Bok, S. 1978. *Lying: Moral choice in public life.* New York: Vintage.

Booth, W. 1982. *The rhetoric of fiction.* Chicago: University of Chicago Press.

Borg-Laufs, M., and L. Duda. 1991. *Zur sozialen Konstruktion von Geschmackswahrnehmung.* Braunschweig: Vieweg.

Borstelman, L. J. 1983. Children before psychology: Ideas about children from antiquity to the late 1800's. In P. H. Mussen, ed. *Handbook of child psychology,* vol. 1: *History, theory and methods,* 4th ed. New York: Wiley.

Bourdieu, P. 1977. *Outline of a theory practice.* London: Cambridge University Press.

Bowers, J. 1991. Time, representation and power/knowledge: Towards a critique of cognitive science as a knowledge-producing practice. *Theory and Psychology,* 4: 543–571.

Bower, G., and T. Trabosso. 1964. *Attention in learning.* New York: John Wiley and Sons.

Boyle, M. 1991. *Schizophrenia: A scientific delusion.* London: Routledge.

Bradley, B. S. 1989. *Visions of infancy: A critical introduction to child psychology.* Cambridge: Polity Press.

——— 1993. A serpent's guide to children's "theories of mind." *Theory and Psychology,* 3: 497–521.

Brice Heath, S. 1983. *Ways with words.* Cambridge: Cambridge University Press.

Briggs, J. L. 1970. *Never in anger: Portrait of an Eskimo family.* Cambridge: Harvard University Press.

Brim, O. G., and J. Kagan. 1980. *Constancy and change in human development.* Cambridge: Harvard University Press.

Britton, B. K., and A. D. Pellegrini, eds. 1990. *Narrative thought and narrative language.* Hillsdale, N.J.: Erlbaum.

Brodsky, A. M., and R. T. Hare-Mustin. 1980. *Women and psychotherapy: An assessment of research and practice.* New York: Guilford.

Brooke-Rose, C. 1981. *A rhetoric of the unreal.* Cambridge: Cambridge University Press.

Broughton, J. M. 1981. Piaget's structural developmental psychology vs. ideology-critique and the possibility of a critical developmental theory. *Human Development,* 24: 382–411.

——— 1986. The psychology, history and ideology of the self. In K. Larsen, ed. *Dialectics and ideology in psychology.* New Jersey: Ablex.

——— 1987. *Critical theories of psychological development.* New York: Plenum.

Brown, C. W., and E. E. Ghiselli. 1955. *Scientific method in psychology.* New York: McGraw-Hill.

Brown, J. 1992. *The definition of a profession: The authority of metaphor in the history of intelligence testing, 1890–1930.* Princeton: Princeton University Press.

Brown, M., and G. Kreps. 1993. Narrative analysis and organizational development. In S. L. Herndon and G. L. Kreps, eds. *Qualitative Research.* Cresskill, N.J.: Hampton Press.

Brown, P. 1973. *Radical psychology.* New York: Harper-Colophon.

Browning, L. D. 1992. Lists and stories as organization communication. *Communication Theory,* 2: 281–302.

Bruffee, K. A. 1993. *Collaborative learning, higher education, interdependence, and the authority of knowledge.* Baltimore: Johns Hopkins University Press.

Bruner, J. 1986. *Actual minds, possible worlds.* Cambridge: Harvard University Press.

———— 1990. *Acts of meaning.* Cambridge: Harvard University Press.

Bruner, J., and C. Feldman. 1990. Metaphors of consciousness and cognition in the history of psychology. In D. Leary, ed. *Metaphors in the history of psychology.* New York: Cambridge University Press.

Buck-Morss, S. 1975. Socio-economic bias in Piaget's theory and its implications for the cultural controversy. *Human Development,* 18: 35–49.

Bugental, J. F. T. 1965. *The search for authenticity.* New York: Holt, Rinehart and Winston.

Bukatman, S. 1993. *Terminal identity: The virtual subject in postmodern science fiction.* Durham, N.C.: Duke University Press.

Burke, K. 1965. *Language as symbolic action.* Berkeley: University of California Press.

Burkitt, I. 1993. *Social selves.* London: Sage.

Burnett, R., P. McGhee, and D. Clarke. 1987. *Accounting for relationships.* London: Methuen.

Burton, R. *The anatomy of melancholy.* Oxford: Clarendon Press. Originally published in 1624.

Bury, M. R. 1987. Social constructionism and the development of medical sociology. *Sociology of Health and Illness,* 9: 137–169.

Buss, A. R. 1979. The emerging field of sociology of psychological knowledge. In A. Buss, ed. *Psychology in social context.* New York: Irvington.

Butler, J. 1990. *Gender trouble: Feminism and the subversion of identity.* New York: Routledge.

Butt, M. 1992. *Psychology, sin and society.* New York: University Press of America.

Butting, R. 1985. Accounts as a reconstruction of an event's context. *Communication Monographs,* 52: 57–77.

Califano speaks on health care costs at Grace Square celebration. 1984. *Psychiatric News,* 14.

Campbell, D. 1969. Ethnocentrism of disciplines and the scale model of omniscience. In M. Sherif and C. W. Sherif, eds. *Interdisciplinary relationships in the social sciences,* pp. 140–152. Chicago: Aldine.

———— 1975. On the conflicts between biological and social evolution and between psychology and moral tradition. *American Psychologist,* 30: 1103–1126.

Campbell, J. 1956. *The hero with a thousand faces.* New York: Meridian. Originally published in 1949.

Cantor, D., and J. Brown. 1981. Explanatory roles. In C. Antaki, ed. *The psychology of ordinary explanations,* pp. 221–242. London: Academic Press.

Cantor, N., and W. Mischel. 1979. Prototypes in person perception. In L. Berkowitz, ed. *Advances in experimental social psychology.* New York: Academic Press.

Caplan, P. 1989. *The cultural construction of sexuality.* London: Routledge.

Caputo, J. D. 1993. *Against ethics.* Bloomington: Indiana University Press.

Carbaugh, D., ed. 1990. *Cultural communication and intercultural contact.* Hillsdale, N.J.: Erlbaum.

Carey, J. 1988. *Media, myths and narratives.* London: Sage.

Carey, S. 1985. *Conceptual change in childhood.* Cambridge: MIT Press.

Carnap, R. 1928. *Knowledge: Theory of ontology.* Berlin: Schlachtensee.

Carr, D. 1984. *Time, narrative and history.* Bloomington: Indiana University Press.

Carrithers, M., S. Collins, and S. Lukes. 1985. *The category of the person.* Cambridge: Cambridge University Press.

Casson, R. W. 1981. *Language, culture and cognition.* New York: Macmillan.

Castel, R., F. Castel, and A. Lovell. 1982. *The psychiatric society.* New York: Columbia University Press.

Chamberlin, J. 1990. The ex-patient's movement: Where we've been and where we're going. *Journal of Mind and Behavior,* 11: 223–226.

Champagne, L. 1990. *Out-from under.* New York: Theatre Communications Group.

Charme, S. L. 1984. *Meaning and myth in the study of lives: A Sartrean perspective.* Philadelphia: University of Pennsylvania Press.

Chodorow, N. 1978. *The reproduction of mothering.* Berkeley: University of California Press.

Chomsky, N. 1968. *Language and mind.* New York: Harcourt, Brace and World.

Churchland, P. M. 1980. A perspective on mind-brain research. *Journal of Philosophy,* 77: 4.

——— 1981. Eliminative materialism and propositional attitudes. *Journal of Philosophy,* 78: 2.

Cicourel, A. V. 1974. *Cognitive sociology: Language and meaning in social interaction.* New York: Free Press.

Cixous, H. 1986. *The newly born woman.* Trans. B. Wing. Minneapolis: University of Minnesota Press.

Clegg, S. 1989. *Frameworks of power.* London: Sage.

Clifford, J. 1983. On ethnographic authority. *Representations,* 2: 132–143.

Clifford, J., and G. Marcus. 1986. *Writing culture.* Berkeley: University of California Press.

Clough, P. T. 1992. *The end(s) of ethnography: From realism to social criticism.* Newbury Park, Calif.: Sage.

Coelho de Amorim, A., and F. G. Cavalcante. 1992. Narrations of the self: Video production in a marginalized subculture. In S. McNamee and K. Gergen, eds. *Therapy as social construction.* London: Sage.

Cohen, E. 1993. Towards a history of physical sensibility: Pain in the later middle ages. Paper presented at the Israel Academy of Sciences and Humanities.

Cohler, B. J. 1982. Personal narrative and the life-course. In P. Battles and O. G. Brim, eds. *Life-span development and behavior*. New York: Academic Press.

Cole, M. 1985. The zone of proximal development: Where culture and cognition create each other. In J. Wertsch, ed. *Culture, communication, and cognition: Vygotskian perspectives*. Cambridge: Cambridge University Press.

Collins, H. M. 1985. *Changing order*. London: Sage.

Collins, H. M., and T. J. Pinch. 1982. *The social construction of extraordinary science*. London: Routledge Kegan Paul.

Connor, S. 1989. *Postmodernist culture*. London: Blackwell.

Cooperrider, D. L. 1990. Positive imagery, positive action: The affirmative basis of organizing. In S. Srivastva, D. Cooperrider, and Associates, eds. *Appreciative management and leadership*. San Francisco: Jossey-Bass.

Cooperrider, D. L., and W. A. Pasmore. 1991. The organizational dimension of global change. *Human Relations*, 44: 763–787.

Cooperrider, D. L., and S. Srivastra. 1987. Appreciative inquiry into organization life. *Research in organizational change and development*, 1: 129–169.

Corbin, A. 1986. *The foul and the fragrant*. Cambridge: Harvard University Press.

Corsaro, W. A. 1985. *Friendship and peer culture*. Norwood, N.J.: Ablex.

Coulter, J. 1979. *The social construction of the mind*. New York: Macmillan.

—— 1983. *Rethinking cognitive theory*. New York: St. Martin's Press.

—— 1989. *Mind in action*. Oxford: Blackwell.

Coupland, N., and J. F. Nussbaum, eds. 1993. *Discourse and lifespan identity*. Newbury Park, Calif.: Sage.

Coyne, J. C. 1976. Toward an interactional description of depression. *Psychiatry*, 29: 28–39.

Craig, R. T., and K. Tracy. 1982. *Conversational coherence*. Beverly Hills, Calif.: Sage.

Crapanzano, V. 1986. Hermes' dilemma: The masking of subversion in ethnographic description. In J. Clifford and G. Marcus, eds. *Writing culture*. Berkeley: University of California Press.

Critchley, S. 1992. *The ethics of deconstruction*. Oxford: Blackwell.

Csikszentmihalyi, M., and O. Beattie. 1979. Life themes: A theoretical and empirical explanation of their origins and effects. *Journal of Humanistic Psychology*, 19: 45–63.

Culler, J. 1982. *On deconstruction*. Ithaca: Cornell University Press.

Curtis, R. C., ed. 1990. *The relational self*. New York: Guilford.

Cushman, P. 1991. Ideology obscured: Political uses of the self in Daniel Stern's infant. *American Psychologist*, 46: 206–219.

Daft, R. 1983. Learning the craft of organizational research. *Academy of Management Review*, 8: 539–546.

Daly, M. 1978. *Gyn/ecology: The metaethics of radical feminism*. Boston: Beacon Press.

Daniels, M. 1988. The myth of self-actualization. *Humanistic Psychology*, 28: 7–38.

Danziger, K. 1990. *Constructing the subject: Historical origins of psychological research.* Cambridge: Cambridge University Press.

Daston, L. 1992. Baconian facts, academic civility, and the prehistory of objectivity. *Annals of Scholarship,* 8: 337–365.

Davidson, D. 1973. On the very idea of a conceptual scheme. *Proceedings of the American Philosophical Association,* 1973–74: 5–20.

Davies, B., and R. Harré. 1990. Positioning: The discursive production of selves. *Journal for the Theory of Social Behaviour,* 20: 43–63.

Davis, K. E., and M. K. Roberts. 1985. Relationships in the real world: The descriptive psychology approach to personal relationships. In K. J. Gergen and K. E. Davis, eds. *The social construction of the person.* New York: Springer-Verlag.

Davis, K. E., and M. Todd. 1981. Friendship and love relationships. In K. E. Davis and T. O. Mitchell, eds. *Advances in descriptive psychology,* vol. 2. Greenwich, Conn.: JAI Press.

Day, J. M. 1991. The moral audience: On the narrative mediation of moral "judgment" and moral "action." In M. B. Tappan, and M. J. Packer, eds. *Narrative and storytelling: Implications for understanding moral development.* San Francisco: Jossey-Bass.

——— 1993. Belief: Language, performance, and narrative in the psychology of religion. *International Journal for the Psychology of Religion,* 3: 213–230.

Deaux, K. 1985. Sex and gender. *Annual Review of Psychology,* 36: 49–81.

Deese, J. 1984. *American freedom and social sciences.* New York: Columbia University Press.

Deetz, S. 1992. *Democracy in an age of corporate colonization.* Albany: State University of New York Press.

DeJean, J. 1991. *Tender geographies: Women and the origins of the novel in France.* New York: Columbia University Press.

Deleuze, G., and F. Guattari. 1986. *A thousand plateaus.* Minneapolis: University of Minnesota Press.

De Man, P. 1979. Shelley disfigured. In H. Bloom, P. De Man, J. Derrida, G. Hartman, and J. H. Miller, eds. *Deconstruction and criticism.* New York: Continuum.

Denzin, N., and Y. Lincoln. 1994. *Handbook of qualitative research.* Thousand Oaks, Calif.: Sage.

DeRivera, J. 1984. The structure of emotional relationships. In P. Shaver, ed. *Review of personality and social psychology.* Beverly Hills, Calif.: Sage.

Derrida, J. 1976. *Of grammatology.* Baltimore: Johns Hopkins University Press.

——— 1978. *Writing and difference.* Trans. A. Bass. Chicago: University of Chicago Press.

de Shazer, S. 1991. *Putting differences to work.* New York: Norton.

de Waele, J. P., and R. Harré. 1976. The personality of individuals. In R. Harré, ed. *Personality.* Oxford: Blackwell.

Dilthey, W. 1984. *Selected writings.* In H. P. Rickman, ed. Cambridge: Cambridge University Press. Originally published in 1914.

Dinnerstein, D. 1976. *The mermaid and the minotaur.* New York: Harper and Row.

Dipple, E. 1988. *The unresolvable plot: Reading contemporary fiction.* London: Routledge.

Donagan, A. 1977. *The theory of morality.* Chicago: University of Chicago Press.

Douglas, M. 1986. *How institutions think.* London: Routledge Kegan Paul.

Douzinas, C., and R. Warrington. 1991. *Postmodern jurisprudence: The law of text in the texts of law.* London: Routledge.

Dreyfus, H. L., and S. E. Dreyfus. 1986. *Mind over machine: The power of human intuition and expertise in the era of the computer.* New York: Free Press.

Duck, S. 1994. Strategies, spoils and a serpent's truth: On the delights and dilemmas of personal relationships. In W. R. Supsch and B. H. Spitzberg, eds. *The darkside of interpersonal communication.* Hillsdale, N.J.: Erlbaum.

Durrant, M., and K. Kowalski. 1993. Enhancing views of competence. In S. Friedman, ed. *The new language of change.* New York: Guilford.

Eagly, A. 1987. *Sex differences in behavior: A social-role interpretation.* Hillsdale, N.J.: Erlbaum.

Eakin, P. J. 1985. *Fictions in autobiography.* Princeton: Princeton University Press.

Edelman, M. 1974. The political language of the helping professions. *Politics and Society,* 4: 295–310.

———— 1988. *Constructing the political spectacle.* Chicago: University of Chicago Press.

Edmondson, R. 1984. *Rhetoric in sociology.* London: Macmillan.

Edwards, D., and N. Mercer. 1987. *Common knowledge: The development of understanding in the classroom.* New York: Methuen.

Edwards, D., and J. Potter. 1993. *Discursive psychology.* London: Sage.

Edwards, D., M. Ashmore, and J. Potter. 1993. Death and furniture: The rhetoric, politics and theology of bottom line arguments against relativism. Unpublished manuscript.

Efran, J., M. Lukens, and R. Lukens. 1990. *Language structure and change.* New York: Norton.

Eiser, J. R. 1980. *Cognitive social psychology.* New York: McGraw-Hill.

Elsbree, L. 1982. *The rituals of life: Patterns in narrative.* Port Washington, N.Y.: Kennikat Press.

Engestrom, Y., and D. Middleton. 1992. *Communal cognition in the workplace.* London: Sage.

Epstein, E. 1991. The problem of individual differences in special education: The social construction of school problems. Ph.D. diss., Union Institute.

Epstein, S. 1980. The self-concept: A review and the proposal of an integrated theory of personality. In E. Staub, ed. *Personality: Basic issues and current research.* Englewood Cliffs, N.J.: Prentice-Hall.

Epston, D., and M. White. 1992. A proposal for a re-authoring therapy. In S. McNamee and K. J. Gergen, eds. *Therapy as social construction.* London: Sage.

Fabian, J. 1983. *Time and the other: How anthropology makes its object.* New York: Columbia University Press.

Farber, S. 1990. Institutional mental health and social control: The ravages of epistemological hubris. *Journal of Mind and Behavior,* 11: 285–300.

———— 1993. *Madness, heresy, and the rumor of angels.* Chicago: Open Court.

Farr, R., and S. Moscovici. 1984. *Social representations.* Cambridge: Cambridge University Press.

Fausto-Sterling, Anne. 1985. *Myths of gender: Theories about women and men.* New York: Basic Books.

Felson, R. 1984. Patterns of aggressive social interaction. In A. Mummenday, ed. *Social psychology of aggression.* Heidelberg: Springer-Verlag.

Festinger, L. 1954. A theory of social comparison processes. *Human Relations,* 7: 117–140.

—— 1957. *A theory of cognitive dissonance.* Evanston, Ill.: Row, Peterson.

Feyerabend, P. K. 1976. *Against method.* New York: Humanities Press.

—— 1978. *Science in a free society.* London: Thetford Press.

Finch, J. 1980. Devising conventional performances: The case of clergymen's wives. *Sociological Review,* 28: 851–870.

Fine, M. 1993. *Beyond silenced voices: Class, race and gender in the United States.* Albany: State University Press of New York.

Fish, S. 1979. Normal circumstances, literal language, direct speech acts, the ordinary, the everyday, the obvious, what goes without saying, and other special cases. In P. Rainbow and W. Sullivan, eds. *Interpretive social science: A reader,* pp. 258–266. Berkeley: University of California Press.

—— 1980. *Is there a text in this class? The authority of interpretive communities.* Cambridge: Harvard University Press.

Fisher, H. In press. Whose right is it to define the self? *Theory and Psychology.*

Fiske, S., and S. Taylor. 1991. *Social cognition.* 2nd ed. New York: McGraw-Hill.

Fivush, R. 1989. Exploring sex differences in the emotional content of mother-child conversation about the past. *Sex Roles,* 20: 675–691.

Flanagan, O. 1991. *Varieties of moral personality.* Cambridge: Harvard University Press.

Flax, J. 1987. Postmodernism and gender relations in feminist theory. *Signs,* 12: 621–43.

Fleck, L. 1979. *Genesis and development of a scientific fact.* Chicago: University of Chicago Press.

Fodor, J. A. 1981. *Representations: Philosophical essays on the foundations of cognitive science.* Cambridge: MIT Press.

Fodor, J., M. Garrett, E. Walker, and C. Parkes. 1980. Against definitions. *Cognition,* 8: 263–267.

Fonow, M. M., and J. A. Cook, eds. 1991. *Beyond methodology: Feminist scholarship as lived research.* Bloomington: Indiana University Press.

Forgas, J. 1979. *Social episodes: The study of interaction routines.* New York: Academic Press.

—— 1981. *Social cognition.* New York: Academic Press.

Foucault, M. 1972. *The archeology of knowledge.* New York: Harper Colophon.

—— 1978. *The history of sexuality.* Vol. 1, *An introduction.* New York: Pantheon.

—— 1979. *Discipline and punish: The birth of the prison.* New York: Random House.

—— 1980. *Power/knowledge.* New York: Pantheon.

Freytag, G. 1895. *Freytag's technique of the drama.* Chicago: Griggs. Originally published in 1863.

Friedman, J. 1991. Further notes on the adventures of Phallus in Blunderland. In L. Nencel and P. Pels, eds. *Constructing knowledge.* London: Sage.

Friedman, S. 1993. *The new language of change.* New York: Guilford Press.

Friedman, S., and M. T. Fanger. 1991. *Expanding therapeutic possibilities: Putting grief psychotherapy to work.* New York: Livingston.

Frindte, W. 1991. Konstruktion von Welten. Unpublished manuscript, Friedrich-Schiller-Universität Jena.

Frisby, D. 1985. *Fragments of modernity.* Cambridge: Polity Press.

Frost, P. J., et al. 1991. *Reframing organizational culture.* Newbury Park, Calif.: Sage.

Frug, M. J. 1992. *Postmodern legal feminism.* New York: Routledge.

Fruggeri, L. 1992. Therapeutic process as the social construction of change. In S. McNamee and K. Gergen, eds. *Therapy as social construction.* London: Sage.

Frye, N. 1957. *Anatomy of criticism.* Princeton: Princeton University Press.

Fuller, S. 1988. *Social epistemology.* Bloomington: Indiana University Press.

―――― 1993. *Philosophy of science and its discontents.* New York: Guilford.

Furby, L. 1979. Individualistic bias in studies of locus of control. In A. Buss, ed. *Psychology in social context.* New York: Halstead Press.

Furnham, A., and V. Lowik. 1984. Lay theories of the causes of alcoholism. *British Journal of Medical Psychology,* 57: 319–332.

Furst, L. R. 1969. *Romanticism in perspective.* London: Methuen.

Gadamer, H. 1975. *Truth and method,* ed. C. Barden and J. Cumming. New York: Seabury. Originally published in 1960.

Gagnon, J., and W. Simon. 1973. *Sexual conduct.* Chicago: Aldine.

Galambos, J. A., R. P. Abelson, and J. B. Black. 1986. *Knowledge structures.* Hillsdale, N.J.: Erlbaum.

Gallie, W. B. 1964. *Philosophy and the historical understanding.* London: Chatto and Windus.

Gardner, C. B. 1994. The social construction of pregnancy and fetal development: Notes on a nineteenth-century rhetoric of endangerment. In T. R. Sarbin and J. I. Kitsuse, eds. *Constructing the social.* London: Sage.

Garfield, J. L. 1988. *Belief in psychology.* Cambridge: MIT Press.

Garfinkel, H. 1967. *Studies in ethnomethodology.* Englewood Cliffs, N.J.: Prentice-Hall.

Geertz, C. 1973. *The interpretation of cultures.* New York: Basic Books.

―――― 1975. On the nature of anthropological understanding. *American Scientist,* 63: 47–53.

Gellatly, A. 1989a. The misleading concept of cognitive competencies. *Theory and Psychology,* 2: 363–390.

―――― 1989b. The myth of cognitive diagnostics. In A. Gellatly, D. Rogers, and J. A. Sloboda, eds. *Cognition and social worlds.* Oxford: Clarendon.

Genette, R. 1980. *Narrative discourse.* Ithaca: Cornell University Press.

Gergen, K. J. 1973. Social psychology as history. *Journal of Personality and Social Psychology,* 26: 309–320.

——— 1984. An introduction to historical social psychology. In K. Gergen and M. Gergen, eds. *Historical social psychology*. Hillsdale, N.J.: Erlbaum.

——— 1985. The social constructionist movement in modern psychology. *American Psychologist*, 40: 266–275.

——— 1988a. Knowledge and social process. In D. Bar-Tal and A. Kruglanski, eds. *The social psychology of knowledge*. Cambridge: Cambridge University Press.

——— 1988b. If persons are texts. In S. B. Messer, L. A. Sass, and R. L. Woolfolk, eds. *Hermeneutics and psychological theory*. New Brunswick, N.J.: Rutgers University Press.

——— 1990. Realities and their relationships. In W. J. Baker, M. E. Hyland, R. van Hezewijk, and S. Terwee, eds. *Recent trends in theoretical psychology: VII*, pp. 51–62. New York: Springer-Verlag.

——— 1991a. Metaphors of the social world. In D. Leary, ed. *Metaphors in the history of psychology*. Cambridge: Cambridge University Press.

——— 1991b. *The saturated self*. New York: Basic Books.

——— 1994. *Toward the transformation in social knowledge*, 2nd ed. London: Sage.

——— In press a. Social construction and the educational process. In L. Steffe, ed. *Alternative epistemologies in education*. Hillsdale, N.J.: Erlbaum.

——— In press b. Mind, text, and society: Self memory in social context. U. Neisser and R. Fivush, eds. *The remembered self*. New York: Cambridge University Press.

Gergen, K. J., and K. E. Davis, eds. 1985. *The social construction of the person*. New York: Springer-Verlag.

Gergen, K. J., and M. M. Gergen. 1983. Narratives of the self. In T. R. Sarbin and K. E. Scheibe, eds. *Studies in social identity*. New York: Praeger.

——— 1986. Narrative form and the construction of psychological science. In T. R. Sarbin, ed. *Narrative psychology: The storied nature of human conduct*. New York: Praeger.

——— 1987. Narratives of relationship. In M. McGhee, D. D. Clarke, and R. Burnett, eds. *Accounting for relationship*. Oxford: Blackwell.

——— 1988. Narrative and the self as relationship. In L. Berkowitz, ed. *Advances in experimental social psychology*. San Diego: Academic Press.

Gergen, K. J., G. Gloger-Tippelt, and P. Berkowitz. 1990. Everyday conceptions of the developing child. In G. Semin and K. J. Gergen, eds. *Everyday understanding: Social and scientific implications*. London: Sage.

Gergen, M. M. 1980. Antecedents and consequences of self-attributional preferences in later life. Ph.D. diss., Temple University.

——— ed. 1988a. *Feminist thought and the structure of knowledge*. New York: New York University Press.

——— 1988b. Toward a feminist metatheory and methodology in the social sciences. In M. Gergen, ed. *Feminist thought and the structure of knowledge*. New York: New York University Press.

——— 1989. Talking about menopause: A dialogic analysis. In L. E. Thomas, ed. *Research on adulthood and on aging: The human sciences approach*. Albany: State University of New York Press.

———— 1992. Life stories: Pieces of a dream. In G. Rosenwald and R. Ochberg, eds. *Telling lives*. New Haven: Yale University Press.

Gewirth, A. 1987. *Reason and morality*. Chicago: University of Chicago Press.

Gibson, J. J. 1979. *The ecological approach to visual perception*. Boston: Houghton Mifflin.

Giddens, A. 1976. *New rules of sociological method*. New York: Basic Books.

———— 1984. *The constitution of society: Introduction of the theory of structuration*. Berkeley: University of California Press.

———— 1991. *Modernity and self-identity*. Stanford: Stanford University Press.

Gigerenzer, G., and D. J. Murray. 1987. *Cognition as intuitive statistics*. Hillsdale, N.J.: Erlbaum.

Gilligan, C. 1982. *In a different voice: Psychological theory and women's development*. Cambridge: Harvard University Press.

Gilligan, C., N. Lyons, and T. Hanmer. 1989. *Making connections*. Troy, N.Y.: Emma Willard School.

Gilly, M. 1980. *Maitres-eleves: Roles institutionnels et representations*. Paris: Presses Universitaires de France.

Gilmour, R., and S. Duck. 1986. *The emerging field of personal relationships*. Hillsdale, N.J.: Erlbaum.

Giorgi, A. 1985. *Phenomenology and psychological research*. Pittsburgh: Duquesne University Press.

Goffman, E. 1959. *The presentation of self in everyday life*. New York: Doubleday.

———— 1961. *Asylums: Essays on the social situation of mental patients and other inmates*. Garden City, N.J.: Doubleday.

———— 1967. *Interaction ritual: Essays in face-to-face behavior*. Chicago: University of Chicago Press.

———— 1969. *Strategic interaction*. Philadelphia: University of Pennsylvania Press.

Goldman, A. 1988. *Moral knowledge*. London: Routledge.

Goodman, N. 1978. *Ways of worldmaking*. New York: Hackett.

Goodnow, J. J. 1984. Parents' ideas about parenting and development: A review of issues and recent work. In M. E. Lamb, A. L. Brown, and B. Rogoll, eds. *Advances in developmental psychology*. Hillsdale, N.J.: Erlbaum.

———— 1988. Parents' ideas, actions, and feelings: Models and methods from developmental and social psychology. *Child Psychology*, 59: 286–320.

Goodnow, J. J., and W. A. Collins. 1990. *Development according to parents*. Hillsdale, N.J.: Erlbaum.

Goolishian, H., and H. Anderson. 1987. Language systems and therapy: An evolving idea. *Journal of Psychotherapy*, 24: 529–538.

———— 1992. The client is the expert: A not-knowing approach to therapy. In S. McNamee and K. Gergen, eds. *Therapy as social construction*. London: Sage.

Goolishian, H., and L. Winderman. 1988. Constructivism, autopoiesis and problem determined systems. *Irish Journal of Psychology*, 9: 130–43.

Gordon, R. 1990. *Anorexia and bulimia*. Cambridge: Basil Blackwell.

Gouldner, A. W. 1960. A norm of reciprocity: A preliminary statement. *American Sociological Review*, 25: 161–178.

Gowen, S. G. 1991. Beliefs about literacy: Measuring women into silence—hearing women into speech. *Discourse and Society*, 1: 297–311.

Grace, G. W. 1987. *The linguistic construction of reality.* London: Routledge.

Graumann, C. F. 1988. Der Kognitivismus in der Sozialpsychologie—Die Kehrseite der Wende, *Psychologische Rundschau,* 39: 83–90.

Graumann, C. F., and M. Sommer. 1984. Schema and inference: Models in cognitive social psychology. In J. R. Royce and L. P. Mos, eds. *Annals of theoretical psychology,* vol. 1. New York: Plenum Press.

Gray, B., M. Bougan, and A. Donnellon. 1985. Organizations as constructions and destructions of meaning. *Journal of Management,* 11: 77–92.

Green, B. 1977. On the evaluation of sociological theory. *Philosophy of the Social Sciences,* 7: 33–50.

——— 1988. *Literary methods and sociological theory.* Chicago: University of Chicago Press.

Greenberg, D. F. 1988. *The construction of homosexuality.* Chicago: University of Chicago Press.

Greenblat, C. S. 1983. A hit is a hit is a hit . . . Or is it? In R. J. Finnkelhor, R. J. Gelles, G. T. Hotaling, and M. A. Strauss, eds. *The dark side of families: Current family violence research,* pp. 132–158. Beverly Hills, Calif.: Sage.

Greenwood, J. D. 1991. *Relations and representations.* London: Routledge.

——— 1992. Realism, empiricism and social constructionism: Psychological theory and the social dimensions of mind and action. *Theory and Psychology,* 2: 131–152.

Gregory, D. 1994. *Geographical imaginations.* Cambridge: Blackwell.

Greimas, A. 1987. *On meaning: Selected writings in semiotic theory.* Minneapolis: University of Minnesota Press.

Groeben, N. 1990. Subjective theories and the explanation of human action. In G. Semin and K. J. Gergen, eds. *Everyday understanding.* London: Sage.

Gross, M. L. 1978. *The psychological society.* New York: Random House.

Gubrium, J., and J. A. Holstein. 1990. *What is a family?* Mountainview, Calif.: Mayfield.

Gubrium, J., J. A. Holstein, and D. Buckholdt. 1994. *Constructing the life course.* Dix Hills, N.Y.: General Hall.

Guerin, B. 1992. Behavior analysis and the social construction of knowledge. *American Psychologist,* 47: 1423–1432.

Gurvitch, G. 1971. *The social frameworks of knowledge.* New York: Harper and Row. Originally published in 1966.

Haan, N., E. Aerts, and B. Cooper. 1985. *On moral grounds.* New York: New York University Press.

Habermas, J. 1971. *Knowledge and human interest.* Boston: Beacon Press.

——— 1975. *Legitimation crisis.* Boston: Beacon Press.

——— 1979. *Communication and the evolution of society.* Boston: Beacon Press.

——— 1983. Modernity—an incomplete project. In H. Foster, ed. *The anti-aesthetic: Essays on postmodern culture.* Port Townsend, Wash.: Bay Press.

Hamilton, D., and T. Rose. 1980. Illusionary correlation and the maintenance of stereotypic beliefs. *Journal of Personality and Social Psychology,* 39: 832–845.

Hampden-Turner, C. 1970. *Radical man: The process of psycho-social development.* Cambridge: Schenkman.

Handler, J. F., and Y. Hasenfeld. 1991. *The moral construction of poverty.* Newbury Park: Sage.

Hankiss, A. 1981. Ontologies of the self: On the mythological rearranging of one's life-history. In D. Bertaux, ed. *Biography and society.* Beverly Hills, Calif.: Sage.

Hanson, N. R. 1958. *Patterns of discovery.* Cambridge: Cambridge University Press.

Haraway, D. 1988. Situated knowledges: The science question in feminism and the privilege of partial perspective. *Feminist Studies,* 14: 575–599.

Hardin, G. 1968. The tragedy of the commons. *Science,* 162: 1243–1248.

Harding, S. 1986. *The science question in feminism.* Ithaca: Cornell University Press.

Harding, S., and M. Hintikka, eds. 1983. *Discovering reality: Feminist perspectives on epistemology, metaphysics, method, and philosophy of science.* Dordrecht: Reidel.

Hardy, B. 1968. Towards a poetics of fiction: An approach through narrative. *Novel,* 2: 5–14.

Hare-Mustin, R., and J. Marecek. 1988. The meaning of difference: Gender theory, postmodernism, and psychology. *American Psychologist,* 43: 455–464.

Harkness, S., and C. M. Super. 1983. The cultural construction of child development. *Ethos,* 11: 222–231.

Harré, R. 1979. Social being: A theory for social psychology. Oxford: Basil Blackwell.

—— 1983. *Personal being.* Cambridge: Harvard University Press.

—— 1986. The social constructionist viewpoint. In R. Harr, ed. *The social construction of emotion.* Oxford: Blackwell.

—— 1988. *Varieties of realism.* Oxford: Oxford University Press.

—— 1992. What is real psychology: A plea for persons. *Theory and Psychology,* 2: 153–158.

Harré, R., and P. Secord. 1972. *The explanation of social behaviour.* Oxford: Blackwell.

Harris, J. F. 1992. *Against relativism: A philosophical defense of method.* La Salle, Ill.: Open Court.

Harris, L. M., K. J. Gergen, and J. W. Lannamann. 1986. Aggression rituals. *Communication Monographs,* 53: 252–265.

Hartmann, H. 1960. *Psychoanalysis and moral values.* New York: International Universities Press.

Harvey, D. 1989. *The condition of postmodernity.* London: Blackwell.

Harwood, H. J., D. M. Napolitano, and P. L. Kristiansen. 1983. *Economic costs to society of alcohol and drug abuse and mental illness.* Research Triangle, N.C.: Research Triangle Institute.

Hawkesworth, M. 1992. From objectivity to objectification: Feminist objections. *Annals of Scholarship,* 8: 451–477.

Heelas, P., and A. Lock. 1981. *Indigenous psychologies: The anthropology of the self.* London: Academic Press.

Hegel, G. W. 1979. *Phenomenology of spirit.* New York: Oxford Press.

Heider, F. 1958. *The psychology of interpersonal relations.* New York: Wiley.

324   *References*

Heller, A., and F. Feher. 1988. *The postmodern political condition.* New York: Columbia University Press.

Hendrick, C., ed. 1989. *Close relationships.* Newbury Park, Calif.: Sage.

Henriques, J., W. Hollway, C. Urwin, C. Venn, and V. Walkerdine. 1984. *Changing the subject: Psychology, social regulation and subjectivity.* London: Methuen.

Henwood, K., and G. Coughlan. 1993. The construction of "closeness" in mother-daughter relationships. In N. Coupland and J. Nussbaum, eds. *Discourse and lifespan identity.* London: Sage.

Herzlich, C. 1973. *Health and illness: A social psychological analysis.* London: Academic Press.

Higgins, T., and J. Bargh. 1987. Social cognition and social perception. *Annual Review of Psychology.* Palo Alto, Calif.: Annual Reviews, Inc.

Hinde, R. A. 1988. *Relationships within families.* New York: Oxford University Press.

Hirsch, E. D. 1967. *Validity in interpretation.* New Haven: Yale University Press.

——— 1976. *The aims of interpretation.* Chicago: University of Chicago Press.

Hirschauer, S. 1991. The manufacture of bodies in surgery. *Social Studies of Science,* 21: 279–319.

Hitler, A. 1943. *Mein Kampf.* New York: Houghton Mifflin.

Hochschild, A. 1983. *The Managed Heart.* Berkeley: University of California Press.

Hoffman, L. 1981. *Foundations of family therapy.* New York: Basic.

——— 1985. Constructing realities: An art of lenses. *Family Process,* 29: 1–12.

——— 1992. A reflexive stance for family therapy. In S. McNamee and K. J. Gergen, eds. *Therapy as social construction.* London: Sage.

Hollis, M. 1977. *Models of man.* London: Cambridge University Press.

Hollway, W. 1989. *Subjectivity and method in psychology.* London: Sage.

Holzkamp, K. 1976. *Kritische Psychologie.* Hamburg: Fischer, Tasch Verlag.

Hopper, R. 1992. *Telephone conversation.* Bloomington: Indiana University Press.

Horkheimer, M., and T. W. Adorno. 1972. *Dialectic of enlightenment.* Trans. J. Cumming. New York: Seabury.

Howard, G. S. 1988. *A tale of two stories.* Notre Dame, Ind.: Academic Press.

Hubbard, R. 1983. Have only men evolved? In S. Harding and M. Hintikka, eds. *Discovering reality: Feminist perspectives on epistemology, metaphysics, methodology, and philosophy of science.* Dordrecht: Reidel.

——— 1988. Some thoughts about the masculinity of the natural sciences. In M. Gergen, ed. *Feminist thought and the structure of knowledge.* New York: New York University Press.

Hull, C. L. 1920. Quantitative aspects of the evolution of concepts: An experimental study. *Psychological Monographs,* 28: 123–125.

——— 1943. *Principles of behavior.* New York: Appleton-Century Crofts.

Hume, K. 1984. *Fantasy and mimesis.* London: Methuen.

Hutschemaekers, G. 1990. *Neurosen in Nederland.* Nijmegen: Sun.

Ibanez, T. G. 1983. Los efectos politicos de la psicologia social. *Cuadernos de Psicologia,* 11: 95–106.

——— 1988. *Ideologias de la vida cotidiana.* Barcelona: Sendai ediciones.

——— 1991. Social psychology and the rhetoric of truth. *Theory and Psychology,* 1: 187–201.

———— 1992. Cómo se puede no ser constructivista hoy en día? *Revista de Psicoterapia*, 3, no. 12: 17–27.

Ingleby, D. 1980. Understanding mental illness. In D. Ingleby, ed. *Critical psychiatry: The politics of mental health*, pp. 23–71. New York: Pantheon.

Ingram, D. 1990. *Critical theory and philosophy*. New York: Paragon House.

Irigaray, L. 1974. *Speculum of the other woman*. Ithaca: Cornell University Press.

Iyengar, S. 1991. *Is anyone responsible? How television frames political issues.* Chicago: University of Chicago Press.

Jaggar, A. 1983. *Feminist politics and human nature*. New York: Rowman.

Jagtenberg, T. 1983. *The social construction of science*. Dordrecht: D. Reidel.

Janssen-Jurreit, M. 1982. *Sexism: The male monopoly on the history of thought.* London: Pluto Press.

Jansz, J. 1991. *Person, self and moral demands*. Leiden: DSWO Press.

Jayyusi, L. 1993. Premeditation and happenstance: The social construction of intention, action and knowledge. *Human Studies*, 16: 435–454.

Jennings, R. 1988. Translation, interpretation and understanding. *Philosophy of Social Science*, 18: 343–353.

Jodelet, D. 1984. The representation of the body and its transformations. In R. Farr and S. Moscovici, eds. *Social representations*. Cambridge: Cambridge University Press.

Johnson, P. B., and I. H. Frieze. 1978. Biases in psychology: What are the facts? In I. Frieze, ed. *Women and sex roles: A social psychological perspective*. New York: Norton.

Johnson-Laird, P. N. 1988. *The computer and the mind*. Cambridge: Harvard University Press.

Jones, E. E. 1990. *Interpersonal perception*. New York: W. H. Freeman.

Josselson, R., and A. Lieblich. 1993. *The narrative study of lives*. London: Sage.

Kagan, J. 1983. Classifications of the child. In P. H. Mussen, ed. *Handbook of Child Psychology*. Vol. 1, *History, Theory and Methods*. New York: Wiley.

Kahn, J., J. C. Coyne, and G. Margolin. 1985. Depression and marital disagreement: The social construction of despair. *Journal of Social and Personal Relationships*, 2: 445–461.

Kant, I. 1956. *Critique of practical reason*. Trans. L. W. Beck. New York: Bobbs-Merrill.

———— 1971. *The doctrine of virtue*. Part 2 of *The metaphysics of morals*. Trans. M. J. Gregor. Philadelphia: University of Pennsylvania Press.

Katz, J. 1989. Rational common ground in the sociology of knowledge. *Philosophy of the Social Sciences*, 19: 257–271.

Kaye, K. 1982. *The mental and social life of babies*. Chicago: University of Chicago Press.

Kaysen, S. 1993. *Girl, interrupted*. New York: Turtle Bay.

Keeney, B. 1983. *Aesthetics of change*. New York: Guilford.

Keller, E. F. 1985. *Reflections on gender and science*. New Haven: Yale University Press.

Kelley, H. H. 1972. *Causal schemata and the attribution process*. New York: General Learning Press.

Kelly, G. A. 1955. *The psychology of personal constructs*. New York: Norton.

Kelly, M. H., and F. C. Keil. 1985. The more things change . . . : Metamorphoses and conceptual structure. *Cognitive Science,* 9: 403–416.

Kelman, H. 1968. *A time to speak: On human values and social research.* San Francisco: Jossey-Bass.

Kermode, F. 1967. *The sense of an ending.* New York: Oxford University Press.

Kessen, W. 1979. The American child and other cultural inventions. *American Psychologist,* 34: 815–820.

——— 1990. *The rise and fall of development.* Worcester, Mass.: Clark University Press.

Kessler, S. J., and W. McKenna. 1978. *Gender: An ethnomethodological approach.* New York: Wiley.

Kiesler, C. A., and A. Sibulkin. 1987. *Mental hospitalization: Myths and facts about a national crisis.* Newbury Park, Calif.: Sage.

Kilduff, M. 1993. Deconstructing organizations. *Academy of Management Review,* 18: 13–31.

Kirk, S., M. Siporin, and H. Kutchins. 1989. The prognosis for social work diagnosis. *Social Casework: The Journal of Contemporary Social Work,* 70: 295–304.

Kirkpatrick, J. 1985. How personal differences can make a difference. In K. J. Gergen and K. E. Davis, eds. *The social construction of the person.* New York: Springer-Verlag.

Kirschner, S. In press. Sources of redemption in psychoanalytic developmental psychology. In G. F. Graumann and K. J. Gergen, eds. *Historical dimensions of psychological discourse.* Cambridge: Cambridge University Press.

Kissling, E. A. 1991. Street harassment: The language of sexual terrorism. *Discourse and Society,* 2: 451–460.

Kitchener, R. F. 1986. *Piaget's theory of knowledge: Genetic epistemology and scientific reason.* New Haven: Yale University Press.

Kitzinger, C. 1987. *The social construction of lesbianism.* London: Sage.

Kleinman, A. 1988. *The illness narratives.* New York: Basic Books.

Knorr, K. D., R. Krohn, and R. Whitley, eds. 1981. *The social process of scientific investigation.* Dordrecht: Reidel.

Knorr-Cetina, K. D. 1981. *The manufacture of knowledge.* Oxford: Pergamon.

Knorr-Cetina, K. D., and M. Mulkay. 1983. *Science observed.* Beverly Hills, Calif.: Sage.

Knudson, R. M. 1985. Marital compatibility and mutual identity confirmation. In W. Ickes, ed. *Compatible and incompatible relationships.* New York: Springer-Verlag.

Koch, S. 1963. Epilogue. In S. Koch, ed. *Psychology: A study of a science,* vol. 3. New York: McGraw-Hill.

Kohlberg, L. 1971. *Collected papers on moral development and moral education.* Cambridge: Moral Education and Research Foundation.

Kohli, M. 1981. Biography: Account, text and method. In D. Bertaux, ed. *Biography and society.* Beverly Hills, Calif.: Sage.

Kondo, D. K. 1990. *Crafting selves: Power, gender and discourses of identity in a Japanese workplace.* Chicago: University of Chicago Press.

Kovel, J. 1980. The American mental health industry. In D. Ingleby, ed. *Crit-*

ical psychiatry: The politics of mental health, pp. 72–101. New York: Pantheon.

——— 1988. *The radical spirit: Essays on psychoanalysis and society.* London: Free Press.

Krausz, M., ed. 1989. *Relativism, interpretation and confrontation.* Notre Dame, Ind.: University of Notre Dame Press.

Krieger, M. 1956. *The new apologists for poetry.* Minneapolis: University of Minnesota Press.

Kruglanski, A. 1992. *Lay epistemics and human knowledge.* London: Plenum.

Kuhn, T. S. 1962. *The structure of scientific revolutions.* Chicago: University of Chicago Press.

——— 1970. *The structure of scientific revolutions.* 2nd rev. ed. Chicago: University of Chicago Press.

——— 1977. *The essential tension.* Chicago: University of Chicago Press.

Kukla, A. 1989. Nonempirical issues in psychology. *American Psychologist,* 44: 785–794.

Kulka, R., J. Veroff, and E. Douvan. 1979. Social class and the use of professional help for personal problems: 1957–1976. *Journal of Health and Social Behavior,* 26: 2–17.

Kurtines, W. M., and J. L. Gewirtz. 1987. *Social interaction and sociomoral development.* New York: Wiley.

Kvale, S., ed. 1992. *Psychology and postmodernism.* London: Sage.

Labov, W. 1982. Speech actions and reactions in personal narrative. In D. Tanner, ed. *Analyzing discourse: Text and talk.* Washington, D.C.: Georgetown University Press.

Lakatos, I. 1970. Falsification and the methodology of scientific research programmes. In I. Lakatos and A. Musgrave, eds. *Criticism and the growth of knowledge.* Cambridge: Cambridge University Press.

Lakoff, G., and M. Johnson. 1980. *Metaphors we live by.* Chicago: University of Chicago Press.

Landau, M. 1991. *Narratives of human evolution.* New Haven: Yale University Press.

Lang, B. 1990. *The anatomy of philosophical style.* London: Basil Blackwell.

Laqueur, T. 1990. *Making sex: Body and gender from the Greeks to Freud.* Cambridge: Harvard University Press.

Larsen, K. 1980. *Social psychology: Crisis or failure.* Montmouth, Oreg.: Institute for Theoretical History.

———, ed. 1986. *Dialectics and ideology in psychology.* New Jersey: Ablex.

Lasch, C. 1979. *The culture of narcissism.* New York: Norton.

Lather, P. 1991. *Getting smart.* London: Routledge.

Latour, B. 1987. *Science in action.* Cambridge: Harvard University Press.

Latour, B., and S. Woolgar. 1979. *Laboratory life: The social construction of scientific facts.* Beverly Hills, Calif.: Sage.

Laudan, L. 1977. *Progress and its problems.* Berkeley, Calif.: University of California Press.

Lax, W. D. 1992. Postmodern thinking in a clinical practice. In S. McNamee and K. J. Gergen, eds. *Therapy as social construction.* London: Sage.

Lazarus, R. S. 1991. Progress on a cognitive-motivational-relational theory of emotion. *American Psychologist*, 46: 819–834.

Leahy, R. L. 1983. *The child's construction of social inequality*. New York: Academic Press.

Leary, D. 1990. *Metaphors in the history of psychology*. Cambridge: Cambridge University Press.

Le Fevre, K. B. 1987. *Invention as a social act*. Carbondale: Southern Illinois University Press.

Leifer, R. 1990. The medical model as the ideology of the therapeutic state. *Journal of Mind and Behavior*, 11: 247–258.

Leppington, R. 1991. From constructionism to social constructionism and doing critical therapy. *Human Systems*, 2: 79–104.

Lessl, T. 1993. Punctuation in the constitution of public identities: Primary and secondary sequences in the Scopes Trial. *Communication Theory*, 3: 91–112.

Leudar, I. 1990. Sociogenesis, coordination and mutualism. *Journal for the Theory of Social Behavior*, 21: 197–219.

Levine, M. 1966. Hypothesis behavior by humans during discrimination learning. *Journal of Experimental Psychology*, 71: 331–336.

Levinson, S. 1982. Law as literature. *Texas Law Review*, 60: 388–411.

Lévi-Strauss, C. 1969. *The raw and the cooked*. Trans. D. Weighton. New York: Harper and Row.

Lincoln, Y. 1985. *Organizational theory and inquiry: The paradigm revolution*. Beverly Hills, Calif.: Sage.

Lipchik, E. 1993. "Both/And" solutions. In S. Friedman, ed. *The new language of change*. New York: Guilford Press.

Lippman, S. 1986. "Nothing but the facts, ma'am": The impact of testimony construction and narrative style on jury decisions. Unpublished senior thesis, Swarthmore College.

Livingstone, M. 1987. The representation of personal relationships in television drama: Realism, convention and morality. In R. Burnett, P. McGhee, and D. Clarke, eds. *Accounting for relationships*. London: Methuen.

London, P. 1986. *The modes and morals of psychotherapy*. New York: Hemisphere Publishing.

Long Laws, J. 1971. A feminist review of marital adjustment literature: The rape of the Locke. *Journal of Marriage and the Family*, 33: 483–517.

Longino, H. 1989. Feminist critiques of rationality: Critiques of science or philosophy of science. *Women's Studies International Forum*, 12: 261–270.

——— 1990. *Science as social knowledge: Values and objectivity in scientific inquiry*. Princeton: Princeton University Press.

Lopes, L. L. 1991. The rhetoric of irrationality. *Theory and Psychology*, 1: 65–82.

Lopez-Pinero, J. M. 1983. *Historical origins of the concept of neurosis*. Trans. D. Berrios. Cambridge: Cambridge University Press.

Lorber, J., and S. A. Farrell. 1990. *The social construction of gender*. Newbury Park, Calif.: Sage.

Loseke, D. R. 1992. *The battered women and shelters: The social construction of wife abuse*. Albany: State University of New York Press.

Luhman, N. 1987. *Love as passion.* Cambridge: Harvard University Press.

Lukacs, G. 1964. *Studies in European realism.* New York: Grosset and Dunlap.

Lukes, S. 1974. *Power: A radical view.* London: Macmillan.

—— 1985. *Individualism.* Oxford: Blackwell.

Lulofs, R. S. 1952. The social construction of forgiveness. *Human Systems,* 3: 183–197.

Lutz, C. 1985. *Depression and the translation of emotional worlds.* In G. White and J. Kirkpatrick, eds. *Person, self and experience: Exploring Pacific ethnopsychologies.* Berkeley: University of California Press.

—— 1986a. The anthropology of emotions. *Annual Anthropology Review,* 15: 405–436.

—— 1986b. Emotion, thought and estrangement: Emotion as a cultural category. *Cultural Anthropology,* 1: 287–309.

—— 1988. *Unnatural emotions.* Chicago: University of Chicago Press.

Lutz, C., and L. Abu-Lughod, eds. 1990. *Language and the politics of emotion.* Cambridge: Cambridge University Press.

Lyons, W. 1986. *The disappearance of introspection.* Cambridge: MIT Press.

Lyotard, J. F. 1984. *The post-modern condition: A report on knowledge.* Minneapolis: University of Minnesota Press.

MacCorquodale, K., and P. E. Meehl. 1948. On a distinction between hypothetical constructs and intervening variables. *Psychological Review,* 55: 95–107.

MacFarlane, A. 1978. *The origins of English individualism.* Oxford: Blackwell.

MacIntyre, A. 1973. Ideology, social science and revolution. *Comparative Politics,* 5: 321–341.

—— 1984. *After virtue.* 2nd ed. Notre Dame, Ind.: University of Notre Dame Press.

Mackie, D. M., and D. L. Hamilton, eds. 1993. *Affect, cognition, and stereotyping: Interactive processes in group perception.* San Diego: Academic Press.

MacKinnon, C. 1987. *Feminism unmodified.* Cambridge: Harvard University Press.

Mahoney, M. 1991. Interactive processes in group perception. *Human change processes.* New York: Basic Books.

Mancuso, J. C., and T. R. Sarbin. 1983. The self-narrative in the enactment of roles. In T. R. Sarbin and K. E. Scheibe, eds. *Studies in social identity.* New York: Praeger.

Mandler, G., and W. Kessen. 1975. *The language of psychology.* Melbourne, Fla.: Krieger.

Mandler, J. M. 1984. *Stories, scripts and scenes: Aspects of schema theory.* Hillsdale, N.J.: Erlbaum.

Mannheim, K. 1951. *Ideology and utopia.* New York: Harcourt Brace. Originally published in 1929.

Marcus, D. K., and M. Wiener. 1989. Anorexia nervosa reconceptualized from a psychological transaction perspective. *American Journal of Orthopsychiatry,* 59: 346–354.

Marcus, G. 1980. Rhetoric and the ethnographic genre in anthropological research. *Current Anthropology,* 21: 507–514.

—— 1982. Ethnographics as text. *Annual Review of Anthropology,* 11: 25–69.

Marcus, G. E., and M. M. J. Fischer. 1986. *Anthropology as cultural critique.* Chicago: University of Chicago Press.

Marcuse, H. 1964. *One-dimensional man: Studies in the ideology of advanced industrial society.* Boston: University Press.

Margolis, J. 1966. *Psychotherapy and morality.* New York: Random House.

——— 1991. *The truth about relativism.* Cambridge, Mass.: Blackwell.

Markman, E. M. 1989. *Categorization and naming in children: Problems in induction.* Cambridge: MIT Press.

Marsh, P., E. Rosser, and R. Harré. 1978. *The rules of disorder.* London: Routledge and Kegan Paul.

Martin, E. M. 1987. *The woman in the body: A cultural analysis of reproduction.* Boston: Beacon Press.

Martin, J. 1990. Deconstructing organizational taboos: The suppression of gender conflict in organizations. *Organization Science,* 1: 339–359.

Martin, W. 1986. *Recent theories of narrative.* Ithaca: Cornell University Press.

Martinez, J. 1984. *Chicano psychology.* New York: Academic Press.

Marx, K., and F. Engels. 1967. *The communist manifesto.* Harmondsworth, U.K.: Penguin.

Maslow, A. H. 1961. Peak-experiences as acute identity experiences. *American Journal of Psychoanalysis,* 21: 254–260.

Masserman, J. 1960. *Psychoanalysis and human values.* New York: Grune and Stratton.

Maturana, U. 1988. Reality: The search for objectivity or the quest for a compelling argument. *Irish Journal of Psychology,* 9: 25–82.

Mayo, E. 1933. *The human problems of an industrial civilization.* New York: Macmillan.

Maze, J. R. 1991. Representationism, realism and the redundancy of mentalese. *Theory and Psychology,* 1: 163–186.

McAdams, D. P. 1985. *Power, intimacy and the life story.* New York: Guilford.

——— 1993. *The stories we live by.* New York: William Morrow and Sons.

McCloskey, D. N. 1985. *The rhetoric of economics.* Madison: University of Wisconsin Press.

McCrea, F. B. 1983. The politics of menopause: The "discovery" of a deficiency disease. *Social Problems,* 31: 111–123.

McGillicuddy-DeLisi, A. V. 1980. The role of parental beliefs in the family as a system of mutual influences. *Family Relations,* 29: 317–323.

McGowan, J. 1991. *Postmodernism and its critics.* Ithaca: Cornell University Press.

McGuire, W. J. 1973. The yin and the yang of progress in social psychology: Seven koans. *Journal of Personality and Social Psychology,* 26: 446–456.

McKay, V. 1993. Making connections: Narrative as the expression of continuity between generations of grandparents and grandchildren. In N. Coupland and J. Nussbaum, eds. *Discourse and lifespan identity.* London: Sage.

McKinlay, A., and J. Potter. 1987. Social representations: A conceptual critique. *Journal for the Theory of Social Behavior,* 17: 471–488.

McLaughlin, M. L. 1984. *Conversation: How talk is organized.* Beverly Hills, Calif.: Sage.

McNamee, S. 1988. Accepting research as social intervention: Implications for a systematic epistemology. *Communication Quarterly,* 36: 50–68.

—— 1992. Reconstructing identity: The communal construction of crisis. In S. McNamee and K. Gergen, eds. *Therapy as social construction.* London: Sage.

McNamee, S., and K. J. Gergen, eds. 1992. *Therapy as social construction.* New York: Macmillan.

Mead, G. H. 1934. *Mind, self and society.* Chicago: Chicago University Press.

Mechanic, D. 1980. *Mental health and social policy.* Englewood Cliffs, N.J.: Prentice-Hall.

Megill, A. 1991. Four senses of objectivity. *Annals of Scholarship,* 8: 301–320.

Mendelsohn, E. 1977. The social construction of scientific knowledge. In E. Mendelsohn and P. Weingert, eds. *The social production of scientific knowledge.* Dordrecht: Reidel.

Meng, K., and V. M. Quasthoff, eds. 1992. *Narrative development in a social context.* Hillsdale, N.J.: Erlbaum.

Menzies, I. 1960. A case study in the functioning of social systems as a defence against anxiety. *Human Relations,* 13: 95–121.

Messer, S. B., L. A. Sass, and R. L. Woolfolk, eds. 1988. *Hermeneutics and psychological theory.* New Brunswick, N.J.: Rutgers University Press.

Middleton, D., and D. Edwards, eds. 1990. *Collective remembering.* London: Sage.

Milgram, S. 1974. *Obedience to authority.* New York: Harper and Row.

Millen, J. H. 1992. The social construction of blame: A mediation case study. *Human Systems,* 2: 199–216.

Miller, G. A., E. Galanter, and K. Pribram. 1960. *Plans and the structure of behavior.* New York: Holt, Rinehart and Winston.

Miller, J. B. 1976. *Toward a new psychology of women.* Boston: Beacon Press.

Miller, P. J., R. Potts, H. Fung, L. Horgstra, and J. Matz. 1990. Narrative practices and the social construction of self in childhood. *American Ethologist,* 17: 292–311.

Mills, C. W. 1940. Situated actions and vocabularies of motives. *American Sociological Review,* 5: 904–913.

Minh-ha, T. T. 1989. *Woman native other.* Bloomington: Indiana University Press.

Mink, L. A. 1969. History and fiction as modes of comprehension. *New Literary History,* 1: 556–569.

Mischler, E. G. 1986. *Research interviewing: Context and narrative.* Cambridge: Harvard University Press.

Mitchell, W. J. T. 1982. *The politics of interpretation.* Chicago: University of Chicago Press.

Mitroff, I. 1974. *The subjective side of science.* Amsterdam: Elsevier.

Moors, A. 1991. Women and the Orient: A note on difference. In L. Nencel and P. Pels, eds. *Constructing knowledge.* London: Sage.

Morawski, J. G. 1979. The structure of psychological communities: A framework for examining the sociology of social psychology. In L. H. Strickland, ed. *Soviet and western perspectives on social psychology.* Oxford: Pergamon Press.

—— 1987. After reflection: Psychologists' uses of history. In H. Stam, T. Rogers, and K. Gergen, eds. *The analysis of psychological theory.* Washington, D.C.: Hemisphere.

————, ed. 1988. *The rise of experimentation in American psychology*. New Haven: Yale University Press.

Morss, J. R. 1990. *The biologizing of childhood: Developmental psychology and the Darwinian myth*. Hove: Erlbaum.

Moscovici, S. 1963. Attitudes and opinions. *Annual Review of Psychology*. Palo Alto, Calif.: Annual Reviews, Inc.

———— 1984. The phenomenon of social representations. In R. Farr and S. Moscovici, eds. *Social representations*. London: Cambridge University Press.

Mulkay, M. 1985. *The word and the world*. London: George Allen and Unwin.

Mulkay, M., and G. N. Gilbert. 1982. What is the ultimate question? Some remarks in defence of the analysis of scientific discourse. *Social Studies of Science*, 12: 309–19.

Mummendey, A. 1982. Zum Nutzen des Aggressionsbegriffs für die psychologische Aggressionsforschung. In R. Hilke and W. Kempf, eds. *Menschliche Aggression: Naturwissenschaftliche Perspektiven der Aggressionsforschung*. Bern-Stuttgart-Wien: Hans Huber.

Mummendey, A., M. Bornewasser, G. Loschper, and V. Linneweber. 1982. It is always somebody else who is aggressive. *Zeitschrift für Sozialpsychologie*, 13: 341–352.

Murray, K. D. 1985a. Justificatory accounts and the meaning of the marathon as a social event. *Australian Psychologist*, 20: 62–74.

———— 1985b. Life as fiction. *Journal for the Theory of Social Behavior*, 15: 189–202.

Myers, F. R. 1979. Emotions and the self: A theory of personhood and political order among Pintupi Aborigines. *Ethos*, 7: 343–70.

Nehamas, A. 1985. *Nietzsche: Life as literature*. Cambridge: Harvard University Press.

Nelson, J. S., A. Megill, and D. McCloskey, eds. 1987. *The Rhetoric of the Human Sciences*. Madison: University of Wisconsin Press.

Nelson, K. 1985. *Making sense: The acquisition of shared meaning*. Orlando: Academic Press.

Nencel, L., and P. Pels, eds. 1991. *Constructing knowledge: Authority and critique in social science*. London: Sage.

Neurath, O. 1933. *Einheitwissenschaft und Psychologie*. Vienna: Gerold.

Newman, F. 1991. *The myth of psychology*. New York: Costillo.

Nietzsche, F. 1979. On truth and falsity in their ultramoral sense. In O. Levy, ed. *The complete works of Friedrich Nietzsche*. New York: Russell and Russell. Originally published in 1873.

Nir, R., and I. Roeh. 1992. Intifada coverage in the Israeli press. *Discourse and Society*, 3: 47–60.

Nisbett, R., and L. Ross. 1990. *Human inference: Strategies and shortcomings of human judgment*. Englewood Cliffs, N.J.: Prentice-Hall.

Norris, C. 1983. *The deconstructive turn*. New York: Methuen.

Novick, P. 1989. *That noble dream*. New York: Cambridge University Press.

Nowell-Smith, P. H. 1977. The constructionist theory of history. *History and Theory: Studies in the Philosophy of History*, 16: 4–12.

Nussbaum, F. 1988. Eighteenth-century women's antibiographical commonplaces. In S. Benstock, ed. *The private self*. London: Routledge.

O'Hanlon, B., and J. Wilk. 1987. *Shifting contexts*. New York: Guilford Press.

Ogilvie, D. M., and R. D. Ashmore. 1991. Self-with-other representation as a unit of analysis in self concept research. In R. C. Curtis, ed. *The relational self*. New York: Guilford.

Olds, L. 1992. *Metaphors of interrelatedness*. New York: State University Press.

Ong, W. J. 1982. *Orality and literacy*. London: Methuen.

Ortega y Gasset, J. 1941. *History as a system*. New York: Norton.

Ossorio, P. 1978. *What actually happens*. Columbia: University of South Carolina Press.

Overton, W. E. 1993. The structure of developmental theory. In P. van Geert and L. P. Mos, eds. *Annals of theoretical psychology*. Vol. 7. New York: Plenum.

Overton, W. R., and H. W. Reese. 1973. Models of development: Methodological implications. In J. R. Nesselroade and H. W. Reese, eds. *Life-span developmental psychology: Methodological issues*. New York: Academic Press.

Packer, M. 1987. Social interaction as practical activity: Implications for the study of social and moral development. In W. Kurtines and J. Gewirtz, eds. *Moral development through social interaction*. New York: John Wiley and Sons.

Packer, M., and R. Addison. 1989. *Entering the circle: Hermeneutic investigation in psychology*. Albany: State University of New York Press.

Palmer, A. 1987. Cognitivism and computer simulation. In A. Costall and A. Still, eds. *Cognitive psychology in question*. New York: St. Martin's.

Parker, I. 1987. Social representations: Social psychology's (mis)use of sociology. *Journal for the Theory of Social Behavior*, 17: 447–470.

———— 1992. *Discourse dynamics*. London: Routledge.

Parker, I., and J. Shotter, eds. 1990. *Deconstructing social psychology*. London: Routledge Kegan Paul.

Parlee, M. B. 1979. Psychology and women. *Signs*, 5: 121–133.

Parsons, T. 1964. *Social structure and personality*. New York: Free Press.

Pasmore, W., and F. Friedlander. 1982. An action research program for increasing employee involvement in problem solving. *Administrative Science Quarterly*, 27: 343–362.

Pawluk, S. J. 1989. The social construction of teasing. *Journal for the Theory of Social Behavior*, 19: 145–168.

Pearce, W. B. 1989. *Communication and the human condition*. Carbondale: Southern Illinois University Press.

———— 1992. A camper's guide to constructionisms. *Human Systems*, 2: 139–162.

Pearce, W. B., and V. E. Cronen. 1980. *Communication action and meaning*. New York: Praeger.

Peeters, H. In press. The historical vicissitudes of mental diseases, their character and treatment. In C. Grauman and K. Gergen, eds. *The historical context of psychological discourse*. New York: Cambridge University Press.

Penn, P., and M. Frankfurt. In press. Creating a participant text: Writing, multiple voices, narrative multiplicity. *Family Process*.

Pennebaker, J., and D. Epstein. 1983. Implicit psychophysiology: Effects of common beliefs and idiosyncratic physiological responses on symptom reporting. *Journal of Personality*, 3: 468–496.

Petrey, S. 1990. *Speech acts and literary theory*. New York: Routledge Kegan Paul.

Pfohl, S. 1992. *Death at the parasite cafe*. New York: St. Martin's Press.

Piaget, J. 1952. *The origins of intelligence in children*. New York: Norton.

——— 1954. *The construction of reality in the child*. New York: Basic Books.

——— 1955. *The language and thought of the child*. New York: Meridian.

Piaget, J., and B. Inhelder. 1969. *The psychology of the child*. New York: Basic Books.

Pinder, C. C., and V. W. Bourgeois. 1982. Controlling tropes in administrative science. *Science Quarterly*, 27: 641–652.

Plon, M. 1974. On the meaning of the notion of conflict and its study in social psychology. *European Journal of Social Psychology*, 4: 389–436.

Plutchik, R. 1980. A general psychoevolutionary theory of emotion. In R. Plutchik and H. Kellerman, eds. *Emotion, theory, research and experience*. New York: Academic Press.

Polkinghorne, D. E. 1988. *Narrative knowing and the human sciences*. Albany: State University of New York Press.

Popper, K. R. 1959. *The logic of scientific discovery*. London: Hutchinson.

——— 1963. *Conjectures and refutations*. New York: Harper.

——— 1968. *The logic of scientific discovery*. New York: Harper and Row.

Porter, T. M. 1992. Objectivity as standardization: The rhetoric of impersonality in measurement, statistics, and cost-benefit analysis. *Annals of Scholarship*, 9: 19–60.

Potter, J., and M. Wetherell. 1987. *Discourse and social psychology: Beyond attitudes and behaviour*. London: Sage.

Potter, J., P. Stringer, and Y. Wetherell. 1984. *Social texts and context*. London: Routledge and Kegan Paul.

Prelli, L. 1989. *A rhetoric of science*. Columbia: University of South Carolina Press.

Pribram, K. H. 1980. The biology of emotions and other feelings. In R. Plutchik and H. Kellerman, eds. *Emotion, theory, research and experience*. New York: Academic Press.

Propp, V. 1968. *Morphology of the folktale*. Austin: University of Texas Press.

Psathas, G. 1979. *Everyday language*. New York: Irvington.

Putnam, H. 1978. *Meaning and the moral sciences*. London: Routledge and Kegan Paul.

——— 1987. *The many faces of realism*. LaSalle, Ill.: Open Court.

Queneau, R. 1981. *Exercises in style*. New York: New Directions.

Quine, W. V. O. 1953. *From a logical point of view*. Cambridge: Harvard University Press.

——— 1960. *Word and object*. Cambridge: MIT Press.

Rabinow, O., and W. M. Sullivan, eds. 1979. *Interpretive social science reader*. Berkeley: University of California Press.

Rawls, J. 1971. *A theory of justice*. Cambridge: Harvard University Press.

Reason, P. 1988. *Human inquiry in action*. London: Sage.

Reber, A. S. 1985. *The Penguin dictionary of psychology*. London: Penguin.

Reed, M. 1985. *Re-directions in organizational analysis*. London: Tavistock.

Regis, E. 1984. *Gewirth's ethical rationalism*. Chicago: University of Chicago Press.

Reinharz, S. 1985. Feminist distrust: Problems of context and content in sociological work. In D. Berg and K. Smith, eds. *Exploring clinical methods for social research*. Beverly Hills, Calif.: Sage.

Reiss, D. 1981. *The family's construction of reality*. Cambridge: Harvard University Press.

Restle, F. A. 1962. The selection of strategies in cue learning. *Psychological Review*, 69: 320–343.

Richards, G. 1989. *On psychological language*. London: Routledge.

Ricoeur, P. 1979. The model of the text: Meaningful action considered as a text. In P. Rabinow and W. Sullivan, eds. *Interpretive social science: A reader*. Berkeley: University of California Press.

———— 1981. *Hermeneutics and the human sciences*. Trans. J. Thompson. New York: Cambridge University Press.

Riesman, C. K. 1990. *Divorce talk: Women and men make sense of relationships*. New Brunswick, N.J.: Rutgers University Press.

Riger, S. 1992. Epistemological debates, feminist voices. *American Psychologist*, 47: 730–740.

Rimmon-Kenan, S. 1983. *Narrative fiction: Contemporary poetics*. London: Methuen.

Ring, K. 1967. Some sober questions about frivolous values. *Journal of Experimental Social Psychology*, 3: 113–123.

Roberts, H. 1981. Doing feminist research. London: Routledge.

Rogoff, B. 1989. *Apprenticeship in thinking*. New York: Oxford University Press.

Rommetveit, R. 1980. On "meanings" of acts and what is meant and made known by what is said in a pluralistic social world. In M. Brenner, ed. *The structure of action*, pp. 108–149. Oxford: Basil Blackwell.

Rorty, R. 1979. *Philosophy and the mirror of nature*. Princeton: Princeton University Press.

———— 1983. Postmodernist bourgeois liberalism. *Journal of Philosophy*, 80: 585–594.

———— 1989. *Contingency, irony, and solidarity*. New York: Cambridge University Press.

———— 1991. *Objectivity, relativism, and truth*. New York: Cambridge University Press.

Rosaldo, M. 1980. *Knowledge and passion: Illongot notions of self and social life*. Cambridge: Cambridge University Press.

Rosaldo, R. 1986. Illongot hunting as story and experience. In V. W. Turner and E. D. Bruner, eds. *The anthropology of experience*. Chicago: University of Chicago Press.

Rosanoff, A. J. 1938. *Manual of psychiatry and mental hygiene*. New York: Wiley.

Rosch, E. 1978. Principles of categorization. In E. Rosch and B. B. Lloyd, eds. *Cognition and categorization*. Hillsdale, N.J.: Erlbaum.

Rose, N. 1985. *The psychological complex*. London: Routledge and Kegan Paul.

———— 1990. *Governing the soul*. London: Routledge.

Rosen, G. 1968. *Madness in society.* Chicago: Chicago University Press.

Rosen, S. 1987. *Hermeneutics as politics.* New York: Oxford.

Rosenau, P. 1992. *Post-modernism and the social sciences.* Princeton: Princeton University Press.

Rosenwald, G. C., and R. L. Ochberg. 1992. Introduction: Life stories, cultural politics, and self-understanding. In G. C. Rosenwald and R. L. Ochberg, eds. *Storied lives: The cultural politics of self-understanding.* New Haven: Yale University Press.

Rosnow, R. L. 1981. *Paradigms in transition.* New York: Oxford University Press.

Rotter, J. 1966. Generalized expectancies for internal versus external control of reinforcement. *Psychological Monographs,* 80: 343–355.

Rummelhart, D. 1977. Understanding and summarizing brief stories. In D. Leberge and S. J. Samuels, eds. *Reading, perception and comprehension.* Hillsdale, N.J.: Erlbaum.

Russell, B. 1924. Logical atomism. In J. H. Muirhead, ed. *Contemporary British philosophy.* London: Allen and Unwin.

Ryder, R. G. 1987. *The realistic therapist: Modesty and relativism in therapy and research.* Newbury Park, Calif.: Sage.

Ryle, G. 1949. *The concept of mind.* London: Hutchinson.

Sabini, J., and M. Silver. 1982. *The moralities of everyday life.* London: Oxford University Press.

Sahlin, N. E. 1991. Baconian inductivism in research on human decision-making. *Theory and Psychology,* 1: 431–451.

Said, E. 1979. *Orientalism.* New York: Random House.

——— 1993. *Culture and imperialism.* New York: Knopf.

Salipante, P., and R. Bouwen. 1990. The social construction of grievances: Organizational conflict as multiple perspectives. Unpublished paper, Weatherhead School of Management, Case Western Reserve University.

Salmond, A. 1982. Theoretical landscapes: On cross-cultural conceptions of knowledge. In D. Parkis, ed. *Semantic anthropology.* London: Academic Press.

Sampson, E. E. 1977. Psychology and the American ideal. *Journal of Personality and Social Psychology,* 35: 767–782.

——— 1978. Scientific paradigms and social values: Wanted—A scientific revolution. *Journal of Personality and Social Psychology,* 36: 1332–43.

——— 1981. Cognitive psychology as ideology. *American Psychologist,* 36: 730–743.

——— 1983. Deconstructing psychology's subject. *Journal of Mind and Behavior,* 4: 135–164.

——— 1988. The debate on individualism. *American Psychologist,* 43: 15–22.

Sanday, P. 1988. The reproduction of patriarchy in feminist anthropology. In M. Gergen, ed. *Feminist thought and the structure of knowledge.* New York: New York University Press.

Sandelands, L. E. 1990. What is so practical about theory? Lewin revisited. *Journal for the Theory of Social Behavior,* 20: 235–262.

Sarbin, T. R. 1968. Ontology recapitulates philosophy: The mythic nature of anxiety. *American Psychologist,* 23: 411–418.

———— 1984. *Narrative psychology: The storied nature of human conduct.* New York: Praeger.

———— 1986. Emotion and act: Roles and rhetoric. In R. Harré, ed. *The social construction of emotions,* pp. 83–98. New York: Basil Blackwell.

Sarbin, T. R., and J. C. Mancuso. 1980. *Schizophrenia: Medical diagnosis or verdict?* Elmsford, N.Y.: Pergamon.

Sarbin, T. R., and K. E. Scheibe, eds. 1983. *Studies in social identity.* New York: Praeger.

Sarnoff, I., and S. Sarnoff. 1989. *Love-centered marriage in a self-centered world.* New York: Hemisphere.

Sassen, G. 1980. Success anxiety in women: A constructivist interpretation of its social significance. *Harvard Educational Review,* 50: 13–24.

Saussure, F. de, 1983. *Course in general linguistics.* Trans. R. Harris. London: Duckworth.

Schacht, T. E. 1985. DSM-III and the politics of truth. *American Psychologist,* 40: 513–521.

Schachter, S. 1964. The interaction of cognitive and physiological determinants of emotional state. In L. Berkowitz, ed. *Advances in experimental social psychology.* Vol. 1. New York: Academic Press.

Schank, R. C., and R. P. Abelson. 1977. *Scripts, plans, goals and understanding.* Hillsdale, N.J.: Erlbaum.

Schapp, W. 1976. *In Geschichten verstrickt zum Sein von Mensch und Ding.* Wiesbaden: Heymann.

Scheff, T. J. 1966. *Being mentally ill.* Chicago: Aldine.

Scheibe, K. E. 1986. Self-narratives and adventure. In T. R. Sarbin, ed. *Narrative psychology.* New York: Praeger.

Scheman, N. 1983. Individualism and the objects of psychology. In S. Harding and M. Hintikka, eds. *Discovering reality.* Dordrecht: Reidel.

Schenk, H. G. 1966. *The mind of the European romantics.* London: Constable.

Scherer, K. 1984. Emotion as a multicomponent process. In P. Shaver, ed. *Review of personality and social psychology.* Beverly Hills: Sage.

Schlegoff, E. A., and H. Sacks. 1973. Opening up closings. *Semiotica,* 7: 289–327.

Schlenker, B. 1985. *The self and social life.* New York: McGraw-Hill.

Schlenker, B. R., and S. W. Darby. 1981. The use of apologies in social predicaments. *Social Psychological Quarterly,* 74: 271–278.

Schlick, M. 1925. *General theory of knowledge.* New York: Springer-Verlag.

Schnitman, D. F., and S. I. Fuks. 1993. Paradigma y crisis: Entre el riesgo y law posibilidad. *Psyckhe,* 2: 33–42.

Scholes, R. 1985. *Textual power.* New Haven: Yale University Press.

Scholes, R., and R. Kellogg. 1966. *The nature of narratives.* New York: Oxford University Press.

Schonbach, P. 1990. *Account episodes: The management and escalation of conflict.* Cambridge: Cambridge University Press.

Schott, R. 1988. *Cognition and eros: A critique of the Kantian paradigm.* Boston: Beacon.

Schutz, A. 1962. *Collected papers: The problem of social reality.* The Hague: Martinus Nijhoff.

———— 1980. *On phenomenology and social relations.* Chicago: Chicago University Press.

Schutze, Y. 1986. Die gute Mutter: Zur Geschichte des normativen Musters *"Mutterliebe."* Bielefeld: Kleine Verlag.

Schwartz, B. 1986. *The battle for human nature.* New York: Norton.

———— 1990. The creation and destruction of value. *American Psychologist,* 45: 7–15.

Searle, J. R. 1970. *Speech acts.* London: Cambridge University Press.

————1985. *Minds, brains and science.* Cambridge: Harvard University Press.

Seidman, S., and D. Wagner. 1992. *Postmodernism and social theory.* Oxford: Blackwell.

Selman, R. L., and L. H. Schultz. 1990. *Making a friend in youth: Developmental theory and pair therapy.* Chicago: University of Chicago Press.

Semin, G., and J. Chassein. 1985. The relationship between higher order models and everyday conceptions of personality. *European Journal of Social Psychology,* 15: 1–16.

Semin, G., and B. Krahe. 1987. Lay conceptions of personality: Eliciting tiers of a scientific conception of personality. *European Journal of Social Psychology,* 17: 199–209.

Semin, G., and A. S. Manstead. 1983. *The accountability of conduct.* Sydney, U.K.: Academic Press.

Sennett, R. 1977. *The fall of public man.* New York: Knopf.

Shailor, J. G. 1994. *Empowerment in dispute mediation: A critical analysis of communication.* Westport, Conn.: Praeger.

Shelley, P. B. 1967. *Shelley's critical prose.* Lincoln: University of Nebraska Press.

Shotter, J. 1975. *Images of man in psychological research.* London: Methuen.

———— 1978. Remembering and forgetting as social institutions. *Laboratory of Comparative Human Cognition,* 9: 11–18.

———— 1980. Action, joint action and intentionality. In M. Brenner, ed. *The structure of action.* Oxford: Blackwell.

———— 1984. *Social accountability and selfhood.* Oxford: Blackwell.

———— 1991. Rhetoric and social construction of cognitivism. *Theory and Psychology,* 1: 495–515.

———— 1993a. *Cultural politics of everyday life.* Toronto: University of Toronto Press.

———— 1993b. *Conversational realities.* London: Sage.

Shotter, J., and K. J. Gergen, eds. 1989. *Texts of identity.* London: Sage.

Shweder, R. A. 1982. Fact and artifact in trait perception: The systematic distortion hypothesis. In B. A. Maher and W. B. Maher, eds. *Progress in experimental personality research.* Vol. 11. New York: Academic Press.

———— 1991. *Thinking through cultures.* Cambridge: Harvard University Press.

Shweder, R. A., and E. Bourne. 1982. Does the concept of the person vary cross-culturally? In A. J. Marsella and G. White, eds. *Cultural conceptions of mental health and therapy.* Boston: Reidel.

Shweder, R. A., and J. G. Miller. 1985. The social construction of the person: How is it possible? In K. J. Gergen and K. E. Davis, eds. *The social construction of the person.* New York: Springer-Verlag.

Shweder, R. A., and N. Much. 1987. Determinations of meaning: Discourse and moral socialization. In W. Kurtines and J. Gewirtz, eds. *Moral development through social interaction*. New York: John Wiley and Sons.

Siegel, H. 1987. *Relativism refuted*. Dordrecht: Reidel.

Sigman, S. 1987. *A perspective on social communication*. Lexington, Mass.: Lexington Books.

Silver, M., and J. P. Sabini. 1978. The social construction of envy. *Journal for the Theory of Social Behavior,* 8: 313–332.

Silver, M., and J. Sabini. 1985. Sincerity: Feelings and constructions in making a self. In K. J. Gergen and K. E. Davis, eds. *The social construction of the person*. New York: Springer-Verlag.

Silverman, H. J. 1990. *Postmodernism, philosophy and the arts*. New York: Routledge.

Simmel, G. 1950. *The sociology of Georg Simmel*. Glencoe, Ill.: Free Press.

Simon, H. A., and K. Kotowsky. 1963. Human acquisition of concepts for sequential patterns. *Psychological Review,* 70: 534–546.

Simons, H. W., ed. 1989. *Rhetoric in the human sciences*. London: Sage.

—— 1990a. *Case studies in the rhetoric of the human services*. Chicago: University of Chicago Press.

—— 1990b. *The rhetorical turn*. Chicago: University of Chicago Press.

Skinner, B. F. 1971. *Beyond freedom and dignity*. New York: Random House.

—— 1989. The origins of cognitive thought. *American Psychologist,* 44: 13–18.

Sless, D. 1986. *In search of semiotics*. Totowa, N.J.: Barnes and Noble.

Smedslund, J. 1988. *Psycho-logic*. New York: Springer-Verlag.

—— 1991. The pseudoempirical in psychology and the case for psychologic. *Psychological Inquiry,* 2: 325–338.

Smith, K., and D. Berg. 1987. A paradoxical conception of group dynamics. *Human Relations,* 40: 633–658.

Smith, M. B. 1969. *Social psychology and human values*. Chicago: Aldine.

Smythies, J. R., and J. Beloff. 1989. *The case for dualism*. Charlottesville: University of Virginia Press.

Solomon, R. C. 1984. *Getting angry*. Boston: Jamesian Theory Press.

Spector, M., and J. I. Kitsuse. 1987. *Constructing social problems*. New York: Aldine.

Spence, D. 1982. *Narrative truth and historical truth: Meaning and interpretation in psychoanalysis*. New York: Norton.

—— 1987. *The Freudian metaphor*. New York: Norton.

Spencer, D. P. 1992. Automythologies and the reconstruction of aging. In J. Okely and H. Callaway, eds. *Anthropology and autobiography*. London: Routledge.

Spender, D. 1980. *Man made language*. London: Routledge.

Spitzer, R. L., and J. B. Williams. 1985. Classification of mental disorders. In H. L. Kaplan and B. J. Sadock, eds. *Comprehensive textbook of psychiatry,* pp. 580–602. Baltimore: Williams and Wilkins.

Squire, C. 1989. *Significant differences: Feminism in psychology*. London: Routledge.

Srivastva, S., and F. J. Barrett. 1988. The transforming nature of metaphors in group development: A study in group theory. *Human Relations,* 41: 31–64.

Stainton Rogers, R., and W. Stainton Rogers. 1992. *Stories of childhood: Shifting agendas of child concern.* Hemel Hempstead, U.K.: Harvester Wheatsheaf.

Stam, H. 1987. The psychology of control: A textual critique. In H. Stam, T. Rogers, and K. Gergen, eds. *Psychological theory,* pp. 131–157. New York: Hemisphere.

——— 1990. Rebuilding the ship at sea: The historical and theoretical problems of constructionist epistemologies in psychology. *Canadian Psychology,* 31: 239–253.

Stearns, P. N. 1989. *Jealousy: The evolution of an emotion in American history.* New York: New York University Press.

Steier, F. 1991. *Research and reflexivity.* London: Sage.

Stein, E., ed. 1990. *Forms of desire, sexual orientation and the social constructionist controversy.* New York: Routledge.

Steiner, I. 1972. *Group process and productivity.* New York: Academic Press.

Stenner, P., and C. Eccleston. 1994. On the textuality of being. *Theory and Psychology,* 4: 85–104.

Stephan, W. G. 1985. Intergroup relations. In G. Lindzey and E. Aronson, eds. *The handbook of social psychology.* New York: Random House.

Sternberg, R. J. 1990. *Metaphors of mind: Conceptions of the nature of intelligence.* New York: Cambridge University Press.

Still, A., and A. Costall, eds. 1991. *Against cognitivism: Alternative foundations for cognitive psychology.* London: Harvester Wheatsheaf.

Stitch, S. 1983. *From folk psychology to cognitive science.* Cambridge: MIT Press.

Stout, J. 1988. *Ethics after Babel.* Boston: Beacon Press.

Stratton, P. 1992. Selling constructionism to market research. *Human Systems,* 2: 253–273.

Strauss, A. 1979. *Negotiations.* San Francisco: Jossey-Bass.

Sulieman, S. R., and I. Crossman. 1980. *The reader in the text.* Princeton: Princeton University Press.

Sullivan, E. V. 1984. *A critical psychology.* New York: Plenum.

Sullivan, H. S. 1953. *The interpersonal theory of psychiatry.* New York: Norton.

Sutton-Smith, B. 1979. Presentation and representation in fictional narrative. *New Directions for Child Development,* 6: 37–60.

Szasz, T. S. 1961. *The myth of mental illness: Foundations of a theory of personal conduct.* New York: Hoeber-Harper.

——— 1963. *Law, liberty and psychiatry: An inquiry into the social uses of mental health practices.* New York: Macmillan.

——— 1970. *The manufacture of madness: A comparative study of the inquisition and the mental health movement.* New York: Harper and Row.

Tappan, M. B. 1991. Narative, authorship, and the development of moral authority. In M. B. Tappan and M. J. Packer, eds. *Narrative and storytelling: Implications for understanding moral development.* San Francisco: Jossey-Bass.

Tavris, C. 1989. *Anger: The misunderstood emotion.* New York: Simon and Schuster.

Taylor, C. 1981. Interpretation and the sciences of man. *Review of Metaphysics.* Cambridge: Harvard University Press.

——— 1989. *Sources of the self.* Cambridge: Harvard University Press.

—— 1991. *The ethics of authenticity*. Cambridge: Harvard University Press.

Tetlock, P. 1991. An alternative metaphor in the study of judgment and choice: People as politicians. *Theory and Psychology*, 1: 451–477.

Thibaut, J., and H. H. Kelley. 1959. *The social psychology of groups*. New York: John Wiley and Sons.

Thomas, D. 1979. *Naturalism and social science: A post-empiricist philosophy of social science*. Cambridge: Cambridge University Press.

Thomas, J. 1993. Doing critical ethnography. *Qualitative Research Methods Series*, 26: 57–69.

Thorndike, E. L. 1933. *An experimental study of rewards*. New York: Columbia University Press.

Tiefer, L. 1992. Social constructionism and the study of human sexuality. In E. Stein, ed. *Forms of desire*. New York: Routledge.

Tolman, C. W., and W. Maiers. 1991. *Critical psychology: Contributions to an historical science of the subject*. Cambridge: Cambridge University Press.

Tololyan, K. 1989. Narrative culture and the motivation of terrorism. In J. Shotter and K. Gergen, eds. *The texts of identity*. London: Sage.

Toulmin, S. 1961. *Foresight and understanding*. New York: Harper and Row.

Toulmin, S., and D. E. Leary. 1985. The cult of empiricism in psychology, and beyond. In S. Koch and D. E. Leary, eds. *A century of psychology as a science: Retrospections and assessments*. New York: McGraw-Hill.

Tracey, D. 1987. *Plurality and ambiguity*. New York: Harper and Row.

Treichler, P. A. 1987. AIDS, homophobia and biomedical discourse: An epidemic of signification. *Cultural Studies*, 1: 263–305.

Trigg, R. 1980. *Reality at risk: A defense of realism in philosophy and the sciences*. Totowa, N.J.: Barnes and Noble.

Tseelon, E. 1992a. What is beautiful is bad: Physical attractiveness as stigma. *Journal for the Theory of Social Behavior*, 22: 295–310.

—— 1992b. Is the presented self sincere? Goffman, impression management and the postmodern self. *Theory, Culture and Society*, 9: 115–128.

Turkington, C. 1985. Support helps schizophrenics meet needs. *American Psychological Association Monitor*, October: 52.

Turner, B. S. 1990. *Theories of modernity and postmodernity*. London: Sage.

Turner, R. 1970. Words, utterances and activities. In J. Douglas, ed. *Understanding everyday life*, 169–187. Chicago: Aldine.

Tyler, S. A. 1986. Post-modern ethnography. From documents of the occult to occult documents. In J. Clifford and G. Marcus, eds. *Writing culture*. Berkeley: University of California Press.

—— 1988. *The unspeakable*. Madison: University of Wisconsin Press.

Unger, R. K. 1983. Through the looking glass: No wonderland yet! (The reciprocal relationship between methodology and models of reality). *Psychology of Women Quarterly*, 8: 19–32.

Urwin, C. 1985. Constructing motherhood: The persuasion of normal development. In C. Steedman, C. Urwin, and V. Walkerdine, eds. *Language, gender, and childhood*. London: Routledge.

Valsiner, J. 1991. Construction of the mental: From the cognitive revolution to the study of development. *Theory and Psychology*, 1: 477–495.

————— 1992. Narratives in the making of histories in psychology. Paper presented at the First Conference for Socio-cultural Research, Madrid.

Vandenberg, B. 1993. Developmental psychology, God and the good. *Theory and Psychology,* 3: 191–205.

van den Berg, J. H. 1961. *Metabletica: Uber die Wandlung des Menschen.* Gottingen: Vadenhoeck and Ruprecht.

van Dijk, T. A. 1992. Discourse and the denial of racism. *Discourse and Society,* 3: 87–118.

van Eemeren, F. H., and R. Grootendorst. 1983. *Speech acts in argumentative discussions.* Dordrecht: Foris.

Van Maanen, J. 1988. *Tales of the field.* Chicago: University of Chicago Press.

von Glasersfeld, E. 1987. The control of perception and the construction of reality. *Dialectica,* 33: 37–50.

————— 1988. The reluctance to change a way of thinking. *Irish Journal of Psychology,* 9: 83–90.

Vuchinich, S. 1984. Sequencing the social structure in family conflict. *Social Psychology Quarterly,* 47: 217–234.

Vygotsky, L. S. 1978. *Mind in society: The development of higher psychological processes.* Cambridge: Harvard University Press.

Walkerdine, V. 1984. Developmental psychology and the child-centered pedagogy. In J. Henriques, W. Holloway, C. Urwin, V. Louze, and V. Walkerdine, eds. *Changing the subject,* pp. 153–202. London: Methuen.

————— 1988. *The mastery of reason.* London: Routledge Kegan Paul.

————— 1993. Beyond developmentalism. *Theory and Psychology,* 3: 451–470.

Wallach, M., and L. Wallach. 1983. *Psychology's sanction for selfishness.* San Francisco: W. H. Freeman.

Watson, J. B. 1924. *Behaviorism.* Chicago: University of Chicago Press.

Watzlawick, P., ed. 1984. *The invented reality.* New York: Norton.

Watzlawick, P., J. Beavin, and D. Jackson. 1967. *Pragmatics of human communication: A study of interactional patterns, pathologies and paradoxes.* New York: Norton.

Waxman, S. 1991. Contemporary approaches to concept development. *Cognitive Development,* 6: 105–118.

Wechsler, I. 1929. *The neuroses.* Philadelphia: Saunders.

Weedon, C. 1987. *Feminist practice and poststructuralist theory.* Oxford: Blackwell.

Weimer, W. B. 1979. *Notes on the methodology of scientific research.* Hillsdale, N.J.: Erlbaum.

Weinstein, A. 1988. *The fiction of relationship.* Princeton: Princeton University Press.

Weisstein, N. 1971. Psychology constructs the female. In V. Gornick and B. K. Moran, eds. *Women in sexist society,* pp. 96–104. New York: Basic.

Wertsch, J. V. 1985. *Vygotsky and the social formation of mind.* Cambridge: Harvard University Press.

————— 1991. *Voices of the mind: A sociocultural approach to mediated action.* Cambridge: Harvard University Press.

Wexler, P. 1983. *Critical social psychology.* Boston: Routledge Kegan Paul.

White, H. 1973. *Metahistory*. Baltimore: Johns Hopkins University Press.

———— 1978. *Tropics of discourse*. Baltimore: Johns Hopkins University Press.

White, M., and D. Epston. 1990. *Narrative means to therapeutic ends*. New York: Norton.

Whorf, B. L. 1956. *Language, thought and reality*. Cambridge: Technology Press of Massachusetts.

Wiener, M. 1991. Schizophrenia: A defective, deficient, disrupted, disorganized concept. In W. F. Flack, Jr., D. R. Miller, and M. Wiener, eds. *What is schizophrenia?* New York: Springer-Verlag.

Wiener, M., and D. Marcus. 1994. A sociocultural construction of "depression." In T. A. Sarbin and J. I. Kitsuse, eds. *Constructing the social*. London: Sage.

Williams, R. 1976. *Keywords: A vocabulary of culture and society*. New York: Oxford University Press.

Wilmot, W., and J. Hocker. 1993. Couples and change: Intervention through discourse and images. In N. Coupland and J. Nussbaum, eds. *Discourse and lifespan identity*. London: Sage.

Winch, P. 1946. *The idea of social science*. London: Routledge Kegan Paul.

Wittgenstein, L. 1953. *Philosophical investigations*. Trans. G. Anscombe. New York: Macmillan.

Wood, L., and H. Rennie. In press. Formulating rape: The discursive construction of victims and villains. *Discourse and Society*.

Woolgar, S., ed. 1988. *Knowledge and reflexivity*. Newbury Park, Calif.: Sage.

Woolgar, S., and D. Pawluck. 1985. Ontological gerrymandering: The anatomy of social problems explanations. *Social Problems,* 32: 218.

Wortham, S. 1985. How justifiable are interpretive ladders? Possibilities for objective knowledge in the social sciences. Senior Honors Thesis, Swarthmore College.

Wright, P., and A. Treacher. 1982. *The problem of medical knowledge: Examining the social construction of medicine*. Edinburgh: University of Edinburgh Press.

Wyer, R. S., and T. K. Srull. 1989. *Memory and cognition in its social context*. Hillsdale, N.J.: Erlbaum.

Young, J., and R. Mathews. 1992. *Rethinking criminology: The realist debate*. London: Sage.

Young, K. 1982. Edgework: Frame and boundary in the phenomenology of narrative. *Semiotica,* 41: 277–315.

————, ed. 1993. *Bodylore*. Louisville: University of Kentucky Press.

Youniss, J. 1980. *Parents and peers in social development*. Chicago: University of Chicago Press.

———— 1987. Social construction and moral development: Update and expansion of an idea. In W. Kurtines and J. Gewirtz, eds. *Moral development through social interaction*. New York: John Wiley and Sons.

Youniss, J., and J. Smollar. 1985. *Adolescent relations with mothers, fathers, and friends*. Chicago: University of Chicago Press.

Zimmerman, D. H., and M. Pollner. 1970. The everyday world as a phenomenon. In J. Douglas, ed. *Understanding everyday life,* pp. 80–104. Chicago: Aldine.

Index

Medical profession, 74–75. *See also* Mental
health professions
Megill, A., 182
Mental deficit terminology, 31; psychological discourse and, 147–151; professional
growth and, 151–155; cycle of progressive infirmity and, 155–161; cultural
modeling and, 158–159; vocabulary expansion and, 159–161; reduction of enfeebling discourse and, 161–164;
destigmatization and, 162–163
Mental health professions: descriptive language and, 31; reality and, 76; psychological discourse and, 147–151; social
hierarchy and, 148–149; community erosion and, 149–150; self-enfeeblement
and, 150–151; professional growth and,
151–155; cycle of progressive infirmity
and, 155–161; demand for services of,
159, 160; alternative vocabularies and,
163–164; modernist context and, 238–
241. *See also* Therapeutic practice
Mental Hygiene (magazine), 157
Mental representations: origins of, 121–
125; actions and, 125–128. *See also* Dualism
Mental states: pictorial *vs.* pragmatic orientation and, 143–146; objectivity and,
145, 167–170; relationship and, 218–
219. *See also* Emotions; Meaning; Psychological discourse
Mercer, N., 140
Metaphor: Western epistemology and, 40;
in scientific accounts, 41–42; morality
and, 107; psychological reality and, 140–
141; distending, 174–175; relational realities and, 214–215; of language as lens,
246; of individual as information processor, 255
Metatheory: as justificatory discourse, 6, 7;
post-empiricist stage in, 21; critiques of
empiricism and, 22–25; rationalist-
empiricist debate in, 23, 25; rationalist
theory of knowledge and, 23–24; power
and, 73–74; constructionist, 113. *See also*
Empiricism; Logical empiricism; Rationalism
Methodology: social constructionism and,
51–52, 61–62; cultural transformation
and, 61–62. *See also* Dialogic methodology; Experimental methodology

Micro-narratives, 203
Microsocial process: emotions and, 217,
218; relatedness and, 217; therapeutic
practice and, 217–218; meaning and,
268; truth and, 277–278
Middleton, D., 219
Milgram, S., 61
Miller, P. J., 139
Mind: as hypothetical construct, 18;
constructionism and, 70; moral discourse and, 94; monitoring of, 169–170
Misunderstanding: concept of, 269; sources
of, 269–271. *See also* Mental states
Mitroff, I., 43
Modernism: morality and, 94, 97–102; narrative form and, 193; therapeutic practice
and, 238–241, 252; challenges to, 242;
hermeneutics and, 257–259; problem of
meaning and, 259–260. *See also* Postmodernism
Monomyth, and narrative form, 194
Moore, G. E., 95
Moral discourse: ideological critique and,
24, 34; sciences and, 24, 34, 57–58; constructionism and, 57–59, 102–105, 108–
112, 287; romanticism and, 94, 95–97;
Darwin and, 96; modernism and, 97–
102; problems of, 105–108; culture and,
107–108; retribution and, 109–111; principles *vs.* practices and, 111–112; self-
narrative and, 207–208; emotions and,
222–223; deceit and, 286–290. *See also*
Deceit
Moral relativism: critiques of constructionist thought and, 79–82, 112–114; constructionist thought and, 93–94, 108–
112
Morawski, J., 59
Moscovici, S., 134–135
Mulkay, M., 61
Multiplicity: concept of, in self-narrative,
202–204; pragmatics of self-narrative
and, 204–207; interknitting of identities
and, 207–209; misunderstanding and,
270; deceit and, 277–281; in interdependency, 284. *See also* Laminations of reality; Relational nuclei
Mummendey, A., 139

Nagel, T., 178
Narrative. *See* Self-narrative

Propp, V., 41
Psychoanalysis. *See* Mental health professions; Therapeutic practice
Psychological constructs, 136. *See also* Mental states; Mind; Psychological discourse
Psychological discourse: pictorial orientation in, 143–146, 153; cultural context and, 145, 146–148; pragmatic orientation to, 146, 147; language of mental deficit and, 146–151; social hierarchy and, 148–149; growth of mental health professions and, 151–155; cycle of progressive infirmity and, 155–161; deficit translation and, 156; cultural dissemination and, 156–158; common language and, 158–159; vocabulary expansion and, 159–161; deceit and, 275–276. *See also* Mental states
Psychological processes, 69–72
Psychological science: empiricism as metatheory in, 5, 6, 7–8; supporting bodies of discourse and, 5, 6–8, 27–28; discursive dimension of paradigm shift and, 11–14; theoretical transformation in, 14–27; moral discourse and, 94, 100–102; conceptions of the self and, 211–212; intersubjectivity and, 254–256. *See also* Behaviorism; Cognitive psychology; Human science; Developmental theory; Social psychology
Public institutions, and conceptions of the self, 211–212

Queneau, R., 171
Quine, W. V. O., 13, 32, 33, 51

Radical behaviorism, 17–18
Rationalism: psychological science and, 5; as intelligibility nucleus, 9–10; critique of logical empiricism and, 23–24; cognitive psychology and, 25, 119–120; morality and, 99–102
Rationality, and relationship, 218–219. *See also* Enlightenment rationality
Rawls, J., 94, 100
Reader response theory, 260
Reagan, Ronald, 281–286
Realism: constructionism and, 72–76; selective, 78
Reality, laminations of, 282–286

Reasoning. *See* Rationality
Reciprocity, imperative of, 226
Reconstruction: of science, 46–48; cultural transformation and, 63
Reflecting team, 251
Reflexivity: social constructionism and, 48, 143; social psychology and, 131–133; in therapeutic practice, 251
Reframing, 231–232
Regressive narrative, 195–196, 198, 201, 206–207
Reichenbach, H., 33
Reinforcement: concept of, 18; concept development and, 121–123
Reiss, D., 140
Relational nuclei: deceit and, 277–281; laminations of reality and, 282–286; conflicting allegiances and, 288
Relationship: identity and, 202–204; ideology of individualism and, 212–214; as by-product of individual selves, 214–218; intersubjectivity and, 216–217; microsocial perspective and, 217; mental states and, 218–219; emotions and, 222–224; language and, 253; meaning in, 262–271; human development and, 271–274; laminations of reality and, 282–286
Relativism: ontological, 76–79; moral, 79–82, 93–94, 108–112; conceptual, 82–84; postmodern accounts of reality and, 249
Religion, and moral discourse, 95–96
Remorse, 231–232
Restle, F. A., 122
Retribution, imperative to, 226
Rhetorical studies: objectivity and, 40–42, 170–172; dislodgement and, 59. *See also* Literary-rhetorical critique
Ricoeur, P., 192
Riger, S., 139
Romance, as narrative form, 194
Romanticism: morality and, 94, 95–97; hermeneutics and, 256–257
Rorty, R., 40, 81, 121
Rosanoff, A., 161
Rosch, E., 123
Rose, N., 139, 148
Rosenwald, G. C., 193
Rule-role theorists, 187–188
Russell, B., 32
Ryle, G., 119, 121

Sampson, E. E., 119, 132
Sarbin, T. R., 140–141, 147
Sarnoff, I., 213
Sarnoff, S., 213
Satire, 194
Saussure, F. de, 9, 38, 49
Schacht, T. E., 148
Schachter, S., 118
Schank, R. C., 188–189
Schapp, W., 209
Scheibe, K. E., 197
Scheler, M., 42
Schlick, M., 32
Schnitman, D. F., 140
Scholarly writing: cultural transformation
   and, 61; experiential presence and, 177–
   178
Scholarship of dislodgement, 58
Schutz, A., 49, 69
Schwartz, B., 132
Science: supporting bodies of discourse and,
   6–8; paradigm shift in, 11–14;
   hypothetical-deductive model and, 19;
   morality and, 24, 34, 57–58, 97, 98–99;
   descriptive claims in, 31–33, 35–36, 38–
   39; reconstruction of, 46–48; predictive
   function of, 50–51, 87–88; practice of,
   55–57, 84–92; transcendental realism
   and, 75–76; theory evaluation and, 88–
   92. See also Human science; Psychological science
Scientific description: critiques of objectivity
   of, 31–33, 35–36, 38–39; metaphor and,
   41–42; social processes and, 42–44; as
   performative, 84–87; felicity and, 86–87;
   objectivity as rhetorical achievement in,
   170–172; techniques for achieving rhetorical objectivity and, 172–180; modernist therapeutic practice and, 238–241
Searle, J. R., 119
"Selective realism," 78
Self: relational conception of, 210, 214–
   218; historical discourse on, 210–211;
   theories of, 211; ideology of individualism and, 212–214; as constituent of the
   whole, 215–216; intersubjectivity and,
   216–217. See also Self-narrative
Self-enfeeblement, 150–151
Self-justification, 152
Self-narrative, 185–209; character of, 187–
   189; concept of, 187–189; structuring of

narrative accounts and, 189–193; personal coherence and, 193–194, 205; varieties of narrative form and, 193–197;
   generation of drama and, 197–199; forms
   of intelligibility and, 199–202; adolescents and, 200–201; processes of, 202–
   204; multiplicity in, 202–209; pragmatics
   of, 204–207, 245–247; functions of,
   205–207; context and, 208–209; emotions and, 224; modernist therapeutic
   practice and, 238–241; postmodern therapeutic practice and, 241–245; utility of,
   in therapeutic practice, 245–247. See also
   Narrative form
Semantics, and social constructionism,
   52–53
Semiotics: poststructuralism and, 39–40;
   problem of meaning and, 263, 265
Semiotic square, 9–10, 22
Sennett, R., 213
Sheff, T. J., 159
Shotter, J., 49, 132, 141, 265
Simon, H. A., 122
Skepticism, 76–79
Skinner, B. F., 17–18, 119
Smedslund, J., 136
Smith, E., 41
Social constructionism: as metatheoretical
   critique, 24–25; assumptions behind,
   48–54; objectivity and, 49–50, 77–79;
   potential for human science and, 54–63;
   as social construction, 76–77; truth
   claims and, 77–79; moral discourse and,
   102–105. See also Constructionist
   thought
"Social constructivism," 68–69
Social critique: of empiricism, 24; objectivity and, 42–44; reconstruction of science
   and, 46, 47–48; problems with, 48; human science and, 58; dislodgement and,
   59; social psychology and, 131–133
Social epistemology, 128–130, 141
Social exchange theory, 215
Social hierarchy, and psychological discourse, 148–149
Social process: meaning and, 46–47, 263–
   271; language and, 47, 51–52; social constructivist theories and, 68–69; moral
   action and, 109; constructionist inquiry
   and, 138–141; relational realities and,
   214; therapeutic practice and, 243